Biblical Law

BEING A TEXT OF THE STATUTES, ORDINANCES, AND
JUDGMENTS ESTABLISHED IN THE HOLY BIBLE—
WITH MANY ALLUSIONS TO SECULAR LAWS:
ANCIENT, MEDIEVAL AND MODERN—DOCU-
MENTED TO THE SCRIPTURES, JUDICIAL
DECISIONS AND LEGAL LITERATURE

By
H. B. CLARK
LAW EDITOR

THE LAWBOOK EXCHANGE, LTD.
Clark, New Jersey

ISBN 9781584770626 (hardcover)
ISBN 9781616192426 (paperback)

Lawbook Exchange edition 2000, 2011

The quality of this reprint is equivalent to the quality of the original work.

THE LAWBOOK EXCHANGE, LTD.

33 Terminal Avenue
Clark, New Jersey 07066-1321

*Please see our website for a selection of our other publications
and fine facsimile reprints of classic works of legal history:*
www.lawbookexchange.com

Library of Congress Cataloging-in-Publication Data

Clark, H.B. (Harold B.), 1893-
Biblical law : being a text of the statutes, ordinances, and
judgments established in the Holy Bible—with many allusions
to secular laws—ancient, medieval, and modern—documented
to the Scriptures, judicial decisions, and legal literature/by
H.B. Clark.
    p. cm.
Originally published: Portland : Binfords & Mort, c1943.
Includes bibliographical references and index.
ISBN 1-58477-062-7 (cloth: acid-free paper)
1. Bible and law. 2. Jewish law. I. Title.

BS680.L33 C53 2000
220.8'34—dc21   99-053316

Printed in the United States of America on acid-free paper

Biblical Law

BEING A TEXT OF THE STATUTES, ORDINANCES, AND
JUDGMENTS ESTABLISHED IN THE HOLY BIBLE—
WITH MANY ALLUSIONS TO SECULAR LAWS:
ANCIENT, MEDIEVAL AND MODERN—DOCU-
MENTED TO THE SCRIPTURES, JUDICIAL
DECISIONS AND LEGAL LITERATURE

By
H. B. CLARK
LAW EDITOR

Published by BINFORDS & MORT
PORTLAND, OREGON

PRINTED IN U.S.A. BY METROPOLITAN PRESS, PORTLAND, OREGON

PREFACE

"A PANDECT of Profitable Laws, against Rebellious Spirits!"
Thus the Scriptures are described in the Preface to the King
James' Version.[1] Indeed, the Holy Bible is, not only a repository of early laws; it is the code at once most ancient and best
known by those who have been observers of the Christian
Creed;[2] and to it our later laws and governmental processes
are, in essential and enduring parts, immediately indebted.[3]

Nor is the Bible simply a collection of rules; it is the history
and literature of an ancient people as well as a text of morals
and religion. Such being the pattern of the Scriptures, the
author—in order that Biblical Law may be easy of access—
has extracted the many commandments, precedents and customs which are to be found throughout the Sacred Writings
and has sought to present them logically and systematically,
in the style of a modern law book.

During the centuries, millions of devout Christians, according to their knowledge and understanding, have respected the
precepts of the Scriptures; and this textbook has been mainly
contrived for other millions who now, and in the days to come,
would follow "the ancient paths"[4] and "adhere to the teachings of their fathers"[5]—and who therefore need and will
hereafter need further light that they may properly "shew
the work of the law."[6]

The attainment of another objective has, also, actuated the
author. He has sought to resolve the question as to whether
Biblical Law, when better understood and observed, may re-
place or at least point a way to simplification of present-day
secular law, with its wilderness of words, "so many as the
stars of the sky in multitude, and as the sand which is by the
sea shore innumerable."[7]

Generally it will be seen that Biblical Law is no less sound
and useable today than when it first was written. And one
who will carefully examine its rules and attempt to trace their
workings will be astonished to find how completely they cover

---

1 The Translators to The Reader (1611)
2 7 Va. L. Reg. [N.S.] (1922) 777
3 10 West. Jur. (1876) 89 (Bowman)
4 Jer. 18:15

5 Juilliard v Greenman (1884) 110 US
421, 470, 28 L ed 204, 215 (Field,J, dissenting)
6 Rom. 2:15
7 Heb. 11:12

the entire field of civil, domestic, and even social life.[8] But
it is evident that Biblical Law was designed primarily for an
agrarian society, and that many details must be supplied to
make it sufficient for the modern commercial and industrial
world—if it be conceded that such a world can lawfully exist.[9]

This work is based primarily upon the King James' Version, translated in 1604-1611, which is generally accepted as
the best from a literary point of view, though not definitely
prescribed by the doctrines of any church.[10] But the so-called
Apocryphal books of the Old Testament also have been freely
drawn upon, and numerous references are made to judicial
decisions and other legal literature.

Secular laws of various nations—ancient, medieval and
modern—including those of Babylon and Rome, England and
America, and the Hebrews or Jews, are occasionally noticed
by way of comparison with Biblical Law. Otherwise no attempt is made to consider or treat of the Hebrew or Jewish
law as such.

In conclusion, the author acknowledges his indebtedness to
many writers who have preceded him—who are mentioned in

---

8 28 Unit. Rev. 293, 294

9 See infra §245 et seq.

10 See 11 Cal LR (1923) 185, 186; Evans
v Selma Union High School Dist. (1924)
193 Cal. 54, 222 P 801, 31 ALR 1121;
Herald v School Directors (1915) 136
La. 1034, 68 So. 116, LRA1915D 941, 943
(Sommerville,J)

Concerning versions of the Bible, the
following statement appears in the
opinion of the court in the Evans case,
supra:

". . . the original manuscripts of the
Bible have been lost for centuries.
Those available for translation are
themselves "versions," and either copies
or translations of still older texts.
There have been numerous English
translations, but those most generally
in use to-day are the King James' version and its subsequent English and
American revisions, and the Douai version.

"The Douai version consists of a
translation of the New Testament made
in the English College at Rheims, published there in 1582, and of the Old
Testament published at Douai in 1609.

"The King James' version is a translation made at the direction of James
I of England, and published at London
in 1611. The work was done by a commission of forty-seven scholars, drawn
largely from the universities of Oxford
and Cambridge. The work of its revi-

sion by English and American commit-
tees was begun in 1870, and the revised
New Testament published in 1881, and
the revised Old Testament in 1884.

"The Douai version is based upon the
text of the Latin Vulgate, the King
James' version on the Hebrew and
Greek texts. There are variances in
the rendering of certain phrases and
passages. The Douai version incorpor-
ates the Apocrypha, which are omitted
from the texts of the Testaments in
the King James' version, though in
many editions they have been printed
between the two Testaments. The Douai
version was the work of Catholics, and
is the translation used by the Roman
Catholic Church in English-speaking
countries. The King James' version
and its revisions are the work of Pro-
testants, and are used in Protestant
churches.

"The contention that the Bible in the
King James' translation is a book of
a sectarian character rests on the fact
that there are differences between it
and, among others, the Douai version;
that it is of Protestant authorship;
that it is used in Protestant churches;
and that it is not approved by the
Catholic Church. According to such a
test the Bible in any known version or
text is sectarian. In fact, until all
sects can agree upon the manuscript
texts that should be used, no English
version of the Bible not "sectarian" in
this view can be produced."

the footnotes—and to Bancroft-Whitney Company and the Lawyers Cooperative Publishing Company for permission to make use of their publications.

H. B. CLARK

Alameda, California,
January 4, 1943

TABLE OF CONTENTS

ANALYSIS OF PARTS

PART I

Introduction and General Principles

CHAPTER 1

Definitions and Sources of Law

CHAPTER 2

Kinds of Law

CHAPTER 3

Divisions of Biblical Law

CHAPTER 4

Burden, Goodness, and Objects of the Law

CHAPTER 5

Application and Bindingness of the Law

CHAPTER 6
Interpretation and Operation of Laws

CHAPTER 7
Conflicts and Changes In the Law

CHAPTER 8
The Writing, Reading and Teaching of the Law

CHAPTER 9
Law Observance

CHAPTER 10
Relation of Biblical Law to Modern Laws

PART II
Political Law

CHAPTER 11
In General

CHAPTER 12
Forms of Government

CHAPTER 13
Public Officers

CHAPTER 14
Official Functions

CHAPTER 15
Civil Obedience and Respect of Officials

CHAPTER 16
International Law

CHAPTER 17
Warfare and Military Law

PART III
Civil Law

CHAPTER 25
Sales, Exchanges and Leases

CHAPTER 26
Suretyship

CHAPTER 27
Trespasses

DIVISION B
Domestic Relations

CHAPTER 28
Introduction

CHAPTER 29
Marriage

CHAPTER 30
Divorce

CHAPTER 31
Husband and Wife

CHAPTER 32
Parent and Child

CHAPTER 33
Master and Servant

CHAPTER 34
Host and Guest

PART IV
Economics and Welfare

CHAPTER 35
Introduction

CHAPTER 36
Labor—The Law of Employment

CHAPTER 45
Food and Drink—Rules of Etiquette

CHAPTER 46
Health, Healing, and Physicians

CHAPTER 47
Prostitution

CHAPTER 48
Religion

CHAPTER 49
"Strangers"—Aliens

CHAPTER 50
Women

PART VI
Penal Law—Crimes and Punishments

CHAPTER 58
Offenses Against Property

CHAPTER 59
Offenses Against Religion

CHAPTER 60
Sexual Offenses

CHAPTER 61
Punishments

PART VII
Procedure—Administration of Law

CHAPTER 62
Introduction

CHAPTER 63
The Judges

CHAPTER 64
Civil Suits

CHAPTER 65
Criminal Prosecutions

KEY TO ABBREVIATIONS AND SIGNS USED IN THE FOOTNOTES

¶—Paragraph
§—Section
2d—Second Series
A or Atl.—Atlantic Reporter
ABA—American Bar Association
AC or ACA—Advance California or California Appellate Reports
AD or AmDec—American Decisions
A.D.—Anno Domini
adv opns—Advance opinions
Ala.—Alabama
ALR—American Law Reports
Am.—American
Am Jur—American Jurisprudence
Anc.—Ancient
Ann Cas—Annotated Cases
App.—Appeals or Appellate Reports
AR—American Reports
Ariz.—Arizona
Ark.—Arkansas
Art.—Article
ASR—American State Reports
Atty.Gen.—Attorney General
B.C.—Before Christ
Bel—Bel and the Dragon
Bl. Com.—Commentaries on the Laws of England by Sir William Blackstone, published 1765-1769
C—Commissioner
Cal.—California
Cal. Jur.—California Jurisprudence
ch.—chapter
Chron.—Chronicles
Cir.J.—Circuit Judge
Civ.—Civil
Civ.App.—Civil Appeals
CJ—Chief Justice
Co.—Company
Col.—Colossians
Colo.—Colorado
Com.App.—Commission of Appeals
Conn.—Connecticut
Const.—Constitution
Cor.—Corinthians
Crim.—Criminal
Crim. Rep.—Criminal Reports
Dan.—Daniel

Dec.—Decisions
Deut.—Deuteronomy
Dist.—District
DJ—District Judge
ed.—edition
Eph.—Ephesians
Eq.—Equity
Esd.—Esdras
Est.—Esther
Ex.—Exodus
Ezek.—Ezekiel
F or Fed.—Federal Reporter
Fed.Cas.—Federal Cases
Fla.—Florida
F. Supp.—Federal Supplement
Ga.—Georgia
Gal.—Galatians
Gen.—Genesis
Geo.—Georgetown
Gr. B.—Green Bag
Hab.—Habakkuk
Hag.—Haggai
Harv.—Harvard
Heb.—Hebrews
Ill.—Illinois
Ind.—Indiana
Internat. L.—International Law
Isa.—Isaiah
J—Justice or Judge
Jer.—Jeremiah
Josh.—Joshua
Jour.—Journal
Jur.—Jurisprudence
Kan.—Kansas
Ky.—Kentucky
L—Law
La.—Louisiana
Lam.—Lamentations
L ed—Lawyer's edition of United States Supreme Court Reports
Lev.—Leviticus
LJ—Law Journal
LQ—Law quarterly
LR—Law Review or Law Reports
LRA—Law Reports Annotated
LRANS—Lawyers' Reports Annotated, New Series
L.Reg.—Law Register

Mac.—Maccabees
Maine's Anc. L.—Ancient Law by Sir Henry Sumner Maine, published in London, January, 1861. References are to Fourth American from Tenth London Edition, 1906
Mal.—Malachi
Mass.—Massachusetts
Matt.—Matthew
Md.—Maryland
Me.—Maine
Mich.—Michigan
Miss.—Mississippi
Mo.—Missouri
Mont.—Montana
n—note
NC—North Carolina
ND—North Dakota
NE—Northwestern Reporter
Neb.—Nebraska
Neh.—Nehemiah
Nev.—Nevada
NH—New Hampshire
NJ—New Jersey
NM—New Mexico
No.—Number
NS—New Series
Num.—Numbers
NY—New York
NYS—New York Supplement
NW—Northwestern Reporter
Obad.—Obadiah
Okla.—Oklahoma
Or.—Oregon
p—Page
P—President (of court)

P or Pac—Pacific Reporter
Pa.—Pennsylvania
Pet.—Peter
Phil.—Philippians
PJ—Presiding Justice
Prob.—Probate
Prov.—Proverbs
Ps.—Psalms
RCL—Ruling Case Law
Rev.—Revelation
R.I.—Rhode Island
Rom.—Romans
Sam.—Samuel
SC—South Carolina
Sch.—School
S.Ct.—Supreme Court
SE—Southeastern Reporter
So.—Southern Reporter
Spec.CJ—Special Chief Justice
St.—Saint or State
SW—Southwestern Reporter
Tenn.—Tennessee
Tex.—Texas
Tex. Jur.—Texas Jurisprudence
Thess.—Thessalonians
Tim.—Timothy
US—United States or United States Supreme Court Reports
v—versus or verse
Va.—Virginia
Wash.—Washington
West.Jur.—Western Jurist
Wis.—Wisconsin
W. Va.—West Virginia
Zech.—Zechariah
Zeph.—Zephaniah

PART I

INTRODUCTION AND GENERAL PRINCIPLES

CHAPTER 1

DEFINITIONS AND SOURCES OF LAW

1 Definitions 2 Enforceability of rule as affecting its character 3 Sources of law
4 Custom

[§1] The Bible is a book of principles rather than definitions. Though it abounds in legal doctrine, it may be searched in vain for a definition of law. Blackstone[1] defined law as a rule of human action or conduct.[2] Holmes[3] considered it as a prediction or prophecy of what a court or officer would do to a man if he did or omitted to do certain things.[4] In this book law means a rule or a body of rules for the government of human life,[5] prescribing rights and duties and regulating conduct.[6] Law embraces custom, and includes expressions showing the attitude or policy of the law-maker as to certain matters. Biblical law also contains some rules pertaining to thought or emotion as distinguished from purely physical action or conduct.

[§2] The question may arise as to whether Biblical doctrines actually are law, for it has been said that a law must be prescribed by an authority that citizens or subjects are bound to obey, and that there must be a court or officer to administer and enforce it.[7] But these sayings are not necessarily true.[8] A rule prescribed by an authority that persons ought to obey may properly be considered as law.[9] A rule may also be established by common consent or agreement of the people that it shall be binding upon them in their dealings among themselves. A law does not lose its legal charac-

1 Sir Wm. Blackstone (1723-1780) English jurist, author of "Commentaries on the Laws of England"
2 1 Bl. Com. 38, 39
3 Oliver Wendell Holmes (1841-1935) American jurist, Associate Justice US Supreme Court 1902-1932
4 Holmes' Collected Legal Papers (1920) Path of the Law
"Law is a statement of the circumstances in which the public force will be brought to bear upon men through the courts." American Banana Co. v United Fruit Co. (1908) 213 US 347, 53 L ed 826, 832 (Holmes,J)
5 27 ABA Journal (1941) No. 2, 78

6 "In general, laws are meant to regulate and direct the acts and rights of citizens." United States v Hoar (1821) 2 Mason 311, 314, Fed.Cas.No.15373 (Story,Cir.J)
7 Dickinson v Dickinson (1819) 7 NC 327; 30 Harv.LR (1917) 284
8 It is not always the case that enforcement in courts is necessary to make a rule law. See 28 Yale LJ (1918-19) 842
9 "This is Law, to which all men ought to yield obedience for many reasons." Demosthenes, Adv. Aristogeiton I § 774

ter because violations are punished mildly or, in practice, are not punished at all, nor even though there is no physical means by which obedience can be presently enforced.[10]

[§3]   Law is found in statutes and judgments,[11] and in custom.   Statutes—or ordinances, as they are sometimes called[12]—are expressions of a law-maker, usually commanding or forbidding that certain things be done.   Judgments are decisions of judges which expound or apply rules of law in settling disputes.[13]   The ruling of a judge or court may become a general law, as in the case of the Daughters of Zelophehad.[14] And custom consists in rules arising out of common usages and practices of the people—for which the law has great regard.[15]

[§4]   Custom is a fruitful source of law.[16]   Error is not to be sanctioned because it has once got a footing.[17]   But when a custom is not evil in itself nor in contravention of any law, it is accepted as a certain kind of law,[18] upon the theory that the law-making power commanded what it permitted over a long period of time.   Ordinarily a custom must be common and well established before it has the binding effect of law. But "all Scripture . . . is profitable for doctrine, for reproof, for correction, for instruction in righteousness,"[19] and the recording of an act without comment on the part of a Biblical writer may therefore be taken, in a proper case, as an indication that it accords with the law or conformed with the custom of the time.[20]

CHAPTER 2

KINDS OF LAW

5 Various classes of law   6 Divine or revealed law   7 Moral law   8 Natural law
9 Human or secular law

[§5]   The field of law has been called a seamless whole,[21] meaning that any particular rule ought to be read in connec-

---

10   The Prometheus (1906) 2 Hongkong 207
11   Ezek. 20:11
12   Ex. 15:25; Eph. 2:15
13   "From the decisions rules are drawn."   Carpenters & Joiners Union v Ritter's Cafe (1942) 315 US 722, 86 L ed —— (Reed,J, dissenting)
14   See infra §139
15   Carson v Blazer (1810) 2 Binney (Pa.) 475, 487 (Yeates,J), observing further that "the law itself" is "nothing else but common usage, with which it complies, and alters with the exigency of affairs"
16   Dewey, Philosophy of Law (1941) 78
17   Brown v Phoenix Ins. Co. (1812)

4 Binney (Pa.) 445, 478 (Brackenridge, J)
  Mere custom or usage cannot make lawful conduct that is actually unlawful.   Milton v Motor Coach Co. (1942) 53 Cal.App. 2d 566, 570, 128 P 2d 178 (Shinn,J) saying that custom cannot make due care out of conduct that is in fact negligence.
  Nor should ancient custom be stubbornly adhered to when this will prevent changes for the better. 10 Cornell LQ (1925) 106 (Rosbrook)
18   Gratian, Decretum, Canons 4, 5
19   2 Tim. 3:16
20   13 Gr.B. (1901) 38 (Amram)
21   1 Street's Foundations (1906) xxviii

tion with the whole body of the law. Yet some division is necessary for purposes of investigation or study. Law may be classified on the one hand as divine or revealed, on the other as human or secular. From other standpoints it is international or municipal, public or private, general or special, civil or criminal, statutory or judicial; and mandatory, permissive or declaratory. International law governs the relations between nations; municipal law, the domestic or internal affairs of a nation, state or city. Public or general law consists of rules of general application; private or special law, rules applicable to particular persons, things or localities. Civil law pertains to civil rights and their enforcement; criminal law, to crimes and their punishments. Statutory law is that which is enacted by legislators; judicial law, that which is formulated by judges in the decision of controversies. Law is mandatory, permissive or declaratory, when it either commands or permits a thing to be done or left undone or when it declares or defines a right, duty or policy.

[§6] Divine or revealed law is that which, according to the Scriptures, God gave directly to man.[22] As Blackstone said:

"Divine Providence . . . hath been pleased at sundry times and in divers manners to discover and enforce its laws by an immediate and direct revelation. The doctrines thus discovered we call the 'revealed' or 'divine' law, and they are to be found only in the Holy Scriptures."[23]

Much of the revealed law of the Old Testament appears to have been "spoken" by the Lord or Jehovah, and some of the law of the New Testament is contained in the teachings of Jesus. Many other provisions of revealed law are found in the sayings, writings and acts of human authorities, both ecclesiastical and civil, such as prophets, disciples, apostles, kings, judges and governors.

The law was revealed in several ways:

1. By commandments to do or not to do certain things;
2. By judgments pronounced in particular cases;
3. By statements commending or reproving certain conduct; and
4. By the absence of comment upon conduct seeming to merit commendation or reproval.

But in the sense that "all scripture is given by inspiration of God,"[24] all law contained in the Bible is to be regarded as divine or revealed, regardless of the particular manner or circumstances of its revelation.

---

[22] 1 Bl. Com. 41

[23] 1 Bl. Com. 42
[24] 2 Tim. 3:16

"It is . . . a fault of presumption, either to reject any of those things that are written, or to bring in any of those things that are not written."[25]

Nothing is to be allowed or considered "against the law of God, but what is prohibited in holy writ."[26]

[§7] Moral law consists in a body of ethical or moral rules for the conduct of man, "to secure him the greatest happiness in harmony with the conditions of his existence"[27]—rules once regarded as "eternally and universally binding upon mankind."[28]   Judge Dillon,[29] in his commentary on the Laws and Jurisprudence of England and America, says:

"Not less wondrous than the revelations of the starry heavens, and much more important, and to no class of men more so than lawyers, is the moral law which Kant found within himself, and which is likewise found within, and is consciously recognized by, every man. This moral law holds its dominion by divine ordination over us all, from which escape or evasion is impossible. This moral law is the eternal and indestructible sense of justice and right written by God on the living tablets of the human heart and revealed in his Holy Word."[30]

Many of the precepts of the moral law relate to mankind as members of an organized society and impose duties upon individuals which are of the same kind as those imposed by the human authority of the state.   Others relate only to mankind as individuals, prescribing duties toward each other and toward God which human law does not and cannot recognize or enforce.   The divine law as expounded in the Scriptures has, by some writers, been characterized as the moral law,[31] and it has been said:

"If our reason were always, as in our first ancestor before his transgression, clear and perfect, unruffled by passions, unclouded by prejudice, unimpaired by disease or intemperance, . . . we should need no other guide. . . . But every man now finds the contrary in his own experience—that his reason is corrupt and his understanding full of ignorance and error."[32]

[§8]   Natural law is a moral system supposedly conformable to nature[33] that has been framed by ethical writers.[34] It is said to be inherent in man,[35] in that, according to St.

25   Preface to King James' Version (1611) "The Translators to the Reader," quoting S.Basil
   "The Scriptures were from Moses' time to the time of the apostles and evangelists, in whose ages . . . the book of Scriptures was shut and closed, so as not to receive any new additions, and . . . the church hath no power after the Scriptures to teach and command anything contrary to the written Word." Bacon
26   Anderson v Winston (1736) Jefferson's (Va.) Reports, 27, citing 1 Hawk. 245

27   Moore v Strickling (1899) 46 W.Va. 515, 33 SE 274, 50 LRA 279 282 (Dent,P)
28   Anderson v Winston (1736) Jefferson's (Va.) Reports, 24
29   John F. Dillon (1831-1914) American jurist and author
30   Moore v Stricklin, ante
31   1 Pomeroy's Eq.Jur. (1881) 5th ed. (1941) §§63, 64
32   Moore v Strickling, ante, quoting Blackstone
33   Cicero
34   1 Bl. Com. 39
35   22 Geo.LJ (1934) 420

Paul, the Lord has put it in the minds and written it into the hearts of men.[36] Its precepts "are not to be rummaged for among old parchments or musty records. They are written with a sunbeam, in the whole volume of human nature by the hand of divinity itself, and can never be erased or obscured by mortal power."[37]

"Things required by natural law are marriage, succession, bringing up of children, one common security for all, one liberty for all, and the right to acquire those things which are capable of possession in air, earth and sea."[38]

[§9] Human or secular law is that which has been made by human legislators or judges. "It is formed and perfected in the mind and will of man" and therefore is "a law of man and not of God Himself."[39] Yet it has often been considered as a development or reflection of divine law. So it has been said that human law is the offspring of divine law,[40] and that the municipal laws of nations and of communities are, in their origin and intrinsic force, no other than the rules of being given us by God.[41] Human law should doubtless be just, moral and righteous, conforming to the "eternal" and to the "design in nature."[42] But in practice it does not, and perhaps cannot, in all respects satisfy the morality of a Christian community.

CHAPTER 3
DIVISIONS OF BIBLICAL LAW

10 Development of law   11 Primitive law   12 Mosaic law   13 —— The Ten Commandments   14 —— Versions   15 —— The Talmud   16 —— Mosaic interpretation of law   17 Christian law   18 —— Love as a rule of law   19 —— Love as fulfillment of the law   20 —— Transgressions as arising in the mind or heart   21 —— The Law of Liberty   22 —— Observance of the law by nature   23 —— The Golden Rule   24 —— Christian interpretation of law

[§10] Law is not a manufacture, but a growth.[43] In other words, it does not spring up instantaneously like Minerva out of the head of Jove, but is developed through years of human experience—by trial and error—according to the needs of the people and the wisdom of their law-makers.[44]

36 Heb. 8:10, 10:16
37 1 Hamilton's Works, Lodge ed. (1903) 113
38 St.Isadore, Etymologies, v 4
39 22 Geo.LJ (1934) 419
40 See Equitable Life Assur. Soc. v Weightman (1916), 61 Okla. 106, 160 P 629, LRA 1917B 1210
41 10 West.Jur. (1876) 89
42 22 Geo.LJ (1934) 419
"Every law is a discovery and gift of God." Demosthenes, Adv.Aristogeiton, I, §774
43 4 Harv.LR (1890-91) 365
44 "The body of the law is like a great river, ever moving—sometimes swiftly and sometimes it appears very slow." 13 Miss.LJ (1941) 668
The development of Anglo-American law "has gone on for nearly a thousand years, like the development of a plant, each generation taking the inevitable next step, mind, like matter, simply obeying a law of spontaneous growth." Holmes' Collected Legal Papers (1920) "Path of the Law"
New rules are evolved (or borrowed) to meet new situations. Kerby v Hal Roach Studios (1942) 53 ACA (Cal.) 226, 229 (Shaw, J pro tem, discussing the recently developed law of privacy)

This was doubtless true of Biblical law, which first appeared in the ancient world and continued its development to a time near the end of the first century after Christ. Historically, the law of the Bible is of three parts: Primitive, Mosaic, and Christian.

[§11] Primitive law preceded history. It arose in the very mists of antiquity, extending from the time of the First Chapter of the Book of Genesis to that of the beginnings of Mosaic law as recorded in the Book of Exodus, or presumably about the year 1490 B.C.[45] Like other ancient law, this law was unwritten and consisted for the most part in traditional usages and forms which had the force of law. Nearly all of our information concerning it is found in Genesis, which contains "traditions hoary with age, reflecting conditions of law and society remotely anterior to the legislation found in the Pentateuch, and to the condition of society described in the Books of the Kings."[46] But Primitive law was not so much concerned with individuals as with the independent family groups of ancient society, each of which was ruled by its own head or patriarch. Having been supplemented by the commands of the heads of households, Primitive law did not develop a complete system of rules.[47]

[§12] Mosaic law comprises the greater part of the law of the Old Testament. According to the Scriptural record it was promulgated by Moses,[48] who is said to have commanded,[49] given[50] or written[51] the law, and to have "delivered it unto the priests . . . and unto all the elders of Israel."[52] It is chiefly found in the second to the fifth books of the Pentateuch or Five Books of Moses, and is called Mosaic law, not because it differs so much from Primitive law or Christian law, but to distinguish it from the law of other periods.[53] This is the ancient and divine authority[54] to which later writ-

---

45 Primitive law has existed for a much longer period than either Mosaic or Christian law. It continued to have force in some respects long after Moses.
46 13 Gr.B. (1901) 37
47 See Maine's Anc. L., pp 122, 147, 250
48 In his Panorama of World's Legal Systems, Library ed. (1936) p 107, Wigmore says that modern research tells us that these texts of the Pentateuch were only gradually built up during some eight centuries of development. Others think, and not without much reason, that Moses only codified for the newly organized nation of Israel the laws which had long been known. In Genesis, 26:5, it appears that the Lord said of Abraham that he "kept my charge, my commandments, my statutes, and

my laws." Thus it is seen that there were "laws" more than four centuries before Moses.
49 Deut. 33:4
50 John 1:17, 7:19
51 Deut. 31:9
52 Deut. 31:9; and see Heb. 7:11, saying that the people received the law under the Levitical priesthood.
53 See Wigmore's Panorama, p 103 et seq.
  Chapters 20 to 23 of Exodus presumably date from the 15th century, B.C. But the law found in Deuteronomy probably was not promulgated until the reign of King Josiah of Judah, about 624 B.C.
54 Hart v Geysel (1930) 159 Wash. 632, 294 P 570, 573 (Holcomb,J., dissenting)

ers—including those of the New Testament—usually refer when they speak of the law[1]

[§13] ——— The Ten Commandments are the basis of Mosaic law—the constitution of the Mosaic dispensation.[2] They have been called the greatest short moral code ever formulated[3] and the idealized model of all law,[4] and it has been argued that the whole of natural law may be deduced from them.[5]

"These commandments, which, like a collection of diamonds, bear testimony to their own intrinsic worth, in themselves appeal to us as coming from a superhuman or divine source, and no conscientious or reasonable man has yet been able to find a flaw in them. Absolutely flawless, negative in terms, but positive in meaning, they easily stand at the head of our whole moral system, and no nation or people can long continue a happy existence in open violation of them."[6]

[§14] ——— ——— The Scriptures contain two versions of the Ten Commandments, one in Exodus (chap. 20, verses 3-17) and the other in Deuteronomy (chap. 5, verses 7-21). The preferred version in Exodus reads thus:

I. Thou shalt have no other gods before me.
II. Thou shalt not make unto thee any graven image, or any likeness of any thing that is in heaven above, or that is in the earth beneath, or that is in the water under the earth: thou shalt not bow down thyself to them, nor serve them.
III. Thou shalt not take the name of the Lord thy God in vain.
IV. Remember the sabbath day, to keep it holy. Six days shalt thou labour, and do all thy work: but the seventh day is the sabbath of the Lord thy God: in it thou shalt not do any work, thou, nor thy son, nor thy daughter, thy manservant, nor thy maidservant, nor thy cattle, nor thy stranger that is within thy gates.
V. Honour thy father and thy mother.
VI. Thou shalt not kill.
VII. Thou shalt not commit adultery.
VIII. Thou shalt not steal.
IX. Thou shalt not bear false witness against thy neighbour.
X. Thou shalt not covet thy neighbour's house, thou shalt not covet thy neighbour's wife, nor his manservant, nor his maidservant, nor his ox, nor his ass, nor any thing that is thy neighbour's.

1 In the writings of St.Paul frequent references are made to "the law," meaning the law of Moses.
2 3 Ala.LJ (1928) 258
The oldest code of laws in the world, of which we are aware, was promulgated by king Hammurabi of Babylon, B.C. 2285-2242, and was discovered in 1902. Hughes v Medical Examiners (1926) 162 Ga. 246, 134 SE 42, 49 (Hill, J)
The earliest code of Roman law was known as the "Twelve Tables," of which mere fragments have been preserved. The text of the tables probably did not survive the sixth century, A.D. They were the local law for Rome and its citizens. School boys were required to commit them to memory, so that each citizen might know the laws of his country. At the end of the Roman Republic, the Roman civil law had taken the place of the Twelve Tables. See 14 Ill.LR (1919-1920) 243
3 Wigmore's Panorama, p 105
"The laws of spiritual life, of civil life, and of moral life are all set forth in the ten commandments." 42 Wash. LR (1914) 770
4 10 Or.LR (1934-35) 91
5 27 Harv. LR (1915) 612, saying Melanchthon so argued.
6 Moore v Strickling (1899) 46 W.Va. 515, 33 SE 274, 50 LRA 279, 282

[§15] —— The Talmud is the body of Jewish civil and canonical law.

"Mosiac law was studied carefully for generations. Extensions and refinements in that law were made by scholars and orally transmitted to their students. This process continued until 189 A.D., when the oral law was set down in writing and called the Mishnah. Later scholars commented and elaborated upon the Mishnah and orally handed down their opinions to their students. In 500 A.D., these oral commentaries were compiled in a new work called the Gemara. The Mishnah and the Gemara together comprise the Talmud. It treats of civil and religious law, history, mathematics, astronomy, medicine, metaphysics, and theosophy. It passes from law to myth, from jest to earnest. It is replete with chaste diction, legendary illustration, touches of pathos, bursts of genuine eloquence, finished rhetoric, and flashes of wit and sarcasm. It has been justly called 'a microcosm embracing heaven and earth.' "[7]

[§16] —— The Mosaic concept or interpretation of law has been said to be founded "on absolute justice between man and man."

"It is made necessary by the bold assumption that every man belongs to himself, and has the right to do as he pleases with himself, so long as he accords the same right to others, and does nothing hurtful to interfere with their enjoyment thereof. In short, that he does not do unto others what he would not have them do unto him. If he does so, he is guilty of immorality, which may be slight or gross, according to circumstances. This interpretation demands 'life for life, eye for eye, tooth for tooth, hand for hand, foot for foot, burning for burning, wound for wound, stripe for stripe.' "[8]

[§17] Christian law is found in the New Testament, and mainly in the Gospels of Matthew, Mark, Luke and John, and and in the Epistles of St. Paul. After the New Testament, the oldest repository of Christian law which has come down to us is "The Tract on the Two Ways" from the "Doctrine of the Twelve Apostles," written in Greek by an unknown author near the beginning of the second Christian century.[9]

Strictly speaking, Christian law consists in the legal teaching of Jesus and his Disciples and Apostles.[10] But the New Testament also reaffirms and emphasizes much of the law laid down in the Old,[11] and that law, though made originally for

7 38 Case & Comment (1932) No. 2, p 2
8 Moore v Strickling, ante, quoting Exodus 21:23-25
See also Ruse v Williams (1913) 14 Ariz. 445, 130 P 887, 45 LRANS 923, 926 (Franklin, CJ) saying that "Among the Anglo-Saxon race the idea strongly prevails that each man is an individual by himself, and is to be dealt with as such; that the individual is the social unit."
9 Ante-Nicene Fathers, pp 377-382, Roberts and Donaldson
10 "Where can the purest principles of morality be learned so clearly or so perfectly as from the New Testament? Where are benevolence, love of truth, sobriety, and industry, so powerfully and irresistibly inculcated as in the sacred volume?" Vidal v Girard's Executors (1844) 2 Howard (US) 127, 200, 11 L ed 205, 235 (Story,J)
11 State v District School Board of Edgerton (1890) 76 Wis. 177, 20 ASR 41, 49 (Lyon, J) saying that "The New Testament . . . reaffirms and emphasizes the moral obligations laid down in the Ten Commandments."

Israelites only, has therefore been adopted and followed by Christians throughout the world, thus becoming a law to them as a result of custom.[12] However, Jesus repudiated provisions of the old law pertaining to divorce, the emancipation of children, and oaths; and other provisions relating to religion were discarded by the early church.[13]

[§18] —— Love of one's brother or neighbor is the fundamental rule of Christian law. In the teachings of Jesus —also those of John the Baptist[14]—"brotherly" or "neighbourly" love[15] is made a duty, to be fulfilled by charity,[16] forgiveness,[17] mercy,[18] non-resistance to personal wrongs,[19] patience,[20] and practice of the Golden Rule. Yet this commandment that we love one another is one that "we had from the beginning."[21] Mosaic law had commanded that "thou shalt love thy neighbour as thyself;"[22] and charity and mercy had been commended or lack thereof denounced in numerous passages of the Old Testament.[23] But the concept of "love" as a basis of law—as an essential requisite to civilization— was not understood nor fully appreciated until the time of Jesus.

[§19] —— It is recognized in the New Testament that "the law made nothing perfect,"[24] also that without observance of the commandment of "love" the law as a whole failed of its purpose, and that, on the other hand, by its observance all the law would be fulfilled in one word.[25] And Jesus, avowedly desiring to fulfill rather than destroy the law,[26] repeated the commandment that "Thou shalt love thy neighbour as thyself,"[27] calling it the second "of all the command-

---

12 Even today, in some quarters, the moral or non-ceremonial law of the Old Testament, as modified by the New, is recognized as in force. 22 Geo.LJ (1934) 501
13 See infra §39
14 See Luke 16:16, saying that "The law and the prophets were until John: since that time the kingdom of God is preached."
15 Heb. 13:1
16 See Matt. 5:42; Luke 6:30; Acts 20:35; 1 Cor. 13:13; Col. 3:14; Heb. 13:3
"The very essence" of religion is "that charity that suffereth long and is kind, which vaunteth not itself, doth not behave unseemly, is not easily provoked, and not only believeth and hopeth, but beareth and endureth all things." Poor v Poor (1836) 8 NH 207, 29 AD 664, 668 (Richardson,CJ)
17 See Matt. 18:35; Luke 6:37, 23:34
18 See Matt. 23:23; Luke 6:36
19 Matt. 5:38,39; Luke 6:28,29; see also Two Ways 1:4
20 See 1 Thess. 5:14
"If when ye do well and suffer for it,

ye take it patiently, this is acceptable with God, says the Bible." Poor v Poor, ante, n 16
21 2 John v 5
22 Lev. 19:17,18; and see Tobit 4:13 ("love thy brethren"); Ecclesiaticus 10:6 ("Bear not hatred to thy neighbour for every wrong"), 27:17 ("Love thy friend, and be faithful unto him"), 28:2 ("Forgive thy neighbour the hurt that he hath done unto thee"), 28:7 ("Bear no malice to thy neighbour")
23 See, for example, Prov. 25:21; Isa. 58:7-10; Jer. 22:16; Zech. 7:9; Tobit, 4:7,8,16 and 14:9; Ecclesiasticus 4:5
24 Heb. 7:19
25 Gal. 5:14; and see Rom. 13:8, "he that loveth another hath fulfilled the law."
26 Matt. 5:17
27 Matt. 19:19, 22:39; Mark 12:31; Luke 6:27 ("love your enemies, do good to them which hate you"); John 15:12 ("love one another, as I have loved you"); Rom. 13:9; James 2:8; see also Two Ways 1:2

ments,"[28] and one of two "on which hang all the law and the prophets."[29] St. Paul also observed that "Love worketh no ill to his neighbour: therefore love is the fulfilling of the law."[30] The meaning of the Christian teaching seems unmistakable. The commandment of "love" was given as a basic law—or, more properly speaking, as a higher law—to be taught to the people and to be observed by each individual in his dealings with his fellows. Two thousand years of human experience in disregard of this commandment have shown the inadequacy of law without love.

[§20] —— That transgressions arise out of the human mind or heart,[31] is recognized in Christian law, for Jesus said:

". . . from within, out of the heart of men, proceed evil thoughts, adulteries, fornications, murders, thefts, covetousness, wickedness, deceit, lasciviousness, an evil eye, blasphemy, pride, foolishness. All these evil things come from within, and defile the man."[32]

Therefore the law is concerned with respect to the mental and spiritual condition of the individual who, as the blind Pharisee, should "cleanse first that which is within . . . that the outside . . . may be clean also."[33]

[§21] —— The "Law of Liberty" is mentioned in the Epistle of James,[34] and from the context of the Epistle it appears that this law is the commandment to "love thy neighbour as thyself,"[35] which James called the "royal law according to the Scripture."[36]

The doctrine of the law of liberty is that "what things soever the law saith, it saith to them who are under the law,"[37] and that "whoso looketh unto the perfect law of liberty, and continueth therein, he being not a forgetful hearer, but a doer of the word,"[38] has ceased to be "under" the numerous rules against wrong-doing. Doubtless one who loves his fellow man will not purposely harm or wrong him and it may be said of one who observes this higher and affirmative law that as to him the object of all other law is attained and the necessity therefor has ceased.[39]

---

28 Matt. 22:39; Mark 12:31
  As to "the first and great commandment," see infra §322
29 Matt. 22:40; and see Rom. 13:9, noting that the various commandments are "briefly comprehended in this saying, namely, Thou shalt love thy neighbour as thyself."
30 Rom. 13:10
  "Thou shalt hate no man, but some thou shalt reprove, and for some thou shalt pray, and some thou shalt love more than thy soul." Two Ways 2:7
31 See Matt. 5:22,28
32 Mark 7:21-23; and see Matt. 15:19

33 Matt. 23:26
34 James 1:25, 2:12 ("So speak ye, and so do, as they that shall be judged by the law of liberty")
35 See supra §§18, 19
36 James 2:8
37 Rom. 3:19
38 James 1:25
39 When the object of a rule is attained, the necessity for the rule ceases. Watkins v Roth (1941) 47 Cal. App. 2d 693, 118 P2d 850
  Also, "when the reason of the law ceases, the law ceases." Holmes v Inhabitants of Paris (1884) 75 Me. 559 (Peters,CJ)

[§22] —— A similar doctrine is that a righteous man who knows and keeps the law or who, though not knowing the law, observes its requirements by nature, is not under the law but walks at liberty. The notion is not peculiar to the New Testament, for it is said in Psalms:

"So shall I keep thy law continually for ever and ever. And I will walk at liberty: for I seek thy precepts."[40]

St. Paul recognized this principle when he declared that "if ye be led of the spirit, ye are not under the law,"[41] that "where the Spirit of the Lord is, there is liberty,"[42] and that the law "was not made for a righteous man, but for the lawless and disobedient."[43] Its influence is also seen in St. Paul's statement—

". . . when the Gentiles, which have not the law, do by nature the things contained in the law, these, having not the law are a law unto themselves:

"Which shew the work of the law written in their hearts, their conscience also bearing witness, and their thoughts the mean while accusing or else excusing one another."[44]

[§23] —— The Golden Rule has been called the most perfect expression of the moral law,[45] and it has been said that there is no principle of wider application and of higher wisdom.[46] This commandment, as found in Matthew, is that—

". . . all things whatsoever ye would that men should do to you, do ye even so to them: for this is the law and the prophets."[47]

It is also written in Luke in these words:

". . . as ye would that men should do to you, do ye also to them likewise."[48]

The rule logically follows the commandment to "love thy neighbour as thyself,"[49] in which all other rules are said to be "briefly comprehended."[50]

It is required of one who would observe the "Golden Rule" that he do to others as he would be done by, but not that he accede to every demand made upon him, for the rule does not say that one shall do to others as they would have him do. And while it has been intimated that damages are imposed against a wrongdoer for the purpose of teaching him to do in the future as he would be done by, the rule can hardly be made effective by the force of the law,[51] any more than the duty of

40 Ps. 119:44,45
41 Gal. 5:18
42 1 Cor. 3:17
43 1 Tim. 1:9
44 Rom. 2:14,15
45 Furst-Edwards & Co. v St.Louis Southwestern R.Co. (1912) 146 SW (Tex. Civ.App.) 1025, 1028 (Jenkins,J)
46 Donahoe v Richards (1854) 38 Me. 379, 69 AD 256,275 (Appleton,J)

47 Matt. 7:12
In the Tract on the Two Ways, the Golden Rule is given in negative form: "Whatsoever thou would not have done to thyself, do not thou either to another." Two Ways 1:2
48 Luke 6:31
49 See supra §§18,19
50 Rom. 13:9
51 4 Jn. Marshall LQ (1939) 482, quoting Atty.Gen. Marshall that "The Gol-

one to love his neighbour can be enforced. Nor does it justify an argument by an attorney to a jury that they should put themselves in the situation of his client and do by him as they would be done by. Such an argument is fallacious since it does not say, "Do unto me as you would have me do unto you," but rather, "Do to my opponent for me as you would like me to do to him for you if you were in my place."[1]

[§24] —— The Christian interpretation of law according to Judge Dent in the celebrated case of Moore v Strickling—

"is founded on the broad fundamental principle that no man belongs to himself, or has the right to do as he pleases with himself, but that he holds his body, mind, soul, and property of every description, by divine grant, in trust for the benefit of his fellowman. It requires the doing of good at all times, the love of enemies, the giving to him that asketh, the loaning to anyone that would borrow without the expectation of any return, and the complete devotion of self to the commonweal of humanity and the establishment of a kingdom of perfect righteousness. It condemns resistance to evil. War under any plea, even for humanity's sake, it does not justify, but condemns in unmistakable terms. It goes still further, enters the human heart as the foundation of all evil, and denounces the very conception thereof without overt act. It destroys all distinction between morality and religion. It makes the laws of morality concur fully with the laws of religion. According to it, he who serves man best worships God best, and he who worships God best serves man best. All other religion it denounces as pure hypocrisy. Because of their incapacity to understand it, through inability to live it, men deny it or wrest its meaning to suit their living, of whom it is said:

'Ye are they which justify yourselves before men, but God knoweth your hearts; for that which is highly esteemed among men is an abomination in the sight of God.'[2]

Its ostensible purpose is to make men perfect in all their conduct as their Creator is perfect. Man's environment, including his heritage and hereditary traits of character, customs, laws, business relations, and acquired necessities, is to an almost immeasureable degree directly opposed thereto. Hence they are immoral, not being in conformity with the will of God, and render man immoral. Thus have mankind woven around themselves, thread by thread, an invisible web, which they are powerless to break. Nor does this interpretation admit of degrees of morality; for all disobedience is equally heinous in the sight of God, and all immorality gross immorality.

'Why callest thou me good? There is none good, but one; that is God. But, if thou wilt enter into life, keep the commandments.'[3]

To accept it, we are compelled to admit at once that all mankind, either consciously or unconsciously, are guilty of gross immorality. Hence, most men reject it; for they would rather be blind, and leaders of the blind and perish in the same pit, than sit in condemnation of their own lives. To live in accordance with it in the present condition of the world's affairs requires a complete surrender of self, the giving up of worldly pleasures and enjoyments, the repression of all lustful passions and ambitions, and an entire devotion of time, service, and energies to

den Rule cannot be made effective by United States marshals."
1 Leonard Bros. v Newton (1934) 71 SW

2d (Tex.Civ.App.) 613 (Lattimore,J)
2 Luke 16:15
3 Matt. 19:17

the elevation of mankind, in regaining for them that greater liberty which must follow when the knowledge of truth fills the earth as the waters cover the sea. This interpretation . . . has never been accepted as, or become a part of, the law of the land. If such were the case we would have no need of prosecuting attorney, judge or court."[4]

CHAPTER 4

BURDEN, GOODNESS AND OBJECTS OF THE LAW

25 The doctrine of freedom   26 —— The burden of law   27 The goodness of the law   28 Objects of the law   29 —— Law as a protection for the righteous   30 —— Law as a means for keeping peace   31 —— Law as an instrument of justice

[§25]   Nature has not made men slaves, but free, with an intrinsic right to liberty,[5] when they infringe not the equal freedom of others.[6] This also seems to be a divine principle,[7] that men should "walk at liberty,"[8] each being "permitted to keep his own . . . and not compelled to do anything contrary to principles of right."[9] Jesus recognized that it is lawful for a man to do what he wills with his own,[10] when he thereby commits no wrong to others.[11] And modern English and American law recognizes that every citizen should be permitted to pursue that mode of life which is dictated by his own conscience.[12] All opinions are tolerated and entire freedom of action allowed, unless such interferes in some way with the rights of others.[13]

[§26]   —— It follows that no greater burden of law should be laid upon the people than is necessary for the general welfare.[14]

4 Moore v Strickling (1899) 46 W.Va. 515, 33 SE 274, 50 LRA 279, 282
"If we open our eyes, and if we will honestly acknowledge to ourselves what we discover, we shall be compelled to confess that all the life and efforts of the civilized people of our times are founded on a view of the world which is directly opposed to the view of the world which Jesus had." Ruse v Williams (1913) 14 Ariz. 445, 130 P 887, 45 LRA NS 923, 926 (Franklin, CJ) quoting Strauss, der Alter und der Neue Glaube, p 74
5 "Liberty in its broad sense means the right, not only of freedom from actual servitude, imprisonment, or restraint, but the right of one to use his faculties in all lawful ways, to live and work when he will, to earn his livelihood in any lawful calling, and to pursue any lawful trade or avocation." In re Aubrey (1904) 36 Wash. 308, 78 P 900
"Freedom includes "freedom from" as well as "freedom to." Thus one has a right to freedom from unwarranted attack by others upon his liberty, property and reputation. See Melvin v Reid (1931) 112 Cal. App. 285, 291, 297 P 91 (Marks,J)
6 Spencer, Justice, §27
But in former times one could "sell" himself—i.e., surrender his freedom and become a bond-servant. See Isa. 52:3 ("ye have sold yourselves for naught . . .")
7 Internoscia's Internat. L. (1910) xxviii
8 Ps. 119:45
9 27 Harv. LR (1915) 613, quoting Melanchthon's definition
10 Matt. 20:15; Heath v Wilson (1903) 139 Cal. 362, 366, 73 P 182; Ferguson v Larson (1934) 139 Cal.App. 133, 33 P2d 1061.
11 See Matt. 20:13, ("Friend, I do thee no wrong"); and see 1 Root's (Conn.) Reports (1789-1793) pp x, xi
12 State v. Amana Society (1906) 132 Iowa 304, 8 LRANS 909, 916, 109 NW 894, 11 AnnCas 231 (Ladd,J)
13 Ruse v Williams (1913) 14 Ariz. 445, 130 P 887, 45 LRANS 923, 927 (Franklin,J)
14 See Acts 15:28

"It is not within the competency of government to invade the privacy of a citizen's life and to regulate his conduct in matters in which he alone is concerned, or to prohibit him any liberty the exercise of which will not directly injure society."[15]

But the liberty that is sanctioned in the Scriptures is not a liberty to "walk every one after the imagination of his evil heart,"[16] nor a liberty to be used "for a cloak of maliciousness."[17] And one may properly be deprived of his liberty as punishment for an offense against the law,[18] or he may lose it by being captured in warfare.[19]

[§27] King David seemingly looked upon the law—Mosaic law—as a supreme good. His views are expressed in numerous passages.[20] And Solomon, who is said to have been wiser than all men,[21]—though there were some things past his comprehension[22]—spoke of the law as a "light,"[23] and again as a "fountain of life."[24] Finally St. Paul observed that "the law is holy, and the commandments holy, and just and good,"[25] and that he delighted "in the law of God after the inward man."[26] But he also saw that the law, however good of itself, might be misused; hence his statement: "we know that the law is good, if a man use it lawfully."[27] And while the meaning of the word "use" is not altogether clear,[28] it is plain that the law should never be permitted to become "a weapon of offense by law-breakers."[29]

[§28] The immediate object of laws is to govern human actions,[30] though they are sometimes made for the purpose of controlling or molding men's minds,"[31] It has been said also that "the law was our schoolmaster,"[32] signifying that it is a function of the law to teach proper conduct—to smooth and perfect civilization.[33] But to what ends are men governed and for what purposes are they taught? As to these things, views have differed through the ages.

---

15 Commonwealth v Campbell (1909) 133 Ky. 50, 117 SW 383, 19 AnnCas 159, 24 LRANS 172
16 Jer. 16:12; and see Baruch 1:22
17 1 Pet. 2:16
18 See infra §§419,420
19 See infra §122
20 Ps. 19:7, 19:8, 119:72, 119:77,174, 119:163
21 1 Kings 4:31
22 Ex parte Harkins (1912) 7 Okla. Crim. Rep. 464, 124 P 131, 940 (Furman, J) citing Proverbs 30:18,19
23 Prov. 6:23
24 Prov. 13:14
25 Rom. 7:12
26 Rom. 7:22
27 1 Tim. 1:18
"A human law is good or bad as it agrees or does not agree with the law of God as indicated by the principle of utility." 1 Austin, Lectures on Jurisprudence (1875) 86
28 1 Stephen, English Utilitarians (1900) 271
29 Burgess v State (1931) 161 Md 162, 155 A 153, 75 ALR 1471, 1475; People v Kilpatrick (1926) 79 Colo. 303, 245 P 719, 720
Nor should it be so used as to "penalize the diligent and place a premium on laziness." McCarthy v Palmer (1939) 29 F. Supp. 585,586 (Moscowitz,DJ)
30 Reynolds v United States (1879) 98 US 145, 166, 25 L ed 244, 250, (Waite,CJ); Nicholls v Lynn (1937) 297 Mass. 65, 7 NE2d 474, 110 ALR 377, 382
31 See supra §§1, 18, 19
32 Gal. 3:24
33 9 Am.L.Sch.Rev. (1942) 1297 (Posey)

[§29] —— According to St. Paul, "all Scripture"—which necessarily includes the law—"is given . . . that the man of God may be perfect, thoroughly furnished unto all good works."[34] Therefore, it has been said of Christian law that it was "intended to secure perfection," whereas Mosaic law was "intended for the government of an imperfect, self-willed, ignorant, stubborn, and hard-hearted people, and for the suppression of vice, injustice, and wrong among them."[35] St. Paul stated further that the law "was not made for a righteous man,"[36] inasmuch as "the desire of the righteous is only good,"[37] and no law is needed to keep him from doing evil.[38] On the contrary the law was made—

"for the lawless and disobedient, for the ungodly and for sinners, for unholy and profane, for murderers of fathers and murderers of mothers, for manslayers.

"For whoremongers, for them that defile themselves with mankind, for menstealers, for liars, for perjured persons, and if there be any other thing that is contrary to sound doctrine."[39]

So it is evident that law may properly be considered as a means—and law is only a means, not an end[40]—by which the wicked shall be "bridled and restrained from outrageous behavior, and from doing of injuries, whether by fraud or by violence,"[41] so that "there shall no evil happen to the just,"[42] and "the rod of the wicked shall not rest upon the lot of the righteous."[43]

[§30] —— In its broadest sense, as including rules of conduct and also the agencies by which they are made and enforced, law is designed to enable men to live together in peace.[44] Primitive law was essentially a device to keep the

34 2 Tim. 3:16,17
35 Moore v Strickling (1899) 46 W.Va. 515, 33 SE 274, 50 LRA 279, 282 (Dent.P)
36 1 Tim. 1:9
"For were the impulses of conscience clear, uniform and irresistibly obeyed, man would need no other law-giver." Th. Paine, Common Sense (1776)
37 Prov. 11:23
38 "If all people were truly moral, human laws and government would be unnecessary; for the laws of nature written in their hearts, and perfectly understood by them, would be a sufficient guidance in their dealings with each other. Where no wrongs are committed there exists no necessity for punishment, compensation, or restitution, and human enactments in relation thereto become obsolete. No man need say to his neighbor, 'Know the law;' for all would know it, from the least unto the greatest. But where society is constituted on such an immoral basis as to continually increase the wants and arouse the selfish propensities of mankind, and yet render them proportionally harder of attainment and satisfaction, human law becomes of increasing necessity, to suppress and control these wants and propensities for the common good, otherwise a state of immoral anarchy would be the result, deserving the just condemnation, once requiring his extinction, that 'the imaginations of a man's heart are evil continually from his youth up.'" Moore v Strickling (1899) 46 W.Va. 515, 33 SE 274, 50 LRA 279, 282 (Dent.P)
39 1 Tim. 1:9,10
40 9 Am.L.Sch.Rev. (1942) 1297 (Posey)
41 Preface to King James' Version, 1611
42 Prov. 12:21
43 Ps. 125:3
44 See 13 Fla.LJ (1939) 120
"Peace means quiet of mind, and there cannot be quiet of mind where one has not practical certainty, that is high probability, of security as to life, liberty, property, etc." 30 Geo.LJ (1942) 527, n 70

peace, giving to those who were injured or wronged a substitute for revenge, thus serving to avert private vengeance and to prevent feuds.[45] Mosaic law was also given, no doubt, that the people might "dwell in a peaceable habitation, and in sure dwellings, and in quiet resting places."[46] Similarly, the Christian teachings are called a "gospel of peace,"[47] and St. Paul observed that it is "good and acceptable in the sight of God" that all men "lead a quiet and peaceable life."[48]

[§31] —— In the modern view, the aims of law are justice, liberty and peace, and the happiness and welfare of the people.[49] Primarily it is the purpose of law, as always, to maintain peace and order,[50] or, as it has been said, "to insure domestic tranquility."[51] Justice and law, as words, have no necessary connection, nor is the law necessarily an instrument by which justice is attained.[52] Yet even under Mosaic law, justice was an ideal, as is seen by the statement of Absalom:

"Oh that I were made judge in the land, that every man which hath any suit or cause might come unto me, and I would do him justice."[1]

It is also regarded as an ideal, if not the ultimate object, of modern law.[2] "For what is law," it has been said, "but the enforcement of justice amongst men?"[3] Justice has been defined as "the constant, perpetual disposition to render to every man his due."[4] But man's conception of justice—of what is one's legal due—in particular circumstances and in the various human relations, differs from age to age.[5] It is coming to mean, not only justice as between the parties to a dispute, but also political, social and economic justice, especially "a more equitable distribution of goods among all the families of the world."[5a]

---

45 27 Harv.LR (1914) 199 (Pound), observing further that "Where modern law seeks a rational mode of trial that will bring forth the exact truth, archaic law sought an acceptable mechanical mode of trial, which would yield a certain, unambiguous result, without opportunity for controversy and consequent disturbance of the peace."
46 Isa. 32:18
47 Rom. 10:15; Eph. 6:15
48 1 Tim. 2:2,3
49 See Preambles to U.S. and Texas constitutions; also 1 Root's (Conn.) Reports (1789-1793) xvi
50 See 14 Or.LR (1934-35) 455
"The triumph of the law is not in always ending conflicts rightly, but in ending them peaceably. And we may be certain that we do less injustice by the worst processes of the law than

would be done by the best use of violence." Robt. H. Jackson, Associate Justice US Supreme Court, address before Amer. Bar Assn., Indianapolis, Oct. 2, 1941
51 See note 49, supra
"The law is, after all simply a method of social control." 9 Am.L.Sch.Rev. (1942) 1284 (Shepherd)
52 28 Yale LJ (1918-19) 842, 843
1 2 Sam. 15:4
2 Shaw, CJ, Mass., (1781-1861) eulogizing his predecessor, Parker, CJ
3 McAllister v Marshall (1814) 6 Binney (Pa.) 338, 6 AD 458, 464 (Brackenridge,J)
4 Justinian, Institutes, I, i
5 See 13 Fla.LJ (1939) 120
5a Bishop de Andrea: see Pathfinder (1942) No. 2542, p 9

CHAPTER 5

APPLICATION AND BINDINGNESS OF THE LAW

[§32]   Generally the law applies to, or operates upon, all persons and things that are subject to the authority of the law-giver.[6]   But it is not always easy to determine who or what is subject to such authority.   This may depend upon the character of the law as being, on the one hand a law of the blood—designed for the government of the people of a particular family or tribe wherever they may be—or, on the other hand, a law of the land—for the government of the people in a particular locality or territory whatever their tribe or race.

[§33]   ——— Primitive law was a law of the family or tribe, and was considered as binding the individual members by reason of an actual or supposed blood relationship.   When a tribe moved from place to place, they took with them, not only their cattle and their goods, as did Jacob when he went down into Egypt,[7] but also their law.   Similarly when members of a tribe departed, like Abram and Lot, from their own country and from their kindred and went to another land,[8] they continued—in theory, at least—to be bound by the tribal laws, though they might of necessity be subject also to the law of the people among whom they sojourned.   Mosaic law became a kind of tribal law that was doubtless more or less observed as custom and also for the sake of religion among captive Israelites and Jews after the fall of the kingdoms of Israel about 721 B.C.[9] and Judah about 588 B.C.[10]   It has also been observed among the dispersed Jews in various parts of the world since the destruction of Jerusalem by Titus in A.D. 70.   This is the kind of law, supported by the bond of blood or religion, of which it may properly be said that "it hath dominion over a man as long as he liveth."[11]

---

6 See 25 RCL 778 et seq. Union Pac. R.Co v Anderson (1941) 120 P2d (Ore.) 578 (Lusk,J)
7 Gen. 46:6.
8 Gen. 12:1 et seq.
9 2 Kings 17:6
10 2 Kings 24:14; 2 Chron. 36:20
The Israelites or Jews were sometimes allowed a measure of self-government according to Mosaic law. See 1 Mac. 6:58-60 (covenant of Eupator with the Jews, "that they shall live after their laws, as they did before"); 2 Mac. 11:31 (command of Antiochus that "the Jews shall use their own kind of meats and laws, as before").   But see Mac. 1:42 (where Antiochus commanded that the Israelites give up their law), and 2 Mac. 6:1 (where "the king sent an old man of Athens to compel the Jews to depart from the laws of their fathers")
11 Rom. 7:1

[§34] —— On the other hand, it has come to be generally accepted that the authority of a state or nation, which occupies a definite place upon the earth, is coextensive with the land or territory so occupied. Its law is obligatory upon all persons and things within its borders, and with respect to persons it is binding upon them whether they are citizens or aliens, or whether they are permanent or temporary residents or mere travellers.[11a] This law is thus the law of the land,[12] of which it may be said that "it hath dominion over a man" not "as long as he liveth" but "as long as he dwelleth or sojourneth in the domain." Mosaic law was at one time a law of this character; it was declared as a national law for the Israelites when they had conquered and taken possession of Canaan;[13] and was to be observed by "men, and women, and children, and thy stranger that is within thy gates."[14] Like the laws of most of the modern nations, Mosaic law was a law of the land, binding within but not beyond its borders or "gates."

[§35] But Biblical law as a whole—including the Primitive law as found in Genesis, the Mosaic law contained in Exodus and the ensuing books of the Old Testament, and the Christian law of the New Testament—may be considered neither as a law of the blood nor as a law of the land among Christian nations or peoples, except as its provisions have been adopted or recognized by human or secular law-makers. Yet the law of the Bible, other than that pertaining to ceremonies and observances, may properly be deemed a law of the faith, binding for the sake of religion upon adherents of Christianity even as the commandments of the Old Testament are still regarded by orthodox Jews as binding upon themselves. Moreover, many of the rules of Biblical law are rules of universal jurisprudence which are essential to the existence of any organized society and which, had they not come down to us in the Scriptures or in some other ancient writing, we would have been obliged to formulate or invent for ourselves. "They are," it has been said, "part of an ancient common law, older than that of England."[15]

11a The law of the land is "binding on every citizen and every court and enforceable wherever jurisdiction is adequate for the purpose." Miles v Illinois Central R. Co. (1942) 315 US 698, 86 L ed —— (Reed,J)

12 Gen. 47:26 ("and Joseph made it a law over the land of Egypt . . .")
 The Constitution of the United States (1787) is declared to be the "supreme Law of the Land." Art. VI, ¶2
 The notion that English statutes bind British subjects everywhere has found expression in modern times. American Banana Co. v United Fruit Co. (1908) 213 US 347, 53 L ed 826, 832 (Holmes,J)

13 See Deut. 12:1, "These are the statutes and judgments, which ye shall observe to do in the land, which the Lord God of thy fathers giveth thee to possess it, all the days that ye live upon the earth."

14 Deut. 31:12

15 See 38 Case & Comment (1932) No. 2, p 24

[§36] —— So, though the law of Moses was proclaimed to a particular people,[16] much of it has become a universal law to mankind, not of its own force but because—

(1) Christ came not "to destroy . . . but to fulfill" the law,[17] "and by precept and example to illustrate and make plain its true meaning and force according to the divine will;"[18]

(2) The law was not made "void" but was rather established "through faith;"[19]

(3) The early Christians adopted the sacred books of the Jews as their Old Testament; and

(4) With the rise and spread of Christianity, the Scriptures were carried to all parts of the earth and thus became the most influential law book of all times, having profound effect upon the customs and institutions of many peoples.

[§37] —— —— The question as to whether or not converts from among the "Gentiles" must "be circumcised after the manner of Moses"[20] and otherwise "keep the law of Moses" arose among the early Christians, and being the cause of "no small dissention and disputation,"[21]—being in fact the first great Christian controversy—it was considered by the apostles and elders at Jerusalem in a council held in A.D. 46 and decribed in the Fifteenth Chapter of The Acts of the Apostles. The decision or "sentence" of the council, pronounced by James,[22] was embodied in letters reading thus:

"The apostles and elders and brethren send greeting unto the brethren which are of the Gentiles in Antioch and Syria and Cilicia:

"Forasmuch as we have heard, that certain which went out from us have troubled you with words, subverting your souls, saying, Ye must be circumcised, and keep the law; to whom we gave no such commandment:

"It seemed good unto us, being assembled with one accord, to send chosen men unto you with our beloved Barnabas and Paul,

"Men that have hazarded their lives for the name of our Lord Jesus Christ.

"We have sent therefore Judas and Silas, who shall also tell you the same things by mouth.

"For it seemed good to the Holy Ghost, and to us, to lay upon you no greater burden than these necessary things;

"That ye abstain from meats offered to idols, and from blood, and from things strangled, and from fornication: from which if ye keep yourselves, ye shall do well. Fare ye well."[23]

[§38] —— —— Many of the early Christian communities existing not only in Asia Minor but also in Cyprus and in Rome down to the fourth Christian century, did not literally

16 Anderson v Winston (1736) Jefferson's (Va.) Reports, 24
17 Matt. 5:17
18 Moore v Strickling (1899) 46 W.Va. 515, 33 SE 274, 50 LRA 279, 282 (Dent,P)
19 Rom. 3:31, "Do we then make void the law through faith? God forbid: yea, we establish the law."
20 Acts 15:1
21 Acts 15:2
22 Acts 15:19,20
23 Acts 15:23-29

accept the decision of the council of Jerusalem. These Christians, who came to be called Ebionites, held that converts were subject to Mosaic law, that Christianity fulfilled but did not abrogate the law, and that Jesus supplemented the law by his own commandments.

Moreover it appears from a letter of Pliny the Younger to the Emperor Trajan, written near the beginning of the second Christian century, that the Christians of Bithynia observed some, even if not all, of the provisions of Mosaic law. For Pliny quotes an apostate's description of a Christian assembly in that province as follows:

"They met on a certain stated day, before it was light, and addressed themselves in a form of prayer to Christ, as to some god, binding themselves, by a solemn oath, not for the purpose of any wicked design, but never to commit fraud, robbery or adultery, nor to break faith, nor to deny the existence of a deposit when called upon to deliver it up; after which it was their custom to separate and then re-assemble to eat in common a harmless meal."[24]

[§39] —— —— A proper interpretation of the judgment of the council of Jerusalem requires the consideration not only of the question presented to the council and its decision thereon, but also the circumstances of the controversy so far as they can be perceived.[25] It is evident that the dissension arose between two groups of Jewish Christians, one of which regarded Christianity as a new faith in which there should be "no difference between the Jew and the Greek"[26] or Gentile, while the other viewed it as a new Jewish sect into which Gentiles might be admitted by becoming adopted Jews, that is, by being circumcised and by keeping Mosaic law. The council chose the former position, relieving the Christians from the necessity of circumcision and the observance of the rules of Mosac law pertaining to religion, except as to "meats offered to idols, . . . blood, and . . . things strangled," but requiring them to "abstain from fornication,"[27]—a requirement not of Mosaic law but one which seems to have been made necessary by a weakness for that offense among Christians.[28]

[§40] —— —— It will hardly be urged that the council intended that Christians might freely commit the various offenses denounced in Mosaic law—as that, while they must abstain from fornication, they might, with impunity, commit adultery—or that they might disregard the many civil rules embodied in Mosaic law. Had they so intended, their decision

24 Plinius ad Trajanum, Lib.X, Epistle XCVII (Donaldson's trans., Edinburgh, 1762, 11:251)
25 "The language of a court must always be read in view of the facts before it." Sharon v Sharon (1888) 75 Cal. 1, 16 P. 345, 356 (McKinstry,J)
26 Rom. 10:12
27 See §37 supra
28 See 1 Cor. 5:1; Eph. 5:3

would properly have been regarded as "void," for they would thereby have "destroyed" the law in so far as Christians were concerned, in violation of the pronouncement of Jesus that he did not come for that purpose. It must always be considered that Jesus is the highest authority as to Christian law,[29] and that His plain teaching is not to be contradicted and cannot be overcome by any other doctrine.

But even if Christians were not obliged in conscience to observe the non-ceremonial laws of Moses as such, they can scarcely ignore those "things . . . written for our admonition"[30] in the Old Testament, since that part of the Scripture is so intimately connected with the New Testament that both are considered as one work.

CHAPTER 6

INTERPRETATION AND OPERATION OF LAWS

[§41] "Like all other ancient writings the Scriptures present many difficulties."[31] Sometimes the meaning of a law is obscure, as though seen "through a glass darkly."[32] More often, questions arise as to whether or how it should be applied. In these circumstances the law must doubtless be interpreted or construed, as the intent of the lawmaker and the conditions of life compel.[33] To interpret a law, like any other thing expressed in words, is to discover and declare its true meaning. To construe a law, on the other hand, is to apply it to a particular situation or state of facts.[34] If the language

---

29 Matt. 28:18, "And Jesus came and spake unto them (the eleven disciples) saying: All power is given unto me in heaven and in earth."
30 1 Cor. 10:11
31 "Some of these (difficulties) are not easy of solution, while others may be satisfactorily explained. The existence of difficulties in such a book was to be expected, and therefore cannot be wondered at. It is a matter of astonishment, indeed, that there are not more found in it. This must be evident to any one on reflecting that 'the books of Scripture were written by different persons, in almost every variety of circumstance; that they refer to people whose customs and habits were totally dissimilar to our own; that they narrate histories of which we possess no other authentic document which might reflect light on some obscurity of expression or vagueness of description; that they

were written in other languages than those in which we now possess them; and that, in addition to the mutability of language, there are the difficulties of translation out of one tongue into another.' " Holman's Bible, 1881
32 1 Cor. 13:12   33 12 Gr.B (1900) 7
But bearing in mind that the law does not contemplate or require impossibilities. Magnolia Petroleum Co. v Still (1942) 163 SW2d (Tex.Civ.App.) 268, 270 (Johnson,CJ)
Nor vain things. State v Wallace (1942) 131 P2d (Or.) 222, 253 (Kelly,CJ, dissenting)
34 1 Davids NY Law of Wills (1923) 733: "The ascertainment of . . . intention . . . is defined as 'interpretation,' whereas the legal effect of the instrument is described as 'construction.' The court first must interpret the writing, and thereafter may proceed to construe it."

is so plain that "a wayfaring man, yea any who can read, need not err therein,"[35] there is no room for interpretation outside the words themselves.[36] When the wording is clear and admits but one meaning, it should be given that meaning and none other.[37]

[§42] —— But when interpretation is needed a law should be interpreted "in newness of spirit, and not in the oldness of the letter,"[38] for "the letter killeth, but the spirit giveth life."[39] The basic rule of interpretation and construction is to find the intent of the law-maker in the whole law, considered in the light of the circumstances under which it was made and the purpose it was intended to serve, and to give proper effect to that intent, though this may result in a departure from the literal meaning of the words used.[40] Yet it is not often permissible when interpreting a law either to add to or take away from the words thereof.[41]

[§43] —— It is to be taken for granted that a law was made for a wholesome purpose, and ordinarily that it was designed to suppress some prevalent wickedness or wrongdoing.[42] If its wording admits of different interpretations, and its purpose is evident or can be seen by those who will "inquire wisely,"[43] it should be so interpreted as to cure the evil toward which it was directed, even though this involves some departure from its literal meaning.[44] On the other hand, it should not be interpreted in such manner as to create other evils. Paraphrasing certain Scriptural passages,[45] where a law "would seek to cast out one evil spirit" it should not be given an interpretation or construction that "would take into the political house thus swept and garnished . . . other more dangerous spirits," thus making "the last condition . . . worse than the first,"[46]

35 Isa. 35:8
36 State v District School Board of Edgerton (1890) 76 Wis. 177, 20 ASR 41, 49 (Lyon,J)
37 Deno v Standard Furniture Co. (1937) 190 Wash. 1, 66 P2d 1158, 1162 (Willard,J dissenting)
38 Rom. 7:6
39 2 Cor. 3:6; Wortham v Walker (1939) 128 SW 2d (Tex.) 1138, 1150 (Samuel,Spec.CJ); 42 Wash. LR (1914) 773
40 See 25 RCL 961 et seq.; 23 Cal. Jur. 719; 39 Tex.Jur. 155
"Courts are not limited to the lifeless words of a statute but may with propriety recur to the history of the times when it was passed." Great Northern Ry Co. v United States (1941) 315 US 262, 86 L ed —— (Murphy,J)
41 See Deut. 4:2; Rev. 22:18,19; also

Two Ways, 4:13, "Thou shalt . . . keep what thou did receive, neither adding thereto nor taking aught away." And see supra §6
42 So the fact that a nation has many laws signifies that its people are lawless. Law is not made when the people are righteous, but when they are lawless and disobedient. See §29 supra.
43 Ecclesiastes 7:10
44 See §42 supra
45 Matt. 12:43-45; Luke 11:24-26
46 See Stackpole v Hallahan (1895) 16 Mont. 40, 40 P 80, 28 LRA 502, 510
A useful and legitimate statute should not be so construed "as to make of it an instrument of positive fraud and oppression." Keller v Downey (1942) 161 SW2d (Tex.Civ.App.) 803,811 (Combs, J, dissenting)

[§44] ——— Much of the law of the Bible is written in broad and general language, and it may therefore be considered as of universal application.[47] The duty to observe this law, like "the obligation to do no hurtful thing toward our fellow man," is one which "rests upon all alike."[48]

"In commandments, such as 'Thou shalt not kill' and 'Thou shalt not steal,' the 'thou,' whatever it may have meant originally, undoubtedly now refers to every human being. Every single person is addressed and . . . is commanded to refrain from these acts. It could not be clearer or more peremptory."[49]

But many provisions of Biblical law concern or are directed to particular persons or classes of persons, such as the king, husbands and wives, parents and children, and masters and servants, and such rules are applicable only to those persons or classes.

[§45] ——— When a secular law is to be interpreted, the court may consider the character of the people, as well as the circumstances existing when the law was made. It has been declared that—

"A literal interpretation of a statute which denies to it the historical circumstances under which it was drawn is to make mummery of its provisions."[50]

So in a proper case a court will consider the fact that Americans are a religious or Christian people. For this reason, "no purpose of action against religion can be imputed to any legislation."[51]

"The court starts with the historical fact in view that this nation (the United States) is a religious nation, a Christian people; and therefore accepts, as a conclusive presumption that Congress, or the State legislature, had the same historical fact in view when it passed the act which is to be construed, and that it did not intend to do anything contrary to that accepted condition."[52]

[§46] Having seen that law generally operates either upon all persons of the blood or upon all within the domain of the law-maker,[1] it is appropriate here to inquire as to exemptions and certain other matters relating to the operation of laws. Under the Mosaic law, no one was exempt from obedience. Inasmuch as the law was God's, though given by Moses, the priesthood and even the king were bound to obey it.[2] But it does not follow that a rule must be applied in every situation.[3]

47 See §32 supra
48 Loyd v Pierce (1935) 89 SW2d (Tex. Civ.App.) 1035, 1039 (Martin,J)
49 14 Or.LR (1934) 91, 92 (Radin)
50 Wortham v Walker (1939) 128 SW2d (Tex.Sup.Ct.) 1138, 1150 (Samuels,Spec. CJ)
51 Holy Trinity Church v United States

(1892) 143 US 457, 36 L ed 226 (Brewer, J)
52 42 Wash.LR (1914) 772 (Barnard)
1 See § 34 et seq., supra
2 See §49 infra
3 "It is impossible to lay down a rule which will govern in every case." Heatherly v Hill (1874) 67 Tenn. 170, 171 (Nicholson,CJ)

On the contrary, it is an axiom that "circumstances alter cases,"[4] and it is plain that there are situations in which the application of a given rule, however wholesome it may ordinarily be, would defeat the very purpose of the law-maker.[5] So while no rule is of more general force than the commandment that "Thou shalt not kill," yet there are circumstances in which this fundamental rule does not apply, as where killing is a social or political necessity.[5a]

[§47] —— The priesthood and also the kings and princes of Israel, after the kingdom had been established, were obligated to keep the law of Moses,[6] though no physical means or procedure existed by which they might be compelled to do so. Similarly in the Roman Empire, priests were amenable to the law of the state as well as the canons of the church,[7] and the emperor was supposedly answerable to the civil and criminal laws.[8] Concerning the bindingness of the law upon the sovereign, it was reasoned that—

"It is just that the prince should obey his own laws. For the authority of his voice is just, only if he is not permitted to do what he has forbidden to the people."[9]

But under the common law it is considered that a rule does not apply to the English king nor to an American government or state, without express words to that effect.[10] It has been said that "there can be no legal right as against the authority that makes the law on which the right depends,"[11] but the better view seems to be merely that the common law, unlike the civil law of Rome, provides no remedy against the king or the government.[12]

[§48] —— In deciding whether one is properly amenable to a rule of Biblical law for a thing that he has done or left undone, it is admissible to consider his knowledge both of law and fact. For in this law it appears that a man is responsible according to that which he knew or should have known. Gen-

4 Payn, Market Overt (1895) xxxix The law or its application "varies with circumstances." Christie v Callahan (1941) 124 F2d 825, 827 (Rutledge,J)
"The character of every act depends upon the circumstances in which it is done." Kersten v Young (1942) 52 Cal. App.2d 1, 125 P2d 501 (White,J)
And each particular case must rest (or stand or turn) upon its own facts. Murphy v. St.Claire Brewing Co. (1940) 41 Cal.App.2d 535, 107 P2d 273, 276 (Peters, PJ); Gates v Bisso Ferry Co. (1937) 172 So. (La.App.) 829, 835 (McCaleb,J); Heron v Ramsey (1941) 45 NM 491, 117 P2d 247 (Zinn,J)
5 "An impeccably 'right' legal rule applied to the 'wrong' facts yields a decision which is as faulty as one which

results from the application of the 'wrong' legal rule to the 'right' facts." United States v Forness (1942) 125 F2d 928, 942, 943 (Frank,Cir.J)
5a See infra §367
6 See Neh. 9:34 ("neither have our kings, our princes, our priests, nor our fathers, kept thy law"); Wisdom of Solomon, 6:4 (condemning rulers because they had not "judged aright nor kept the law")
7 See 7 Cal.LR (1918) 101 (Sherman)
8 See 13 Ill.LR (1918-1919) 443 (Zane)
9 St.Isadore of Seville, Sententiae, III: 51
10 See 25 RCL 783 et seq.
11 Kawananakoa v Polybank (1907) 205 US 349, 51 L ed 834 (Holmes,J)
12 30 Harv.LR (1917) 21 (Maguire)

erally one is not to be held accountable or molested for a thing "ignorantly done,"[13] whether his ignorance pertained to the law itself or to the nature and consequences of the thing done.[14] Thus it is seen that Ezra was commanded merely to judge "all those that know the law,"[15] and that Jesus prayed in behalf of those who crucified him, saying "Father forgive them; for they know not what they do."[16] But one who is "willingly ignorant,"[17]—who has "rejected knowledge"[18] and scorned the law—may not be held guiltless.

[§49] —— —— The reason for the Biblical doctrine of non-responsibility for things done in ignorance doubtless was that in former times the whole of the law could be read and explained to the people in seven days, so that with proper observance of the directions concerning the reading and teaching of the law to the people they might actually have known and understood the rules by which they were governed. But this reason does not obtain in modern legal systems, and no distinction is recognized, therefore, between those who know the law and those who do not. On the contrary, it is now held that every man must know and conform to the laws of his country.[19] As a practical expedient, "every man is presumed to know the law,"[20] and a violator is not permitted to assert his lack of knowledge.[21]

[§50] —— It is a principle of antiquity that the law should be equal[22] and impartial,[23] and that all should be treated equally[24] "without prefering one before another" either "in words or in deeds."[25] As bearing upon this doctrine, it has been said:

"If the fortunes of all cannot be equal, if the mental capacities of all cannot be the same, at least the legal rights of all those who are citizens of the same state ought to be equal."[26]

13 2 Mac. 11:31, command of King Antiochus
Ignorance is not "a legal crime." Smith,CJ dissenting in Johnson v State (1942) 163 SW2d (Ark.) 153, 158
But if one, through ignorance violates any commandment "concerning things which ought not to be done" he is guilty "when he knoweth of it," within the laws relating to sin offerings. Lev. 4:2, 5:3
14 See Gen. 9:21. It is said that by the judgment of the fathers Noah was not guilty of "sin" in being overcome by wine, because he knew not the strength of it.
15 Ezra 7:25; 1 Esd. 8:23
16 Luke 23:34   17 2 Pet. 3:5
18 Hosea 4:6
19 Bixler v Baker (1811) 4 Binney (Pa.) 213, 221 (Yeates,J)
20 Harris v Clap (1805) 1 Mass. 308, 2 AD 27, 32 (Strong,J)

21 10 RCL 873
22 Cicero, Topica, 23, "Justice requires that in equal cases there should be an equal law."
23 See Mal. 2:9, "I . . . have made you contemptible . . . according as ye . . . have been partial in the law."
24 People v Coleman (1942) 53 Cal.App. 2d 18,34, 127 P2d 309 (Ward,J)
"True, the deceased was a Chinaman, a foreigner and a heathen . . . but still he was a human being, and in the estimation of the law his life was as precious, and as much entitled to protection, as that of the most exalted and best beloved citizen of our own State." Duran v State (1883) 14 Tex.Crim.Rep. 195, 199 (Willson,J)
25 1 Tim. 521 "I charge the . . . observe these things without prefering one before another, doing nothing by partiality."
26 Cicero, De Leg., 2:32,12

The principle first appears in Exodus, in reference to discrimination against aliens or "strangers," that—

"One law shall be to him that is homeborn, and unto the stranger that sojourneth among you."[27]

It is also embodied in various statements concerning "respect of persons,"[28] as that "Thou shalt not respect persons"[29] and that "It is not good to have respect of persons in judgment."[30] Whether one be poor and friendless or rich and mighty, he is entitled to the same consideration and protection before the law. So, in administering the law, it is improper to show partiality to the rich[31] or to "turn aside the poor in the gate from their right."[32] On the other hand it is also unlawful to "respect the person of the poor."[33]

[§51] —— —— But even the doctrine of equality is not applicable in every situation. So, though the general rule declared that the homeborn (native) and the stranger (foreigner) should be governed by "one law," yet it was expressly provided that a stranger should not "eat of the passover"[34] or "enter into the congregation."[35] Moreover, the requirement of impartiality does not mean that the righteous and the unrighteous are to receive equal treatment at the hands of the law. On the contrary, a man is to be judged according to his works[36] and recompensed "according to the cleanness of his hands."[37] The law approves of those who "work righteousness"[38] and condemns those who "work wickedness."[39] It will not "accept the person of the wicked, to overthrow the righteous in judgment."[40]

CHAPTER 7
CONFLICTS AND CHANGES IN THE LAW

52 Reconciliation of conflicting rules 53 —— Last pronouncement as law 54 —— Inferior prevails not against superior 55 —— Human not to contradict divine laws 56 Changes in the law 57 —— Ancient law as unchangeable 58 —— Fundamentals not alterable 59 —— Supplementals subject to change

[§52] There will occasionally be found two rules, in the same body or system of law, that conflict or seem to conflict,

27 Ex. 12:49. See also Lev. 24:22; Num. 9:14, 15:15,16
28 "God is no respecter of persons." Acts 10:34. See also Ecclesiasticus 35:12; Rom. 2:11; Eph 6:9; Col. 3:25; 1 Pet. 1:17
"For he which is Lord over all shall fear no man's person, neither shall he stand in awe of any man's greatness: for he hath made the small and great, and careth for all alike." Wisdom of Solomon 6:7
29 Deut. 16:19
30 Prov. 24:23; 3 Ky.St.BJ, No.4, p 22
31 James 2:1-7   32 Amos 5:12
33 Lev. 19:15   34 Ex. 12:43
35 Deut. 23:3, "An Ammonite or Moabite shall not enter into the congregation." And see Neh. 13:1
36 Prov. 24:12; Ecclesiasticus 16:12; 1 Pet. 1:17
"By their fruits ye shall know them." Matt. 7:16, 20. In re Kirk (1925) 130 Atl. (N.J.) 569, 570 (Minturn,J)
"Even a child is known by his doings." Prov. 20:11
37 2 Sam. 22:21
38 Ps. 146:8; Acts 10:35
39 Tobit 4:17; Ecclesiasticus 12:6
40 Prov. 18:5

one with the other. In such a case, the rules should, if possible, be interpreted so that they will harmonize and so that proper effect may be given to both, as near as may be.[41] But conflicting rules cannot always be reconciled by sound reasoning, and this will more often be true of rules made at different times or by different authorities. Accordingly the difficulty can usually be solved by giving effect to the more recent rule or to the rule pronounced by the higher authority, if it is apparent that one is superior to the other.

[§53] —— "The latest pronouncement of the law-maker is the law."[42] According to this axiom where two laws have been made by the same authority, or by different authorities of the same dignity, the one last made will prevail over the earlier one in so far as the two conflict. Applying this principle to Biblical law, when a rule of the Old Testament disagrees with one of the New, the older rule must be considered as "abrogated" or "repealed" and the newer rule as being the effective and existing law. So even if a commandment of Jesus were regarded as of the same authority as one given by Moses, the new commandment nevertheless is of greater force and supersedes the old by virtue of its being the latest expression of the law-maker.[43]

[§54] —— But the doctrine of the supremacy of the most recent law is controlled by one even more fundamental, that an inferior may not be permitted to prevail as against his superior,[44] and consequently that a command of supreme authority is not overcome by that of a subordinate. For example, it is not to be considered that a rule announced by Moses is abrogated or limited by any subsequent pronouncement of a lesser authority. Nor may any notion based upon the saying of an apostle be regarded as valid if it is seen to conflict with a plain doctrine of Jesus.[45]

[§55] —— "No human laws," said Blackstone, "should be suffered to contradict" the law of revelation.[46] In the first American colonial grant in 1584 authority was conferred to enact statutes for the government of the proposed colony provided that "they be not against the true Christian faith."[47]

41 A "repeal by implication" is never favored or presumed (25 RCL 918). The intent to repeal must clearly appear (25 RCL 917), and if, by any reasonable construction an early rule and a later one can be reconciled and so construed that both may stand, this must be done (39 Tex Jur 141, 142)
42 25 RCL 914
43 It follows, for example, that Christians are bound to observe the teachings of Jesus concerning divorce, rather than the earlier rule of Moses on that subject. See infra §204
44 22 Geo.LJ (1934) 426
45 See §42 supra
46 1 Bl.Com. 42
47 See Holy Trinity Church v United States (1892) 143 US 457, 36 L ed 226, 230 (grant by Queen Elizabeth to Sir Walter Raleigh)

And it may be argued that no law-making body has ever been invested with power to enact statutes in violation of Biblical law. At all events it has been recognized that "there are . . . fundamental principles of morality and justice which no legislature is at liberty to disregard."[48] But this does not mean that an individual may properly set at naught a secular law of the land in which he lives because he considers that it conflicts with the law of the Bible.[48a]

[§56] Since time immemorial some have desired permanency and stability in human affairs, while others have sought change and progress. This struggle has centered about the law, for law can be an instrument either of stability or progress. Doubtless "it is of great consequence that the law should be settled,"[49] and it has been asserted:

"We must not by any whimsical conceits, supposed to be adapted to the altering fashions of the times, overturn the established law . . . It descended to us as a sacred charge, and it is our duty to preserve it."[50]

On the other hand, the law—as Jesus said of the sabbath[51] —was made for man, and not man for the law,[52] and it has been declared that—

"As the usages of society alter, the law must adapt itself to the various situations of mankind."[53]

[§57] —— Ancient law-makers assumed to speak for all time, and the law was regarded as eternal and unchangeable. Thus it appears in the Scriptures that at the time of Darius, about 537 B.C., "according to the law of the Medes and Persians, which altereth not,"[1]—"no decree nor statute which the king establisheth may be changed."[2] Also it seems that Jesus conceded the everlastingness of Mosaic law in his saying that, "till heaven and earth pass, one jot or one tittle shall in

---

48 License Tax Cases (1867) 5 Wall. (US) 462, 18 L ed 497, 500, (Chase,CJ); Appeal of Allyn (1909) 81 Conn. 534, 71 A 794, 23 LRANS 630, 632
"What is morally wrong cannot be made legally right." Lincoln

48a See infra §105

49 Coggs v Bernard (1703) Lord Raym. 909, 917, 918, 920, 5 English Ruling Cases 247, 260, Smith's Leading Cases, 8th ed., 199 (Holt,CJ) saying, "I have said thus much in this case, because it is of great consequence that the law should be settled in this point, but I don't know whether I may have settled it, or may not rather have unsettled it. But however that happen, I have stirred these points, which wiser heads in time may settle."
"It is not of so much importance what the rule is, as that it be settled." Adams v Delaware Ins. Co. (1811) 3 Binney (Pa.) 287, 294 (Brackenridge,J)

See also Clayton v Clayton (1811) 3 Binney (Pa.) 476, 491 (Yeates,J)
50 Clayton v Adams (1796) 6 Durnford & East's Reports 604 (Lord Kenyon)
"Stability . . . and permanency in the laws, are positive blessings. Any change, unless absolutely required by the exigencies of the particular case, is in itself an evil." 18 Mass.LQ (1933) No. 4, p 163 (Inaugural address of Governor Clifford, 1853)
51 Mark 2:27   52 12 Gr.B (1900)
53 Barwell v Brooks (1784) 3 Douglas's Reports 371 (Lord Mansfield)
"Law . . . must adjust itself to the changing needs of . . . life." 27 ABA Journal (1941) No. 2, p 78
"New times demand new measures . . . The old advances and in time outgrows the laws that in our forefathers' day were best." (Lowell) 20 Tex. LR (1942) No. 7, p 62
1 Dan. 6:8,12; see also Est. 1:19
2 Dan. 6:15

no wise pass from the law, till all be fulfilled."[3]   Similarly it was prophesied of the Roman Jus Gentium, that it should not be "one law for Rome, another law for Athens, one law today, another law tomorrow, but one eternal and immutable law for all nations and for all ages."[4]   And in some nations "it was made a capital crime, once to motion the making of a new law for the abrogating of an old, though the same were most pernicious."[5]

[§58]   —— From the old idea of the immutability of law, it is a far cry to the modern notion of law as something to vary with the fashions of the hour and the shifting currents of politics.[6]   The truth, no doubt, is to be found somewhere between these extremes, for parts of the law repose upon fundamental facts of human nature, while other parts are less securely grounded or were designed to meet transitory conditions.   Fundamentals—"the weightier matters of the law"[7]— "admit of no substantial change, save in finding the best form of expression."[7a]   The basic rules of Biblical law, as finally established in the New Testament, may properly be considered as fundamental and therefore unalterable.

[§59]   —— But not all rules, even of Biblical law, are of that character.   Many provisions—the greater portion, indeed, of secular law—are merely supplemental to the more fundamental principles, and were intended to apply those principles in certain particulars to the conditions of the time. Such rules will not necessarily fit all people at all times, nor satisfy their sense of justice in all circumstances.[8]   On the contrary, they must change from time to time to meet the changing conditions of life—though not so rapidly as to endanger peace and security.   This is the law that is meant when it is said "the law must progress,"[9] and that it must adapt itself "to the new relations and interests which are constantly springing up in the progress of society."[10]

---

3 Matt. 5:18; 42 Wash.LR (1914) 773
4 Cicero, De Republica
5 Preface to King James' Version, 1611
6 4 J. Marshall LQ (1939) 576
7 Matt. 23:23; Robinson v State (1870) 33 Tex. 342 (Walker,J)
7a 30 Harv. LR (1917) 796, 797
8 13 Fla.LJ (1939) 121
"Since experience is of all teachers the most dependable, and since experience also is a continuous process, it follows that a rule . . . at one time thought necessary . . . should yield to the experience of a succeeding generation whenever that experience has clearly demonstrated the fallacy or unwisdom of the old rule." Funk v United States (1933) 290 US 371, 78 L ed 369 (Sutherland,J)

9 38 Case & Comment (1932) No. 1, p 9, per Wm. M. McKinney, saying, "But the law must progress; new legislation is needed to meet changed conditions; fresh interpretations must come from the courts; early precedents must now and then be overruled or given applications to modern circumstances; and lawyers will ever seek and rely upon the latest pronouncements and the newest discussions."

10 Hodges v New England Screw Co. (1850) 1 R.I. 312, 356 (Green,CJ)
History shows that it has been in time of war and crisis that the great forward steps in law and government have been made. 20 Tex.LR (1942) No. 7, p 7, quoting Judge John J. Parker.

CHAPTER 8

THE WRITING, READING AND TEACHING OF THE LAW

[§60] "The law is in the heart of a righteous man."[11] It is said to be written in the hearts of those who "do by nature the things contained in the law,"[12]—"written not with ink, but with the Spirit of the living God; not in tables of stone, but in fleshly tables of the heart."[13] But the words of the law have also been engraved in stone, lettered in manuscripts, and printed in books, that it might more readily be handed down to posterity and disseminated throughout the earth.

[§61] —— According to the Scriptural record, Primitive law was traditional, which is to say that it was not in writing but was carried in memory and handed down by word of mouth until the time of Moses, to whom we may attribute the recording of such fragments or portions as are now found in the book of Genesis. Mosaic law, on the other hand, "God spake" unto Moses,[14] "and Moses wrote all the words of the Lord,"[15] in the books of Exodus, Leviticus, Numbers and Deuteronomy. The teachings of Jesus, like the primitive commandments and judgments, were given orally and after many years were partially reduced to writing, in the "Four Gospels" of Matthew, Mark, Luke and John.

[§62] —— In Exodus it appears that the Lord "gave unto Moses, when he had made an end of communing with him upon Mount Sinai, two tables of testimony, tables of stone, written with the finger of God."[16] But when "Moses turned, and went down from the mount," seeing the molten calf which the people had made, his "anger waxed hot, and he cast the tables out of his hands, and brake them beneath the mount."[17] Thereafter, at the command of the Lord, Moses hewed two other "tables of stone like unto the first," and again "went up unto Mount Sinai," where he re-wrote "upon the tables the words of the covenant, the ten commandments."[18] A similar account is contained in Deuteronomy,[19] where it is said, however, that the Lord "wrote on the tables, according to the first writing, the ten commandments,"[20] and that Moses, upon coming down from the mount, "put the tables in the ark" which

11 Ps. 37: 31
12 Rom. 2:14,15
13 2 Cor. 3:3
14 Ex. 24:4
15 Ex. 20:1 et seq.
16 Ex. 31:18
17 Ex. 32:15,19
18 Ex. 34:1,4,28
19 Deut. 5:22, 9:15-17
20 Deut. 10:4

he had made, "and there they be, as the Lord commanded me."[21]

[§63] —— Mosaic law directed that when the people of Israel passed over the river Jordan they should set up "great stones and plaister them with plaister," and that they should write thereon "all the words of this law very plainly."[22] This commandment was performed by Joshua, who set up stones in mount Ebal, and wrote "there upon the stones a copy of the law of Moses . . . in the presence of the children of Israel."[23]

[§64] —— The Bible from the press of Johann Gutenberg in 1454 was the first book to be printed from movable type. Since that time it has been "published according to the language of every people,"[24]—it has been reproduced more frequently and distributed more universally than any other book.[25] Thus it has been said:

"There is . . . no book that is so widely used and so highly respected as the Bible; no other that has been translated into as many tongues; no other that has had such marked influence upon the habits and life of the world . . . Many translations of it, and of parts of it, have been made from time to time, since two or three centuries before the beginning of the Christian era. And since the discovery of the art of printing and the manufacture of paper in the sixteenth century, a great many editions of it have been printed."[26]

[§65] The law must be made known to the people in order that they may support it and that ignorance of its requirements may be inexcusable.[27] This is recognized in the Scriptures, which teach that the law should be publicly read and expounded from time to time. Mosaic law commands:

"At the end of every seven years, in the solemnity of the year of release, thou shalt read this law before all Israel in their hearing. Gather the people together, men and women, and children, and thy stranger that is within thy gates, that they may hear and that they may learn . . . and observe to do all the words of this law."[28]

21 Deut. 10:5
22 Deut. 27:2-4,8
The code of Hammurabi was inscribed on a monument—a block of black diorite —nearly 8 feet high, which was discovered in Babylonia in 1902. Hughes v Medical Examiners (1926) 162 Ga. 246, 134 SE 42, 49 (Hill,J)
23 Josh. 8:30-32
The "stone Ezal" is mentioned in 1 Sam. 20:19
24 See Est. 1:22, stating that Ahasuerus, king of the Medes and Persians, commanded that the law that a man should bear rule in his own house be published according to the language of every people.
25 In 121 years (1816-1936) the American Bible Society distributed 276,371,654 volumes of Scriptures, and it is said that "The total number of languages in which the Bible or some part of it has been published has now reached the

notable figure of 991; the complete Bible in 176 languages; the New Testament in an additional 214; portions consisting of at least one complete book in 520 more; and selections of Scripture, less than a complete book, in still 81 more languages." Report of Board of Managers (1936) p 32
26 Hacket v Brooksville School District (1905) 120 Ky. 608, 9 AnnCas 36, 37
27 22 Geo.LJ (1934) 417; 4 Jn. Marshall LQ (1939) 482
28 Deut. 31:10-12
The Lord "established a testimony . . . and appointed a law . . . which he commanded our fathers, that they should make them known to their children, that the generation to come might know them, even the children which should be born, who should arise and declare them unto their children." Ps. 78:5,6

We are not enlightened as to the observance of this provision, but the public reading of the law upon several occasions is mentioned. Thus, it is said that Joshua—

"read all the words of the law . . . before all the congregation of Israel, with the women, and the little ones, and the strangers that were conversant among them."[29]

Shaphan the scribe read unto king Josiah the book of the law found in the house of the Lord,[30] and the king read or caused it to be read to "all the men of Judah and all the inhabitants of Jerusalem . . . and the priests, and the prophets, and all the people, both small and great."[31]

Similarly, during the reign of Artaxerxes of Persia, Ezra the chief priest and reader brought the law before the people upon the first day of the seventh month and read "from morning unto midday"[32] for seven days, "before the men and the women, and those that could understand."[33] And the priests and Levites "caused the people to understand the law: . . . they read . . . distinctly, and gave the sense, and caused them to understand the reading."[34]

[§66] As to the teaching of the law, the Mosiac provision is that—

"Thou shalt teach them (the commandments) diligently unto thy children, and shalt talk of them when thou sittest in thine house, and when thou walkest by the way, and when thou liest down, and when thou risest up. . . . And thou shalt write them upon the posts of thy house, and on thy gates."[35]

The foregoing provision imposes a duty upon parents to instruct their children in the law; other provisions speak of teaching the law to the people, meaning no doubt the public reading and expounding of the law (see §65). Thus it appears that Jehosaphat sent his princes, and with them Levites and priests, and they taught the law throughout all the cities of Judah;[36] also that Artaxerxes, king of Persia, commanded Ezra that "all those that know . . . (the law) thou shalt teach."[37]

---

29 Josh. 8:34,35
30 2 Kings 22:10
In the reign of Josiah, Kilkiah the priest "found the book of the law in the house of the Lord," which he delivered to Shaphan the scribe, who carried it to the king and read it before the king. 2 Chron. 34:14-18
31 2 Kings 23:2
32 1 Esd. 9:41; and see Neh. 9:3, stating that on the twenty and fourth day of this month they "read in the book of the law . . . one fourth part of the day."
33 Neh. 8:1-18; 1 Esd. 9:38-41
34 Neh. 8:7,8
35 Deut. 6:7-9
36 2 Chron. 17:7-9
37 1 Esd. 8:23; Ezra 7:25

CHAPTER 9

LAW OBSERVANCE

67 In general   68 Rewards for obedience   69 Punishments for disobedience

[§67]   It is not enough that the people "with their lips do honour"[38] the law, "for not the hearers . . . but the doers of the law shall be justified."[39]   And surely it is no excuse for disobedience of the law to say that men have never obeyed it as they should.   Many passages throughout the Scriptures show a deep and constant apprehension—which history shows to have been warranted—that the law would not be properly observed.[40]   In varying phraseology the commandment is re-iterated to "do,"[41] "fulfill,"[42] "keep,"[43] "observe,"[44] "remember,"[45] and "forget not" the law,[46] the "commandments,"[47] the "ordinances"[48] or "statutes,"[49] and the "judgments."[50] In ancient times obedience to law was encouraged by blessings and enforced by curses.[1]   And, as we shall presently see, rewards are promised to those who keep Biblical law and punishments are threatened to those who violate it.

[§68]   To them that keep the law, the Scriptures promise the blessings of fruitfulness,[2] happiness,[3] health,[4] longevity,[5]

38 Isa. 29:13; Matt. 15:8
39 Rom. 2:13
"Who is the upright man? He who keeps the decrees of the fathers, the legislation, and the customs." Horace, Epistles, I, 16, 40
40 See Deut., chaps. 11, 28; Lev., chap. 26; Jer., chap. 7; Ezek., chap. 18; and other citations in notes to this section
41 Lev. 19:37, 20:8,22, 25:18; Deut. 27:10, 30:8; Josh. 23:6 ("do all that is written in the book of the law of Moses")
42 1 Chron. 22:13
43 Lev. 18:30, 19:19, 20:8,22, 25:18; Deut. 5:17, 7:11, 11:1; Josh. 23:6; 1 Chron. 28:8; Prov. 3:1; Ps. 119:4; Ecclesiasticus 28:6 ("abide in the commandments")
44 Lev. 19:37; Deut. 8:1
"Ye shall observe to do therefore as the Lord your God hath commanded you: ye shall not turn aside to the right hand or to the left." Deut. 5:32
45 Mal. 4:4 ("Remember ye the law"); Ecclesiasticus, 28:7 ("Remember the commandments")
46 Prov. 3:1 ("My son, forget not the law"); 2 Mac. 2:1-3 (. . . Jeremy the prophet . . . charged them not to forget the commandments . . . and with

other such speeches he exhorted them, that the law should not depart from their hearts")
47 Deut. 5:17, 7:11, 8:1, 11:1; 27:10, 30:8; 1 Chron. 28:8; Prov. 3:1; Tobit 14:19; Ecclesiasticus 28:6,7; 2 Mac. 2:1-3; Matt. 19:17; John 14:21-24
48 Lev. 18:30
49 Lev. 18:26, 19:19,37, 20:8,22, 25:18; Deut. 5:17, 7:11, 11:1, 27:10; Mal. 4:4
50 Lev. 18:26, 19:37, 20:22, 25:18; Deut. 7:11; 11:1; Mal. 4:4
1 See 14 Harv.LR (1901) 509
2 Deut. 7:14 ("Thou shalt be blessed above all people: there shall not be male or female barren among you, or among your cattle"); Deut. 30:9 ("And the Lord thy God will make thee plenteous in every work of thine hand, and in the fruit of thy body, and in the fruit of thy cattle, and in the fruit of thy land, for good")
3 Prov. 29:8 ("he that keepeth the law, happy is he")
4 Deut. 7:15 ("the Lord will take away from thee all sickness")
5 Prov. 3:1,2 ("My son . . . keep my commandments, for length of days, and long life . . . shall they add to thee")

peace,[6] prosperity,[7] and safety.[8] Thus in Leviticus it is declared:

"If ye walk in my statutes, and keep my commandments, and do them:
"Then I will give you rain in due season, and the land shall yield her increase, and the trees of the field shall yield their fruit.
"And your threshing shall reach unto the vintage, and the vintage shall reach unto the sowing time: and ye shall eat your bread to the full, and dwell in your land safely.
"And I will give peace in the land, and ye shall lie down, and none shall make you afraid: and I will rid evil beasts out of the land, neither shall the sword go through your land.
"And ye shall chase your enemies, and they shall fall before you by the sword.
"And five of you shall chase a hundred, and a hundred of you shall put ten thousand to flight: and your enemies shall fall before you by the sword.
"For I will have respect unto you, and make you fruitful, and multiply you, and establish my covenant with you.
"And ye shall eat old store, and bring forth the old because of the new.
"And I will set my tabernacle among you: And my soul shall not abhor you.
"And I will walk among you, and will be your God, and ye shall be my people."[9]

Similar expressions may be found in the book of Deuteronomy.[10] And in the New Testament, Jesus declares:

". . . whosoever heareth these sayings of mine, and doeth them, I will liken him unto a wise man, which built his house upon a rock:
"And the rain descended, and the floods came, and the winds blew, and beat upon that house: and it fell not: for it was founded upon a rock."[11]

Nevertheless it should be remembered that, in a spiritual sense, one is "not justified by the works of the law," that is, Mosaic law, "but by the faith of Jesus Christ."[12]

[§69] On the other hand, a "curse" is pronounced against those "that confirm not all the words of this law to do them,"[13] and the consequences of disregard and disobedience of the law are set forth at length. For example, it is said:

". . . if ye will not hearken unto me, and will not do all these commandments;
"And if ye shall despise my statutes, or if your soul abhor my judg-

6 Prov. 5:2; Isa. 32:17 ("the work of righteousness shall be peace; and the effect of righteousness quietness and assurance for ever")
"Great peace have they which love thy law." Ps. 119:165
7 Lev. 25:19 ("the land shall yield her fruit, and ye shall eat your fill"); Deut. 30:9; 1 Chron. 22:13 ("Then shalt thou prosper, if thou takest heed to fulfill the statutes and judgments which the Lord charged Moses concerning Israel")
8 Lev. 25:19 ("ye shall . . . dwell . . .

in safety"); Tobit 12:7 ("Do that which is good, and no evil shall touch you")
"Blessed" are they "who walk in the law of the Lord." Ps. 119:1
9 Lev. 26:3-12
"He that keepeth the law bringeth offerings enough." Ecclesiasticus 35:1
10 Deut. 5:33, 7:12,13, 11:1-32, 28:1-13; 14 Harv.LR (1901) 510, quoting Deut. 7:12,13, 11:22 et seq.; and see Isa. 33:15, 16; Ezek. 18:5-9
11 Matt. 7:24
12 Gal. 2:16
13 Deut. 11:28, 27:26; Gal. 3:10

ments, so that ye will not do all my commandments, but that ye break my covenant:

"I also will do this unto you; I will even appoint over you terror, consumption, and the burning ague, that shall consume the eyes, and cause sorrow of heart: and ye shall sow your seed in vain, for your enemies shall eat it.

"And I will set my face against you, and ye shall be slain before your enemies: they that hate you shall reign over you; and ye shall flee when none pursueth you.

"And if ye will not yet for all this hearken unto me, then I will punish you seven times more for your sins.

"And I will break the pride of your power; and I will make your heaven as iron, and your earth as brass:

"And your strength shall be spent in vain: for your land shall not yield her increase, neither shall the trees of the land yield their fruits.

"And if ye walk contrary unto me, and will not hearken unto me; I will bring seven times more plagues upon you according to your sins.

"I will also send wild beasts among you, which shall rob you of your children, and destroy your cattle, and make you few in number: and your high ways shall be desolate.

"And if ye will not be reformed by me by these things, but will walk contrary unto me;

"Then will I also walk contrary unto you, and will punish you yet seven times for your sins.

"And I will bring a sword upon you, that shall avenge the quarrel of my covenant: and when ye are gathered together within your cities, I will send the pestilence among you; and ye shall be delivered into the hand of the enemy.

"And when I have broken the staff of your bread, ten women shall bake your bread in one oven, and they shall deliver you your bread again by weight: and ye shall eat, and not be satisfied.

"And if ye will not for all this hearken unto me, but walk contrary unto me;

"Then I will walk contrary unto you also in fury; and I, even I, will chastise you seven times for your sins.

"And ye shall eat the flesh of your sons, and the flesh of your daughters shall ye eat.

"And I will destroy your high places, and cut down your images, and cast your carcasses upon the carcasses of your idols, and my soul shall abhor you.

"And I will make your cities waste, and bring your sanctuaries unto desolation, and I will not smell the savour of your sweet odours.

"And I will bring the land into desolation: and your enemies which dwell therein shall be astonished at it.

"And I will scatter you among the heathen, and will draw out a sword after you; and your land shall be desolate, and your cities waste."[14]

Moreover it is stated in the New Testament that "Whosoever transgresseth (revolteth), and abideth (continueth) not in the doctrine of Christ, hath not God."[15]

---

14 Lev. 26:14-33; and see Deut. 28:15-68; Isa. 24:5,6; Jer. 35:17; 14 Harv.LR (1901) 510, quoting from Deut. chaps. 27 and 28
15 2 John, v 9, quoted in Ruse v Williams (1913) 14 Ariz. 445, 130 P 887, 45 LRA NS 923, 928 (Franklin,J)
"Whosoever therefore shall break one of these least commandments, and shall teach men so, he shall be called the least in the kingdom of heaven: but whosoever shall do and teach them, the same shall be called great in the kingdom of heaven." Matt. 5:19

CHAPTER 10

RELATION OF BIBLICAL LAW TO MODERN LAWS

70 Biblical law as the connecting link between and the source of modern laws
71 Scriptural influence upon American law 72 America as a Christian land
73 Christianity as a part of the common law 74 Simplicity and complexity in the
law 75 Fundamental precepts

[§70] "Israel's law is the connecting link between the earliest and the latest legal systems and has proved itself one of the most influential forces in the evolution of the world's law."[16] The Scriptures embody fundamental principles that have attained legal effectiveness among nearly all peoples and in remote parts of the earth—principles without which human societies can scarcely continue to exist[17]—and it is not unreasonable to suppose that in many instances these principles were borrowed from the Scriptures or were obtained through contact with those who observed Biblical law.[18] At all events, much of the common law of England was founded upon Mosaic law.[19] The primitive Saxon Codes re-enacted certain precepts taken from the Holy Scriptures,[20] and King Alfred in his Doom Book adopted the Ten Commandments and other selections from the Pentateuch, together with the Golden Rule in the negative form, as the foundation of the early laws of England."[21]

[§71] The Scriptures doubtless have been a potent influence upon American law. In the early colonial period, the Bible seems to have been commonly regarded among the people as law. Several of the colonies formally adopted provisions of Mosaic law.[22] For example, Plymouth Colony in 1636 adopted a "small body of Lawes" largely based upon the

---

16 4 China LR (1931) 362 (Lobingier)
17 See 42 Wash.LR (1914) 773 (Barnard) saying that "Without the knowledge of right and wrong that is taught by the Lord in the New Testament, in the Sermon on the Mount, and His other sayings and parables, and by His life, men would not know today what laws ought to be established."
18 But see 28 Yale LJ (1919) 782 (Keller) stating that "Human societies are nearly enough alike to be obliged, as a condition of self-preservation, to taboo practices that might be termed antisocial. Such taboos might be thought to be the result of acculturation (contagion, borrowing) if any possible agency of communication could be discovered or even imagined between remote parts of the earth in primitive ages. The better explanation of concurrences is that they are parallelisms—taboos that have sprung up under sim-

ilar conditions as the only adequate response to them."
19 42 Wash.LR (1914) 770 (Barnard)
". . . our English law never appeared in its strength until after the reformation; until it had come in contact with a free Bible; until it had been softened, subdued and leavened by Bible teaching and Bible precepts, and, by these unmanacled from many of its glaring absurdities and heathenisms and unjust distinctions and inhuman punishments. It was not until then that civil liberty was reinstated after the downfall of the Jewish theocracy." 10 West. Jur. (1876) 92 (Bowman)
20 1 Pomeroy's Eq.Jur. (1881) 5th ed. (1941) §10
21 Moore v Strickling (1899) 46 W.Va. 515, 33 SE 274, 50 LRA 279, 282 (Dent, P); 4 China LR (1931) 359 (Lobingier)
22 See Data of Jurisprudence, Miller, p 416

laws of Israel.[23]   And New Haven Colony in 1639 resolved that "the word of God shall be the only rule to be attended to in ordering the affairs of government in this plantation,"[24] and in 1655 adopted a code in which 47 out of 79 topical statutes were based on the Bible."[25]

Many provisions of Biblical law are still to be seen in American statutes and court decisions.[26]   Allusions to the Bible are contained in the reported cases.[27]   It has been characterized as "a very ancient authority not inappropriate."[28]   "At one time . . . no book was oftener quoted in argument before a jury," but "it is seldom referred to now."[29]

[§72]   There is difference of opinion as to whether America is now a Christian land.[30]   But it doubtless was so in former times, when the people were predominately Christian and Protestant.[31]   As in Rome after 379 A.D.,[32] Christianity was the established and legally recognized faith among the colonies and also, at first, among the states.[33]   Many colonial documents, the Declaration of Independence,[34] the Articles of

23   4 China LR (1931) 360
"Historians have emphasized the Biblical element in the founding of Massachusetts. It was to be a Bible commonwealth, a theocracy, the Genevan experiment writ large. Without question the law and theory of the ancient Hebraic order were large factors in shaping and guiding the public polity of the Bay Colony. The influence of the scriptural element is clearly evident in the book of laws (of 1648)." 15 Iowa LR (1930) 181 (Root)
24   10 Encyc. Amer., New Haven Colony (Osborn)
25   Jewish influence on Christian Reform Movements, Newman, p 642
In the early history of Connecticut, the Bible was a rule of political government "in the case of the defect of the law in any particular case." Appeal of Allyn (1909) 81 Conn. 534, 71 A 794, 23 LRANS 630, citing Col. Rec. of Conn., 1, 509
26   42 Wash.LR (1914) 771 (Bernard) also saying that "lawyers and judges frequently refer to and quote from the Bible in the trial of cases."
"The laws" of the Christian system, as embraced in the Bible, "must be respected as of high authority in all our courts. And it cannot be thought improper for the officers of such (our) government to acknowledge their obligation to be governed by its rules." Judge Nathaniel Freeman's Charge to the Grand Jury at the Court of General Sessions of the Peace, holden at Barnstable, Mass. March Term, 1802
27   29 Case & Comment (1923) No. 1, p 3 (Brown) stating that "allusions to the Bible are perhaps more frequent than to any book other than profes-

sional law treatises and previous decisions."
"It has been recognized in the courts that generally we acknowledge with reverence the duty of obedience to the will of God." United States v Macintosh (1931) 283 US 605, 75 L ed 1302; Harfst v Hoegen (1942) 163 SW2d (Mo.) 609, 612 (Douglas,J)
28   Moore v Indian Spring Channel Gold Mining Co. (1918) 37 Cal.App. 370, 381, 174 P 378 (Chipman,PJ)
29   7 Va.L.Reg.(N.S.) (1922) 777
30   See Harold v Parish School Directors (1915) 136 La. 1034, 68 So. 116, LRANS1915D 941, 945
31   Ex parte Newman (1858) 9 Cal. 502, 523 (Field,J) dissenting, saying that "Christianity is the prevailing faith of our people; it is the basis of our civilization; and that its spirit should infuse itself into and humanize our laws, is as natural as that the national sentiment of liberty should find expression in the legislation of the country."
32   7 Cal.LR (1918) 100, 101 (Sherman) observing that "By decree of Constantine the Great in 313 A.D., Christianity was made a lawful Roman religion. In the time of Theodosius the Great, about 379, the pagan religion was completely prescribed and Christianity became the only lawful Roman religion."
33   Runkel v Winemiller (1799) 4 Harris & McHenry (Md.) 429, 1 AD 411, 417 (Chase,J) saying that "By our form of government, the Christian religion is the established religion."
34   In the Declaration of Independence, God is acknowledged as over all and the giver of all good gifts. Herold v Parish School Directors (1915) 136 La. 1034, 68 So. 116, LRA1915D 941, 945

Confederation,[35] state constitutions,[36] and even the Federal constitution,[37] attest to the religious character of early America.[38] It has been declared:

> "There is a universal language pervading them all, having one meaning; they affirm and reaffirm that this is a religious nation. These are not individual sayings, declarations of private persons; they are organic utterances; they speak the voice of the entire people."[39]

As to the original constitutions of the various states, it has been said:

> "The constitution of South Carolina adopted in 1778 declared that the 'Christian Protestant religion' was the 'established religion' of that state; but that was modified in 1790, so as to secure freedom and prevent discrimination or preference in worship or religion. The constitution of North Carolina of 1776 excluded from office all non-believers in the Protestant religion or the divine authority of the Old or New Testament; while the constitution of Delaware of the same year made every official subscribe to a confession of faith; but that was abrogated sixteen years afterwards, and equal protection was extended to all sects. So the first constitutions of Maryland, Massachusetts, and New Hampshire, and later, of Connecticut, provided for the support, by taxation or otherwise, of the Christian or Protestant Christian religion, with more or less toleration guaranteed to other sets. Such direct sanction and toleration seems to have been inspired by a lingering attachment for, or a sympathy with, the European theory of union between church and state. But the several states of New Jersey, New York, Pennsylvania, Vermont, and Virginia, from the first, and later, Maine and Rhode Island, of the New England States, and every, or nearly every, state admitted

---

35 God was recognized in the Articles of Confederation (Art.No.13)

36 Holy Trinity Church v United States (1892) 143 US 457, 36 L ed 226 (Brewer,J)

In many states, the constitutions assume Christianity to be the religion of the state and that equality of religions refers to equality among Christian sects. 11 Cal.LR (1923) 186

The Delaware Constitution of 1776 (art.22), prescribed the following formal oath: "I, A.B., do profess faith in God the Father, and in Jesus Christ, His only Son, and in the Holy Ghost, one God, blessed forevermore; and I do acknowledge the Holy Scriptures in the Old and New Testament to be given by divine inspiration."

Preamble to the Constitution of Georgia: "We, the people of Georgia, relying upon the protection . . . of Almighty God, do ordain and establish this constitution." Wilkerson v Rome (1922) 152 Ga. 762, 110 SE 895, 20 ALR 1334, 1343

The Massachusetts Constitution, "in language strong and energetic" established "the religion of Protestant Christians." Avery v People of Tryingham (1807) 3 Mass. 160, 3 AD 105 (Sedgwick,J)

In the preamble to the Constitution

of Missouri (1875) the people acknowledge their "profound reverence for the Supreme Ruler of the Universe" and their gratitude for His goodness. Harfst v Hoegen (1942) 163 SW 2d (Mo.) 609, 612 (Douglas,J)

37 God is referred to in the date of the Constitution of the United States.

"In our original Federal Constitution no mention was made of the Bible, or of religion; but religious freedom was what inspired our colonial ancestors to come to this new country, and to declare their independence; and the First Amendment to the Constitution provided that 'Congress shall make no law respecting an establishment of religion, or prohibiting the free exercise thereof'." 42 Wash.LR (1914) 772, 773 (Barnard)

38 42 Wash.LR (1914) 772 (Barnard)

Our government "originating in the voluntary compact of a people, who in that very instrument profess the Christian religion, it may be considered, not as republican Rome, was a Pagan, but a Christian republic." Judge Nathaniel Freeman's Charge to the Grand Jury, 1802

39 Holy Trinity Church v United States (1892) 143 US 457, 36 L ed 226, 231 (Brewer,J)

into the Union after the organization of the federal government, expressly secured, in effect, in their respective state constitutions, the equal freedom of every religious sect, organization, and society, with a guaranty against preference or discrimination."[40]

[§73] Similarly there is a conflict of authority as to whether Christianity is a part of the common law. Many of the early cases hold that it is.[41] In an early Pennsylvania decision it is said:

"The declaration that Christianity is part of the law of the land is a summary description of an existing and very obvious condition of our institutions. We are a Christian people, in so far as we have entered into the spirit of Christian institutions, and become imbued with the sentiments and principles of Christianity; and we cannot be imbued with them, and yet prevent them from entering into and influencing, more or less, all our social institutions, customs, and relations, as well as all our individual modes of thinking and acting. It is involved in our social nature, that even those among us who reject Christianity cannot possibly get clear of its influence, or reject those sentiments, customs, and principles which it has spread among the people, so that, like the air we breathe, they have become the common stock of the whole country, and essential elements of its life."[42]

Also, in a Wisconsin case, the court conceded an argument of counsel that—

"the Christian religion is part of the common law of England; that the same was brought to this country by the colonists, and by virtue of the various colonial charters was embodied in the fundamental laws of the colonies; that this religious element or principle was incorporated in the various state constitutions, and in the ordinance of 1787 for the government of the Northwest Territory, by virtue of which ordinance it became the fundamental law of the territory of Wisconsin."[43]

However, the ecclesiastical law was not adopted in America,[44] and some authorities even deny that Christianity is a

40 State v District School Board of Edgerton (1890) 76 Wis. 177, 20 ASR 41, 57 (Cassoday,J)
The Constitution of Louisiana, "in the preamble, places God before the state, in the following language: 'We, the people of the state of Louisiana, grateful to Almighty God for the civil, political and religious liberties we enjoy and desiring to secure the continuance of these blessings, do ordain and establish this Constitution.'" Herold v Parish School Directors (1915) 136 La. 1034, 68 So. 116 LRA1915D 941, 946
41 See 49 AD 608, AnnCas1913E 1227
42 Mohney v Cook (1855) 26 Pa.St. 342, 67 AD 419
"It is also said, and truly, that the Christian religion is a part of the common law of Pennsylvania. But this proposition is to be received with its appropriate qualifications, and in connection with the bill of rights of that State, as found in its constitution of government." Vidal v Girard's Execu-

tors (1844) 2 Howard (US) 127, 198, 11 L ed 205, 234 (Story,J)
43 State v District School Board of Edgerton (1890) 76 Wis. 117, 20 ASR 41, 46 (Lyon,J), saying further: "Numerous quotations are given by him (counsel) from the above documents, from the utterances of Congress and legislatures, and from the writings of our early statesmen, to prove these propositions. . . . More than that, counsel have proved that many, probably most, of those charters, and some of the state constitutions, not only ordained and enforced some of the principles of the Christian religion, but sectarian doctrines as well."
44 Burtis v Burtis (1825) 1 Hopk. (N Y) 557, 564; Hodges v Hodges (1916) 22 NM 192, 159 P 1007; and see 17 Am Jur p 149, §6
But it does not follow that none of the principles of the ecclesiastical law of divorce are to be applied by an American divorce court. See 30 Harv. LR (1917) 283, 284

part of the common law in England and America. Thus, in Thomas Jefferson's Reports it is argued that the common law began with the settlement of the Saxons in England about the middle of the fifth century, and that Christianity was not introduced in England till the seventh century, and was never adopted into the common law by legislative authority.[45] The doctrine that Christianity is part of the common law was rejected in Ohio,[46] and it has been only partially accepted in other states.

Whichever view is taken, it is certain that many of the principles and usages, constantly acknowledged and enforced in courts of justice rest upon the Christian religion.[47]

[§74] Plainness and simplicity are qualities greatly to be desired in law, which ought to be so plain that "he may run that readeth it"[48] and so simple that "wayfaring men, though fools, shall not err therein."[49] Biblical law answers these requirements, for it is a law of fundamentals. Other legal systems, beginning with fundamentals, have developed a maze of rules and forms in which the fundamentals have been buried and lost sight of.[49a] Modern laws, like those of the Romans, have grown "contradictory, some obsolete, some unpractical, some obscure, and the whole bulk of them too voluminous."[50] As Bentham[1] asserted:

"That which we have need of (need we say it?) is a body of law, from the respective parts of which we may each of us, by reading them or hearing them read, learn, and on each occasion know, what are his rights, and what his duties."[2]

And it has been said that—

". . . all the massive bulk of our English and American law may be reduced to a very few grand principles underlying the whole and which were enunciated by Moses, and which Bracton, Blackstone, Kent and the host of our English and American commentators have found a common labor in explaining. And the all but fabulous heaps of our statutes, reports and digests, are but amplifications and applications of these great principles to the various conditions of society."[3]

45 Reports of General Court of Virginia, 1730-1740, 1768-1822, published at Charlottesville in 1829; and see 12 Gr.B. (1900) 441
46 Bloom v Richards (1853) 2 Ohio St. 387
47 City Council v Benjamin (1846) 2 Strobhart (SC) 508, 49 AD 608, 609, (O'Neall,J) ; and see Dunn v Jones (1926) 192 NC 251, 134 SE 487 (1928) 195 NC 354, 142 SE 320
48 Hab. 2:2
49 Isa. 35:8
49a The law has become "encrusted with a mass of barnacles." From a simple set of rules of conduct it has been gradually transformed into a highly technical system composed of tens of thousands of provisions and pronouncements 'meticulously dealing with minutiae." See 2 FRD (1942) 495 (Holtzoff) speaking of the NY Code of Civ. Proc.
50 Rolle's Abridgement (1668) Preface
1 Jeremy Bentham (1748-1832) English philosopher and jurist
2 18 Harv.LR (1905) 276 (Beale)
3 10 West. Jur. (1876) 91 (Bowman)
But see 28 Cal.LR (1940) 578, (Holdsworth) saying that "the complexity of life, and therefore of the rules of law needed to regulate it, must increase with the complexity of civilization, so that . . (the) ideal of a code of substantive and adjective law, so simple that it could be understood by all" is illusory.

[§75]   The antediluvians are supposed to have had seven great laws, one positive—to do justice, and six negative—not to blaspheme, nor to commit idolatry, murder, incest or robbery, nor to eat the flesh of living animals.[4]   The prophet Micah reduced Biblical law to three rules, saying—

". . . what doth the Lord require of thee, but to do justly, and to love mercy, and to walk humbly with thy God?"[5]

And according to the Institutes of Justinian:

"The precepts of right and law are three: to live honorably, not to injure another, and to give to every one his own."[6]

But secular law-makers have not ordinarily required that one should do good, or even refrain from doing wrong except in specific instances.   So it has been said that "Human laws, as a general rule, do not attempt to enforce the positive moral obligation that we should do good, but they do undertake to restrain us from doing harm,"[7] in (it should be added) "certain respects."

---

[4]   13 Gr.B. (1901) 202
[5]   Micah. 6:8
"If a man be just, and do that which is lawful and right . . . he shall surely live." Ezek. 18:5,9
[6]   Institutes, I, i, §3
The following sections, based upon maxims of Biblical law, are offered as a substitute for present-day laws:
Section 1. Everyone within the jurisdiction shall, at all times and in all circumstances, do justly and speak the truth.
Sec. 2. Whoever shall violate this law, by doing wrong or speaking falsely to another, shall be liable to the person injured thereby in double the amount of damages actually sustained;

and in case of a malicious or wilful violation he shall be subject also to a fine, imprisonment or other punishment, in such amount, for such time, and in such manner, as the judge in his discretion, and in the same proceeding, shall decree.
[7]   Furst-Edwards & Co. v St.Louis Southwestern Ry. Co. (1912) 146 SW (Tex.Civ.App) 1024, 1028, error refused (Jenkins,J) observing further that "Our duty in specific instances is written in our statute books, but before human statutes were written, before the law was given at Sinai, the law of God had written upon the hearts of all men the injunction not to harm his fellow man."

PART II

POLITICAL LAW

CHAPTER 11

IN GENERAL

76 Necessity of government   77 Its purposes   78 The source of power   79 Citizenship

[§76]   At certain times the people have lived without government, "every man," it is said, doing "that which was right in his own eyes."[8] But "there was government before there was anything we could call law,"[9] for man has ordinarily chosen to live among his fellows, and experience has long since demonstrated the necessity of government "because all are not willing to be legitimately controlled or . . . to make personal concessions for the general welfare."[10] Government, like law (§29), is not an end in itself; at best it is "but a necessary evil,"[11] to which people submit that they may obtain the benefits which government should confer. Yet it has been said, and truly it seems, that "the laws of God" entitle a people to establish their own government.[12]

[§77]   The first purpose of government, as of law,[13] is to insure tranquility, and then, no doubt, to establish justice, for, as St. Augustine said: "If justice be taken away, what are governments but great bands of robbers?"[14]

It has been well said that the chief ends of government are "the safety, the health, the morals, the good order, and the general welfare of the people.[15]

8 Judges 17:6, 21:25 ("In those days there was no king in Israel, but every man did that which was right in his own eyes")

"In the old days before there was a king of Israel, the elders of the towns were the only authority." 12 Gr.B (1900) 196

9 14 Or. LR (1934-35) 94
10 7 Tex. LR (1929) 261 (Saner)
11 Th. Paine, Common Sense, 1776
12 American Declaration of Independence (1776) ¶1

"Where a people are gathered together the word of God requires that to maintain the peace and union . . . there should be an orderly and decent Government established according to God." Preamble, Connecticut Constitution (1639)

13 See supra §§30,31
14 De Civ.Dei, IX:4
"Justice is the goal of all free government . . . and 'good faith is the foundation of justice'." 31 Cal.LR (1942) 58 (Munro) quoting Cicero.
"The right of courts to exist and function rests upon their power to mete out fundamental justice." State v Ramirez (1921) 34 Idaho 623, 636, 203 P 279, 29 ALR 297 (Budge,J)
If, through courts of justice, a man can be chiseled out of his property . . . then it would be well to abolish courts, and let every man, like the 'heathen,' rage' and be 'a law unto himself.'" Latta v Wiley (1905) 92 SW 433, 437 (Neill,J)
15 Leisy & Co. v Hardin (1890) 135 US 100, 34 L ed 128, 149 (Gray,J, dissenting)

According to some writings governments are also instituted to facilitate "the pursuit of happiness."[16] So it has been said:

"The great end of civil government is social happiness; to induce us to respect the rights, interests, and feelings of others as our own, conformable to that great command in the law, which is the foundation of all relative duties from man to man; to love our neighbour as ourselves, and to do to all as we would that they should do to us; knowing that the rights and enjoyments of others are the same to them as ours are to us, and that all men are brethren, have one father, who is God, created in his image, and connected in one great family under the government of their illustrious head the Prince of Peace and of the potentates and powers of the earth."[17]

[§78] It is a doctrine of both Mosaic and Christian law that governments are divinely ordained and derive their powers from God. In the Old Testament it is asserted that "power belongeth unto God,"[18] that God "removeth kings and setteth up kings,"[19] and that "the Most High ruleth in the kingdom of men, and giveth it to whomsoever he will."[20] Similarly in the New Testament it is stated that ". . . there is no power but of God, the powers that be are ordained of God."[21]

In Roman law it was originally considered that the emperor's power had been bestowed upon him by the people, but when Rome became a Christian state his power was regarded as coming from God.[22] In America also God has been recognized as the source of government,[23] though it is commonly thought that in a republican or democratic government "all power is inherent in the people."[24]

[§79] Primitive family groups were bound together by an actual or supposed blood relationship, and this notion of relationship persisted when families became tribes, and tribes nations. Citizens of a primitive nation believed that they were

But "Government is not the custodian of the people and their welfare, and no government is called upon to remove or prevent all of the hazards of life." Samson v California (1942) 55 ACA (Cal.) 229,233 (Doran,J., dissenting)
16 American Declaration of Independence (1776) ¶2
The right to pursue happiness "includes the right to live free from unwarranted attack of others upon one's liberty, property, and reputation." Melvin v Reid (1931) 112 Cal.App. 285, 291, 297 P 91 (Marks,J)
17 1 Root's (Conn.) Reports (1789-1793) Introduction, xvi, xvii, saying further that "A practice universally adopted agreeable to these principles and rules would, without the intervention of penal laws, render the security of individuals perfect, and advance the harmony, beauty, and happiness of society, beyond the power of language to describe."
18 Ps. 62:11
19 Dan. 2:21
20 Dan. 4:32
21 Rom. 13:1
22 13 Ill.LR (1918-1919) 444
23 Appeal of Allyn (1909) 81 Conn. 534, 71 A 794, 23 LRANS 630, 631 (Baldwin,CJ) observing that "The preamble of the constitution of Connecticut, gratefully acknowledging the good providence of God, in having permitted them to enjoy a free government, is a recognition of God as the source of that government."
24 Donahoe v Richards (1854) 38 Me. 379, 61 AD 256, 262 (Appleton,J)

related to one another, as did the Israelites.[25]　Strangers, though tolerated and protected, had no rights.[26]　But Mosaic law provided for the adoption or naturalization of strangers by a ceremony that was believed to create kinship.[27]　The law declared that—

"... when a stranger shall sojourn with thee, and will keep the passover to the Lord, let all his males be circumcised, and then let him come near and keep it; and he shall be as one that is born in the land ..."[28]

Ruth, a Moabitess, is said to have become a naturalized citizen of Judah, by her action in following Naomi to Bethlehem, and by her words in adopting Naomi's country, her God and her domicile.[29]

On the other hand, individuals might be "cut off from the people,"—that is, excommunicated and thereby deprived of their citizenship or civil rights,—for breaking the ceremonial law or committing certain offenses.　Thus it is declared that in the time of the Passover "whosoever eateth leavened bread from the first day until the seventh day, that soul shall be cut off from Israel."[30]　Similarly it is provided that "Ye shall eat the blood of no manner of flesh ... whosoever eateth it shall be cut off."[31]　The "cutting off" or excommunication of nonconformists was practiced even in England and in the American colonies.[32]

CHAPTER 12

FORMS OF GOVERNMENT

80 In general　81 Patriarchy　82 Theocracy　83 Monarchy　84 Republic　85 Democracy　86 Separation of church and state　87 Separation of government into departments

[§80]　Nearly every form of government existed at one time or another during the Biblical ages.　First to appear was the family, and shortly, the tribal, government.　A priesthood developed and theocracy became the next form of government. That, in turn, was succeeded by monarchy, usually absolute

25　14 Harv. LR (1901) 513
26　14 Harv. LR (1901) 516
27　See 14 Harv. LR (1901) 514 (Thayer) noting further that "St.Paul made use of the primitive idea of national kinship in framing his theory of Christian communion. He says, 'The bread which we break, is it not the communion of the body of Christ? For we being many are one bread and one body; for we are all partakers of that one bread.' 1 Cor. 10:16,17"
28　Ex. 12:48
Foreigners not permitted to become citizens until the third generation: Deut. 23:8

29　Ruth 1:14-22; 13 Gr.B. (1901) 315
30　Ex. 12:15
31　Lev. 17:14
32　In the government framed by the Puritans, the Old Testament doctrine as to "cutting off" was received with favor.　A non-communicant could not vote; a militia officer was complained of, as being unfit for his position, because corrupt in his judgment with reference to the Lord's Supper, and a man was excluded from communion and afterwards prosecuted before the County Court for denying baptism to his infant child. 14 Harv. LR (1901) 517 (Thayer) citing Brooks Adams' Emancipation of Massachusetts, pp 26, 81, 119

but sometimes, in fact, limited. Democracies arose in Greece, and the Romans established a Republic which was later transformed to an Empire, ruling conquered provinces by governors sent from Rome.

[§81]   The unit of primitive society was not the individual, but the family—a group of related individuals ruled by its elder or patriarch. After the death of a patriarch, the families of his sons separated, as did those of Esau and Jacob,[33] or they held together, as did the children of Jacob,[34] and became a house, an aggregation of houses or a tribe, and finally an aggregation of tribes or a nation.

In the primitive family, the patriarch was the father, or, if there was more than one in the group, the eldest male parent; and he exercised supreme authority over the family.[35] He had the power of life and death over its members[36] and administered its property. His word was the family law, and from his decision there was no appeal.[37] On the other hand, he was answerable for trespasses and offenses committed by members of the family against others, though he might deliver up an offending member in satisfaction of a wrong. His last acts of authority were the apportionment of family property among the children, and the naming of his successor as the head of the family.[38]

The house and the tribe were but larger families, and were ordinarily governed by the eldest male of the eldest line. But in certain circumstances the succession might pass over to a younger son or to an uncle. In the most ancient times, before either the hierarchy or the kingdom was organized, the elders or patriarchs were the only authorities.[39] Patriarchal rule remained in full force as long as the Israelites lived a nomadic life, and even in some respects after they had settled in Palestine.[40]

[§82]   Theocracy—meaning a government by the Lord[41] acting through human agents—is seemingly the government that most nearly meets with Scriptural approval. The theocracy of Israel was established by Moses, who was divinely selected to rule the people,[42] and who created the priesthood[43] and proclaimed the laws by which the nation was governed.

33 Gen. 36:6,7
34 See Gen., ch. 49
35 13 Gr.B. (1901) 38
36 14 Gr.B. (1902) 83
37 13 Gr.B. (1901) 38
38 14 Gr.B. (1902) 233
   The "blessing" of Jacob by his father Isaac, as described in Gen. 27:28,29, was evidently a mode of naming the patriarchal successor, and not a will.
39 12 Gr.B. (1900) 197, 199
40 13 Gr.B. (1901) 39
41 Judges 8:23
42 Ex. 3:10 et seq.
43 Ex. 28:1 et seq.

When Moses had grown old and the Israelites were about to invade Canaan, Joshua was selected to succeed him, and Moses "took Joshua, and set him before Eleazar the priest, and before all the congregations: and he laid his hands upon him, and gave him a charge, as the Lord commanded."[44] After the death of Joshua, the people were governed by "judges"[45] for "about the space of four hundred and fifty years, until Samuel the prophet."[46]

Actually theocracy was a government or "kingdom" of priests,[47] who were the custodians, readers and teachers of the law, and who ruled, indirectly if not directly, in the name of the Lord and through judges usually chosen from their own number. This government was doubtless well adapted to the people in the beginning, but it seems to have become intolerable after four and a half centuries, when the Israelites demanded a king, though conceding that to do so was "evil."[48]

[§83] Moses was the first king of Israel—"he was king in Jeshurun, when the heads of the people and the tribes of Israel were gathered together."[49] His successor was Joshua, but he is not spoken of as a king.

Mosaic law provided for the establishment of a kingdom after the conquest of Canaan.[50] But before the land had been completely subdued, the Israelites asked Gideon to become their ruler, which he declined to do, saying: "I will not rule over you, neither shall my son rule over you: the Lord shall rule over you."[1]

After a long rule by "judges," the people again expressed their desire for a monarchy. When the prophet Samuel had become old, and after "he made his sons judges over Israel"[2]—

". . . all the elders of Israel gathered themselves together, and came to Samuel unto Ramah, "And said unto him. Behold, thou art old, and thy sons walk not in thy ways: now make us a king to judge us like all the nations."[3]

Though "the thing displeased Samuel,"[4] he yielded to the demand of the elders and "made them a king,"[5] in the person of Saul, "and all the people shouted, and said, God save the king."[6] Subsequently, when Saul had shown himself unfit for rulership, Samuel annointed David,[7] who became king after the death of Samuel[8] and the suicide of Saul.[9]

---

44 Num. 27:12-23
45 1 Chron. 17:10 (the Lord "commanded judges to be over my people")
46 Acts 13:20
47 Ex. 19:6
48 1 Sam. 12:19
49 Deut. 33:5
50 Deut. 17:14
1 Judges 8:23
2 1 Sam. 8:1
3 1 Sam. 8:4,5
4 1 Sam. 8:8
5 1 Sam. 8:22, 12:1
6 1 Sam. 10:24; and see 1 Sam. 11:14, 15, as to "renewal" of the kingdom.
7 1 Sam. 16:13
8 1 Sam. 25:1
9 1 Sam. 31:4

From the beginning, the monarchy was, in a sense, constitutional. The powers and duties of the king were in some respects defined in a covenant with the people and prescribed by Mosaic law. Thus, it appears that at the time of the accession of Saul, "Samuel told the people the manner of the kingdom, and wrote it in a book, and laid it up before the Lord."[10] David made a "league" or "covenant" with the "elders" before they "anointed" him king.[11] And Jehoiada the priest made a "covenant" between himself and the people and the king (Jehoash).[12] But Rehoboam refused to covenant with the people to make less grievous the "yoke" placed upon them by Solomon, for which the people, other than those of the tribe of Judah, rebelled and established a separate kingdom."[13]

[§84] Republican government—in which the people govern themselves by chosen representatives—has been characterized as "the most rational form of government for free men."[14] The nearest approach to such government in ancient times appears to have been the occasional gatherings of "elders" or tribal heads for consultation as to national problems. But the Roman Republic was in existence at the time of the Maccabees, and it is mentioned approvingly in the Apochryphal writings. It is said to have been told Judas of the Romans—

". . . how they had made for themselves a senate house, wherein three hundred and twenty men sat in council daily, consulting alway for the people, to the end they might be well ordered:

"And that they committed their government to one man every year, who ruled over all their country, and that all were obedient to that one, and that there was neither envy nor emulation among them."[15]

[§85] Democracy is a government in which all, or nearly all, of the people participate on a basis of equality.[16] It has been asserted that Moses intended to institute a "democratical government" by preserving some kind of equality in property through laws against usury and the alienating of land forever, and the law of jubilee."[17] Also it has been declared that—

10 1 Sam. 10:25
11 2 Sam. 5:3; 1 Chron. 11:3
12 2 Kings 11:17; 2 Chron. 23:16
13 1 Kings 12:1-20
14 Richard Cobden (1804-1865) English statesman and economist
15 1 Mac. 8:15,16
16 The doctrine of democracy is the "supremacy of the people." Donahoe v Richards (1854) 38 Me.379, 61 AmDec 256, 272 (Appleton,J)
     That a majority shall control, but that the minority is still entitled to representation and to the protection of law. People v Chambers (1937) 22 Cal.App2d 687,706, 72 P2d 746

And that "the material rights of no man shall be subject to the mere will of another." Railroad Commission v Shell Oil Co. (1942) 161 SW2d (Tex.) 1022, 1025 (Alexander,CJ)
     "A common wealth is called a society or common doing of a multitude of free men collected together and united by common accord and covenauntes among themselves, for the conservation of themselves as well in peace as in warre." 1 Smith's De Republica Anglorum (1683) ch. 10, p 20
17 Anderson v Winston (1736) Jefferson's (Va.) Reports 24

". . . democracy . . . finds its highest expression in the teachings of the Savior, who saw that institutions exist for men and not men for institutions, and that the happiness of the poor and the humble is of as much importance as the happiness of the great and the proud."[18]

But the Scriptures give no direct encouragement to this type of government, recognizing that wisdom which is required in governmental affairs "is not manifest unto many"[19] and teaching that "folly" ought not to be "set in great dignity."[20] Matters of state are not for artisans, craftsmen and laborers.

"All these trust to their hands: and every one is wise in his work.
"Without these cannot a city be inhabited: and they shall not dwell where they will, nor go up and down:
"They shall not be sought for in publick counsel, nor sit high in the congregation: they shall not sit on the judges' seat, nor understand the sentence of judgment; and they shall not be found where parables are spoken.
"But they will maintain the state of the world, and (all) their desire is in the work of their craft."[21]

Democracy was not for primitive peoples; it is possible only "among a population . . . imbued with conceptions of justice and equality before the laws."[22]

[§86] The doctrine of the separation of church and state is a modern development.[22a] In primitive society, the patriarch was both priest and temporal ruler. And "in most ancient communities, the priest was also king and judge."[23] Theocracy, as we have seen (§82), was a government of priests. And notwithstanding the establishment of the monarchy of Israel, the hierarchy continued to exercise great influence. The tenure of the king largely depended upon his continued acceptability to them. Thus we find that after the death of Ahaziah and the seizure of power by Athaliah his mother, Jehoiada the priest took Joash, one of the sons of Ahaziah who had escaped being slain, and made him king, and commanded that Athaliah, who had made herself queen, be killed.[24] Also at other times, the priests "made" or "unmade" kings or procured "covenants" between the king and themselves and the people.[25]

Constantine the Great adopted and practiced the principle that the church was subservient to the state, and his imperial

18 41 Case & Comment (1934) No.2, p 4 (U.S.Cir.J. Parker)
19 Ecclesiasticus 6:22
20 Ecclesiasticus 10:6
"I have seen servants upon horses, and princes walking as servants upon the earth." Ecclesiastes 10:7
21 Ecclesiasticus 38:31-34
22 13 Ill.LR (1918-1919) 448
22a There is abundant historical evidence . . . that the pioneers . . . of American colonial government did not have in mind to bring about a complete separation of church and state. Wilkerson v Rome (1922) 152 Ga. 762, 110 SE 895, 20 ALR 1334, 1338 (Gilbert,J)
23 14 Harv. LR (1901) p 517 (Thayer)
24 2 Kings 11:12,13
25 See supra §83

successors always maintained that principle.[26] In the American colonies, church and state were closely related, but the founders of the federal and most of the state governments were careful "to distinguish exactly the business of civil government from that of religion, and to settle the just bounds that lie between the one and the other."[27]

[§87] The separation of government into three branches— legislative, executive and judicial—is also of recent origin and is still, perhaps, an experiment. Formerly it was not considered improper that the three basic functions of government— those of making the law, enforcing the law, and interpreting the law in the settlement of controversies[28]—should be exercised by one supreme authority, and such is still the practice in many parts of the world. Thus it will be seen that Moses not only made or promulgated the law, but also that he was leader or king, and that he sat as a judge. But it is now recognized that "the spheres of operation of the three powers are essentially different," though they overlap to some extent, and it is thought that they should ordinarily be separately and independently exercised.[29] And so they have been in England and America, though the present tendency is to entrust many governmental activities to agencies which exercise all three powers within restricted fields.[30]

CHAPTER 13

PUBLIC OFFICIALS

88 In general   89 Authority and duties   90 The king—Selection   91 —— Anointing   92 —— Oath or promise of allegiance   93 —— Succession   94 —— Powers and restrictions thereon   95 —— Duties   96 —— Wrongs and offenses

[§88] A government acts through officers, all of whom, taken together, actually are the government.[31] With regard to the qualifications of officers, the Scriptures declare that:

"When the righteous are in authority, the people rejoice: but when the wicked beareth rule, the people mourn."[32]

"The people have the right . . . that public offices shall be filled by upright and moral men."[33] Formerly it was required, even in America, that an officer be an adherent of the

26   7 Cal. LR (1918) 101 (Sherman)
27   John Locke's "Letter Concerning Toleration" 1689
"The complete separation of the church from the state did not really come until the formation of our federal system of government, although the Virginia Bill of Rights had earlier guaranteed freedom of worship." Harfst

v Hoegen (1942) 163 SW2d (Mo.) 609, 611 (Douglas,J)
28   See 6 RCL 144 et seq.
29   13 Ill. LR (1918-1919) 436 (Zane)
30   See 42 AmJur 291
31   14 Or. LR (1934-35) 94
32   Prov. 29:2
33   Moore v Strickling (1899) 46 W.Va. 515, 33 SE 274, 50 LRA 279, 283 (Dent,P)

prevailing religious belief,[34] but the federal Constitution prohibits any religious test as a qualification for office.[35] The statutes generally provide, however, that office holders should ask the help of God to discharge their duties in an oath of office closing with the words: "So help me God."[36]

[§89]   Concerning official authority[37] and duties, the Scriptures declare to those "that rule the people"—that is, to officers—that "power is given you of the Lord, and sovereignty from the Highest, who shall try your works and search out your counsels."[38]   It is required that an officer "rule" diligently[39] and justly.[40]   He should exact no more than that which is appointed him.[41]   He should not be rebellious, a companion of thieves, a lover of gifts, a follower after rewards, nor a withholder of justice from the fatherless or the widow.[42]   If he causes an innocent person to be slain without cause he may properly be punished as a murderer.[43]

[§90]   In a monarchy, the king is the supreme officer,[44] as the president is the supreme officer in a republic or democracy.[44a]   According to Biblical law, the king was required, in the first instance, to be chosen by the Lord from among the "brethren."

"Thou shalt in any wise set him king over thee, whom the Lord thy God shall choose: one from among thy brethren shalt thou set king over thee: thou mayest not set a stranger over thee, which is not thy brother."[45]

Thus, in the Scriptural view, the king was divinely selected and the kingly rulership was ordained of God.[46]

[§91]   —— Upon the accession of a new king, custom required him to be formally "anointed."   So Samuel first anointed Saul to be king,[47] and later anointed David to be king in his stead.[48]   Subsequently, "the men of Judah came" to Hebron, and "anointed David king over the house of Judah,"[49] and "all the elders of Israel came to the king to Hebron . . .

34 Religious belief as affecting the right to hold office in America: Hale v Everett (1868) 53 NH 9, 16 AR 82, 168
35 US Const. (1789) Art. VI, ¶3
36 Herold v School Directors (1915) 136 La. 1034, 68 So. 116, LRA1915D 941, 946 (Sommerville,J)
37 In ancient times a key was the symbol of official authority. See Isa. 9:5, 22:22; Matt. 16:19
And ballots were cast by using white and black stones. "To him that overcometh will I give . . . a white stone." Rev. 2:17
38 Wisdom of Solomon 6:2,3
39 Rom. 12:8
40 2 Sam. 23:3
41 Luke 3:13 (command of John the Baptist to the publicans)

42 Isa. 1:23 (referring to "princes")
43 2 Mac. 4:38
44 1 Pet. 2:13
44a See supra §§ 84,85
Daniel was the first "president." "It pleased Darius to set over the kingdom an hundred and twenty princes, which should be over the whole kingdom; and over these three presidents; of whom Daniel was first . . ." Dan. 6:1,2
45 Deut. 17:15
46 See supra §78
47 1 Sam. 10:1 ("Samuel took a vial of oil, and poured it upon his head, and kissed him, and said, Is it not because the Lord hath anointed thee to be captain over his inheritance?")
48 1 Sam. 16:13
49 2 Sam. 2:4

and they anointed David king over Israel."[50] Before the death of David and at his command—

". . . Zadok the priest, and Nathan the prophet, and Benaiah the son of Jehoiada, and the Cherethites, and the Pelethites, went down, and caused Solomon to ride upon David's mule, and brought him to Gihon.

"And Zadok the priest took a horn of oil out of the tabernacle, and anointed Solomon. And they blew the trumpet; and all the people said, God save king Solomon.

"And all the people came up after him, and the people piped with pipes, and rejoiced with great joy, so that the earth rent with the sound of them."[1]

And upon the coronation of Jehoash, Jehoiada the priest "put his crown upon him, and gave him the testimony; and they made him king and anointed him; and they clapped their hands, and said, God save the king."[2]

[§92] —— The answer given Joshua by the Reubenites, the Gadites, and the half tribe of Manasseh, is a form of oath or promise of allegiance. In response to his appeal for help—

". . . they answered Joshua, saying, All that thou commandest us we will do, and whithersoever thou sendest us, we will go.

"According as we hearkened unto Moses in all things, so will we hearken unto thee: only the Lord thy God be with thee, as he was with Moses.

"Whosoever he be that doth rebel against they commandment, and will not hearken unto thy words in all that thou commandest him, he shall be put to death: only be strong and be of good courage."[3]

[§93] —— Ordinarily upon the death of a king, his eldest son succeeded to the throne.[4] But a younger son was sometimes made king in place of his father. For example, David made Solomon king before his death,[5] and the inhabitants of Jerusalem made Ahaziah, the youngest son of Jehoram, king in his stead.[6] But it was not thought desirable that a young child should be king.[7] In some instances, a person outside the established royal line became king by popular choice,[8] or usurpation.[9] At one time the kingdom of Judah was governed by a queen,[10] and upon another occasion the people in Edom were ruled by a deputy.[11] During the reign of David, his sons were "chief" about him,[12] and after king Azariah became a leper his son Jotham was "over the house, judging the people of the land."[13]

---

50 2 Sam. 5:3; 1 Chron. 11:3
1   1 Kings 1:38-40   2   2 Kings 11:12
3 Josh. 1:16-18
   Pledge of allegiance in schools, see infra §296
4 See 1 Kings 11:43, 14:20,31, 15:8,24, 16:28, 22:40,50; 2 Chron. 21:3 (Jehoshaphat gave the kingdom on his death to Jehoram "because he was the firstborn")
5 1 Chron. 23:1

6 2 Chron. 22:1 ("for the band of men . . . had slain all the eldest")
7 Ecclesiastes 10:6 ("woe unto thee, oh land, when thy king is a child")
8 See 1 Mac. 9:30,31, 13:8,9
9 See Judges, chap. 9
10 2 Kings 11:1-3; 2 Chron. 22:12
11 1 Kings 22:47 ("There was then no king in Edom; a deputy was king")
12 1 Chron. 18:17
13 2 Kings 15:15; and see 2 Chron. 26:21

[§94] —— Generally speaking the king possessed and exercised all the powers of government—executive, legislative and judicial.[14] He had "dominion" over the bodies of his subjects and over their property (cattle) at his pleasure.[15] But he was not regarded as being "above the law."[16] Mosaic law declared that—

"he (the king) shall not multiply horses to himself, nor cause the people to return to Egypt, to the end that he should multiply horses . . . "Neither shall he multiply wives to himself, that his heart turn not away: neither shall he greatly multiply to himself silver and gold."[17]

Orders of the king were issued in his name and were sealed with his seal.[18]

[§95] —— The first duty of the king was to study and observe the law. It was provided that—

". . . when he sitteth upon the throne of his kingdom, . . . he shall write him a copy of this law in a book out of that which is before the priests the Levites:
"And it shall be with him, and he shall read therein all the days of his life: that he may learn to fear the Lord his God, to keep all the words of this law and these statutes, to do them:
"That his heart be not lifted up above his brethren, and that he turn not aside from the commandment, to the right hand, or to the left . . ."[19]

The king was legally bound to "keep the charge of the Lord . . . to walk in his ways, to keep his statutes, and his commandments, and his judgments, and his testimonies, as it is written in the law of Moses."[20] And it was recognized that the king should be just, "ruling in the fear of God,"[21] and executing "judgment and justice among all his peoples;"[22] that he should—

"execute . . . judgment and righteousness, and deliver the spoiled out of the hand of the oppressor: and do no wrong, do no violence to the stranger, the fatherless, nor the widow, neither shed innocent blood."[23]

---

14 See supra §87
15 Neh. 9:37
16 See supra §47
"While regularly and in a political sense the king rules over his people, he is bound to the observance of the laws as he swears at his coronation." Fortescue, De Laudibus, cap. 34
17 Deut. 17:16,17
18 See 1 Kings 21:8
19 Deut. 17:18-20
20 1 Kings 2:3 (charge by David to Solomon)
King Josiah "stood in his place, and made a covenant before the Lord, to walk after the Lord, and to keep his commandments, and his testimonies, and his statutes, with all his heart, and with all his soul, to perform the words of the covenant which are written in this book." 2 Chron. 34:31

21 2 Sam. 23:3 ("He that ruleth over men must be just, ruling in the fear of God")
22 1 Chron. 18:14 (David "executed judgment and justice among all his people")
23 Jer. 22:3
"Thus saith the Lord God; Let it suffice you, O princes of Israel: remove violence and spoil, and execute judgment and justice, take away your exactions from my people, saith the Lord God." Ezek. 45:9
". . . the throne is established by righteousness." Prov. 16:12
"He does not rule who does not rule rightly; therefore the name of king is held on condition of doing right and is lost by wrongdoing." St.Isidore, Etymologies, IX:3

With respect to law-enforcement, it was the king's duty to "scatter the wicked and bring the wheel over them."[24] And it is said that when Jonathan began to govern the people, he "destroyed the ungodly men out of Israel,"[25] and that Simon "strengthened all those of his people that were brought low: the law he searched out; and every contemner of the law and wicked person he took away."[26]

[§96] —— On the other hand, it was improper for the king to "frame mischief by a law"[27] or to oppress his people.[28] Nor was it proper for him "to drink wine; nor for princes (to drink) strong drink, lest they drink, and forget the law, and pervert the judgment of any of the afflicted."[29]

And though it was "an abomination to kings to commit wickedness,"[30] many of them appear to have been men of evil spirit, unfit for their high office. They were sometimes punished or reprimanded for offenses. For example, it is said that—

"... Saul died for his transgressions, which he committed against the Lord, even against the word of the Lord, which he kept not, and also for asking counsel of one that had a familiar spirit, to enquire of it;

"And enquired not of the Lord; therefore he slew him, and turned the kingdom unto David the son of Jesse."[31]

David, in turn, committed adultery and homicide, and was reproved by Nathan the prophet.[32] Solomon "loved many strange women," who turned "his heart . . . away from the Lord God of Israel," and the Lord reprimanded him.[33] Jeroboam was condemned to lose his kingdom "for thou hast gone and made thee other gods, and molten images."[34] And Ahab was reproved for taking the vineyard of Naboth.[35]

CHAPTER 14

OFFICIAL FUNCTIONS

97 In general   98 Law-making   99 Census   100 Famine relief   101 Taxation
102 —— Tribute   103 —— Exemption   104 —— Payment

[§97] The three basic functions of government, as we have seen, are the making, the enforcement, and the interpretation of law (§87). Law-making is considered in the next section. The duties of the chief executive—that is, the king—with respect to the enforcement of law (§95), and general

24   Prov. 20:26
25   1 Mac. 9:73
26   1 Mac. 14:14
27   Ps. 94:20 ("the throne of iniquity . . . frameth mischief by a law")
28   Ezek. 45:8 ("my princes shall no more oppress my people")
29   Prov. 31:4,5
30   Prov. 16:12
31   1 Chron. 10:13,14
32   2 Sam. 12:13-18
33   1 Kings 11:1-12
34   1 Kings 14:9
35   1 Kings 21:1-22

rules as to the interpretation of law (§§43-47), are discussed in preceding sections. Punishments for offenses, damages for civil wrongs, and procedures for the settlement of controversies and for the enforcement of penal laws, are treated in subsequent chapters (Parts VI and VII).

In addition to its primary functions, a government may engage in other activities. For example, it may enumerate the inhabitants of the country (§99), it may adopt measures to prevent or relieve against famine (§100), and it may levy and collect taxes (§§101-103). It may also enter into treaties (§112), and it may engage in warfare (Chap. 17).

[§98] Legislation or law-making has a large place in every governmental system. According to the Scriptures this is an exalted and important function, to be exercised with divine guidance or at least by wise and righteous men. In the main the legal provisions of the Bible emanated from the Lord or from Jesus, or were proclaimed by persons speaking with divine authority—prophets, disciples or apostles. As regards Mosaic law, it is said that "the Lord talked with Moses"[36] upon numerous occasions; the Lord "spake" unto him[37] and he "spake" unto the Lord,[38] and twice he was "with the Lord forty days and forty nights" on mount Sinai.[39] Jesus possessed an unusual knowledge of law at an early age, for it is said that when his parents were returning from a feast of the passover at Jerusalem and failed to find their child, then 12 years old, among their kinsfolk and acquaintances, they turned back again and "after three days they found him in the temple, sitting in the midst of the doctors (of law), both hearing them, and asking them questions."[40] And quite evidently St. Paul was "profoundly instructed" in both the Hebrew and the Roman law of his time."[41]

A law should doubtless be so made as that it "shall be honest, just, possible, according to nature and the custom of the country, convenient to the time and place, plain, written not for some private advantage, but for the common benefit of the citizens."[42] But it is not invalid because it prohibits what a citizen may conscientiously think right or requires what he may conscientiously think wrong.[43]

36 See Ex. 33:9
37 See for example Ex. 20:1, 30:11,17,22, 31:1,12
38 Num. 27:15 39 Ex. 24:18, 34:28
40 Luke 2:41-46
41 Hockaday v Lynn (1906) 200 Mo. 456, 98 SW 585, 118 ASR 672 (Lamm,J) observing that St.Paul was "himself a lawyer profoundly instructed in Hebrew jurisprudence."

42 St.Isidore, Etymologies, V:21
A law may be made to protect "one set of men from another set of men—the one from their station and condition being liable to be imposed upon by the other." Miller v California Roofing Co. (1942) 55 ACA (Cal.) 170,178 (Wagler,J pro tem)
43 Donahoe v Richards (1854) 38 Me. 379. 61 AD 256, 272 (Appleton,J)

[§99]　The Scriptures mention several censuses. The first census of the Israelites was taken by divine command "in the second year after they were come out of the land of Egypt."[44] The order to take this census and the results thereof are thus stated:

"Take ye the sum of all the congregation of the children of Israel, after their families, by the house of their fathers, with the number of their names, every male by their polls;

"From twenty years old and upward, all that are able to go forth to war in Israel: thou and Aaron shall number them by their armies.

"And with you there shall be a man of every tribe: every one head of the house of his fathers."[45]

"So were all those that were numbered of the children of Israel, by the house of their fathers, from twenty years old and upward, all that were able to go forth to war in Israel;

"Even all they that were numbered were six hundred thousand and three thousand and five hundred and fifty.

"But the Levites after the tribe of their fathers were not numbered among them.

"For the Lord had spoken unto Moses, saying

"Only thou shalt not number of the tribe of Levi, neither take the sum of them among the children of Israel."[46]

After the death of Aaron, a second census was taken by Moses and Eleazar the son of Aaron, also by divine command, and at that time there were "numbered of the children of Israel, six hundred thousand and a thousand seven hundred and thirty."[47]

A third census was taken by king David without divine sanction. Concerning this census, it appears that—

". . . the king said to Joab the captain of the host, which was with him, Go now through all the tribes of Israel, from Dan even to Beersheba, and number ye the people, that I may know the number of the people.

". . . And Joab and the captains of the host went out from the presence of the king, to number the people of Israel.

". . . when they had gone through all the land, they came to Jerusalem at the end of nine months and twenty days.

"And Joab gave up the sum of the number of the people unto the king: and there were in Israel eight hundred thousand valiant men that drew the sword; and the men of Judah were five hundred thousand men.

"And David's heart smote him after that he had numbered the people. And David said unto the Lord, I have sinned greatly in that I have done: and now, I beseech thee, O Lord, take away the iniquity of thy servant; for I have done very foolishly.

"For when David was up in the morning, the word of the Lord came unto the prophet Gad, David's seer, saying,

"Go and say unto David, Thus saith the Lord, I offer thee three things; choose thee one of them, that I may do it unto thee.

"So Gad came to David and told him, and said unto him, Shall seven years of famine come unto thee in thy land? or wilt thou flee three months before thine enemies, while they pursue thee? or that there

[44] Num. 1:1　　[45] Num. 1:2-4　　[46] Num. 1:45-50　　[47] Num. 26:1-52

be three days' pestilence in thy land? now advise, and see what answer I shall return to him that sent me.

"And David said unto Gad, I am in a great strait: let us fall now into the hand of the Lord; for his mercies are great: and let me not fall into the hand of man.

"So the Lord sent a pestilence upon Israel from the morning even to the time appointed: and there died of the people from Dan even to Beer-sheba seventy thousand men."[48]

Subsequently Amaziah "numbered" the men of Judah and Benjamin "from twenty years old and above, and found them three hundred thousand choice men, able to go forth to war, that could handle spear and shield."[49]

The people in former times objected to the census because it was "obviously the forerunner of conscription into the army and was also a survey to determine how many people there were who could be taxed and how much tax they could bear." Resentment against the census has continued down through the centuries. "The first count of population in the United States was undertaken in New York in 1712, but had to be left unfinished, so violent was the opposition. New Jersey, a few years later, wanted to take a census but it did not dare begin."[50]

[§100] A government may doubtless adopt necessary measures for the protection or relief of the people against famine. But the Scriptural example shows that such measures may end in their impoverishment or enslavement. In this case it appears that when Joseph had foretold seven years of plenty to be followed by seven years of famine, he was appointed Pharaoh's administrator. In that office he appropriated one fifth of all food grown in Egypt during the seven years of plenty. When the famine had begun and the people had exhausted their own stores, he sold them food from the stores of Pharaoh, and when their money was exhausted he took their cattle and finally their lands in exchange for food. Subsequently all the people were removed into the cities, but were given seed and directed to sow the lands and turn over one fifth of their crops to Pharaoh.[1]

[§101] Taxation was probably unknown in primitive society, and it does not appear that taxes were imposed upon the Israelites during the theocratic regime, apart from the tithes and offerings which were designed for the maintenance of the priesthood. But when a separate temporal government was established it became necessary to subject the people to various assessments or exactions for it support. According to the

48 2 Sam. 24:2-15 (in part); and see 1 Chron. 21:1-8

49 2 Chron. 25:5

50 4 S.F.Bar (1940) No. 2, p 3 (McAtee)

1 See Gen., chaps. 41, 47

Scripture, Samuel warned the Israelites that a king would "take the tenth of your seed, . . . your vineyards . . . and . . . your sheep: and ye shall be his servants."[2] Solomon, in particular, made the "yoke grievous" upon the people,[3] and they petitioned his son to "make the grievous servitude of thy father, and his sore yoke lighter."[4]

[§102] —— Tribute was levied upon subject people. Solomon made "the people that were left of the Hittites, and the Amorites, and the Perizites, and the Hivites, and the Jebusites, which were not of Israel . . . to pay tribute."[5] Much later, the Romans took custom or tribute, not from their "children" or citizens, but from "strangers" who had been subjugated.[6] In the time of Augustus Caesar, "a decree" is said to have gone out "that all the world should be taxed" and that "every one" should go "into his own city" to be taxed.[7]

[§103] —— The priesthood have long been considered exempt from taxation. This exemption was recognized by the Persian king Artaxerxes, who commanded Ezra to—

"require no tax, nor any other imposition, of any of the priests, or Levites, or holy singers, or porters, or ministers of the temple, or of any that have doings in this temple, and that no man have authority to impose any thing upon them."[8]

In Roman law also it is probable that the earliest immunity of the clergy was to relieve them from the public burdens of taxes and personal services to which all other citizens were subject.[9]

[§104] —— As to the payment of taxes or tribute, the Scriptures seem to teach that when a tax has been levied and is due, it ought to be paid,[10] and more especially if it can be paid without hardship, as where the tax money can be found in the mouth of "the fish that first cometh up when a hook is

---

2 1 Sam. 8:15,17
"Taxation is but the means by which the Government distributes the burden of its costs among those who enjoy its benefits." Feist v Young (1942) 46 F. Supp. 622,630 (Schwellenbach,DJ)
3 2 Chron. 10:4
In ancient times it was sometimes necessary to borrow money to pay taxes "There were also that said, We have borrowed money for the king's tribute, and that upon our lands and vineyards." Neh. 5:4
4 1 Kings 12:4
5 2 Chron. 8:7,8
6 Matt. 17:24-26 ("And when they were come to Capernaum, they that received tribute money came to Peter, and said, Doth not your master pay tribute? He saith, Yes. And when he was come into the house, Jesus prevented him, saying What thinkest thou, Simon? of

whom do the kings of the earth take custom or tribute? of their own children or of strangers? Peter saith unto him, Of strangers. Jesus saith unto him, Then are the children free")
7 Luke 2:1-3 ("this taxing was first made when Cyrennius was governor of Syria")
8 1 Esd. 8:22; and see Ezra 7:24
9 7 Cal.LR (1918) 101
10 See Matt. 22:18-21, quoted in Scopes v Tennessee (1927) 154 Tenn. 105, 289 SW 363, 53 ALR 821, 831 (Chambers,J); to same effect, Mark 12:15-17; Luke 20:23-25
"It is the high duty of every citizen to pay lawful taxes . . . because in doing so he helps to maintain the institutions of his country." Bashara v Saratoga School Dist. (1942) 163 SW2d (Tex.Com.App.) 631, 633 (Brewster,C)

cast in the sea."[11] In writing the saints at Rome, St. Paul directed them to "render . . . to all their dues: tribute to whom tribute is due, custom to whom custom (is due)."[12] Failure to pay taxes has been called a "mortal sin," on the ground that taxation is necessary for the well-being of the state, but Jesus directed the payment of tribute "lest we should offend them . . . that received tribute money."[13]

CHAPTER 15

CIVIL OBEDIENCE AND RESPECT OF OFFICIALS

[§105] The Scriptures definitely teach civil obedience, that is, that one should obey the secular authority and its laws.[14] Thus in the Old Testament it is counselled to "keep the king's commandments."[15] And in the New Testament, Jesus observed that "the scribes and Pharisees sit in Moses' seat,"[16] and commanded that—

"All therefore whatsoever they bid you observe, that observe and do; but do not ye after their works: for they say, and do not."[17]

St. Paul also directed "all that be in Rome,"[18] to subject themselves "unto the higher powers," saying:

". . . there is no power but of God: the powers that be are ordained of God.

"Whosoever therefore resisteth the power, resisteth the ordinance of God: and they that resist shall receive to themselves damnation.

"For rulers are not a terror to good work, but to evil. Wilt thou then not be afraid of the power? do that which is good, and thou shalt have praise of the same:

"For he is the minister of God to thee for good. But if thou do that which is evil, be afraid; for he beareth not the sword in vain: for he is the minister of God, a revenger to execute wrath upon him that doeth evil.

"Wherefore ye must needs be subject, not only for wrath, but also for conscience sake."[19]

11 Matt. 17:27 ("go thou to the sea, and cast an hook, and take up the fish that first cometh up; and when thou hast opened his mouth, thou shalt find a piece of money; take that, and give unto them for me and thee")
12 Rom. 13:7
13 Matt. 17:27
14 Religion teaches obedience to law. State v District School Board of Edgerton (1890) 76 Wis. 177, 20 ASR 41 54 (Lyon,J)
15 Ecclesiastes 8:2; and see Baruch 2:21 ("Thus saith the Lord, Bow down your shoulders to serve the king of Babylon")
16 Matt. 23:2
17 Matt. 23:3
18 Rom. 1:7
19 Rom. 13:1-5; and see Titus 3:1 ("Put them in mind to be subject to principalities and powers, to obey magistrates, to be ready to every good work"); Heb. 13:7 ("Remember them which have the rule over you"); Heb. 13:17 ("Obey them that have the rule over you, and submit yourselves")

Similarly, Peter wrote the "scattered strangers" that they should—

"Submit . . . to every ordinance of man for the Lord's sake: whether it be of the king, as supreme;
"Or unto governors, as unto them that are sent by him for the punishment of evildoers, and for the praise of them that do well.
"For so is the will of God, that with well doing ye may put to silence the ignorance of foolish men:
"As free, and not using your liberty for a cloak of maliciousness, but as the servants of God."[20]

[§106]   —— The doctrine of civil obedience is contained in the commandment of Jesus to "Render . . . unto Cesar the things which are Cesar's,"[21] which may properly be understood as meaning that one should obey the secular authority— even though an alien conqueror like Caesar—as well as that he should pay taxes or tribute. And the remark of St. Paul that "ye must needs be subject" to civil or secular law "for conscience sake"[22] implies that such law is binding in conscience and that its violation is a sin or wrong.

The secular law may be considered as resting upon "the authority of the divinely ordained state" rather than upon "an authoritative universal law.[23] It has been reasoned that the law is to be obeyed as the collective wisdom of the state, intended for the benefit of the people, individually and collectively,[24] and that "it becomes no prudent man to overstep the line which the wisdom of the community has drawn."[25]

[§107]   —— But it does not seem that Biblical law obligates one to submit to oppression[26] or to obey any secular rule that conflicts with its requirements in matters of conscience or religion. To the contrary, we are commanded not alone to "render unto Cesar the things which are Cesar's," but likewise to render "unto God the things that are God's."[27] So far as the Scriptures are concerned, a commandment or ordinance of the secular authority may be disregarded if it interferes with the practice of religion. Thus we find that Mattathias said:

"We will not hearken to the king's words, to go from our religion, either on the right hand, or the left."[28]

20 1 Pet. 2:13-16
21 Matt. 22:21; Mark 12:17; Luke 20:25; City of Manchester v Leiby (1941) 117 F2d 661, 666 (Magruder,Cir.J); Schriber v Rapp (1836) 5 Watts (Pa.) 351, 30 AD 327, 329 (Gibson,CJ)
22 Rom. 13:5
23 27 Harv.LR (1914) 611 (Pound) saying that "The most significant feature of the reformation, from a legal standpoint, was its replacement of the universal empire of Roman law and canon law by the civil law of each state"
24 42 Wash. LR (1914) 770
25 Lewis v England (1811) 4 Binney (Pa.) 5, 16 (Yeates,J)
26 "Oppression is illegal, even if done under the form of law. It is not treasonable to resist laws contravening inalienable rights, whether made by kings or parliaments, by a popular majority or a preponderant opinion, for such laws are made merely by arbitrary force masquerading as lawful authority." 28 Va. LR (1942) 487 (Simms)
27 See note 21 supra 28 1 Mac. 2:22

Nor did Peter and other apostles regard themselves as bound by an order of the council that they should not "speak at all nor teach in the name of Jesus."[29]   When charged with the violation of this order, they "answered and said, We ought to obey God rather than men."[30]

[§108] —— In America, the federal Constitution declares that no law may be made "prohibiting the free exercise of religion.[31]   And it has been asserted that in this country—

"Conscience is subject to no human law . . . so long as its dictates are obeyed, consistently with the harmony, good order and peace of the community."[32]

"It is not within the province of any department of the government . . . to determine what ought or ought not to be a fundamental of religious belief, so long as the professed creed is not subversive of the peace and good order of society."[33]

In other words, it is for each individual to decide for himself what to him is religious.

"No man . . . is empowered to censor another's religious convictions or set bounds to the areas of human conduct in which those convictions should be permitted to control his actions, unless compelled to do so by an overriding public necessity . . ."[34]

But it is for the civil authority to say what laws are necessary for the peace and welfare of the state, and it can never concede that regulations which are generally accepted as being reasonable and proper, and which are not directed against any particular sect or creed, are inapplicable to persons who may object to their observance upon religious grounds.[35]

[§109]   Biblical law requires that secular officials be respected.   Thus, we are admonished to render unto the powers that be "fear to whom fear; honour to whom honour" is due,[36] and, more specifically, to fear[37] and honour[38] the king.   This demands obedience, for it is only by obedience that proper

29 Acts 4:18
30 Acts 5:29
31 US Const., 1st Amendment (1791)
32 Waite v Merrill (1826) 4 Greenleaf (Me.) 102, 16 AD 238, 245 (Mellen,CJ)
33 Ruse v Williams (1913) 14 Ariz. 445, 130 P 887, 45 LRANS 923, 927 (Franklin,CJ)
34 Gobitis v Minersville School District (1937) 21 F Supp. 581 (Maris,DJ)
35 City of Manchester v Leiby (1941) 117 F2d 661, 666 (Magruder,Cir.J) citing Hamilton v Regents (1934) 293 US 245, 268, 55 S Ct 197, 79 L ed 343 (Cardozo,J) and saying that the regulations of the National Prohibition Act as to the use of sacramental wine "were no doubt applicable even to persons who might have believed it a gross impiety to apply for a civil permit before partaking of a divine sacrament. Similarly,

as to the sacrament of marriage—one must get a marriage license from the civil authority, and in some states a brief waiting period is mandatory after the license is issued. These may be regarded as instances of rendering unto Caesar the things which are Caesar's; certainly no insult to the Almighty is implied."
36 Rom. 13:7
37 Prov. 24:21 ("My son, fear thou the Lord and the king")
38 1 Pet. 2:17
Respect for the Court was also demanded in the olden days. It was held to be a crime to be disrespectful to a judge. "If a man curses a judge he violates two commandments, the commandment against cursing a judge (Ex. 22:28), and the commandment against cursing an ordinary man (Lev. 19:14)."
5 Docket (1941) No. 9, p 4179

respect can be shown to a superior having a right to command.[39]

It is forbidden to "curse"[40] or "speak evil of the ruler of thy people."[41] But it is seemingly a good defense to a charge of speaking evil of the ruler that the person charged with this offense did not know that the one to whom, or of whom, he spoke was the ruler.[42] In the reign of Ahaseurus, king of the Medes and Persians, it was unlawful for one "whether man or woman," even to "come unto the king into the inner court," unless called.[43]

[§110] —— In the case of Shimei, it is said that "when king David came to Bahurim, behold, thence came out a man . . . whose name was Shimei . . .; he came forth and cursed still as he came. And he cast stones at David, and at all the servants of king David . . . And David said . . . let him curse; for the Lord hath bidden him."[44] But David remembered the incident, and shortly before his death charged Solomon in reference to Shimei to "hold him not guiltless . . .; but his hoar head bring thou down to the grave with blood."[45] Accordingly Solomon called for Shimei and instructed him to "build an house in Jerusalem, and dwell there, and go not forth thence any wither,"[46] under penalty of death. Shimei obeyed the order for three years, at the end of which he "arose . . . and went to Gath to Achish to seek his servants."[47] When this was told to Solomon, he commanded Benaiah, captain of the host, "which went out and fell upon him (Shimei), that he died."[48]

CHAPTER 16

INTERNATIONAL LAW

111 In general   112 Treaties   113 —— Violations   114 Leagues of nations

[§111] "International law is the result of international association, and consists in those rules which should be observed in the mutual relations of nations in time of peace and

39 Legal Tender Cases (1871) 79 US 457-680, 20 L ed 287, 354 (Field,J, dissenting) saying that "It is only by obedience that affection and reverence can be shown to a superior having a right to command. So thought our great Master when he said to his disciples: 'If ye love me, keep my commandments.'"
40 Ex. 22:28; and see Ecclesiastes 10:20
41 Acts 23:5
42 Acts 23:4,5
43 See Est. 4:11 ("All the king's servants, and the people of the king's province, do know, that whosoever, whether man or woman, shall come unto the king into the inner court, who is not called, there is one law of his to put him to death, except such to whom the king shall hold out the golden sceptre, that he may live")
44 2 Sam. 16:5,6,11
45 1 Kings 2:9
46 1 Kings 2:36
47 1 Kings 2:40
48 1 Kings 2:46

in time of war."[49] It has been defined as "the sum of the rules or usages which civilized states have agreed shall be binding upon them in their dealings with one another."[50]

[§112] Treaties are the principal source of international law.[1] A treaty is an agreement or contract between two or more states.[2] The Scriptures refer to many such contracts. In the patriarchal age, the so-called "covenants," like those between Abram and Lot, Abraham and Abimelech, Isaac and Abimelech,[3] and Jacob and Hamor,[4] were treaties between tribal leaders. During the life of the original kingdom of Israel, and later that of the separate kingdoms of Israel and Judah, treaties were made with surrounding nations. For exmple, Ahab made a covenant with Ben-hadad of Syria after defeating him in battle.[5] In later times, Judas Maccabeus made a treaty with Rome.[6] Jonathan renewed the treaty, and "sent letters also to the Lacedemonians, and to other places, for the same purpose."[7] After the death of Jonathan, Simon again renewed the Roman treaty.[8] The Lacedemonians also sent a letter to Simon and the people of the Jews, to renew friendship with them.[9]

[§113] —— Violations of treaties have often occurred. In ancient times, as well as modern, the most solemn compacts were treated as "scraps of paper" when that seemed expedient. The first recorded instance of treaty violation is that of the covenant between Jacob and Hamor. Two of the sons of Jacob repudiated the compact three days after it was made and suddenly slew all the male members of Hamor's house, captured their women and children, and appropriated their property.[10]

[§114] A league of nations is an agreement of two or more nations by which they associate themselves to effect some common object, usually of a military character. Such agreements or alliances were not uncommon in Biblical times. Thus the kings of the Hittites, the Amorites, the Canaanites, the Perizzites, the Hivites and the Jebusites, made a league and "gathered themselves together, to fight with Joshua and with Israel, with one accord."[11] Joshua, on the other hand, made a league with the Hivites, whose ambassadors represented that they had come from a far country.[12] Solomon

49 15 RCL 94 (Davids)
50 Lord John Russell (1792-1878) English statesman
1 15 RCL 96
2 15 RCL 147
3 See infra §148
4 Gen. 34:6-19
5 1 Kings 20:34; 2 Chron. 16:2-4
6 1 Mac. 8:22-30
7 1 Mac. 12:1,2
8 1 Mac. 14:24
9 1 Mac. 14:20-23
10 Gen. 34:25-29
11 Josh. 9:1,2
12 Josh. 9:15

"made affinity (alliance) with Pharaoh king of Egypt, and took Pharaoh's daughter,"[13] and Hiram king of Tyre and Solomon "made league together."[14] Simon "sent Numenius to Rome with a great shield of gold of a thousand pound weight to confirm the league with them."[15]

The Scriptures do not approve of reliance upon leagues with foreign nations. Asa king of Judah was reprimanded because he "relied not on the Lord," but made a league with Ben-hadad of Syria against Baasha of Israel. Of this it is said that—

". . . Hanani the seer came to Asa king of Judah, and said unto him, Because thou hast relied on the king of Syria, and not relied on the Lord thy God, therefore is the host of the king of Syria escaped out of thine hand.

"Were not the Ethiopians and the Lubims a huge host, with very many chariots and horsemen? yet, because thou didst rely on the Lord, he delivered them into thine hand.

"For the eyes of the Lord run to and fro throughout the whole earth, to shew himself strong in the behalf of them whose heart is perfect toward him. Herein thou hast done foolishly: therefore from henceforth thou shalt have wars."[16]

CHAPTER 17

WARFARE AND MILITARY LAW

[§115] Many Scriptural passages pertain to warfare and military law,[17] and, without attempting to notice all of them, it seems desirable briefly to discuss the subject. In general, the Sacred Writings may not be said to approve of war, but they recognize that "these things must come to pass"[18] in an evil world, and that the waging of war may be justifiable in some circumstances. So it is said that there is "a time of war, and a time of peace."[19] And whereas the destruction of human life is ordinarily indefensible,[20] it may become a practical necessity for a righteous people to arise and fight for their lives and their laws.[21]

According to the Scriptures, "there is no peace unto the wicked,"[22] and it is futile to cry "peace, peace, when there is no peace."[23] If men would have peace, they must "seek first

13 1 Kings 3:1
14 1 Kings 5:12   15 1 Mac. 14:24
16 2 Chron. 16:7-9
17 Law of sieges: Deut. 20:10-20
18 Matt. 24:6; Mark 13:7
19 Ecclesiastes 3:8
20 Internoscia's Internat. L. (1910) xxvii

21 1 Mac. 2:40 ("If we all do as our brethren have done, and fight not for our lives and our laws against the heathen, they will now quickly root us out of the earth")
22 Isa. 48:22, 57:21
23 Jer. 6:14

the kingdom of God, and his righteousness,"[24] for peace is the "work of righteousness"[25] and there can be no lasting and universal peace until "righteousness and peace have kissed each other."[26] It is "in the last days"[27] and when "the Lord alone shall be exalted"[28] that—

". . . the nations . . . shall beat their swords into ploughshares, and their spears into pruning-hooks: nation shall not lift up sword against nation, neither shall they learn war any more."[29]

[§116] —— Inasmuch as there have been "wars and rumors of war"[30] since time immemorial, it may not be said that the inspired writers were unacquainted with warfare. Therefore had they considered it proper, they would doubtless have outlawed war in no uncertain terms. Yet not one unequivocal statement is to be found denouncing wars or forbidding individuals to participate therein. The commandment against man-killing—"Thou shalt not kill"—may not rightly be understood as prohibiting warfare, for it is plainly a precept of civil law—intended to govern relations between individuals of the same tribe or nation—and not a rule of international law. John the Baptist commanded certain soldiers to "do violence to no man,"[31] signifying perhaps that he disapproved of warfare. But, according to Moses, "The Lord is a man of war,"[32] who goes with his people, to fight for them against their enemies.[33] And it is said of the war which was made by the sons of Reuben, and the Gadites, and half the tribe of Manasseh, with the Hagarites, that "the war was of God."[34]

[§117] Doubtless a nation ought not to make war against another save for a just cause nor without considering whether it is able to withstand the power of the enemy.[35] But when it has been determined to go to war, the entire people are bound to take part according to their ability and the necessities of the occasion. The Scriptures sanction both military training and service. The "hands" of men who are liable to service should be taught to "war."[36] So it appears that David commanded that the children of Judah be taught the use of the bow.[37] And when war impends, or hostilities have begun, the

24 Matt. 6:33
25 Isa. 32:17
26 Ps. 85:10 (There shall be peace when "the inhabitants of the world . . . learn righteousness")
27 Isa. 2:2
28 Isa. 2:11
29 Isa. 2:4
30 Matt. 24:6; Mark 13:7
31 Luke 3:14
32 Ex. 15:3
33 Deut. 20:4; and see Num. 21:4 (re-

ferring to "the book of the wars of the Lord")
34 1 Chron. 5:22
35 Luke 14:31 ("What king, going to make war against another king, sitteth not down first, and consulteth whether he be able with ten thousand to meet him that cometh against him with twenty thousand?")
36 Ps. 144:1 ("Blessed be the Lord my strength, which teacheth my hands to war, and my fingers to fight")
37 2 Sam. 1:18

obligation rests upon "all that are able to go to war,"[38] who are "from twenty years old and upward"[39] and are not exempt from service,[40] to go forth as they are required "armed to battle."[41] Those who willfully sit at home while their brethren go to war,[42] and thereby discourage the heart of the people,[43] may be regarded as having "sinned against the Lord."[44]

[§118] —— Under Mosaic law, certain classes of persons were excused "before battle," that is, deferred or temporarily exempted from military service. The "officers" were directed to "speak unto the people," saying—

". . . What man is there that hath built a new house, and hath not dedicated it? let him go and return to his house, lest he die in the battle, and another man dedicate it.

"And what man is he that hath planted a vineyard, and hath not yet eaten of it? let him also go and return unto his house, lest he die in the battle, and another man eat of it.

"And what man is there that hath betrothed a wife, and hath not taken her? let him go and return unto his house, lest he die in the battle, and another man take her.

". . . What man is there that is fearful and fainthearted? let him go and return unto his house, lest his brethren's heart faint as well as his heart."[45]

It is further provided that a man who "hath taken a wife . . . shall not go out to war, . . . but . . . shall be free at home one year . . ."[46]

According to this law, Gideon proclaimed to the people who were with him, before attacking the Midianites, that ". . . Whosoever is fearful and afraid, let him return and depart early from mount Gilead."[47] And it appears that Judas Maccabeus, before joining battle with the army of Lysias, commanded "such as were building houses, or had betrothed wives, or were planting vineyards, or were fearful" to "return, every man to his own house."[48]

[§119] When the officers had finished speaking to the people concerning those who were excusable "before battle," they were required to "make captains of the armies to lead the people."[49] So Judas Maccabeus—

38 Num. 26:2
39 Num. 26:2,4
40 See infra §118
41 Num. 32:29
42 Num. 32:6
43 Num. 32:7
44 Num. 32:23
"The spirit" of one who refuses to serve in the army "is one of rebellion against the laws . . . such citizens are at heart traitors to their country." Ex parte Billings (1942) 46 F. Supp. 663,668 (Hopkins,DJ)
45 Deut. 20:5-8
46 Deut. 24:5
47 Judges 7:2,3
48 1 Mac. 3:56
49 Deut. 20:9

"ordained captains over the people, even captains over thousands, and over hundreds, and over fifties, and over tens."[50]

And though the law forbids work on the Sabbath, it was decided not to be wrongful to fight against those who "make battle with us on the Sabbath day."[1]

[§120] —— Mosaic law directs that a "charge" be given by the "priest" when the people—that is, the army—"are come nigh unto battle."

". . . the priest shall approach and speak unto the people.
"And shall say unto them, Hear, O Israel, ye approach this day unto battle against your enemies: let not your hearts faint, fear not, and do not tremble, neither be ye terrified because of them;
"For the Lord your God is he that goeth with you, to fight for you against your enemies, to save you."[2]

[§121] —— The Scriptures prescribe sanitary regulations to be observed in time of war.

"When the host goeth forth against thine enemies, then keep thee from every wicked thing.
"If there be among you any man, that is not clean by reason of uncleanliness that chanceth him by night, then shall he go abroad out of the camp, he shall not come within the camp:
"But it shall be, when evening cometh on, he shall wash himself with water: and when the sun is down, he shall come into the camp again.
"Thou shalt have a place also without the camp whither thou shalt go forth abroad:
"And thou shalt have a paddle upon thy weapon: and it shall be, when thou wilt ease thyself abroad, thou shalt dig therewith, and shalt turn back and cover that which cometh from thee:
"For the Lord thy God walketh in the midst of thy camp, to deliver thee, and to give up thine enemies before thee; therefore shall thy camp be holy: that he see no unclean thing in thee, and turn away from thee."[3]

[§122] —— In ancient times, prisoners of war were put to death or enslaved. Later it became a practice to allow them their freedom upon the payment of "ransom money" or to exchange prisoners on one side for those on the other. Moses made two rules concerning the taking of prisoners, one applying to nearby enemies and the other to enemies "which are very far off." As to the former it was ordered that—

". . . thou shalt save alive nothing that breatheth:
"But thou shalt utterly destroy them, namely, the Hittites, and the Amorites, the Canaanites, and the Perizzites, the Hivites, and the Jebusites; as the Lord thy God hath commanded thee."[4]

But with regard to distant enemies it was prescribed that—

50 1 Mac. 3:55
1   1 Mac. 2:41
2   Deut. 20:2-4

3   Deut. 23:9-14, quoted in 14 Harv. LR (1901) 510
4   Deut. 20:16,17

"... thou shalt smite every male thereof with the edge of the sword: "But the women, and the little ones, and the cattle, and all that is in the city, even all the spoil thereof, shalt thou take unto thyself."[5]

[§123] —— —— In some cases it was forbidden to "save" even the women of the enemy "alive."[6] But special rules were prescribed as to the treatment of female captives in cases where they were permitted to be taken.

"When thou goest forth to war against thine enemies, and the Lord thy God hath delivered them into thine hands, and thou has taken them captive,

"And seest among the captives a beautiful woman, and hast a desire unto her, that thou wouldest have her to thy wife:

"Then thou shalt bring her home to thine house; and she shall shave her head, and pare her nails;

"And she shall put the raiment of her captivity from off her, and shall remain in thine house, and bewail her father and her mother a full month: and after that thou shalt go in unto her, and be her husband, and she shall be thy wife.

"And it shall be, if thou have no delight in her, then thou shalt let her go whither she will; but thou shalt not sell her at all for money, thou shalt not make merchandise of her, because thou hast humbled her."[7]

[§124] —— In ancient warfare, it was considered a natural right that soldiers of a conquering army should take spoils, "every man for himself;"[8] in other words, that they should seize the property of their vanquished enemies. But in some instances the taking of spoils was forbidden.[9] Following his victory over the Amalekites, king David ruled that those who "tarry by the stuff" should share equally in the spoils. It is related that—

"... David took all the flocks and the herds, which they drave before those other cattle, and said, This is David's spoil.

"And David came to the two hundred men, which were so faint that they could not follow David, whom they had made also to abide at the brook Besor: and they went forth to meet David, and to meet the people that were with him: and when David came near to the people, he saluted them.

"Then answered all the wicked men and men of Belial, of those that went with David, and said, Because they went not with us, we will not give them ought of the spoil that we have recovered, save to every man his wife and his children, that they may lead them away and depart.

"Then said David, Ye shall not do so, my brethren, with that which the Lord hath given us, who hath preserved us, and delivered the company that came against us into our hand.

5 Deut. 20:13,14
"... the laws of war, of 34 centuries ago, given by Moses to the Israelites, and reported in the 20th chapter of Deuteronomy, make even the atrocity pictures and stories of the present day appear humane." 45 Case & Comment

(1939) No. 3, p 7 (C.A. Beardsley, Pres. Am.Bar Assn.)
6 See for example Num. 31:6-18; Deut. 20:16,17; Josh. 6:17,21, 8:25,26, 11:14
7 Deut. 21:10-14
8 Num. 31:53
9 See infra §125

"For who will hearken unto you in this matter? but as his part is that goeth down to the battle, so shall his part be that tarrieth by the stuff: they shall part alike.

"And it was so from that day forward, that he made it a statute and an ordinance for Israel unto this day."[10]

[§125] —— —— Achan's case arose at the seige of Jericho, where it was expressly forbidden to take spoils, save that "the silver and gold, and vessels of brass and iron" should "come into the treasury of the Lord."[11] Achan took certain spoils and, being confronted by Joshua, confessed that he had taken "a goodly Babylonish garment, and two hundred shekels of silver, and a wedge of gold of fifty shekels weight," and had hidden them in his tent.

"So Joshua sent messengers, and they ran unto the tent; and, behold, it was hid in his tent, and the silver under it.

And they took them out of the midst of the tent, and brought them unto Joshua, and unto all the children of Israel, and laid them out before the Lord.

"And Joshua, and all Israel with him, took Achan the son of Zerah, and the silver, and the garments, and the wedge of gold, and his sons, and his daughters, and his oxen, and his asses, and his sheep, and his tent, and all that he had: and they brought them unto the valley of Achor.

"And Joshua said, Why hast thou troubled us? the Lord shall trouble thee this day. And all Israel stoned him with stones, and burned them with fire, after they had stoned them with stones."[12]

10 1 Sam. 30:20-25
11 Josh. 6:17-19

12 Josh. 7:21-25

PART III

CIVIL LAW

CHAPTER 18

INTRODUCTION

126 Definitions   127 The two elementary rules

[§126]   The civil law pertains to private rights and duties in respect of persons and property.[13]   A right may be said to be a claim or license that the law will—or should—recognize and protect.[14]   It cannot be founded upon a wrong.[14a]   But if one has a right, he does not lose it by asserting or exercising it; it may be exercised nine (many) times as well as once.[14b]

It is elementary knowledge that rights and duties are correlative, in the sense that where one has a right there is a corresponding duty owing from another or others.[15]   It is also a fundamental principle that one who receives the benefit of a transaction should bear its burden.[15a]

[§127]   The civil law of the Bible is founded upon two elementary rules: first, that one should "do justly"[16] and second, that one should "speak the truth."[17]   These rules are variously expressed in many passages to the effect that one should "do justice,"[18] "follow that which is good"[19] or "just,"[20] and "abstain from all appearance of evil;"[21] also in other provisions forbidding one to do "evil,"[22] to "render evil

---

13 "Civil law" is also understood as meaning the civil or municipal law of the Roman Empire.

14 See Acts 25:16, where St.Paul speaks of the "license" of an accused person "to answer for himself concerning the crime laid against him."

Rights of the individual are not absolute. They must always be exercised with reasonable regard for the conflicting rights of others. Hitchman Coal & Coke Co v Mitchell (1917) 245 US 229, 38 S Ct 65, 62 L ed 260, 277, LRA1918C 497, Ann Cas 1918B 461 (Pitney,J)

Such rights must give way when they come into conflict with other rights granted for the protection, safety and general welfare of the public. Ex parte Kanai (1942) 46 F.Supp. 286 (Duffy,DJ); United States v Hirabayashi (1942) 46 F.Supp. 657, 660 (Black,DJ)

14a People v LaBarre (1924) 193 Cal. 388, 224 P 750 (Seawell,J)

14b Near v Minnesota (1930) 283 US 697-738, 75 L ed 1357, 1369 (Hughes,CJ)

15 "There can be no rights without corresponding duties." Sharron v Sharron (1888) 75 Cal. 1, 16 P 345, 361 (McKinstry,J)

15a See Rom. 15:27 ("For if the Gentiles have been made partakers of their spiritual things, their duty is also to minister unto them in carnal things")

16 Micah 6:8 ("What doth the Lord require of thee, but to do justly . . . ?")

17 Zech. 8:16; Eph. 4:25

18 Prov. 21:3 ("To do justice . . . is more acceptable than sacrifice"); Isa. 56:1 ("Thus saith the Lord . . . do justice")

19 1 Thess. 5:15; Titus 2:7 ("In all things shew . . . thyself a pattern of good works")

20 Deut. 16:20 ("That which is altogether just shalt thou follow")

21 1 Thess. 5:22

22 Ps. 34:14, 37:27; Prov. 3:7

for evil,"[23] to "lie,"[24] and to "oppress" others.[25] And concerning the speaking of the truth, it has been noted that "One may speak as plainly and effectually by his acts and conduct as he can by word of mouth."[26]

As one is bound to do justly and speak the truth, so is he entitled to receive justice at the hands and truth from the lips of his neighbour. The fact that the law is not always able to enforce this right is no reason to deny its existence.[27]

DIVISION A

Property, Contracts and Trespasses

CHAPTER 19

PROPERTY—GENERALLY

128 Divine ownership   129 Nature of man's right   130 Common or joint ownership   131 Individual or private rights   132 How rights were acquired   133 Lost property

[§128] Under Scriptural law, all property—the whole earth—belongs to God, who is the only owner of property.[28] Thus in the Old Testament it is asserted that "all the earth is mine (God's)."[29]

". . . I am God . . .

". . . every beast of the forest is mine, and the cattle upon a thousand hills.

". . . the wild beasts of the field are mine.

". . . the world is mine, and the fulness thereof."[30]

The rule is repeated in the New Testament, where it is said that "the earth is the Lord's, and the fulness thereof,"[31] and that "all things are of God."[32]

In particular "the land,"[33] "the silver" and "the gold" are God's.[34] And it appears that Jesus had no property, other than His garments which the soldiers "parted" among them-

23 1 Thess. 5:15 ("See that none render evil for evil unto any man")
24 Lev. 19:11; Ps. 101:7, 119:163; Prov. 6:16,17, 12:22, 13:5; Hosea 4:2; Ecclesiasticus 7:12,13, 20:24, 41:17; Eph. 4:25; Col. 3:9
"Keep thee far from a false matter." Ex. 23:7
"A thief is better than a man that is accustomed to lie." Ecclesiasticus 20:25
"Be not a liar, for the lie guideth to theft." Two Ways 3:5
25 See infra §246
26 Atwood v State (1927) 146 Miss. 662, 111 So. 865, 51 ALR 836 (Anderson,J)
And often "one may learn more from what has been done than from what has been said." 65 Law Notes (1941) No. 3, p 9
27 United States v American Bell Tel.

Co. (1897) 167 US 224, 42 L ed 144, 147, argument of Atty. Gen. Harmon
28 " . . . wise men die, likewise the fool and the brutish person perish, and leave their wealth to others. Their inward thought is, that their houses shall continue for ever, and their dwelling places to all generations: they call their lands after their own names. Nevertheless man . . . abideth not: he is like the beasts that perish . . . For when he dieth he shall carry nothing away: his glory shall not descend after him." Ps. 49:10-12,17
29 Ex. 19:5
30 Ps. 50:7, 10-12
31 1 Cor. 10:26,28
32 2 Cor. 5:18
33 Lev. 25:23
34 Aggeus 2:9

selves after the crucifixion,[35] for it is related that He had "not where to lay his head."[36]

[§129]   But the Scriptures give man the right to "subdue" the earth and to have "dominion over the fish of the sea . . . the fowl of the air, and . . . every living thing that moveth upon the earth."[37]   This is a common right given to all men over all things, and not to particular individuals to be exercised by them to the exclusion of others.

"God intended the earth as a common fund for all mankind and that the fruits thereof should sustain all men."[38]

"The first of mankind had in common all those things which God had given to the human race. This community was . . . called a negative community, which resulted from the fact that those things which were common to all belonged no more to one than to the others."[39]

Thus, while it may be said that "all things are for your (man's) sakes,"[40] one may not properly say that anything is his own[41]—unless it be something made by his own hands[41a]— in the sense of having any permanent right in the thing itself.

"The idea of absolute property forever in any particular owner . . . is a fiction. There can be no such thing . . . as absolute property forever, in the true sense of the term."[42]

[§130]   Contrary to the modern notion, said to have been bequeathed to us by the Romans, common or joint ownership of property by groups of men—rather than separate ownership by individuals—is the natural and normal state. So in the patriarchal age property was owned by family or tribal groups, and the property of each group was held either by its patriarch as trustee for all of its members, or jointly by the male members for the use and benefit of all.[43]   Where property was held and used separately by an individual, he could not convey it away, especially to a stranger, without the consent of the tribal council.[44]   And, as we shall see, a community ownership of property was established by the early Christians.[45]

35 Matt. 27:35; Mark 15:24; Luke 23:34; John 19:23,24
36 Matt. 8:20; Luke 9:58; Ruse v Williams (1913) 14 Ariz. 445, 130 P 887, 45 LRANS 923, 926 (Franklin,CJ)
37 Gen. 1:28; Ecclesiasticus 17:2,4
"Thou hast put all things in subjection under his (man's) feet. For in that he put all in subjection under him, he left nothing that is not put under him. But now we see not yet all things put under him." Heb. 2:8
38 St.Ambrose
"If we are all here by the equal permission of the Creator, we are all here with an equal title to his bounty— with an equal right to all that nature so impartially offers." Henry George (1839-1897) American political economist
39 Rock Creek Ditch & Flume Co. v

Miller (1933) 93 Mont. 248, 17 P2d 1074, 89 ALR 200, 203 (Callaway,CJ) quoting Pothier
40 2 Cor. 4:15
41 Two Ways 4:8
41a One has the sole and exclusive right to the fruits of his labor—"to every cow her calf." Finian v Colomba, decided by King Dermott in the halls of Tara, A.D. 567
42 11 Harv. LR (1897) 69
43 See Maine's Anc. L. 251-253
Continued existence of a family depends on its having property. Without common property, the family disintegrates. Individual ownership of property has undermined the modern family. Its place has been taken in some respects by corporations.
44 12 Gr B (1900) 90 **45** See infra §248

[§131]   In ancient times, individual or private rights as to property were very limited. But there seems to be an inherent desire in natural man to "lay up treasure for himself,"[46] that is, to possess material things and to exclude others, even members of his own family, therefrom. The law doubtless took cognizance of this desire—as did Moses of the hardness of the hearts of men when he suffered them to put away their wives[47]—by recognizing private property rights, which have been regarded as based upon the commandment that "Thou shalt not steal."[48]   Inasmuch as this commandment forbids and thereby makes wrongful the "stealing" of property from another, it may be regarded as establishing a right of the latter in respect of property over which he has personal dominion.[49]   It is his right for the time being to possess and use the property according to his needs[50] and as he wills,[1] so long as he does not thereby injure others[2] and thus misuse his own.[3]

In the first sale of land, the true subject-matter of the transaction was recognized as being the possession or right to possession of the property.[4] In later passages also land is referred to as a "possession."[5]

[§132]   Property rights were originally acquired by occupancy or possession. The first occupant or possessor—whether a family or tribe, or an individual—was regarded as having a kind of transient right that lasted so long as the occupancy or possession continued, and no longer. As Blackstone said—

"The earth and all things therein were the general property of mankind from the immediate gift of the Creator . . . Thus the ground was in common, and no part was the permanent property of any man in particular; yet whoever was in the occupation of any determined spot of it, for rest, for shade, or the like, acquired for the time a sort of ownership, from which it would have been unjust and contrary to the law of nature to have driven him by force, but the instant that he quitted the use or occupation of it, another might seize it without injustice."[6]

It has been noted that the Biblical patriarchs did not attempt permanently to appropriate the land over which they grazed their flocks and herds.[7]

46 Luke 12:21
47 Matt. 19:8; Mark 10:5
48 27 Harv. LR (1914) 613
49 28 Yale LJ (1919) 782 (Killer) observing that "Thou shalt not steal (from a tribal brother) establishes the right to property, thus excluding aggressions, reprisals, and consequent chaos and disorganization."
50 Acts 2:45
1 Matt. 20:15

2 See infra §176
"Individuals in the enjoyment of their own right must be careful not to injure the rights of others. License Cases, 5 Howard (US) 504, 12 L ed 256, 295 (McLean,J)
3 Gaius 1:53 ("One ought not to misuse his right")
4 Gen. 23:3-20
5 See for example Ecclesiasticus 28:24; Acts 5:1
6 2 Bl.Com. 4
7 Maine's Anc. L. 245

[§133] The Mosaic law of "lost property' is that "all lost things of thy brother's, which he hath lost, and thou hast found,"[8] "thou shalt bring . . . again unto thy brother."[9]

"And if thy brother be not nigh unto thee, or if thou know him not, then thou shalt bring it (the lost thing) unto thine own house, and it shall be with thee until thy brother seek after it, and thou shalt restore it to him again."[10]

This rule applies to animals which have gone astray, to "raiment," and any other lost thing.[11] And as regards the concealment of property that has been found, the law provides that—

"If a soul . . . have found that which was lost and lieth concerning it, and sweareth falsely, . . . he shall restore . . . the lost thing which he found . . . and shall add the fifth part more thereto."[12]

CHAPTER 20

DISPOSITION OF PROPERTY UPON THE OWNER'S DEATH

[§134] "A good man," it has been said, "leaveth an inheritance"[13] and "inheritance flows naturally with the blood."[14] In other words, a man's children are his natural and proper heirs,[15] and their rightful inheritance ought not to be turned to strangers.[16]

According to Biblical law, the property that a man possessed at the time of his death ordinarily passed to his son or sons,[17] to the exclusion of daughters. If a man left several sons, the eldest was entitled to a double portion; and this rule applied though the decedent had had two wives, one beloved and the other hated, and the firstborn was the son

8 Deut. 22:3
9 Deut. 22:1
10 Deut. 22:2
11 Deut. 22:3
12 Lev. 6:2-5
13 Prov. 13:22
14 Hole v Robbins (1881) 53 Wis. 514, 10 NW 617 (Taylor,J)
The tie of blood makes one the heir of another. Hehr's Adm'r v Hehr (1941) 157 SW2d (Ky.) 111, 113 (Stanley,C)
15 Rom. 8:17 ("if children, then heirs")
". . . men . . . leave the rest of their substance to their babes." Ps. 17:14

16 Lam. 5:2 ("Our inheritance is turned to strangers")
"There is nothing in Jewish law to warrant the belief that the King or the State had any right to inherit property upon the death of the owner without lawful heirs." 12 Gr.B. (1900) 506. See also §422 infra
17 Gen. 15:4 ("he that shall come forth out of thine own bowels shall be thine heir"), 25:5 ("And Abraham gave all that he had unto Isaac") See also Tobit 14:13 showing that Tobias inherited the substance of his father- and mother-in-law as well as that of his father.

of the hated wife.[18] But a firstborn son was not preferred over a younger son where he had "sold" his birthright[19] or where some other sufficient reason existed for giving preference to the younger.[20]

[§135] —— In England lands formerly descended to the eldest son, and personal property at one time became the property of the church, which devoted a portion to masses, and paid the debts and distributed the residue, if any, to the next of kin.[21] Later the lands of one dying intestate were equally divided among his sons, except that the eldest took a double share. In early American law the property was equally divided among all the children, including daughters. At first the eldest son took a double portion, but this preference was soon abolished.[22] The object of the law, it has been stated, was—

". . . to make an equal division among all the children, with regard to the value of the estate. But as the right of choice must be given to some, where the land cannot be divided amongst all, it was judged most reasonable to give preference first to the male sex and next to priority of birth."[23]

[§136] Under Primitive law the illegitimacy of a son seemingly did not alter his legal status as an heir.[24] He was entitled to inherit from his natural father though his mother was a bondmaid, a concubine or a harlot, and not a legal wife. But the rights of illegitimates were defeated in some instances by "sending" them "away." Thus Abraham sent away Ishmael, his son by Hagar the bondmaid, "that he should not be . . . heir with Isaac,"[25] and he gave gifts unto the sons of his concubines and sent them away while he yet lived.[26]

Under Mosaic law it is probable that an illegitimate child was not permitted to inherit, since he could not enter into the congregation. It is declared that "A bastard shall not enter the congregation of the Lord; even to his tenth generation shall he not enter into the congregation of the Lord."[27] And it appears that the sons of Gilead's wife thrust out Jephthah, whom Gilead begat of an harlot, saying unto him:

---

18 Deut. 21:15-17 ("he may not make the son of the beloved firstborn before the son of the hated, which is indeed the firstborn: but he shall acknowledge the son of the hated for the firstborn, by giving him a double portion of all that he hath")
19 Gen. 25:29-34, 27:18-29
20 See Gen. 48:18,19 (where Israel pronounced his blessing upon the second son of Joseph)

21 14 Harv. LR (1901) 521
22 Findlay's Lessee v Riddle (1810) 3 Binney (Pa.) 139, 158 (Yeats,J)
23 Kline v Grayson (1811) 4 Binney (Pa.) 225, 226 (Tilghman, CJ)
24 14 Gr.B. (1902) 83
25 Gen. 21:9-14
26 Gen. 25:6
27 Deut. 23:2

"Thou shalt not inherit in our father's house; for thou art the son of a strange woman."[28]

Concerning the Christian law it has been observed that "it nowhere appears in Sacred Writ that the Great Teacher made any distinction in regard to the paternity of the children."[29]

[§137] —— But the common law visited the penalty of disinheritance upon the child of an unmarried woman.[30] An illegitimate was not considered as the child of his father within the inheritance law. Indeed, it has been said that, in law, he is the child of nobody,[31] "a living example of the exceedingly old and right bitter adage (doubted, as unfair, even when in use); 'The fathers have eaten a sour grape, and the children's teeth are set on edge.' "[32] Such is still the law of England and of some of the American states.

"The reasons for the . . . rule were doubtless twofold. One is the ostracism and odium which have been universally visited upon the illegitimate since the days of Moses. The other is the possibility of the assertion of fraudulent claims to heirship by those born 'out of wedlock.' "[33]

[§138] It has often happened that a man had no sons, or, though he had sons, that he outlived them. To meet these situations, Mosaic law prescribed rules of succession:

". . . If a man die, and have no son, then ye shall cause his inheritance to pass unto his daughter.

"And if he have no daughter, then ye shall give his inheritance unto his brethren.

"And if he have no brethren, then ye shall give his inheritance unto his father's brethren.

"And if his father have no brethren, then ye shall give his inheritance unto his kinsman that is next to him of his family, and he shall possess it."[34]

---

28 Judges 11:2

29 Hastings v Rathbone (1922) 194 Iowa 177, 188 NW 960, 23 ALR 392, 395 (Faville,J)

30 Hastings v Rathbone, supra (observing that the common law "frowns upon the guiltless child with the disdain of a Pharisee")

31 "At the common law an illegitimate child . . . had no inheritable blood. He was cut off completely from his ancestors, including his father and mother." Gossett's Estate (1942) 129 P2d 56, 58 (Brice,CJ)

"The common law was so rigorous that it regarded a child born out of wedlock as nullius filius—the son of no one, having no father and no mother—and ignored its existence. The more humane attitude of the present age and sympathetic concept closer to the Christian ideal has led to an advancement in bestowing legal rights and remedies in the child's favor by statutory provisions for his maintenance by the father and inheritance from the mother and her kindred." Hehr's Adm'r v Hehr (1941) 157 SW2d (Ky.) 111, 114 (Stanley,C)

32 Jer. 31:29; Hockaday v Lynn (1906) 200 Mo. 456, 98 SW 585, 118 ASR 672, 683 (Lamm,J)

33 Hastings v Rathbone, supra (saying that "The harshness of this inexorable command has been somewhat, but not wholly, dissipated as civilization has advanced through the succeeding ages")

34 Num. 27:8-11; 14 Harv. LR (1901) 509

As to gifts by a prince and the inheritance thereof, see Ezek. 46:16-18

[§139] —— In the "Case of the Daughters of Zelophehad" it is related that Zelophehad left five daughters and no son, and that the daughters came before Moses, Eleazar the priest, the princes and all the congregation and petitioned that a possession be allotted to them, saying—

"Why should the name of our father be done away from among his family, because he hath no son? Give unto us therefore a possession among the brethren of our father."[35]

Moses took the cause before the Lord, who directed that the daughters of Zelophehad be given "a possession of an inheritance among their father's brethren," and that "the inheritance of their father" should "pass unto them."[36]

The chief fathers of the families of the children of Gilead next petitioned for a rule as to the marriage of the daughters of Zelophehad, so as to prevent their inheritance from passing to another tribe. In reply it was thus decreed:

". . . Let them marry to whom they think best; only to the family of the tribe of their father shall they marry.

"So shall not the inheritance of the children of Israel remove from tribe to tribe: for every one of the children of Israel shall keep himself to the inheritance of the tribe of his fathers.

"And every daughter, that possesseth an inheritance in any tribe of the children of Israel, shall be wife unto one of the family of the tribe of her father, that the children of Israel may enjoy every man the inheritance of his fathers.

"Neither shall the inheritance remove from one tribe to another tribe; but every one of the tribes of the children of Israel shall keep himself to his own inheritance."[37]

It has been said that this was a special case, decided according to a custom peculiar to the tribe of Manasseh, and that it was not until afterwards that the decision became a general law.[38]

[§140] When a man believes that death is imminent, whether from extreme age or serious illness, common prudence dictates that he "set his house in order,"[39] and this may include the appointment of his successor as head of the family (§142), the distribution of his property before death, or a declaration as to who shall have it after his death (§141). Concerning the distribution of property, it has been recom-

35 Num. 27:4
36 Num. 27:7
37 Num. 36:6-9; and see Joshua 17:1-6
See also 5 Docket (1939-40) No. 4, p 4060, referring to the case as one "wherein the equity powers of the court were invoked" and calling attention to "the similarity between the law as modified by the exception, and the present laws of descent."
38 12 Gr. B. (1900) 7
39 Isa. 38:1
"Common prudence dictates to every man the necessity of settling his temporal concerns while it is in his power." Letter of George to Martha Washington, Philadelphia, June 19, 1775

mended that one "distribute" his inheritance "at the time when thou shalt end thy days and finish thy life,"[40] and it appears to have been customary among the ancient Israelites, before wills were thought of, for a man to give away his property before death.[41] Thus is appears that "Jacob called unto his sons, and said, Gather yourselves together, that I may tell you that which shall befall you in the last days,"[42] and he preferred Joseph above his other sons by giving him an additional portion "which I took out of the hand of the Amorite with my sword and with my bow."[43]   So also Judith, "before she died," distributed her goods "to all them that were nearest of kindred to Manasses her husband, and to them that were the nearest of her kindred."[44]   But it was recognized that one should not be hasty in distributing his property, lest he recover from his illness[45] and be dependent upon others for support.[45a]   It is said to "beware of thine own children"[46] for "better it is that thy children should seek to thee, than that thou shouldest stand to their courtesy."[47]

[§141]   A "will" or "testament," in its true meaning, is a declaration or "witnessing" of the "mind" of one who has property, concerning who shall have it after his death.[48] The first wills disposing of property—like the ceremony by which a patriarch designated his successor (§142)—were doubtless made orally, but it has long been a legal requirement that a will be in writing, unless it be the will of a soldier or sailor and made in fear or peril of death.[49]

In justification of wills, it has been argued that "the lord of the vineyard has the right to do with his own as he pleases,"[50] and it has been asserted that without wills society can scarcely be supposed capable of holding together.[1]   On the other hand, it has been said that a will is a device by which an old man can keep his property from those who are naturally and justly entitled to it.[2]   But whether wills

---

40 Ecclesiasticus 33:23; 5 S.F. Bar (1941) No. 1, p 3

41 14 Ill. LR (1919) 101

42 Gen. 49:1

43 Gen. 48:22

44 Judith 16:24

45 Ecclesiasticus 33:19
As a matter of common knowledge, most men do not divest themselves of their whole estates . . . except as the result of . . . contemplation of death." In re Schweinler's Estate (1934) 117 NJ Eq. 67, 175 A 71; Newman's Estate (1942) 52 Cal.App.2d 126, 136, 125 P2d 908

45a See infra §162

46 Ecclesiasticus 32:22

47 Ecclesiasticus 33:21

48 See 28 RCL 58
Strictly speaking, a will disposes of realty and a testament of personalty. But the words are commonly used as synonymous.

49 See Cal.Prob.Code (1931) §54

50 Matt. 20:1-15

1 Sir Henry Maine (1822-1888) English jurist and historian

2 Wills were not originally intended to enable one to pass his property "to strangers to his blood." See Clark v Payne (1942) 157 SW2d (Ky.App.) 63, 67 (Tilford,J)

can be justified or not, it is generally agreed that no one has any natural or inherent right to make a will, but only a privilege which the law may give or take away.[3]

[§142] —— The ancient ceremony or proceeding by which the head of a family, believing himself about to die, designated his eldest son—or possibly a younger son or some other member of the family—to be his successor, constituted the primitive form of will.[4] In this manner the aged patriarch transferred his authority over the household. Originally he could make no will in respect of property, for the property belonged not to him but to the family as a sort of corporation.[5] In the Scriptures the succession ceremony is called a "blessing." In the blessing of Jacob, who had impersonated his elder brother Esau, their father Isaac declared that he should "be lord over thy brethren, and let thy mother's sons bow down to thee."[6] Subsequently, when Jacob had become old and was upon his death bed, he conferred his blessing upon his fourth son Judah, rather than upon his firstborn son Reuben, saying: "thou art he whom thy brethren shall praise; . . . thy father's children shall bow down before thee."[7]

[§143] —— There is evidence of the use of wills in ancient Egypt. The oldest written will as yet discovered was made in that country about 2550 B.C., by one Sekhenren in favor of his brother, a priest of Osiris. But it appears that wills were unknown in the law of Babylon and in the old law of Israel.[8] Mosaic law originally contemplated that a man should dispose of his property during his lifetime;[9] otherwise that it should pass at the time of his death according to the rules of descent or succession.[10] But in later times the testamentary disposition of property was allowed when all of the kindred entitled to inherit under Mosaic law had failed or were undiscoverable.[11] Wills were commonly recognized and understood by the beginning of the Christian era, and those of Christians were often deposited in churches for safekeeping.[12]

---

3 Matter of Delano (1903) 176 N Y 486, 68 NE 871, 872, 64 LRA 279; Watson's Estate 1919) 226 N Y 384, 123 NE 758, 761

4 Maine's Anc. L. 185, 200

5 11 Harv.LR (1897) 75 (Bigelow)

In Primitive law the family property belonged not alone to the head of the family, but also to his wife or wives and children. So Rachel and Leah "answered and said" that all the riches acquired by their husband Jacob from their father Laban "is ours and our children's." Gen. 31:16

6 Gen. 27:29

7 Gen. 49:8

8 14 Ill. LR (1920) 540

9 See supra §140

10 See supra §§138, 139

11 Maine's Anc. L. 191

12 7 Cal. LR (1918) 102

[§144] —— The Romans have been credited with the invention of the will, but it seems more likely that they borrowed the idea and developed it to conform with their notions of property rights. The "Twelve Tables" recognized and permitted wills in case of failure of children and near kindred, but they were regarded only as a device for making better provisions for members of the testator's family and not a means of giving property to others.[13] It has been said that "the substance of a Roman testament consisted in the designation of some person" as "the heir or universal successor of the testator, and a time was allowed him in which to decide whether he would accept or reject the inheritance."[14] It is from the Roman law that the early Christians gained their understanding of wills.

[§145] —— For centuries the common law has recognized the propriety of allowing a man to control the distribution of his property after death.[15] At one time, indeed, a person who died under normal conditions without leaving a will was regarded as infamous, and unfit to be buried in consecrated soil, for the making of the last will preceded the last confession and it was thought that one who left no will must have died unconfessed.[16] But the privilege of making a will has been hedged about with restrictions. In some American states, the law does not allow one to disinherit his natural heirs. In others it forbids bequests or devises for charitable uses unless the will was made a certain length of time before the death of the testator.[17] And in one state a recent law prohibits a man from giving his estate to a second wife to the detriment of children born of his first wife.[18]

[§146] —— Though the language of a will, like that of other instruments, is interpreted according to the time when it was made and the circumstances then existing, it is an old

13 Maine's Anc. L. 184-211
It has been said that "the practice of executing wills in writing was the result of an enactment of the Emperor Marcus Aurelius." (1 David's New York Law of Wills [1923] 4). This is doubted, however, since wills were in use among the Romans at the time of St. Paul, nearly two centuries before Aurelius.

14 2 Pomeroy's Eq. Jur., 5th ed. (1941) §463

15 "Wills of land were lawful and in constant use in England before the Norman conquest (1066)." 11 Harv. LR (1897) 75, n 1 (Biglow)
At common law, two witnesses are required to witness a will. 15 Harv. LR (1901) 85

16 If he had confessed, the priest would have persuaded him to make a will, bestowing a portion of his goods upon the church and the poor for the repose of his soul. 18 Harv. LR (1904) 120, 121

17 See Cal.Prob.Code (1931) §41

18 Florida Laws, 1939, ch. 18999

and settled rule that the will takes effect or "speaks" only when the testator has died.[19]

"During his life, it is subject to his control, and until it was consummated by his death, no one had, in a legal view, any interest in it."[20]

This rule is found in the New Testament, where St. Paul says that—

"Where a testament is, there must also of necessity be the death of the testator. For a testament is of force after men are dead: otherwise it is of no strength at all while the testator liveth."[21]

CHAPTER 21

CONTRACTS—GENERALLY

[§147] In a very broad sense, the term "contract' includes all the various dealings and transactions between persons which give rise, on the one hand, to rights, and, on the other, to duties; and the law of contracts may thus be regarded as the foundation of human society.[22] But a contract is commonly understood as "an agreement to do or refrain from doing some particular thing."[23] Ordinarily the agreement must be made voluntarily,[24]—the parties, as it is said, being "well pleased,"[25]—and it must be supported by mutual consideration,[26] that is, by some benefit moving from or detriment suffered by each of the parties.[27] When so made, a contract becomes a sort of law that binds and governs its parties.[28]

[§148] But our present concept of contracts has not always been known. In Primitive law, it seems likely that men were bound only by oaths or vows, and not by mere promises.[29]

19 See 28 RCL 234; Gorham v Chadwick (1938) 200 A (Me.) 500, 117 ALR 805, 808 (Sturgis,J)

A will "speaks" or takes effect from the date of the death of the testator, but his intent is determined from the date when he made the will. Carter's Estate (1942) 49 Cal.App.2d 251, 254, 121 P2d 540 (Ward,J)

20 Jackson v Kniffen (1806) 2 Johnson (NY) 31, 3 AD 390, 394 (Livingston,J)

21 Heb. 9:16,17
22 1 Parsons' Contracts (1853) 3
23 See 2 Bl.Com. 442

24 See 6 RCL 592
25 See Tobit 5:16
26 12 AmJur 564
27 12 AmJur 570
28 But see Hullgren v Amoskeag Mfg. Co. (1926) 82 NH 268, 133 A 4, 46 ALR 380,384 (Allen, J) saying "A contract is not a law."

29 See 14 Harv.LR (1901) 312, quoting Deut. 23:21-23

Formerly at common law simple promises, as distinguished from covenants, were not recognized as creating legal rights. 12 AmJur 496

Moreover, the original contract—called a "covenant"—was not usually made between ordinary individuals, but between heads of families[30] or other organized groups of men,[31] who dealt with each other as sovereigns.[32]

The Scriptures refer to many such contracts or covenants.[33] For example, Abram and Lot agreed to separate themselves and their flocks and herds.[34] Later, Abraham covenanted with Abimelech that he would not deal falsely with him, nor his son, nor his son's son, but "according to the kindness that I have done unto thee, thou shalt do unto me, and to the land wherein thou hast sojourned."[35] Other early contracts were those of Isaac and Abimelech,[36] Jacob and Laban,[37] Joshua's spies and Rahab the harlot,[36] David and Johnathan,[39] and Solomon and Hiram of Tyre.[40]

[§149] Contracts are often said to be "express" or "implied," meaning that they are stated in words, spoken or written, or that they arise out of acts rather than words.[41] The earliest express contract was an oral agreement solemnized by an oath[42] or some other ceremony, such as a formal sacrifice or the eating of a sacred meal.[43] But written contracts were made as far back as the time of king Solomon, about 1000 B.C., for it appears that a contract between Solomon and Hiram of Tyre was in writing.[44] Such contracts were also made in the time of Simon, about 140 B.C. It is said that "the people began to write in their instruments and contracts, In the first year of Simon the high priest, the governor and leader of the Jews."[45] Thus we see that since time immemorial it has been considered wise that the words of a contract be put down in writing[46] and everything made so clear as to leave no room for law suits.[47]

[§150] An oath, according to Biblical law, consisted in the invocation of God to witness the covenant or promise of

---

30 13 Gr. B (1901) 408
31 Maine's Anc. L. 263
32 13 Gr B (1901) p 408
33 As to treaties, see supra §112
34 Gen. 13:5-11
35 Gen. 21:23
36 Gen. 26:28-31
37 Gen. 29:19-20, 26, 30 (contracts of Jacob to serve Laben seven years for his younger daughter Rachel, and upon the completion of the service and substitution of the elder daughter Leah, a second contract to serve another seven years for Rachel); Gen. 31:44 et seq. (boundary contract)
38 Josh. 2:12-22,25
39 1 Sam. 18:3, 20:16, 23:18

40 1 Kings 5:1-11 and 2 Chron., chap 2 (contract for building materials)
41 12 AmJur 499
42 See infra §150
43 13 Gr. B. (1901) p 408
44 2 Chron. 2:11
The Israelites were acquainted with the use of seals. See Solomon's Song 8:6
45 1 Mac. 13:42
Written accounts were also kept at an early period. See Ecclesiasticus 42:7, recommending to "put all in writing that thou givest out, or receivest in."
46 Gloria, Cod. dipl. Padovano, II, n 42, a 1100; 13 Ill. LR (1919) 595
47 Moore v Lessee of Bickham (1811) 4 Binney (Pa.) 1, 4. (Tilghman,CJ)

the person taking it and to take vengeance upon him if he should fail to keep his word. Thus it was not the mere taking of an obligation to testify truly, but was a method of solemnizing a promise to do or not to do a certain thing and which, without an oath, was not considered binding.[48] In some respects, the ancient promise with an oath corresponds to an agreement under seal at common law.[49]

The first oath of which we have record was taken by Abraham from his eldest servant:

"And Abraham said unto his eldest servant . . . Put, I pray thee, thy hand under my thigh:
"And I will make thee swear by the Lord, the God of heaven, and the God of the earth, that thou shalt not take a wife unto my son of the daughters of the Canaanites, among whom I dwell:
"But thou shalt go unto my country, and to my kindred, and take a wife unto my son Isaac.
"And the servant put his hand under the thigh of Abraham his master, and sware to him concerning that matter."[50]

In similar manner, an oath was also taken by Jacob (Israel) from his son Joseph:

"And the time drew nigh that Israel must die: and he called his son Joseph, and said unto him, If now I have found grace in thy sight, put, I pray thee, thy hand under my thigh, and deal kindly and truly with me; bury me not, I pray thee, in Egypt:
"But I will lie with my fathers, and thou shalt carry me out of Egypt, and bury me in their burying place. And he said, I will do as thou hast said.
"And he said, Swear unto me. And he sware unto him."[1]

Among other oaths mentioned in the Scriptures is one taken by Joseph of the children of Israel, that "ye shall carry up my bones from hence,"[2] and another taken by Saul from David, "that thou wilt not cut off my seed after me, and that thou wilt not destroy my name out of my father's house."[3]

[§151] —— In Mosaic law, oaths were doubtless considered legal and proper. The law prescribed that "Thou shalt . . . swear by his (the Lord thy God's) name,"[4] and provided

---

48 See Heb. 6:16, saying that ". . . men verily swear by the greater; and an oath for confirmation is to them an end of all strife."
Compare Respublica v Newell (1802) 3 Yeates (Pa.) 407, 2 AD 381, 384, (Smith,J) citing 1 Atk. 20, and saying "What is universally understood by an oath is, 'the person who takes it imprecates the vengeance of God upon him, if the oath he takes is false.'"

49 See 6 RCL 651
50 Gen. 24:2-4,9
1 Gen. 47:29-31
2 Gen. 50:25; and see Ex. 13:19 and Josh. 24:32 as to the performance of this oath
3 1 Sam. 24:21
4 Deut. 6:13, 10: 20
". . . make no mention of the name of other gods, neither let it be heard out of thy mouth." Ex. 23:13

for the taking of an oath in case of the loss or injury of animals delivered to another to keep.[5]

But the practice of "swearing" or "taking oaths" fell into disrepute in the course of time, for Christian law expressly forbids all "swearing," the plain commandment of Jesus being to—

"Swear not at all . . . But let your communciation be, Yea, yea; Nay, nay: for whatsoever is more than these cometh of evil."[6]

This commandment would seem to prohibit oaths, though it is commonly held to be merely a precept against profanity. It was repeated and emphasized by James, in his epistle "to the twelve tribes which are scattered abroad," saying:

". . . above all things, my brethren, swear not, neither by heaven, neither by the earth, neither by any other oath: but let your yea be yea; and your nay, nay; lest ye fall into condemnation."[7]

[§152]   The basic rules of the civil law, as stated in a preceding section (§127), apply to contracts. The law requires that one who enters into a contract or otherwise deals with his fellow man should do justly and speak the truth. These requirements are expressed in various ways. Thus it is said that one should deal "faithfully"[8] and "truly,"[9] and that he should "do that which is honest"[10] and "upright."[11] Conversely the law, in substance, forbids that one deal "deceitfully,"[12] "falsely,"[13] "treacherously"[14] or "unjustly,"[15] or that he "scorn" to "give and take."[16]

[§153]   Men ought no doubt to renounce "the hidden things of dishonesty" and to walk not "in craftiness,"[17] for it is said that "the man that deceiveth his neighbour" is "as a mad man who casteth firebrands, arrows and death."[18]   One who

---

5 See infra §155

6 Matt. 5:34,37
"The frequency of oaths detracts from their solemnity. They become a matter of course." Vanatta v Anderson (1811) 3 Binney (Pa.) 417, 426 (Brackenridge, J)

7 James 5:12; and see Zech. 5:3 (". . . every one that sweareth shall be cut off . . .")

8 Ecclesiasticus 29:3

9 Prov. 12:22 ("They that deal truly" are the delight of the Lord); Tobit 4:6 ("For if thou deal truly, thy doings shall prosperously succeed to thee, and to all them that live justly"); Ecclesiasticus 29:3, 40:12 ("true dealing shall endure for ever")

10 2 Cor. 13:7 ("ye should do that which is honest")

11 Tobit 4:5 ("do uprightly all thy life long, and follow not the ways of unrighteousness")

12 Ps. 101:7; Prov. 24:28, 26:18,19

13 Lev. 19:11 ("ye shall not . . . deal falsely")

14 Isa. 33:1 ("Woe to thee that . . . dealest treacherously and they dealt not treacherously with thee"); Mal. 2:10 ("Have we not all one father? hath not one God created us? why do we deal treacherously every man against his brother?")

15 Ecclesiasticus 41:17,18

16 Ecclesiasticus 41:19

17 2 Cor. 4:1,2

18 Prov. 26:18,19

deals deceitfully with another, misleading or taking advantage of him, is said to be guilty of fraud, and the transaction is tainted therewith.[19] Fraud commonly consists in "the getting of treasures by a lying tongue,"[20] and Biblical law bans it, commanding that one "defraud not" another "in any matter"[21] —"Thou shalt not defraud thy neighbour"[22]—and "deceive not with thy lips."[23] Though one need not ordinarily speak at all, if he does speak, the law requires that he speak the truth, lest the voice be the voice of Jacob but the hand be that of Esau.[24]

A contract induced by fraud "shall not stand," but "shall be disannulled."[25] And where one has obtained property from his neighbour by deceit, "he shall restore the thing which he hath deceitfully gotten . . . and shall add the fifth part more thereto."[26]

[§154] One of the first principles of law is that contracts must be performed, for if solemn and voluntary agreements are not kept there can be no orderly society.[27] Biblical law requires that one keep his word,[28] and that he be "stedfast" in his "covenant" and "conversant therein."[29] Though one may properly decline to make a contract that he may be unable or unwilling to perform, if he voluntarily enters into a contract or makes a covenant or promise—not being induced thereto by fraud[30]—he should scrupulously perform it even though it may be "to his own hurt" to do so.[31] "Every man's contract, wherever it is possible, should . . . be performed as it was intended,"[32] that it may be said of him as Solomon said

19 One who obtains the promise of another by fraud ought not to be heard to say that the promise should be performed. He is estopped.
20 Prov. 21:6
21 Mark 10:19; 1 Cor. 7:5 ("Defraud ye not one the other, except it be with consent for a time"); 2 Cor. 7:2; 1 Thess. 4:2,6 ("For ye know what commandments we gave you . . . that no man go beyond and defraud his brother in any matter")
22 Lev. 19:13
23 Prov. 24:28; and see Ps. 101:7 ("He that worketh deceit shall not dwell within my house")
24 United States Pipe & F. Co. v Waco (1937) 108 SW2d (Tex.) 432, 434 (Martin,C)
But see Gen. 27:1-40, where no disapproval is shown of the deceit practiced by Jacob upon his blind father for the purpose of wrongfully securing the blessing to which Esau was legally entitled.
25 Isa. 28:18
26 Lev. 6:2-5
27 22 Geo.LJ (1934) 424 (Scott)
The underlying idea of the rule that one who has undertaken a duty, in legal form, must fully and exactly perform it, at all events, is that "a man of full age must take care of himself. . . . If he has made a foolish bargain he must perform his side like a man, for he has but himself to blame; if he has acted, he has done so at his own risk with a duty of keeping his eyes open, and he must abide the appointed consequences, . . . But the whole point of view is that of primitive society." 27 Harv.LR (1913) 212 (Pound)
28 Ecclesiasticus 29:3
"Thy word shall not be false, nor empty, but fulfilled in deed." Two Ways 2:5
29 Ecclesiasticus 11:20; and see Ecclesiasticus 5:10 ("Be stedfast in thy understanding; and let thy word be the same")
30 See supra §153
31 Ps. 15:4, commending him "that sweareth to his own hurt, and changeth not."
32 Thompson's Lessee v White (1789) 1 Dallas (Pa.S.Ct.) 424, 1 AD 252, 256, (McKean,CJ)

of the Lord, that he "hath with his hands fulfilled that which he spake with his mouth."[33]

CHAPTER 22

BAILMENTS, LOANS AND PLEDGES

[§155] A bailment arises when one entrusts personal property to another.[34] The Scriptures contain provisions in reference to property that is delivered to another for safe-keeping and property that is loaned to another for the latter's benefit.[35]

"The law concerning things given to be kept" is "that they should be safely preserved for such as had committed them to be kept."[36] As to "money or stuff" delivered to another to be kept, it is provided that—

"If a man shall deliver unto his neighbour money or stuff to keep, and it be stolen out of the man's house; if the thief be found, let him pay double.

"If the thief be not found, then the master of the house shall be brought unto the judges, to see whether he have put his hand unto his neighbour's goods.

". . . whom the judges shall condemn, he shall pay double unto his neighbour."[37]

Concerning animals which have been delivered to another to be kept, the law prescribes that—

"If a man deliver unto his neighbour an ass, or an ox, or a sheep, or any beast, to keep; and it die, or be hurt, or driven away, no man seeing it:

"Then shall an oath of the Lord be between them both, that he hath not put his hand unto his neighbour's goods; and the owner of it shall accept thereof, and he shall not make it good.

"And if it be stolen from him, he shall make restitution unto the owner thereof.

"If it be torn to pieces, then let him bring it for witness, and he shall not make good that which was torn."[38]

In case one to whom property has been delivered for keeping shall "lie unto his neighbour in that which was delivered

---

33 2 Chron. 6:4
    "That which is gone out of thy lips, thou shalt keep and perform." Deut 23:23
34 See 6 Am Jur 140

35 See infra §157
36 2 Mac. 3:15
37 Ex. 22:7-9
38 Ex. 22:10-13, cited in 42 Wash.LR (1914) 772

him to keep . . . he shall restore . . . that which was delivered to him to keep . . . and shall add the fifth part more thereto."[39]

[§156] —— The deposit by Tobit at Rages is an early example of bailment. It is related that Tobit "went into Media, and left in trust with Gabael the brother of Gabrias, at Rages a city in Media, ten talents of silver,"[40] and that after many years Tobit called his son Tobias and directed him to go and repossess the deposit. Tobias answered and said, "how can I receive the money, seeing I know him not?"[41] Tobit "then . . . gave him the handwriting (receipt), and said unto him . . . go and receive the money."[42] After reaching Ecbatane, "Tobias called Raphael (supposing him to be Azarias his servant), and said unto him, . . . go to Rages of Media to Gabael, and bring me the money."[43] And so "Raphael went out, and lodged with Gabael, and gave him the handwriting; who brought forth bags which were sealed up, and gave them to him."[44]

[§157] Loans are of two kinds: those of things—animate or inanimate—and those of money. Both are for the benefit of the borrower; but the loan of a thing is a bailment (see §155) and the thing loaned is to be restored or returned to the lender, whereas a loan of money is to be "repaid." In general, the Scriptures approve of lending to the needy, but not of borrowing. It is declared that "A good man sheweth favour, and lendeth,"[45] that "He that hath pity upon the poor lendeth unto the Lord,"[46] and even that one should "lend, hoping for nothing again."[47]

Nevertheless, it is recognized that a "loan" is not a "gift,"[48] and that a lender ought not to be defrauded.[49] The law demands the timely return or repayment of a loan, the rule being to "lend to thy neighbour in time of his need, and pay thou thy neighbour again in due season."[50] As to the liability of borrowers, it is provided that—

"if a man borrow ought of his neighbour, and it be hurt, or die, the owner thereof being not with it, he shall surely make it good. But if the owner thereof be with it, he shall not make it good; if it be an hired thing it came for his hire."[1]

39   Lev. 6:2-5
40   Tobit 1:14
41   Tobit 5:1,2
42   Tobit 5:3
43   Tobit 9:1,2
44   Tobit 9:5
45   Ps. 112:5
46   Prov. 19:17
47   Luke 6:35
48   See infra §161
49   Ecclesiasticus 29:4,7,8, "Many, when a thing was lent them, reckoned it to

be found, and put them to trouble that helped them. . . . Many therefore have refused to lend for other men's ill dealing, fearing to be defrauded. . . . Yet have thou patience with a man in poor estate, and delay not to show him mercy."
50   Ecclesiasticus 29:2
"The wicked borroweth, and payeth not again." Ps. 37:21
1   Ex. 22:14,15; and see supra §155

[§158] A pledge is a deposit or pawn as security for a debt[2] In Biblical law, the taking of a pledge is doubtless permissible in some circumstances.[3] But pledges are ordinarily merciless transactions, and they were subjected to restrictions in Mosaic law. Thus it was forbidden to "take the nether or the upper millstone to pledge,"[4] or to "take a widow's raiment to pledge."[5]

With respect to the manner of taking a pledge, the law prescribes that—

"When thou dost lend thy brother any thing, thou shalt not go into his house to fetch his pledge.

"Thou shalt stand abroad, and the man to whom thou dost lend shall bring out the pledge abroad unto thee.

"And if the man be poor, thou shalt not sleep with his pledge;

"In any case thou shalt deliver him the pledge again when the sun goeth down that he may sleep in his own raiment . . ."[6]

When the loan is returned or repaid, it becomes the duty of the pledgee to restore the thing pledged.[7] Failure to do so was at one time, not only a civil wrong, but also a crime punishable by death. It is said that he that "hath not restored the pledge . . . shall surely die."[8]

CHAPTER 23

CORPORATIONS AND PARTNERSHIPS

159 Corporations   160 Partnerships

[§159] A corporation is an artificial legal person created or recognized by the state. It is usually formed of persons associated together for some common purpose, such as conducting a business or holding and managing property. But the law regards it as a separate being or entity, apart from its members or stockholders, so that, though they die, it may continue to live under its own name.[9] It is thought that corpora-

---

2 21 RCL 630

3 See Gen. 38:18, where it appears that Judah gave pledges to his daughter-in-law, supposing her to be a harlot.

4 Deut. 24:6

5 Deut. 24:17; and see Job 24:3, stating, as though it were wrongful, that "some . . . take a widow's ox for a pledge."

6 Deut. 24:10-13; and see Ex. 22:26 ("If thou at all take thy neighbour's raiment to pledge, thou shalt deliver it unto him by that the sun goeth down") Also Job 24:9 observing that some "take a pledge of the poor."

7 21 RCL 682

8 Ezek. 18:12,13

9 See 13 Am Jur 157

tions are derived from the Roman law, though similar organizations doubtless existed among other ancient and medieval peoples.[10] The primitive family group was a sort of corporation, whose "head" or "patriarch" was like a corporation president and whose members were related by blood or adoption.[11]

[§160] A partnership is an association of persons for carrying on some business or other undertaking.[12] Partnerships have been known since ancient times; their existence is recognized in both the Old and the New Testaments.[12a] In the Book of Proverbs, it is observed that "Whoso is partner with a thief hateth his own soul."[13] James and John, the sons of Zebedee, were partners with Simon, in the fishing business.[14] St. Paul stated that "Titus . . . is my partner,"[15] and he besought Philemon to receive Onesimus, saying "If thou count me therefore a partner, receive him as myself."[16]

CHAPTER 24

GIFTS

[§161] A gift is a free handing over of property by one to another, without any consideration or compensation,[17] that is, "without money and without price."[18] Many gifts are mentioned in the Scriptures, and it is said to be "more blessed to give than to receive."[19] It is usually proper, no doubt, to make a gift to a member of one's family, such as a son,[20]

10 1 Fletcher's Cyclopedia of the Law of Private Corporations (1917) 2-7
11 Maine's Anc. L. pp 178, 179; 11 Harv.LR (1897) 75; and see supra §186
12 40 Am Jur 126
12a "Be ashamed . . . of unjust dealing before thy partner." Ecclesiasticus 41:17,18
"Be not thou ashamed . . . of reckoning with thy partners." Ecclesiasticus 42:1,3
13 Prov. 29:24
14 Luke 5:10
15 2 Cor. 8:23
16 Philemon 17
17 12 RCL 923
Gifts by prince, see Ezek. 46:16-18
18 Isa. 55:1
19 Acts 20:35; Muellhaupt v Strow-

bridge Estate Co. (1932) 140 Or. 484, 487, 14 P2d 282 (Campbell,J)
See also Ex. 23:8 ("thou shalt take no gift"); Deut. 16:19 ("Thou shalt not . . . take a gift"); Prov. 15:27 ("he that hateth gifts shall live"); Dan. 5:17 ("Let thy gifts be to thyself")
"Woe to him that receiveth, for if one receiveth because he hath need, he shall be guiltless; but he that hath no need shall render account why he received and for what, and being cast into straits shall be examined concerning what he did, and shall not come out thence till he hath paid the uttermost farthing." Two Ways 1:5
20 Gen. 25:6 ("unto the sons of the [his] concubines . . . Abraham gave gifts") And see supra §136

daughter[21] or brother,[22] or to one who is poor or in distress.[23] But not all giving is commendable, for "a gift doth blind the eyes of the wise, and pervert the words of the righteous."[24] In particular, it is improper to make gifts to one who is rich[25] or who occupies a position of "judgment,"[26] or to "a strange nation."[27]

[§162] It is doubtless laudable to "give to the poor,"[28] and, more especially, to one "that asketh."[29] And one who is able to give to a neighbour to whom it is due—who is needy and worthy—should not put him off, saying, "Go, and come again, and to-morrow I will give."[30] But charitable gifts are not to be made carelessly or indiscriminately. One should know to whom he is giving.[31] Gifts should be made to the worthy and not to the wicked.[32] The rule is to "give to the godly man, and help not a sinner."[33] Moreover, aged persons should refrain from giving away their property, so as to become dependent upon charity.[34]

"Give not thy son and wife, thy brother and friend, power over thee while thou livest, and give not thy goods to another: lest it repent thee, and thou intreat for the same again.

"As long as thou livest and hast breath in thee, give not thyself over to any."[35]

[§163] The "Case of Ananias and Sapphira" arose out of a practice of the early Christian church under which those desiring to enter into the fellowship sold their property and gave the price to the church.[36] It establishes the rule that

21 Gen. 29:24,29 (gifts of handmaid by parent to daughter on marriage of the latter)
22 Gen. 32:13-15 (gift of livestock by Jacob to Esau) ; 33:11 (acceptance of gift by Esau)
23 See infra §273
24 Deut. 16:19; cited in State v Coyle (1913) 8 Okla. Crim. Rep. 686, 130 P 316 (Furman,J) ; Ex. 23:8
"A gift destroyeth the heart." Ecclesiastes 7:7
25 Prov. 22:16 ("he that giveth to the rich shall surely come to want")
26 See infra §352
27 Baruch 4:3 ("Give not . . . the things that are profitable unto thee to a strange nation")
28 Matt. 19:21; Mark 10:21
"Be not one that holdeth out his hands to receive and shutteth them for giving." Two Ways 4:5
29 Matt. 5:42
"Give to every one that asketh thee, and ask it not again." Two Ways 1:5
30 Prov. 3:27,28
"Thou shalt not doubt to give, nor shalt thou murmur when thou givest." Two Ways 4:7
31 Two Ways 1:6 ("But about this it hath also been said: Let thine alms

sweat into thy hands, until thou know to whom thou art to give")
32 Tobit 4:17 ("Pour out thy bread on the burial of the just, but give nothing to the wicked")
33 Ecclesiasticus 12:4
"Do well unto him that is lowly, but give not to the ungodly: hold back thy bread, and give it not unto him, lest he overmaster thee thereby. Give unto the good, and help not the sinner." Ecclesiasticus 12:5,7
34 See supra §140
35 Ecclesiasticus 33:19,20
36 Schriber v Rapp (1836) 5 Watts (Pa.) 351, 30 AD 327, 332 (Gibson,CJ) saying that "these contributions were not merely voluntary . . . it is not to be credited that they [Ananias and Sapphira] would have been permitted to exercise their right of separate ownership and remain in Christian fellowship. Ananias was emphatically told that he had 'lied not unto man, but unto God;' a distinction evincive of the origin of the duty, and the nature of the being who had set him to perform it; and showing that the law for whose violation he was to be struck dead, was not human, but divine."

deceit or hypocrisy is not countenanced even in the making of gifts.[37] It is related that "a certain man named Ananias, with Sapphira his wife, sold a possession"—

"And kept back part of the price, his wife also being privy to it, and brought a certain part, and laid it at the apostles' feet.

"But Peter said, Ananias, why hath Satan filled thine heart to lie to the Holy Ghost, and to keep back part of the price of the land?

"While it remained, was it not thine own? and after it was sold, was it not in thine own power? why hast thou conceived this thing in thine heart? thou has not lied unto men, but unto God.

"And Ananias hearing these words fell down, and gave up the Ghost: and great fear came on all them that heard these things.

"And the young men arose, wound him up, and carried him out, and buried him.

"And it was about the space of three hours after, when his wife, not knowing what was done, came in.

"And Peter answered unto her, Tell me whether ye sold the land for so much? And she said, Yea, for so much.

"Then Peter said unto her, How is that ye have agreed together to tempt the Spirit of the Lord? behold, the feet of them which have buried thy husband are at the door, and shall carry thee out.

"Then fell she down straightway at his feet, and yielded up the ghost: and the young men came in, and found her dead, and, carrying her forth, buried her by her husband."[38]

CHAPTER 25

SALES, EXCHANGES AND LEASES

[§164]   A sale, unlike a gift[39] is a transfer of property from one to another for a price in money,[40] and an exchange is a barter or trade of properties, one for the other, without putting a money price or value upon either.[41]   Nearly all kinds of things, including animals, may be sold (see §165), as may also lands or possessions (see §167). But there are some things that may not properly be bought and sold. For example, Mosaic law provided that "no devoted thing shall be sold."[41a]   The Lord disapproved of a secret plan of Baalam

---

37 Ruse v Williams (1913) 14 Ariz. 445, 130 P 887, 45 LRANS 923, 925 (Franklin,CJ) referring to "the awful fate of Ananias and Sapphira, his wife, for their hypocrisy in concealing part of the price of their property."

38 Acts 5:1-10
39 See supra §161
40 See 23 RCL 1186; 37 Tex.Jur 69
41 18 Tex Jur 470, 471
41a Lev. 27:28

to profit by the use of the divine power with which he was endowed.[42] And when Simon, a sorcerer, offered money to the apostles for power to cure or save by the laying on of hands, Peter rebuked him, saying, "Thy money perish with thee, because thou hast thought that the gift of God may be purchased with money."[43]

[§165]   Sales and exchanges of personal property, such as cattle and horses, corn or food, goods, and servants or slaves, are mentioned in many places in the Scriptures,[44] though no specific rules are laid down as to transactions of this kind.[45] For example, Esau sold his "birthright" to Jacob,[46] Potiphar bought Joseph of the hands of the Ishmaelites,[47] Joseph sold food unto the Egyptians,[48] all countries came into Egypt "for to buy corn,"[49] and David bought oxen of Araunah.[50]

The distinction between a sale and an exchange is recognized. Thus it appears that Joseph sold "corn" for money until he had "gathered up all the money that was found in the land of Egypt, and in the land of Canaan,"[1] and when "money failed in the land, . . . all the Egyptians . . . brought their cattle unto Joseph: and Joseph gave them bread in exchange for horses, and for the flocks, and for the cattle of the herds, and for the asses."[2]   Properly speaking, the so-called "sale" of Esau's "birthright" was an exchange.[3]

[§166]   ——— "All things" are properly delivered "in number and weight."[4]   It is wrongful to use "divers weights and

42 See Num. 22:21-35

43 Acts 8:18-23; State v Buswell (1894) 40 Neb. 158, 58 NW 728, 24 LRA 68 (Ryan,C)

44 See for example Ex. 21:2 (buying of Hebrew servant) 21:7 (sale of daughter to be a maidservant); Prov. 11:26 ("Blessing shall be upon the head of him that selleth" corn); Matt. 10:29 ("Are not two sparrows sold for a farthing"); Luke 12:6 ("Are not five sparrows sold for two farthings"); Acts 2:45 ("all that believed . . . sold their possessions and goods")

During a siege of Samaria, "an ass's head was sold for 'forescore pieces of silver." 2 Kings 6:25

Markets and fairs were held in Tyre. "They traded the persons of men . . . in thy market. They . . . traded in thy fairs with horses and horsemen and mules." Ezek. 27:13,14

45 St.Augustine admits that a merchant can sell at a price higher than the real cost of the goods, provided he does not conceal the real cost with lies or false swearings. See 21 Geo.LJ (1933) 488 (Lardone)

46 Gen. 25:29-34: "Esau came from the field and he was faint. And Esau said to Jacob, feed me . . . for I am faint. And Jacob said, Sell me this day thy birthright. And Esau said, Behold, I am at the point to die; and what profit shall this birthright do to me?   And Jacob said, Swear to me this day; and he sware unto him: and he sold his birthright to Jacob.   Then Jacob gave Esau bread and pottage of lentils." And see supra §134

47 Gen. 39:1

48 Gen. 41:56, 42:6

49 Gen. 41:57

50 2 Sam. 24:24

1 Gen. 47:14

2 Gen. 47:15,17; and see supra §100

3 See supra, this section, n 46

4 Ecclesiasticus 42:7

measures,"[5] a "scant measure"[6] or a "false balance."[7] The law forbids any "unrighteousness . . . in meteyard, in weight, or in measure,"[8] and requires "just balances, just weights, . . . a just ephah, and just hin."[9] Even the possession of "divers weights and measures" and "unjust balances" is prohibited.

"Thou shalt not have in thy bag divers weights, a great and a small.
"Thou shalt not have in thine house divers measures, a great and a small.
"But thou shalt have a perfect and just weight, a perfect and just measure shalt thou have."[10]
"Ye shall have just balances, and a just ephah, and a just bath.
"The ephah and the bath shall be of one measure, that the bath may contain the tenth part of an homer, and the ephah the tenth part of an homer: the measure thereof shall be after the homer.
"And the shekel shall be twenty gerahs: twenty shekels, five and twenty shekels, fifteen shekels, shall be your maneh."[11]

[§167] In former times, as now, real property—land and things appurtenant, such as buildings, fences, and trees—was ordinarily bought and sold for money,[12] but was sometimes exchanged for other property.[13] The first purchaser of land appears to have been Abraham, who bought a field from Ephron, with the cave therein and all the trees that were in the field, for 400 shekels of silver.[14] In later times, Jacob "bought a parcel of a field . . . of the children of Hamor,"[15] David bought the threshingfloor of Araunah,[16] Omri "bought the hill of Samaria of Shemer,"[17] and Judas Iscariot "purchased a field with the reward of iniquity."[18]

5 Prov. 20:10 ("Divers weights, and divers measures, both of them are alike abomination to the Lord")
6 Micah 6:10,11 (" . . . the scant measure . . . is abominable. Shall I count them pure with the wicked balances, and with the bag of deceitful weights?")
7 Prov. 11:1 ("A false balance is abomination to the Lord: but a just weight is his delight"), 20:23 ("Divers weights are an abomination unto the Lord, and a false balance is not good")
8 Lev. 19:35
9 Lev. 19:36
"A just weight and balance are the Lord's: all the weights of the bag are his work." Prov. 16:11
". . . be not thou ashamed . . . of exactness of balance and weights." Ecclesiasticus 42:1,4
10 Deut. 25:13-15, quoted in 42 Wash. LR (1914) 771
11 Ezek. 45:10-12
A cab was 3 pints; an omer, 3 quarts; a hin, about a gallon and 2 pints; a firkin, about 9 gallons; and an ephah or bath, 8 gallons and 5 pints. A farthing was worth a cent and a half; a gerah, about 3 cents; a shekel of gold, 8 dollars; and a shekel of silver about 50 cents.
12 Gen. 33:19 (hundred pieces of money); Josh. 24:32 (hundred pieces of silver); 2 Sam. 24:24 (fifty shekels of silver); 1 Kings 16:24 (two talents of silver); 1 Chron. 21:25 (six hundred shekels of gold by weight); Jer. 32:44 ("Men shall buy fields for money")
13 Gen. 47:20 (Joseph exchanged food for land); Prov. 27:26 ("the goats are the price of the field")
14 Gen. 23:3-17 In this transaction, the sons of Heth "made sure" or "warranted" the possession of the land unto Abraham. See infra §174
15 Gen. 33:19
The bones of Joseph were buried "in a parcel of ground which Jacob bought of the sons of Hamor." Josh. 24:32
16 2 Sam. 24:24; and see 1 Chron. 21:24, saying that David bought the threshing floor of Ornan.
17 1 Kings 16:24
18 Acts 1:18

[§168] —— But lands have not always been considered as disposable. In primitive society, the right of an occupant or possessor of land was probably too ephemeral to be bought and sold.[19] Subsequently an occupant of land was regarded as having a right of possession or property, of which he could dispose in any manner he saw fit.[19a] However, certain restrictions were imposed upon the sale of land, by custom or law. So though Mosaic law generally admits of such sales, it forbids the sale of "the field of the suburbs" of cities of the Levites;[20] it specifies that "land shall not be sold for ever,"[21] and it provides for the redemption of sold-land by a kinsman of the seller[22] or for its reversion to the seller or his heirs in the next year of Jubilee.[23] This law is said to have been intended to preserve "some kind of equality in property,"[24] but it seems more likely that the purpose was to assure the solidarity of family groups by preserving to them their hereditary lands. Under this law, Naboth refused to exchange or sell his vineyard to king Ahab, saying: "The Lord forbid it me, that I should give the inheritance of my fathers unto thee."[25] Also it was seemingly regarded as improper, if not unlawful, to transfer property (houses) to aliens.[26]

[§169] —— Before writing had been invented or had come into common use, land was purchased, sold, and conveyed by a ceremony at the gate of the city or village near or within which it was situated, and in the presence of the public assembly or council of elders.[27] The buyer and seller reached an agreement by an exchange of remarks—usually perhaps in the form of questions and answers—until an offer of one to buy or sell had been accepted by the other.[28] The buyer paid over the purchase money, and the seller, according to the custom at one time, gave his shoes or one of them to the buyer as a symbol of possession.[29] Also it appears once to have been customary for the assembly of elders who witnessed the ceremony, if they consented to the sale, to "make sure" or warrant the buyer's possession.[30]

19 See supra §131
19a An owner of property may dispose of it in any manner he may see fit. Dana v Stanford (1858) 10 Cal. 269, 277 (Field,J); United States v Eleven Parcels of Land (1942) 45 Fed. Supp. 289, 290 (O'Connor,DJ)
20 Lev. 25:34
21 Lev. 25:23
22 See infra §172
23 See infra §269
24 Anderson v Winston (1736) Jefferson's (Va.) Rep. 24
25 1 Kings 21:3; and see 2 Kings 9: 22-26

26 Lam. 5:2
27 12 Gr. B. (1900) 89; Maine's Anc. L. 197, 198
28 12 Gr. B. (1900) 91; 13 Gr. B. (1901) 315
29 Ruth 4:7; 13 Gr. B. (1901) 315
The shoe, as a symbol of possession was equivalent to the old English custom of "livery of seizin." But in later times the shoe ceased to be a symbol of title and became a symbol of contempt of one who refused to marry his brother's widow. 13 Gr. B. (1901) 316
30 Gen. 23:17,18,20; and see infra §170, 174

[§170] —— —— The ceremony by which Abraham purchased the "field of Ephron" is thus described:

"And Abraham stood up . . . and spake unto the sons of Heth, saying,
"I am a stranger and a sojourner with you: give me a possession of a buryingplace with you, that I may bury my dead out of my sight.
"And the children of Heth answered Abraham, saying unto him,
"Hear us, my lord: thou art a mighty prince among us: in the choice of our sepulchres bury thy dead; none of us shall withhold from thee his sepulchre, but that thou mayest bury thy dead.
"And Abraham stood up, and bowed himself to the people of the land, even to the children of Heth.
"And he communed with them, saying, If it be your mind that I should bury my dead out of my sight, hear me, and entreat for me to Ephron the son of Zobar.
"That he may give me the cave of Machpelah, which he hath, which is in the end of his field; for as much money as it is worth he shall give it me for a possession of a buryingplace amongst you.
"And Ephron dwelt among the children of Heth:[31] and Ephron the Hittite answered Abraham in the audience of the children of Heth, even of all that went in at the gate of his city, saying,
"Nay, my lord, hear me: the field give I thee, and the cave that is therein, I give it thee; in the presence of the sons of my people give I it thee: bury thy dead.
"And Abraham bowed down himself before the people of the land.
"And he spake unto Ephron in the audience of the people of the land, saying, But if thou wilt give it, I pray thee, hear me: I will give thee money for the field; take it of me, and I will bury my dead there.
"And Ephron answered Abraham, saying unto him,
"My lord, hearken unto me: the land is worth four hundred shekels of silver; what is that betwixt me and thee? bury therefore thy dead.
"And Abraham hearkened unto Ephron; and Abraham weighed to Ephron the silver, which he had named in the audience of the sons of Heth, four hundred shekels of silver, current money with the merchant.
"And the field of Ephron, which was in Machpelah, which was before Mamre, the field, and the cave which was therein, and all the trees that were in the field, that were in all the borders round about, were made sure
"Unto Abraham for a possession in the presence of the children of Heth, before all that went in at the gate of his city.
"And after this, Abraham buried Sarah his wife in the cave of the field of Machpelah before Mamre: the same is Hebron in the land of Canaan.
"And the field, and the cave that is therein, were made sure unto Abraham for a possession of a buryingplace by the sons of Heth."[32]

[§171] —— —— Long before the Christian era it had become customary, in transferring land, to "subscribe evidences, and seal them, and take witnesses."[33] The manner in which a purchase and conveyance were made, and the method

---

31 The statement that "Ephron dwelt among the children of Heth" should be translated "was sitting" among them at the gate where the proceedings were taking place. 12 Gr. B. (1900) 91
32 Gen. 23:3-20
33 Jer. 32:44

by which a record thereof was preserved, are shown in the account of the purchase of a field by Jeremiah from Hanameel.

"And I bought the field of Hanameel . . . and weighed him the money, even seventeen shekels of silver.

"And I subscribed the evidence, and sealed it, and took witnesses, and weighed him the money in the balances.

"So I took the evidence of the purchase, both that which was sealed according to the law and custom, and that which was open:

"And I gave the evidence of the purchase unto Baruch . . . in the sight of Hanameel . . . and in the presence of the witnesses that subscribed the book of the purchase . . .

"And I charged Baruch before them, saying,

". . . Take these evidences, this evidence of the purchase, both which is sealed, and this evidence which is open; and put them in an earthen vessel, that they may continue many days."[34]

In modern times, real property is transferred by "conveyances" or "deeds," which are recorded in a public office. And in America deeds were formerly addressed to "Christian people."[35]

[§172] —— Mosaic law provided for the redemption of lands and houses that had been sold. As to lands or "fields of the country," the law declared that—

". . . in all the land of your possession ye shall grant a redemption for the land.

"If thy brother be waxen poor, and hath sold away some of his possession, and if any of his kin come to redeem it, then shall he redeem that which his brother sold.

"And if the man have none to redeem it, and himself be able to redeem it;

"Then let him count the years of the sale thereof, and restore the overplus unto the man to whom he sold it; that he may return unto his possession.

"But if he be not able to restore it to him, then that which is sold shall remain in the hand of him that hath bought it until the year of jubilee: and in the jubilee it shall go out, and he shall return unto his possession."[36]

---

34 Jer. 32:9-14
"The purchase price was weighed according to the custom of the times. A deed of conveyance was written and sealed and witnesses were taken to it. The form of law which students of Anglo-Saxon jurisprudence call "livery of seisin" was used. The deed was sealed and placed in an earthen vessel, which, like a modern filing system, securely held the evidence of title. 5 Docket (1939-40) No. 4, p 4060

35 See Gittings' Lessee v Hall (1800) 1 Harris & J. (Md.) 14, 2 AD 502, 503 (Chase,CJ) setting out a copy of a deed of grant, beginning as follows: "To all Christian people to whom these presents shall come. Henry Hill, of Ann Arundel county, in the province of Maryland, sendeth greeting, etc." This deed was executed on July 27, 1737.
36 Lev. 25:24-28

Concerning the redemption of houses in cities and villages, the law provided that—

". . . if a man sell a dwellinghouse in a walled city, then he may redeem it within a whole year after it is sold; within a full year may he redeem it.

"And if it be not redeemed within the space of a full year, then the house that is in the walled city shall be established for ever to him that bought it throughout his generations: it shall not go out in the jubilee.

"But the houses of the villages which have no wall round about them shall be counted as the fields of the country: they may be redeemed, and they shall go out in the jubilee."[37]

Under a special rule, the Levites were authorized to redeem their "cities" and "the houses of the cities of their possession" at any time.[38]

It was the duty of the nearest kinsman to redeem the inheritance of one who had been obliged to part with it.[39] And in doing so, it was incumbent upon him to take the widow also, at least where the decedent left no heir, in order "to raise up the name of the dead upon his inheritance, that the name of the dead be not cut off from among his brethren."[40]

The redemption ceremony was performed in the presence of the "elders" or "ten men of the elders of the city."[41] And "this was the manner in former time in Israel concerning redeeming and concerning changing, for to confirm all things: a man plucked off his shoe, and gave it to his neighbour: and this was a testimony in Israel."[42]

[§173] Lands and houses were mortgaged in cases of necessity, and were also sometimes leased or rented. Thus in Nehemiah it is related that "We have mortgaged our lands, vineyards, and houses, that we might buy corn . . ."[42a] Solomon is said to have had a vineyard at Baal-hamon that "he let out . . . unto keepers; every one for the fruit thereof was to bring a thousand pieces of silver."[43] St. Paul also hired or rented a house in Rome, in which he dwelt two whole years.[44]

---

37   Lev. 25:29-31
38   Lev. 25:25
39   13 Gr. B. (1901) 314
40   Ruth 4:1-13. And see infra §191
41   13 Gr. B. (1901) 314

42   Ruth 4:7
42a   Neh. 5:3
43   Song of Solomon 8:11
44   Acts 28:30

CHAPTER 26

SURETYSHIP

174 Suretyship   175 Attitude of law

[§174] "A contract of suretyship is an accessory agreement, by which one person binds himself for another already bound."[45] Several contracts of this kind are mentioned in the Scriptures.[46] For example, the sons of Heth "made sure" to Abraham the possession of a field purchased from Ephron.[47] Judah became surety to his father for the safe return of his youngest brother Benjamin;[48] and St. Paul assumed a debt of Onesimus to Philemon.[49] The ancient contract of suretyship was made by "striking hands"[50] in the presence of witnesses.[1] In later times such contracts were made in writing.[2]

[§175] The law does not ordinarily favor suretyships.[3] It is improper, or at least unwise, to become a surety for a stranger[4] or to be a surety above one's power.[5] And it has been observed that—

"Almost all who sign as surety have occasion to remember the proverb of Solomon: 'He that is surety for a stranger shall smart for it, and he that hateth suretyship is sure.'[6] But they are nevertheless held liable upon their contracts, otherwise there would be no smarting, and the proverb would fail."[7]

But in some circumstances one may properly become a surety for his neighbour.

"An honest man is surety for his neighbour: but he that is impudent will forsake him.

"Forget not the friendship of thy surety, for he hath given his life for thee.

45 21 RCL 946
46 See Job 17:3 ("Lay down now, put me in a surety with thee") and see other citations infra, this section.
47 Gen. 23:20
48 Gen. 43:8,9: "And Judah said unto Israel his father, Send the lad with me . . . I will be surety for him; of my hand shalt thou require him: if I bring him not unto thee, and set him before thee, let me bear the blame for ever."
49 Philemon 18,19 ("If he hath wronged thee, or oweth thee aught, put that on mine account . . . I will repay it")
50 Job 17:3 ("who is he that will strike hands with me?"); Prov. 6:1,2 ("if thou has stricken thy hand with a stranger, thou are snared with the words of thy mouth"), 17:18 ("A man void of understanding striketh hands"), 22:26 ("Be not thou one of them that strike hands")

1 Prov. 17:18 ("A man void of understanding . . . becometh surety in the presence of his friends")
2 Philemon 19 (" I Paul have written it with mine own hands")
3 Prov. 6:1,2 ("if thou be surety for thy friend . . . thou art snared with the words of thy mouth"), 17:18 ("A man void of understanding . . . becometh surety"), 22:26 ("Be not thou one of them that . . . are sureties for debts")
4 Prov. 11:15, 20:16 ("Take his garment that is surety for a stranger"), 27:13 (same)
5 Ecclesiasticus 8:13 ("Be not surety above thy power: for if thou be surety, take care to pay it")
6 Prov. 11:15
7 Mayo v Hutchinson (1870) 57 Me. 546, 547 (Appleton,CJ)

"Suretyship hath undone many of good estate, and shaken them as a wave of the sea: mighty men hath it driven from their houses, so that they wandered among strange nations.

"Help thy neighbour according to thy power, and beware that thou thyself fall not into the same."[8]

CHAPTER 27

TRESPASS

[§176]   Generally it is unlawful to do "any manner of trespass"[9] or "wrong"[10] against a "neighbour."[11]   A trespass is some "transgression or offense" that injures another.[12] Every one is liable for any injury that his act or omission causes to another, though it may have been unintentional,[12a] as where he did not foresee the consequences of his act[12b] or where he merely acted without due care, or negligently.[13]   But ordinarily a bystander is not required to become a good Samaritan[13a] and prevent injury to others.

"A bystander may watch a blind man or a child walk over a precipice, and yet he is not required to give warning. He may stand on the bank of a stream and see a man drowning, and although he holds in his hand a rope that could be used to rescue the man, yet he is not required to give assistance. He may owe a moral duty to warn the blind man or to assist the drowning man, but being a mere bystander, and in nowise responsible for the dangerous situation, he owes no legal duty to render assistance."[13b]

Some of the more common trespasses are here noticed;

---

8 Ecclesiasticus 29:14-20
9 Ex. 22:9
10 2 Cor. 7:2
11 1 Kings 8:31
12 26 RCL 930
12a Hestonville Ry. Co. v Connell (1879) 88 Pa. St. 520, 32 AR 472, 473 (Gordon,J)
And at common law a husband is answerable for wrongs committed by his wife—if committed in his company he alone is answerable. Poor v Poor (1836) 8 NH 307, 29 AD 664, 669 (Richardson, CJ)
12b Kerby v Hal Roach Studios (1942) 53 Cal.App.2d 207,127P2d 577 (Shaw,J pro tem.)
13 36 Case & Comment (1930) No. 2,

p 14 (Dox): "In a primitive stage of culture one who feels that he has been harmed seeks vengeance on the cause of his harm, whether man, beast or inanimate thing. If a human being causes the harm, he ignores the latter's state of mind. As the law evolves, it begins to distinguish inevitable accident, intent and negligence, and limits the field of absolute liability. There emerges the notion of liability for harm resulting from another's act, later still from another's omission accompanied by the failure to exercise a certain degree of care."
13a Luke 10:33
13b Buchanan v Rose (1942) 159 SW2d (Tex.) 109, 110 (Alexander,CJ)

other wrongs which also constitute crimes are treated in subsequent chapters.[14]

[§177] An "assault," in common parlance, is the beating or striking of another.[15] Under Mosaic law, it is unlawful to "smite" a neighbour "secretly,"[16] or to "lay hands" upon him "suddenly,"[17] and one is responsible for an injury to another though it occurs in course of a mutual combat. The rule is that—

". . . if men strive together, and one smite another with a stone, or with his fist, and he die not, but keepeth his bed:

"If he rise again, and walk abroad upon his staff, then shall he that smote him be quit: only he shall pay for the loss of his time, and shall cause him to be thoroughly healed."[18]

As to an injury resulting in a miscarriage, the law says that—

"If men strive, and hurt a woman with child, so that her fruit depart from her, and yet no mischief follow; he shall . . . pay as the judges determine."[19]

[§178] Burning property of another, or causing it to burn, is a legal wrong for which the owner is entitled to recompense, whether the thing burned be a dwelling house, a growing crop[20] or other property. Mosaic law declares that—

"If fire break out, and catch in thorns, so that the stacks of corn, or the standing corn, or the field, be consumed therewith; he that kindled the fire shall surely make restitution."[21]

Under this rule, one who kindled a fire was absolutely responsible for injury the fire might cause to others.[22]

[§179] Entry upon the lands of another, or into his house, may be a trespass.[23] It is unlawful to set foot within a neighbour's house against his will,[24] to "enter into the fields of the fatherless,"[25] or to cause another man's field or vineyard to

---

14 See infra §361 et seq.
15 But in modern law, an assault is a violent attempt or willful offer to do hurt to another; and the actual doing of the hurt is called a battery. See 4 Am Jur 124
Every man's person is sacred and no other has the right to touch it. 2 RCL 526; Kirland v State (1873) 43 Ind. 146, 13 AR 386, 389 (Buskirk,J) quoting Blackstone's definition of battery.
16 Deut. 27:24
17 1 Tim. 5:22
18 Ex. 21:18,19; Hart v Guysel (1930) 159 Wash. 632, 294 P 570, 573 (Holcomb, J, dissenting)
"This is substantially the law today in damage suits against the aggressor

for assault and battery." 2 Wash.LR (1914) 771 (Barnard,J)
19 Ex. 21:22
20 See 2 Sam. 14:28-32, where Absalom caused his servants to set fire to Joab's field of barley because the latter refused to come when sent for.
21 Ex. 22:6
22 "Later the intervention of a sudden wind-storm was treated as an available excuse for failure to prevent the spread of the fire." See 7 Harv.LR (1894) 448 (Wigmore)
23 See 26 RCL 938
24 Prov. 25:17 ("Withdraw thy foot from thy neighbour's house lest he be weary of thee, and so hate thee")
25 Prov. 23:10

be "eaten" by cattle.[26]   But it is not unlawful merely to enter
another's field or vineyard, nor even to "satisfy one's hunger"
from the grapes or other crop growing therein.

"When thou comest into thy neighbour's vineyard, then thou mayest
eat grapes thy fill at thine own pleasure; but thou shalt not put any
in thy vessel.

"When thou comest into the standing corn of thy neighbour, then
thou mayest pluck the ears with thine hand; but thou shalt not move a
sickle unto thy neighbour's standing corn."[27]

[§180]   Mischief consists in malicious or wilful acts by
which another's property is damaged or destroyed.[28]   The
Scriptures impliedly condemn all such acts, observing that
mischief is the device of a wicked man,[29] and that the Lord
hates "a heart that deviseth wicked imaginations" and "feet
that be swift in running to mischief."[30]   Simeon and Levi
committed mischief when "in their selfwill they digged down
a wall," and for this their father Jacob "cursed" them in his
dying statement.[31]

[§181]   Digging a pit or setting a trap, for the purpose of
causing another to fall in the pit or to be taken by the trap,
is against Mosaic law,[32] as is also the placing of a "stumblingblock" in the path of a blind person.[33]   "And if a man shall
open a pit, or . . . dig a pit, and not cover it, and an ox or an
ass fall therein, the owner of the pit shall make it good."[34]   In
modern law also it is regarded as negligence to leave open a
dangerous pit where any person or domestic animal may fall
into it.[35]

[§182]   Mosaic law provides that a man who seduces a
damsel that is a virgin "shall give unto the damsel's father
fifty shekels of silver, and she shall be his wife;[35] also that a
man who entices a maid that is betrothed "shall surely endow
her to be his wife.[36]   If her father utterly refuse to give her
unto him, he shall pay money according to the dowry of virgins."[37]

Shechem's Case.   But the foregoing rule was not respected
where the seducer was legally ineligible to marry the maid.
In the Shechem Case, though Shechem offered to marry Dinah

26 Ex. 22:5
27 Deut. 23:24,25
28 See 34 Am Jur 688
29 Ps. 36:1,4 ("the wicked . . . deviseth mischief upon his bed") ; Prov. 6:12,
14 ("a wicked man . . . deviseth mischief continually")
30 Prov. 6:16,18
31 Gen. 49:6
32 Ps. 119:85 ("The proud have digged
pits for me, which are not after thy

law") ; Ecclesiasticus 27:26 ("Whoso
diggest a pit shall fall therein: and he
that setteth a trap shall be taken therein")
33 Lev. 19:14
34 Ex. 21:33,34
35 42 Wash.LR (1914) 771
35a Deut. 22:28,29; and see infra §192,
n 1
36 See infra §192
37 Ex. 22:16,17

and to pay any amount of dowry, Simeon and Levi, two of the sons of Jacob, took vengeance for the wrong done their family by slaughtering Shechem, Hamor his father, and all the male inhabitants of their city.[38]

[§183] Slander is the utterance of defamatory words, injuring another's reputation.[39] The wrong is done when one, as it has been said, "with his mouth destroyeth his neighbour."[40] The law, in effect, forbids slander,[41] admonishing that one "keep" his "tongue from evil," and his "lips from speaking guile,"[42] and declaring that one should "speak evil of no man"[43] but should rather "speak the truth[44] in love."[45] It is wrongful to "backbite"[46] or to "speak evil" of another.[47] "He that speaketh evil of his brother and judgeth his brother, speaketh evil of the law, and judgeth the law."[48]

[§184] —— According to Mosaic law, a husband is liable for slandering his wife.

"If any man take a wife, and go in unto her, and hate her,
"And give occasions of speech against her, and bring up evil name upon her, and say, I took this woman, and when I came to her, I found her not a maid:
"Then shall the father of the damsel, and her mother, take and bring forth the tokens of the damsel's virginity unto the elders of the city in the gate:
"And the damsel's father shall say unto the elders, I gave my daughter unto this man to wife, and he hateth her;
"And lo, he hath given occasions of speech against her, saying I found not thy daughter a maid; and yet these are the tokens of my daughter's virginity. And they shall spread the cloth before the elders of the city.
"And the elders of that city shall take that man and chastise him;
"And they shall amerce him in an hundred shekels of silver, and give them unto the father of the damsel, because he hath brought up an evil name upon a virgin of Israel: and she shall be his wife; he may not put her away all his days.

38 Gen. 34:1-31; and see supra §113
It is slanderous to charge one with having an "evil disease." Ps. 41:8
39 33 Am Jur 39
One who lives a life of rectitude has a right to freedom from attacks upon his character. Melvin v Reid (1931) 112 Cal.App. 285, 291, 297 P 91 (Marks,J)
40 Prov. 11:9; Harvey v Territory (1901) 11 Okla. 156, 65 P 837 (Burford, CJ)
"Set a watch, O Lord, before my mouth; and a door round about my lips." Ps. 141:3, quoted in Scott's Estate (1898) 1 Coffey's (Cal.) Prob. Dec. 271,301
41 Ps. 101:5 ("Whoso privily slandereth his neighbour, him will I cut off"); Prov. 10:18 ("he that uttereth a slander, is a fool"); Two Ways 2:3 ("thou shalt not slander")
"The law will not permit a person to go unpunished, who slanders the

reputation of another by finesse." Bornman v Boyer (1811) 3 Binney (Pa.) 515, 518 (Yeates,J)
"The English Star Chamber laid it down that 'libeling and calumnation is an offence against the law of God,' and sought their legal basis in Exodus and Leviticus." Pluknett's History of Common Law, 2d ed., p 431
42 42 Wash.LR (1914) p 722 (Barnard, J) saying that this is the law of slander.
43 Titus 3:2
"Let no corrupt communication proceed out of your mouth." Eph. 4:29
44 Zech. 8:16; Acts 4:20 ("words of truth and soberness")
45 Eph. 4:15
46 Ps. 15:3, condemning one "that backbiteth . . . with his tongue."
47 James 4:11 ("Speak not evil one of another")
48 James 4:12

"But if this thing be true, and the tokens of virginity be not found for the damsel:
"Then they shall bring out the damsel to the door of her father's house, and the men of her city shall stone her with stones that she die: because she hath wrought folly in Israel, to play the whore in her father's house: so shalt thou put evil away from among you."[49]

DIVISION B

Domestic Relations

CHAPTER 28

INTRODUCTORY

185 In general   186 The family

[§185]   The most ancient law is that pertaining to the family or "house" and commonly known as the law of domestic relations. It embraces rules as to marriage, divorce, husband and wife, parent and child, master and servant, and host and guest. Many modern laws governing these matters are based upon Biblical precepts,[50] and some of them have remained virtually unaltered from the earliest times. But there has long been a tendency, shown by acts of law-makers and decisions of judges, to lessen the solidarity of the family. In recent times many of the rules as to master and servant also have become obsolete.

[§186]   The family is the simplest form of society,[1] and it—rather than the individual—was formerly regarded as the basic social unit.[2] The primitive family was a small but nearly independent political body,[3] somewhat like a modern corporation.[4] It was a single group, consisting of (a) blood relatives descended from the same male ancestor, (b) others attached to the group by marriage or adoption, and (c) slaves.[5] The official head of the family was its patriarch— the chief or great father—who was ordinarily the oldest male in the eldest line from the common ancestor. The word of

49 Deut. 22:13-21
50 42 Wash.LR (1914) p 770
1 N J St. Bar Assn.Yr.Bk. (Dec.1939) 125, 128 (Bishop Eustace) observing further that "The family is the most important element in human society, an element that is so important that he

who would destroy the State needs but to destroy the family."
2 13 Gr. B. (1901) 315
3 14 Gr. B. (1902) 490
4 See supra §159
5 Maine's Anc. L. 159, 254, 255

the patriarch was the law of the family.[6] He had control of the lives and property of all its members, and was responsible for their conduct.[7] Upon the death of a patriarch his eldest son usually succeeded him as the family head.[8]

CHAPTER 29

MARRIAGE

[§187] "The children of this world marry and are given in marriage."[9] Marriage or matrimony is the "union of man and woman."[10] In most civilized nations, it is a contract, regulated by law.[11] But it is more than a contract, for it gives the parties a new status and makes of them a new community in which the state is interested.[12] It exists as a legal institution among all peoples who have advanced beyond a condition of savagery.[13]

"From time immemorial marriage has been, in every civilized country, recognized as the foundation of civilization and of the social system.

6 13 Gr. B. (1901) 38 (Amram) saying that in the patriarchal age, "public law took no cognizance of family matters; and family law, so far as it may be called law, was simply the expressed will of the head of the household"

7 Ruse v Williams (1913) 14 Ariz. 445, 130 P 887, 45 LRANS 923, 927 (Franklin,CJ) noting that in China, "it is a common thing . . . for the individual collective family to live in one place for centuries; sometimes the family will number two or three hundred persons, whose labor and property is controlled by the oldest male ancestor for the common good; and for the conduct and behavior of each member of the family the ancestor is held responsible."

8 Maine's Anc. L. 231, observing that, in course of time, the power of the family head was looked upon as ownership, while his duties to the family members were lost sight of.

9 Luke 20:34

10 Justinian, Digest, 23, 2, 1
The marriage also creates a legal relation between the groom and the family of the bride, and between the bride and the family of the groom, but not

between the two families: See infra §227, and see Cortez v State (1942) 161 SW2d 495, 497 (Krueger,J) quoting an "old and familiar adage"—

"The groom and bride each come within
The circle of each other's kin,
But kin and kin are still no more
Related than they were before."

11 Reynolds v United States (1878) 98 US 145, 25 L. ed 244, 250 (Waite,CJ) saying that "Marriage, while from its very nature a sacred obligation, is nevertheless, in most civilized nations, a civil contract, and usually regulated by law. Upon it society may be said to be built; and out of its fruits spring social relations and social obligations and duties, with which government is necessarily required to deal."

12 Justinian, Institutes, 1, 9, 1
Marriage is the civil status of one man and one woman united in law for life, for the discharge to each other and to the community of the duties legally incumbent on those whose association is founded on the distinction of sex. Sharon v Sharon (1888) 75 Cal. 1, 16 P 345, 348 (McKinstry,J)

13 28 Geo.LJ (1940) 809

Neither one of the parties to the marriage can thereafter commit a breach of any of the obligations or duties assumed without a violation of conscience as well as of the law."[14]

[§188] The Scriptures encourage marriage[15] and, in some instances, even command it.[16] So it is said that "Marriage is honourable in all,"[17] that "He that getteth a wife beginneth a possession, a help like unto himself and a pillar of rest,"[18] and that "Whoso findeth a wife findeth a good thing, and obtaineth favour of the Lord,"[19] whereas "He that hath no wife will wander up and down mourning."[20] St. Paul considered it expedient for "younger women" to marry, declaring that—

"I will . . . that the younger women marry, bear children, guide the house, give none occasion to the adversary to speak reproachfully."[21]

But being himself unmarried, he regarded marriage as a "lesser evil," saying—

". . . It is good for a man not to touch a woman.

"Nevertheless, to avoid fornication, let every man have his own wife, and let every woman have her own husband."[22]

"I say therefore to the unmarried and widows, It is good for them if they abide even as I.

"But if they cannot contain, let them marry: for it is better to marry than to burn."[23]

[§189] According to Primitive law, an elder daughter was entitled to be given in marriage before her younger sister.[24] And under Mosaic law, the right to marry a woman was regarded as "appertaining" to one of her kindred.[25] A woman who "possessed" an "inheritance" was entitled to marry whom she thought best, "only to the family of the tribe of her father."[26] The New Testament concedes that a woman—or at any rate a widow—may marry "whom she will."[27] But

---

14 Hilton v Roylance (1902) 25 Utah 129, 60 P 660, 95 ASR 821, 826 (Bartch,J)
15 Ecclesiasticus 26:3,14
Jesus avoided saying that "it is not good to marry." See Matt. 19:10,11
16 Jer. 29:6 ("Take ye wives")
17 Heb. 13:4
18 Ecclesiasticus 36:24
19 Prov. 18:22
20 Ecclesiasticus 36:25
21 1 Tim. 5:14
The principal ends of marriage are to prevent licentiousness and to secure the procreation of children under the shield and sanction of the law. Sharon v Sharon (1888) 75 Cal. 1, 16 P 345, 359 (McKinstry,J)
22 1 Cor. 7:1,2
23 1 Cor. 7:8,9
"In 131 B.C., Q. Caecilius Metellus, Censor, proposed a bill requiring all

Romans to marry. In his speech before the Senate he observed, 'that if it were possible to have no wives at all, everybody would gladly escape that annoyance, but since nature had so ordained that it was not possible to live agreeable with them, nor to live at all without them, regard must be had rather to permanent welfare than to transitory pleasure.'" Bryce, Marriage and Divorce under Roman and English Law (1909) 800

24 Gen. 29:26
25 Tobit 6:11
26 Num. 36:6
27 1 Cor. 7:39
"The very nature of rights of personality is freedom to dispose of one's own person as one pleases." Bonner v Moran (1941) 126 F2d 121, 122 (Groner,CJ)

freedom with respect to marrying has not been generally conceded. It was not until A.D. 451, that a universal prohibition was formulated against violence in compelling marriage. A canon of the Council held at Chalcedon in that year anathematized "all who forcibly carry off women under pretense of marriage."[28]

A husband is at liberty to remarry after the death of his wife;[29] and so is a wife after the death of her husband.[30]

[§190] Biblical law does not prescribe minimum ages at which persons may marry. But the Old Testament indicates that marriage did not take place early in life. Thus it appears that Isaac was 40 years old when he took Rebekah to wife,[31] and that Esau was 40 years old when he took to wife Judith the daughter of Beeri and Bashemath the daughter of Elon.[32] Under Roman law, the minimum ages for marriage were 14 for the boy and 12 for the girl.[33] Also under American law, a boy of 14 and a girl of 12 formerly were capable of marrying by their own consent.[34]

Nor does Biblical law prescribe any age after which men or women are considered too old to marry.[34a] Abraham, after the death of Sarah, though he was old "and well stricken in age"[35] again took a wife.[36] Roman law at first forbade a man of 60 to marry a woman of 50, and afterwards forbade a man of 60 to marry at all. But this rule was later abrogated and no one was considered too old to marry.[37]

---

28 In ancient Rome, both sons and daughters were married off at the sole discretion of the paterfamilias. But from approximately the first century B.C., a son could not be betrothed against his will by his father. Daughters, however, had no choice in the matter of marriage at this time. 7 Va. LR (1939) 73

29 See Gen. 25:1, stating that Abraham took another wife after the death of Sarah.

30 1 Cor. 7:39,40, "The wife is bound by the law as long as her husband liveth; but if her husband be dead, she is at liberty to be married to whom she will, only in the Lord. But she is happier if she so abide, after my judgment: and I think also that I have the Spirit of God." See also Rom. 7:3

31 Gen. 25:20

32 Gen. 26:34
The Talmud approves the opinion of Judah, son of Tamai, that "at five years of age a child should study the Bible, at ten he should study the Mishna, at fifteen he should study the Gemara, and at eighteen he should get married." 30 Harv. LR (1916) No. 2, p 127 (Swindlehurst)

33 Justinian, Institute, Lib. I, tit. XXII

34 But the modern tendency has been to raise the age of consent to 21 years for the male and 18 for the female, but permitting a male under 21 and over 18 and a female under 18 and over 16 to marry with parental consent, and permitting a male under 18 and a female under 16 to marry with such consent and upon obtaining a court order granting them permission to do so.

34a But it was recognized that one might be too old to marry. See Ruth 1:12 where Naomi said "I am too old to have a husband."

35 Gen. 24:1

36 Gen. 25:1

37 30 Harv. LR (1916) No. 2, p 133 (Swindlehurst)

[§191] Under Primitive law one might marry his brother's widow;[38] and in case of a man's death without an heir, but leaving a widow and a younger brother, it was the duty of the brother to take the widow as his wife.[39] In the absence of a brother able and willing to perform this duty, it passed to the next of kin of the deceased husband.[40]

Mosaic law forbade marriage to a brother's widow except where there was no child of the first marriage.[41] In such a case the law provided that—

"If brethren dwell together, and one of them die, and have no child, the wife of the dead shall not marry without unto a stranger: her husband's brother shall go in unto her, and take her to him to wife, and perform the duty of an husband's brother unto her.

"And it shall be, that the firstborn which she beareth him shall succeed in the name of his brother which is dead, that his name be not put out of Israel.

"And if the man like not to take his brother's wife, then let his brother's wife go up to the gate unto the elders, and say, My husband's brother refuseth to raise up unto his brother a name in Israel, he will not perform the duty of my husband's brother.

"Then the elders of his city shall call him, and speak unto him: and if he stand to it, and say, I like not to take her:

"Then shall his brother's wife come unto him in the presence of the elders, and loose his shoe from off his foot, and spit in his face, and shall answer and say, So shall it be done unto that man that will not build up his brother's house.

"And his name shall be called in Israel, The house of him that hath his shoe loosed."[42]

By legal fiction a son born of a marriage to a widow was the son of the deceased husband and continued his family.[43] So when Ruth bore a son by Boaz, he was considered as the son of Mahlon, so as to continue the line of Elimelech. For this reason the neighbor women said, "There is a son born to Naomi."[44]

[§192] Dowry was originally a gift or price paid by a bridegroom to the father of the bride.[45] Jacob gave 14 years of services as the price of Rachel and Leah.[45a] When Shechem

---

38   14 Gr.B (1902) 345 (Amram)

39   See Gen. 38:8,9,11

40   See Ruth 4:1-12; Tobit 3:15-17, 6:11,12, 7:12

At first it was the duty of the nearest kinsman to marry the widow. In later times, only the actual brother of the dead man was obliged to marry the widow. 13 Gr.B. (1901) 316

41   14 Gr.B. (1902) 345

42   Deut. 25:5-10. See also Matt. 22:23-30; Mark 12:18-25; Luke 20:27-35

In Hindu law, if a husband should die without providing for a successor, or should have been so long absent that his death seemed probable, the wife might bear him an heir by a near kinsman. 16 Harv. LR (1902) 26 (Ayer)

43   13 Gr.B. (1901) 314

44   Ruth 4:17; 13 Gr.B. (1901) 315

45   14 Gr.B. (1902) 344 (Amram)

The first money is said to have been used to purchase brides.

45a   Rachel and Leah said unto Jacob their husband that their father "hath sold us" and that they were "counted of him strangers." Gen. 31:15

desired to marry Dinah, "he said unto her father and unto her brethren, Let me find grace in your eyes, and what ye shall say unto me I will give: Ask me never so much dowry and gift, and I will give according as ye shall say unto me: but give me the damsel to wife."[46] And David "slew the Philistines two hundred men; and . . . brought their foreskins, and . . . gave them in full tale to the king, that he might be the king's son in law. And Saul gave him Michal his daughter to wife."[47] In course of time, dowry became a sum of money or other property given to the groom by the parents of the bride, or brought by the wife to her husband at the time of the marriage.[48] This became a part of the property of the new family.[49] In modern law, dowry is a share of the family property to which a widow is entitled.

In a case of seduction we have seen that the law required the seducer to endow the maid to be his wife[50] or to "pay money according to the dowry of virgins."[1]

[§193] Doubtless a marriage should ordinarily be solemnized by a ceremony,[2] before a minister, priest or civil officer, or at least before witnesses, but no particular form of ceremony[3] or vow is prescribed.[4] The wedding of Boaz and Ruth was publicly solemnized at the gate of Bethlehem, in the presence of "ten men of the elders of the city."[5]

"And Boaz said unto the elders and unto all the people, Ye are witnesses this day, that . . . Ruth the Moabitess . . . have I purchased to be my wife . . .

"And all the people that were in the gate, and the elders, said, We are witnesses.

"So Boaz took Ruth, and she was his wife . . ."[6]

---

46 Gen. 34:11,12
47 1 Sam. 18:27
48 See Ecclesiasticus 22:4
49 So according to an old American custom, the father of the bride gave her a cow, which was intended to be the mother of a new herd to supply milk and meat for the new family.
50 See supra §182
1 Ex. 22:16,17 But see Deut. 22:28,29, providing that "If a man find a damsel that is a virgin, which is not betrothed, and lay hold on her, and lie with her, and they be found; then the man that lay with her shall give unto the damsel's father fifty shekels of silver, and she shall be his wife; because he hath humbled her, he may not put her away all his days." See also infra §203
2 During the Middle Ages, a sacramental ceremony was made essential to a marriage in most if not all Christian countries. 14 Harv. LR (1901) 513 (Thayer)

3 Graham v Bennett (1852) 2 Cal. 503
"Sealing ceremony" performed in 1872 according to the tenets of the Mormon Church, see Hilton v Roylance (1902) 25 Utah 129, 60 P 660, 95 ASR 821, 824
4 The form of marriage vow in most general use is:
"I, —— take thee, ——, to be my lawfully wedded wife (or husband), to have and to hold from this day forward, for better, for worse, for richer, for poorer, in sickness and in health, to love and to cherish till death us do part."
5 Ruth 4:2
Among the Jews, ten men are required to attest certain acts, such as a marriage or the granting of a bill of divorce. 13 Gr.B. (1901) 314 (Amram)
6 Ruth 4:9-11,13
This was a lawful marriage and required no further ceremony. 13 Gr.B. (1901) 316

But the wedding of Tobias and Sara was private. It is related that Raguel called his daughter Sara—

"And she came to her father, and he took her by the hand, and gave her to be wife to Tobias, saying 'Behold, take her after the law of Moses, and lead her away to thy father.' And he blessed them; and called Edna his wife, and took paper, and did write an instrument of covenants, and sealed it."[7]

Nor does Christian law expressly require the presence of a pastor, priest, officer or witness, in contracting a marriage.[8] And under the common law it is sufficient that a man and woman, being legally capable of marrying, freely consent to take each other as husband and wife.[9] Their consent may be given by words spoken in the presence of witnesses[10] or by a writing signed and witnessed,[11] or it may be shown by their conduct.

[§194] According to ancient custom, a marriage was celebrated for seven days. So Jacob "fulfilled the week" of his marriage to Leah,[12] and the wedding of Tobias and Sara was kept seven days "with great joy."[13] It was customary to make a feast[14] and to invite guests[15] or to gather together all the men of the place.[16] And it was expected of a guest that

---

7 Tobit 7:13,14

8 If a pastor or priest cannot be had, the marriage may be contracted merely in the presence of two witnesses; if it is impossible to have two witnesses, one will suffice; and if no witnesses are available, a marriage can be celebrated without them.

9 Peet v Peet (1884) 52 Mich. 464, 18 NW 220 (Cooley,CJ)

A ceremony on the high seas in which the ship captain asks the man if he takes the woman as his wife, and asks the woman if she takes the man as her husband, and receives an affirmative answer from each, and thereupon pronounces them man and wife, is held to constitute a valid marriage. Fisher v Fisher (1929) 250 NY 313, 165 NE 460, 61 ALR 1523

10 By the law of nature, marriage can be contracted without witnesses.

11 The ceremony may consist in the signing and witnessing of a writing such as this: "Marriage in the year 1845. Isaac Graham of Santa Cruz, and Catherine Bennet of San Francisco, were married at Lyant, by banns, this twenty-sixth day of September, 1845, by one who was requested to read the ceremony, Henry Ford. This marriage was solemnized between us, Isaac Graham, Catherine Bennet. In presence of William Werm, Henry Ford." Graham v Bennet (1852) 2 Cal. 503

In the Sharon case (1888) 75 Cal. 1, 16 Pac. 345, it appears that the parties signed a declaration of marriage, "in the words and figures following:

"In the city and county of San Francisco, state of California, on the twenty-fifth day of August, A.D. 1880, I, Sarah Althea Hill, of the city and county of San Francisco, state of California, age twenty-seven years, do here, in the presence of Almighty God, take Senator William Sharon, of the state of Nevada, to be my lawful and wedded husband, and do here acknowledge and declare myself to be the wife of Senator William Sharon of the state of Nevada.

SARAH ALTHEA HILL

"I Agree not to make known the contents of this paper, or its existence, for two years, unless Mr. Sharon himself see fit to make it known.

S.A. HILL

"In the city and county of San Francisco, state of California, on the twenty-fifth day of August, A.D. 1880, I, Senator William Sharon, of the state of Nevada, age sixty years, do here, in the presence of Almighty God, take Sarah Althea Hill, of the city and county of San Francisco, Cal., to be my lawful and wedded wife; do here acknowledge myself to be the husband of Sarah Althea Hill.

WILLIAM SHARON, Nevada

12 Gen. 29:28
13 Tobit 11:19
14 Gen. 29:22
15 Matt. 22:3
16 Gen. 29:22

he should come suitably clothed—that he should wear a "wedding garment."[17]

[§195] Mosaic law provided for a "honeymoon" period of one year. The rule is that

"When a man hath taken a new wife, he shall not go out to war, neither shall he be charged with any business: but he shall be free at home one year, and shall cheer up his wife which he hath taken."[18]

[§196] The patriarchal family was polygamous.[19] Lamech,[20] Jacob,[21] and Elkanah[22] had two wives; Esau had three;[23] Gideon[4] and David[25] had "many" wives; Abijah "waxed mighty" and had fourteen,[26] Rehoboam had eighteen[27] and Solomon had seven hundred.[28] Many Biblical characters also had concubines—women who were not recognized as legal wives. Thus it is stated that Jacob,[29] Eliphaz[30] and Gideon[31] had a concubine; Abraham[32] and David[33] had "concubines;" Rehoboam had threescore concubines[34] and Solomon had three hundred.[35] On the other hand, it appears that Adam,[36] Cain,[37] Noah,[38] Abraham,[39] Lot,[40] Isaac,[41] Moses,[42] and doubtless others among the patriarchs, had one wife.[43]

[§197] —— The Bible seems to take polygamy for granted.[44] Biblical law does not condemn it, nor provide for its punishment.[45] So far as it is concerned, a man may decide for himself whether he shall have one or many wives, or the matter may be regulated by the government of the country in which he lives. In ancient times, polygamy was practiced

17 Matt. 22:11,12
18 Deut. 24:5
19 14 Gr.B. (1902) 345
20 Gen. 4:19 ("the name of the one was Adah, and the name of the other Zillah")
21 Gen. 29:15 et seq., stating that Jacob married two daughters of Laban, giving seven years' service for each.
22 1 Sam. 1:1,2
23 Gen. 26:34, 28:9, 36:2
24 Judges 8:30
25 1 Sam. 18:27, 25:39-44; 2 Sam. 5:13, 11:27
26 2 Chron. 13:21
27 2· Chron. 11:21
28 1 Kings 11:3
29 Gen. 35:22
30 Gen. 36:12
31 Judges 8:31
32 Gen. 25:6
33 2 Sam. 5:13
34 2 Chron. 11:21
35 1 Kings 11:3
36 Gen., chaps. 2-4
37 Gen. 4:17
38 Gen. 6:18, 7:7, 8:16,18
39 Gen. 11:29
Note, however, that Sarah, being childless, gave her handmaid Hagar to Abraham to be his wife, in order that she might "obtain children by her." But after the birth of Isaac, Sarah required Abraham to "cast out" Hagar and her son Ishmael.
40 Gen. 19:15,16,26
41 Gen. 24:67
42 Ex. 2:21, 18:2 But Moses later married an Ethiopian woman See Num. 12:1
43 "The old traditions in Genesis assigned but one wife to many of the ancient patriarchs, such as Adam, Cain and Noah. This, however, is merely negative evidence, and does not preclude the idea that they may have had more than one wife, excepting Adam, who was perforce obliged to be a monogamist." 14 Gr.B. (1902) 345 (Amram)
44 14 Gr.B. (1902) 345
45 The Court of Appeal at Jerusalem has recently decided that bigamy is not a crime for Palestine Jews. Jacob Melnik, a Palestine Jew of Tel Aviv who had married three wives in succession, was acquitted on the ground that, in the Jewish religion, there was no express clause forbidding polygamy, although Rabinical edicts forbid it. 2 Leg. Chat. (1939) No. 8 p 23

among the Israelites and their neighbours, and it would doubtless have been expressly forbidden in Bible law had it been deemed wrongful.

But there are indications that monogamy was preferred from the beginning. In various passages the taking of "one wife" was evidently contemplated.[46] Thus in Genesis it is said that "a man shall leave his father and his mother, and shall cleave unto his wife: and they shall be one flesh."[47] Similarly it is stated in Matthew that "they twain shall be one flesh."[48] St. Paul counselled the Corinthians to "let every man have his own wife, and . . . every woman . . . her own husband."[49] But he declared that a bishop or deacon must be "the husband of one wife," meaning no doubt that he may not be the husband of more than one wife.[50] This statement, however, will support an inference that one other than a bishop or deacon might lawfully have more than one wife.

The modern view of polygamy is stated by Chief Justice Waite as follows:

Polygamy has always been odious among the Northern and Western Nations of Europe and . . . was almost exclusively a feature of the life of Asiatic and African people. At common law, the second marriage was always void, and from the earliest history of England, polygamy has been treated as an offense against society. After the establishment of the ecclesiastical courts, and until the time of James I it was punished through the instrumentality of those tribunals, not merely because ecclesiastical rights had been violated, but because upon the separation of the ecclesiastical courts from the civil, the ecclesiastical were supposed to be the most appropriate for the trial of matrimonial causes and offenses against the rights of marriage; just as they were for testamentary causes and the settlement of the estates of deceased persons.

"By the Statute of 1 James I, ch. 11, the offense, if committed in England or Wales, was made punishable in the civil courts, and the penalty was death. As this statute was limited in its operation to England and Wales, it was at a very early period re-enacted, generally with some modifications, in all the Colonies."[1]

---

46 Prov. 5:18 ("rejoice with the wife of thy youth"); Ecclesiastes 9:9 ("Live joyfully with the wife whom thou lovest all the days of the life of thy vanity . . . for that is thy portion in this life"); Eph. 5:33 ("let every one of you in particular . . . love his wife even as himself")

47 Gen. 2:24
This "purely ethical" passage "simply indicates that polygamy was not in the foreground of the writer's mind, and it cannot properly be construed into a legalization of monogamy." 14 Gr.B. (1902) 345 (Amram)

48 Matt. 19:5; see also Mark 10:7,8; 1 Cor. 6:16; Eph. 5:31
49 1 Cor. 7:2
50 1 Tim. 3:2,12

1 Reynolds v United States (1878) 98 US 145, 25 L Ed 244, 250, stating further that ". . . Professor Lieber says: polygamy leads to the patriarchal principle, and which, when applied to large communities, fetters the people in stationary despotism, while that principle cannot long exist in connection with monogamy. . . . An exceptional colony of polygamists under an exceptional leadership may sometimes exist for a time without appearing to disturb the social condition of the people who surround it; but there cannot be a doubt that, unless restricted by some form of constitution, it is within the legitimate scope of the power of every civil government to determine whether polygamy or monogamy shall be the law of social life under its dominion."

A state may forbid polygamy,[2] and it has long been prohibited in all the American states.[3] No one may claim an exemption from the law against polygamy, or freedom from punishment imposed upon its violation, because he may believe that it is an institution founded on the soundest political wisdom and resting on the sure foundation of inspired revelation.[4]

[§198] —— The practice of polyandry—the marriage of a woman to several husbands—is forbidden by necessary implication, since a woman who takes another man during the life of her husband is held to be guilty of adultery.[5]

[§199] Mosaic law forbids the marriage of a man to a woman to whom he is closely related,[6] or to a "strange woman"—one of another race or nation.[7] And it is forbidden to "take a wife and her mother."[8] A priest may not "take a wife that is a whore, or profane," nor "a woman put away from her husband."[9] Nor may the high priest take "a widow, or a divorced woman, or profane, or an harlot, . . . but he shall take a virgin of his own people to wife."[10]

Christian law forbids the marriage of Christians to unbelievers, that they be not "unequally yoked together."[11]

[§200] —— There is a natural revulsion against the marriage of persons closely related by blood. But in the beginning incestuous marriages were permitted. Thus Cain supposedly married Save, a sister.[12] Such marriages were also made long after necessity therefor had ceased. Thus Abraham married his half-sister Sarah, she being the daughter of his father but not the daughter of his mother,[13] and "Amram took him Jochebed his father's sister to wife; and she bare him Aaron and Moses."[14]

Mosaic law forbids marriage between those who are closely related. The provisions relating to this subject are set out in the section dealing with the crime of incest.[15]

2 Donahue v Richards (1854) 38 Me. 379, 61 AD 256, 272 (Appleton,J)

3 The polygamous marriage is void, amounting in law to no marriage, and the parties who participate therein are punishable by imprisonment.

4 Donahue v Richards (1854) 38 Me. 379, 61 AD 256, 272 (Appleton,J)

5 See infra §396

6 See infra §200

7 See infra §201

8 Lev. 20:14

9 Lev. 21:7

10 Lev. 21:14

11 2 Cor. 6:14

But this is sometimes taken to mean that a believer should not remain married to an unbeliever.

In Sweden, as late as 1873, one not confirmed in the Lutheran faith could not be legally married. 14 Harv. LR (1901) 513 (Thayer)

12 Gen. 4:17

13 Gen. 20:12

14 Ex. 6:20

15 See infra §403

[§201] —— A time-honored rule forbids marriages with persons of another nation, race or tribe. Abraham required his eldest servant to swear that he would "not take a wife unto my son of the daughters of the Canaanites, among whom I dwell," but would "go unto my country, and to my kindred, and take a wife unto my son Isaac."[16] And Mosaic law provides that "thou (shalt not) make marriages" with those of other nations, "thy daughter thou shalt not give unto his son; nor his daughter shalt thou take unto thy son."[17] The reason assigned for this rule was that "they will turn away thy son from following me, that they may serve other gods: so will the anger of the Lord be kindled against you, and destroy thee suddenly."[18] But it was doubtless intended also to preserve the racial integrity of the Israelites.

The rule was often violated, not only by particular individuals, but also, at times, by the whole people.[19] For example, it is related that—

". . . king Solomon loved many strange women, together with the daughter of Pharaoh, women of the Moabites, Ammonites, Edomites, Zidonians, and Hittites:

"Of the nations concerning which the Lord said unto the children of Israel, Ye shall not go in unto them, neither shall they come in unto you: for surely they will turn away your heart after their gods: Solomon clave unto these in love.

"And he had seven hundred wives, princesses, and three hundred concubines: and his wives turned away his heart.

"And the Lord was angry with Solomon, because his heart was turned away from the Lord God of Israel.

"Wherefore the Lord said unto Solomon, Forasmuch as this is done of thee, and thou hast not kept my covenant and my statutes, which I have commanded thee, I will surely rend the kingdom from thee, and will give it to thy servant."[20]

16 Gen. 24:3,4; and see supra §150
See also Tobit 4:12, where Tobit commanded his son Tobias to "take a wife of the seed of thy fathers, and take not a strange woman to wife, which is not of thy father's tribe."
17 Deut. 7:3; Ezra 9:12; Neh. 10:30
18 Deut. 7:4
". . . if ye do in any wise go back, and cleave unto the remnant of these nations, even these that remain among you, and shall make marriages with them, and go in unto them, and they to you: know for a certainty that the Lord your God will no more drive out any of these nations from before you; but they shall be snares and traps unto you, and scourges in your sides, and thorns in your eyes, until ye perish from off this good land which the Lord your God hath given you." Josh. 23:12,13

"Mixed marriages" are forbidden because they commonly tend to serious religious disputes between the parties, leading rather often to separation or divorce.

19 See Judges 3:5,6 ("And the children of Israel dwelt among the Canaanites, Hittites, and Amorites, and Perizzites, and Hivites and Jebusites: and they took their daughters to be their wives, and gave their daughters to their sons, and served their gods"); Ezra 9:1,2 ("The people of Israel, and the priests, and the Levites, . . . have taken of their daughters for themselves, and for their sons: so that the holy seed have mingled themselves with the people of those lands: yea, the hand of the princes and rulers hath been chief in this trespass")
20 1 Kings 11:1-3,9,11

Again, in the time of Ezra, "all the men of Judah and Benjamin gathered themselves together unto Jerusalem"—

"And Ezra the priest stood up, and said unto them, Ye have transgressed, and have taken strange wives, to increase the trespass of Israel.

"Now therefore make confession unto the Lord God of your fathers, and do his pleasure: and separate yourselves from the people of the land, and from the strange wives.

"Then all the congregation answered and said with a loud voice, As thou hast said, so must we do.

"But the people are many, and it is a time of much rain, and we are not able to stand without, neither is this a work of one day or two: for we are many that have transgressed in this thing.

"Let now our rulers of all the congregation stand, and let all them which have taken strange wives in our cities come at appointed times, and with them the elders of every city, and the judges thereof, until the fierce wrath of our God for this matter be turned from us.

"Only Jonathan the son of Asahel and Jahaziah the son of Tikvah were employed about this matter: and Meshullam and Shabbethai the Levite helped them.

"And the children of the captivity did so. And Ezra the priest, with certain chief of the fathers, after the house of their fathers, and all of them by their names, were separated, and sat down in the first day of the tenth month to examine the matter.

"And they made an end with all the men that had taken strange wives by the first day of the first month.

"And among the sons of the priests there were found that had taken strange wives; namely, of the sons of Jeshua the son of Jozadek, and his brethren; Maaseiah, and Eliezer, and Jarib, and Gedaliah.

"And they gave their hands that they would put away their wives; and being guilty, they offered a ram of the flock for their trespass."[21]

Similarly, many of the Jews "had married wives of Ashdod, of Ammon, and of Moab," in the days of Nehemiah.

"And their children spake half in the speech of Ashdod, and could not speak in the Jews' language, but according to the language of each people.

"And I (Nehemiah) contended with them, and cursed them, and smote certain of them, and plucked off their hair, and made them swear by God, saying, Ye shall not give your daughters unto their sons, nor take their daughters unto your sons, or for yourselves.

"Did not Solomon king of Israel sin by these things? yet among many nations was there no king like him, who was beloved of his God, and God made him king over all Israel: nevertheless even him did outlandish women cause to sin."[22]

21 Ezra 10:9-19; and see 1 Esdras 9:7 et seq.   22 Neh. 13:23 et seq.

CHAPTER 30

DIVORCE

[§202] Divorce is the cutting off or ending of the marriage relation other than by death.[23] There may be a separation of husband and wife without divorce, but this does not free them from all their marital duties nor permit them to marry others.[24]

In a proper case, a marriage may be annulled. An annulment differs from a divorce; it may be had for causes existing before or at the time of the marriage ceremony and which go to the very essence of the relation, such as that one or both of the parties was not legally capable of marrying or the fact that the husband was impotent, or that the wife had committed fornication and was pregnant by another man, or that she was sterile and, knowing this, concealed it.[25] The decree of annulment declares, in effect, that the parties were not legally united in marriage and are not husband and wife. On the other hand, when a divorce is allowed it is usually for a cause that arose after the ceremony, and it severs the marital relation which has theretofore existed.[26]

[§203] Mosaic law ordinarily "suffered" a man "to write a bill of divorcement and to put . . . away" his wife.[27] The law provided that

"When a man hath taken a wife, and married her, and it come to pass that she find no favour in his eyes, because he hath found some uncleanness in her: then let him write her a bill of divorcement, and give it in her hand, and send her out of his house.[28]

---

23 This is the divorce a vinculo matrimonii or absolute divorce, which dissolves the marriage bond. See 17 Am Jur 147

24 See 17 Am Jur 543

25 "A woman who accepts the hand of her suitor thereby impliedly assures him of her ability, so far as lies within her knowledge, to bear children. Her concealment of her sterility is a fraud that vitiates the marriage contract and justifies annulment, when the man acts promptly upon his discovery of the fraud. There is neither rule of law, principle of equity nor reason arising from public policy which requires the continuance of a marriage resulting from such fraud." Vileta v Vileta (1942) 53 Cal.App.2d 794, 128 P 2d 376 (Gould, J pro tem)

26 See 17 Am Jur 164, 367

27 Mark 10:4
Under ancient Egyptian law, a wife might by contract reserve the sole right of divorce. But under Mosaic law, the husband only has a right to divorce his wife.

28 Deut. 24:1
See also Isa. 50:1, as recognizing divorce: "Thus saith the Lord, Where is the bill of your mother's divorcement, whom I have put away?"
Mosaic law says nothing of any payment by a husband on divorcing his wife. He might send her away empty handed. But under the Code of Hammurabi, a husband was bound to restore his wife's dowry to her, even though she had bourne him no children.

"And when she is departed out of his house, she may go and be another man's wife.

"And if the latter husband hate her, and write her a bill of divorcement, and giveth it in her hand, and sendeth her out of his house; or if the latter husband die, which took her to be his wife;

"Her former husband, which sent her away, may not take her again to be his wife, after that she is defiled; for that is abomination before the Lord . . ."[29]

It was seemingly regarded as proper to divorce a wicked woman. Thus it is said:

"An evil wife is a yoke shaken to and fro: he that hath hold of her is as though he held a scorpion.[30]

"I had rather dwell with a lion and a dragon, than to keep house with a wicked woman.[31]

"If she go not as thou wouldest have her, cut her off from thy flesh, and give her a bill of divorce, and let her go."[32]

On the other hand, it is said that the Lord "hateth putting away"[33] and that one should not "deal treacherously against the wife of his youth."[34] Moreover the law forbids the "putting away" of a wife whom the husband had "humbled" before their marriage,[35] or one whom he had slandered after the marriage.[36]

[§204] According to Christian law a valid and consummated marriage can be terminated only by the death of one of the parties.[37] So Christian law superseded Mosaic law as to divorce[38] and restored the rule of Primitive law.[39] The teaching of Jesus concerning divorce is this:

"It hath been said, Whosoever shall put away his wife, let him give her a writing of divorcement:

"But I say unto you, That whosoever shall put away his wife, saving for the cause of fornication, causeth her to commit adultery: and whosoever shall marry her that is divorced committeth adultery.[40]

". . . Have ye not read, that he which made them at the beginning made them male and female.

"And said, For this cause shall a man leave father and mother, and shall cleave to his wife: and they twain shall be one flesh?

---

29 Deut. 24:1-4
The form of divorce in Jewish courts in Palestine at the present time is said to be practically the same as it was 2000 years ago. The divorce is made by mutual consent of the parties. The function of the court is merely to determine whether the requirements of Jewish law have been observed.

30 Ecclesiasticus 26:7
31 Ecclesiasticus 25:16
32 Ecclesiasticus 25:26
33 Mal. 2:16
34 Mal. 2:15
35 Deut. 22:29 And see §192, n 1

36 Deut. 22:19 And see supra §184
37 Under Christian law, as under the early English law, "the union was absolute, and could end only with the death of one of the parties." 15 Harv. LR (1902) 638 (Peaslee)

But an unconsummated marriage may be dissolved for a just cause, if requested by one or both of the parties. 26 Va. LR (1939) 71

38 See supra §§53,203
39 Matt. 19:8 ("from the beginning it was not so")
40 Matt. 5:31,32; and see Matt. 19:9; Mark 10:11,12; Luke 16:18

"Wherefore they are no more twain, but one flesh. What therefore God hath joined together, let no man put asunder.[41]

". . . Moses because of the hardness of your hearts suffered you to put away your wives: but from the beginning it was not so."[42]

Respecting the subject of separation and divorce, St. Paul wrote—

". . . unto the married I command, yet not I, but the Lord, let not the wife depart from her husband:

"But and if she depart, let her remain unmarried, or be reconciled to her husband: and let not the husband put away his wife.[43]

"But to the rest speak I, not the Lord: If any brother hath a wife that believeth not, and she be pleased to dwell with him, let him not put her away.

"And the woman which hath an husband that believeth not, and if he be pleased to dwell with her, let her not leave him."[44]

"For the woman which hath an husband is bound by the law to her husband as long as he liveth; but if the husband be dead, she is loosed from the law of her husband.

"So then if, while her husband liveth, she be married to another man, she shall be called an adulteress: but if her husband be dead, she is free from that law; so that she is no adulteress though she be married to another man."[45]

It follows that under the Christian law, divorce—or more properly speaking, annulment—is allowable to a husband for the sole cause of "fornication"—which is an offense committed before marriage. A wife, however, is not entitled to a divorce, though she may "depart from her husband."

[§205] Early English and American law, unlike the Roman law[46] did not allow divorce, so as to admit of another marriage—unless by special legislative dispensation—though it did allow a decree of separation from bed and board for adultery or cruelty.[47]

One American state—South Carolina—still adheres to the Scriptural injunction, "Those whom God has joined together let not man put asunder."[48] A few states, in an erroneous view of Christian law, allow a divorce only for adultery.[48a]

---

41 Matt. 19:4-6; and see Mark 10:6-9
42 Matt. 19:8; and see Mark 10:5
43 1 Cor. 7:10,11
44 1 Cor. 7:12,13

According to the so-called Pauline Privilege, based on 1 Cor. 7:12-15, if two unbelievers contracted marriage and then one of them became a Christian and was unable to live as a Christian because of the other's attitude or conduct, the marriage would be dissolved if and when the Christian party married another sacramentally.

45 Rom. 7:2,3

46 The Roman law allowed divorce, with the right of remarriage.
47 15 Harv. LR (1902) 638 (Peaslee)
48 12 Fla. LJ (1938) 336 (Cobb) observing that "one commentator believes that this policy has been to the good of the people and the State in every respect, (1 Bishop "Marriage, Divorce and Separation" §58)
48a Holt v Holt (1935) 77 F2d (App. D.C.) 538, 541 (Hitz,J) saying that a law allowing divorce for adultery only "is now neither adequate nor appropriate to the life of the community and tends to produce a train of perjury, bigamy, and bastardy."

But the law in most of the states more nearly approaches Mosaic law, for they allow a divorce both to the husband and the wife for a variety of causes, such as adultery, desertion, drunkenness, extreme cruelty, and even incompatibility.[49]

CHAPTER 31

HUSBAND AND WIFE

[§206]   "The rights and duties of married persons are manifold."[50]   And these rights and duties come not from any agreement between the spouses, but from the law.[1]   They are fixed by society, in accordance with natural law, and are beyond and above the parties themselves, who cannot modify the terms on which they are to live together, nor superadd to the relation a single condition, except as to property.[2]

[§207]   According to Biblical law, as also under the English and American common law,[3] a husband and his wife are "one" or "one flesh."[4]   And he, being "the head of the

---

49 But even in a "forward-looking" jurisdiction like Nevada, "parties to a divorce may not litigate by day and copulate by night, inter sese and pendente lite." Holt v Holt (1935) 77 F2d 538, 540 (Hitz,J)

That a husband is unduly penurious towards his wife and children does not constitute extreme cruelty. Parney v Parney (1942) 55 ACA (Cal.) 807, 131 P2d 562 (Adams,PJ)

Extreme cruelty by a husband is willful misconduct which endangers the life or the health of his wife—"not mere austerity of temper, petulance of manners, rudeness of language, want of civil attention, or even occasional sallies of temper, if there be no threat of bodily harm."

"Nor is she entitled to be divorced on the ground of ill treatment if it was drawn upon her by her own misconduct. In such a case her remedy is in a reform of her manners. Poor v Poor (1836) 8 NH 307, 29 AD 664, 670, 671 (Richardson,CJ)

Courts will not listen to trivial complaints of ill treatment by a husband. State v Oliver (1874) 70 NC 60-62 (Settle,J)

Indeed, it has been said of a wife, who complained of maltreatment by her husband, that "She has spread her own bed, and there she must be contented to lie, though it may now appear to her a bed of torture." Tiffin v Tiffin (1809) 2 Binney (Pa.) 202, 208 (Yeates,J)

50 Sharon v Sharon (1888) 75 Cal. 1, 16 P 345, 360 (McKinstry,J)

1 Sharon v Sharon (1888) 75 Cal. 1, 16 P 345, 377 (Thornton,J, dissenting)

2 Sharon v Sharon (1888) 75 Cal. 1, 8, 16 P 345, 348 (McKinstry,J)

3 See 13 RCL 983

4 Gen. 2:24; Matt. 19:5; Mark 10:8; 1 Cor. 6:16; Eph. 5:31

"Man and wife are the same flesh." Bracton, fo. 32

In contemplation of law, "the husband and wife are one. Her legal existence and authority are suspended during the continuance of the matrimonial union." Poor v Poor (1836) 8 NH 307, 29 AD 664, 669 (Richardson,CJ)

But the merger theory of husband and wife never obtained under the Roman civil law. See 15 Or. LR (1936) 293 (Daggett)

wife,"[5] is the "one" in whom the "legal identity" of the wife is merged.[6] This is an established maxim, recognized from the most ancient times in all civilized lands.[7] For some purposes it is a mere figure of speech, but it is literally true as regards actions, family government, and property rights.[8]

[§208] "Secrecy sometimes attends the most regular marriages from prudential reasons."[9] And though concealment of the fact of marriage is perhaps a violation of the rule concerning the speaking of the truth,[10] it does not invalidate the marriage.[11] The Scriptures mention several instances in which a husband, to avoid possible harm to himself or his wife, misrepresented her as being his sister. Thus Abram, when entering Egypt, represented Sarai as his sister, and Pharoah took her into his house, but upon learning of the deception expelled them from the country.[12] Subsequently Abraham misrepresented Sarah[13] to Abimelech, who restored her to Abraham when the deception was revealed, gave him a thousand pieces of silver and invited him to dwell in the land where it pleased him.[14] Thereafter Isaac misrepresented his wife Rebekah to Abimelech, doubtless hoping also to receive a gift, but upon discovering the deception Abimelech reproved Isaac and charged the people not to touch Isaac or his wife on penalty of death.[15]

---

5 1 Cor. 11:3 ("the head of the woman is the man"); Eph. 5:23 ("the husband is the head of the wife")

"In scripture the wife is represented as standing, in some respects, in the same relation to the husband as the husband stands to the Redeemer, and the Redeemer to God. The words are: The head of every man is Christ, and the head of the woman is the man, and the head of Christ is God. And in our law the wife is considered as being, in some respects, subordinate to the husband, who is the head of the house." Poor v Poor (1836) 8 NH 307, 29 AD 664, 669 (Richardson,CJ)

6 Kelley v Kelley (1931) 51 R.I. 173, 153 Atl. 314, 74 ALR 135, 137, (Stearns, CJ) saying that "The rule of the common law that the legal identity of the wife was merged in that of her husband has long since been changed . . . The wife, by statute, in many respects is now held to be a distinct legal person; but she is not and never has been held to be in the same legal position as an unmarried woman."

7 And it has been said that the maxim "must continue to be recognized, however much modern laws enlarge the separate rights and privileges of each. Mary Morehead's Estate (1927) 289 Pa. 542, 137 A 802, 52 ALR 1251, 1258 (Frazer,J)

8 Phillips v Barnett (1876) LR 1 QBD 436, 440 (Lush,J); 25 Iowa LR (1940) 352

9 Dalrymple v Dalrymple (1811) 2 Hagg. 54, 4 Eng. Ecc. R 485

Where prudential reasons do not appear, that may cast doubt upon the fact of marriage. Sharon v Sharon (1888) 75 Cal. 1, 16 P 345, 357 (McKinstry,J)

10 See supra §127

11 "It seems to me it is rather late in the Christian era to claim that a secret marriage, or a contemporaneous agreement to keep the marriage secret, is opposed to good morals or public policy, in any sense which will render the marriage . . . void. . . . Such marriages have been held valid throughout Christendom ever since the sixth century, with some few exceptions, made by positive law, within the past two centuries. It goes without saying that there have always been secret marriages. They have always been condemned by the church and by the courts; and yet they have always been held legal. Sharon v Sharon (1888) 75 Cal. 1, 16 P 345, 368 (Temple,J)

12 Gen. 12:14-20

13 Change of names, see infra §280

14 Gen. 20:1-6

15 Gen. 26:7-11

[§209] The law imposes upon husband and wife the duty to "be fruitful and multiply"[16]—to "beget sons and daughters."[17] In point of time, if this be regarded as a "precept" as well as a "blessing," it is the first of all "commandments." It was given in the beginning to Adam and Eve, and was repeated in substance to Noah and his sons[18] and to Jacob.[19] The purpose of the rule is to "replenish the earth."[20] It is said that God "formed" the earth "to be inhabited,"[21] and that "children are a heritage of the Lord."[22] But not foolish[23] thankless,[24] ungodly or unprofitable children.[25] Better it is to die childless than to have such.[26]

[§210] In former times it was considered of much importance that a man, being married, should have children, and especially sons. It was therefore thought proper that a wife who was barren should send her husband to her "handmaid," that she might "have children by her."[27] And such children, being born "upon the knees" of the wife were regarded as her lawful children.[28]

Instances of this practice are not unknown in modern times. For example, one John Wilkinson, being desirous of having children to whom he might leave his property, and not expecting any from his wife, cohabited with a woman of his household, with his wife's knowledge and consent, and three children were born, in the dwellinghouse, which he always acknowledged as his children and which were brought up, maintained and educated at his expense.[29]

[§211] The husband is the head of the house[30] and "should bear rule" therein.[31] He "hath power of the body

---

16 Gen. 1:28
17 Jer. 29:6
18 Gen. 9:1
19 Gen. 35:11
20 Gen. 1:28
21 Isa. 45:18
22 Ps. 127:3
23 Prov. 17:21
24 "How sharper than a serpent's tooth it is to have a thankless child," quoted in Loar v Poling (1929) 107 W.Va. 280, 148 SE 114, 64 ALR 1246, 1249 (Maxwell,J)
25 Ecclesiasticus 16:1 ("Desire not a multitude of unprofitable children, neither delight in ungodly sons")
26 Ecclesiasticus 16:3
27 Gen. 16:1-6, 30:3,9
This was the counterpart of the rule requiring the brother of one dying without an heir to marry his widow. See supra §191.
In Hindu law, if a husband was unable to beget children "a son might

be begotten for him upon his wife by a kinsman appointed for that purpose." 16 Harv. LR (1902) 26 (Ayer)
28 Gen. 30:6 ("and Rachel said, God hath . . . given me a son")
29 Wilkinson v Adam (1813) 1 Ves. & Bea. 422-469, 25 Eng. Rul. Cas. 506
30 Poor v Poor (1836) 8 NH 307, 29 AD 664,669 (Richardson,J)
But not if he and his wife are living in the house of her father. In that case she and her children, if she has any, are under the control of the father-in-law. See Gen. 31:43; 14 Gr.B. (1902) 232 (Amram)
31 Est. 1:22 (decree of king Ahasuerus)
"Whether a man dominates his wife, or vice versa, is sometimes a very debatable question. Many a man fancies that he rules his wife when the reverse is the case." Jennings v Jennings (1919) 212 SW (Tex.Civ.App.) 772, 774 (Higgins,J)

of the wife"[32] and is entitled to obedience.[33] Accordingly it
has been thought to be the privilege of a husband to chastise
or restrain his wife for misbehavior,[34] as though she were
a daughter[35]—but being careful, if he had occasion to punish her, to use a switch no larger than his thumb[36] or a whip
no larger than could be passed through her wedding ring.[36a]
On the other hand it has been asserted that

> "Whatever the old books may say upon the subject, there never was,
> in the relation between husband and wife, when rightly understood, any-
> thing that gave to a husband the right to reduce a refractory wife to
> obedience by blows. And at this day the moral sense of the community
> revolts at the idea that a husband may inflict personal chastisement upon
> his wife, even for the most outrageous conduct."[37]

Concerning the duties of a husband, Biblical law requires
that he "cleave unto his wife"[38] and "forsake her not."[39]
He is bound to love his wife[40] if he can,[41] to "dwell" with
her "according to knowledge, giving honour unto the wife,
as unto the weaker vessel,"[42] and to render her "due benev-

---

32 1 Cor. 7:4
But he has no right to sell her when
he is no longer pleased with her.
Mosaic law put an end to that. 14
Gr.B. (1902) 344 (Amram)

33 See infra §215

34 1 Bl.Com. 445
By the law of England, where a
wife made an undue use of her liberty,
either by squandering away the husband's estate or going into lewd company, it was lawful for him, in order
to preserve his honor and estate, to lay
such a wife under restraint. Rex v
Lister (1721) 1 Strange 478; 15 Harv.
LR (1902) 640 (Peaslee)

35 And so she was, according to the
early Roman law. See 25 Iowa LR
(1940) 352

36 State v Oliver (1874) 70 NC 60,61
(Settle,J); Gill v Board of Commissioners (1912) 160 NC 176, 76 SE 203,
43 LRANS 293, 301 (Clark,CJ,dissenting)

36a Keller v Downey (1942) 161 SW
2d (Tex.Civ.App.) 803, 811 (Combs,J,
dissenting) intimating that the old rule
did not justify a husband's beating his
wife with a cat-o-nine tails on the
theory that that instrument could be
passed through his wife's wedding ring
one tail at a time.
But see Poor v Poor (1836) 8 NH
307, 29 AD 664, 672 (Richardson,CJ)
saying that "we entirely condemn the
use of the whip by the husband, as
unlawful and unmanly."
"It is difficult to conceive how a
man, who has promised, upon the altar
to love, comfort, honor, and keep a
woman, can lay rude and violent hands
upon her, without having malice and

cruelty in his heart." State v Oliver
(1874) 70 NC 60, 62 (Settle,J)

37 Poor v Poor (1836) 8 NH 307, 29
AD 664, 668 (Richardson,CJ) saying
further that "The blow given by the
husband in this case deserves the
severest censure. All must condemn it.
But I am much mistaken if the stubborn obstinacy with which the wife
set him at defiance, and the violence
she used in her rebellion against his
authority, will not, under all the circumstances, be quite as revolting to
the moral sense of an enlightened and
religious community as the unmanly
conduct of the husband."
The old doctrine that a husband may
use on his wife a switch no larger than
his thumb is not law in North Carolina.
The husband has no right to chastise
his wife under any circumstances.
State v Oliver (1874) 70 NC 60, 61
(Settle,J)

38 Gen. 2:24; Matt. 19:5; Mark 10:7,8;
1 Cor. 6:16; Eph. 5:31

39 Ecclesiasticus 7:26 ("Hast thou a
wife after thy mind? forsake her not:
but give not thyself over to a light
woman")

40 Eph. 5:25,33 ("Husbands, love your
wives, . . . let every one of you
in particular so love his wife even as
himself"); Col. 3:19

41 The law does not require impossibilities. Magnolia Petroleum Co. v Still
(1942) 163 SW2d (Tex.Civ.App.) 268, 270
(Johnson,CJ)

42 1 Pet. 3:7
A husband is bound to honor his
wife. Poor v Poor (1836) 8 NH 307,
29 AD 664, 669 (Richardson,CJ)

olence."[43]   And he is not to be "bitter" against her,[44] nor "jealous over" her.[45]   It is further provided that a husband shall not "take a wife to her sister, to vex her, to uncover her nakedness, beside the other in her life time."[46]

[§212]   —— Like the duty of a father to support his children,[47] the natural and primal obligation has been imposed immemorially upon the husband of maintaining and supporting his wife "in sickness and in health during life"[48] —unless she "departs" from him.[49]   It is declared that "if any provide not for his own, and especially for those of his own house, he hath denied the faith, and is worse than an infidel."[50]

[§213]   —— And it is doubtless incumbent upon a surviving husband to give decent burial to his deceased wife. So, although Abraham made no preparations for the burial of his wife Sarah before her death, he afterwards purchased "the field of Machpelah before Mamre"[1] and buried her in the cave thereof.[2]

[§214]   "The rights of the wife are those things which she may claim of her husband."[3]   When wives were purchased[4] or stolen, "as captives taken with the sword,"[5] a wife had no rights that the husband was bound to respect, unless out of fear of her father or brothers.[6]   She was a legal nonentity—not a person in law[7] but a mere chattel like a servant or slave.[8]   But in course of time it came to be recognized that a woman may choose her husband,[9] that

43 1 Cor. 7:3
At common law he had to pay debts that she contracted before their marriage.
44 Col. 3:19
45 Ecclesiasticus 9:1 ("Be not jealous over the wife of thy bosom, and teach her not an evil lesson against thyself")
46 Lev. 18:18   And see infra §403
47 See infra §225
48 Mary Morehead's Estate (1927) 289 Pa. 542, 137 Atl. 802, 52 ALR 1251, 1258, (Frazer,J)
At common law he is bound to support her "in a manner suitable to her situation and his condition." Poor v Poor (1836) 8 NH 307, 29 AD 664, 669 (Richardson,CJ)
49 See supra §204
50 1 Tim. 5:8
1 See supra §170
2 Gen. 23:19
Generally as to burial, see infra §290
3 Sharon v Sharon (1888) 75 Cal. 1, 16 P 345, 361 (McKinstry,J)

The wife's position under the Roman civil law: 15 Or. LR (1936) 291 (Daggett)
4 See supra §192
5 Gen. 31:26
6 See Gen. 31:1,2, 34:5,7
7 See supra §207
8 4 Harv. LR (1891) 353 (Holmes)
In early Roman history a woman became by marriage a daughter of her husband bringing her "under his hand." 25 Iowa LR (1940) 352
"Shakespeare, who was a fairly good lawyer, stated the law of England in his day when he made Petruchio say of his wife (Taming of the Shrew, Act II, Scene 2): 'I will be master of what is mine own, she is my goods, my chattels: she is my house, my household stuff, my field, my barn, my horse, my ox, my ass, my anything.'" Gill v Board of Commissioners (1912) 160 NC 176, 76 SE 203, 43 LRANS 293, 301 (Clark,CJ,dissenting)
9 See supra §189

he owes her certain duties,[10] and—rights and duties being correlative[11]—that she has corresponding rights which he is bound freely and liberally to accord to her.[12] So, for example, it is doubtless the right of a wife that her husband dwell with her[13] and support her,[14] and also that he accord her all reasonable liberty.[15] And it has been said that the wife "hath power" of the "body" of her husband.[16] Thus a wife has ceased to be the mere servant or slave of her husband, and has become "his companion, the partner and sharer of his fortune, in many respects his equal, who in her appropriate sphere is entitled to share largely in his authority."[17]

[§215] —— But a wife also owes duties to her husband. She is expressly commanded to love,[18] honour,[19] reverence[20] and obey him.[21] whether he be great or small,[22] "even as Sara obeyed Abraham."[23] And she is required to render him "due benevolence,"[24] and to "submit"[25] or "be in subjection" to her "own husband,"[26] "in every thing,"[27] as he is subject to the laws under which he lives[28] and "as the

10 See supra §§211, 212
11 See supra §126
12 "A husband is bound to accord to his wife freely and liberally all her rights, and to guarantee to her the full and free enjoyment of all her just privileges and prerogatives as the mistress of the family. In a particular manner he is bound to leave her free to enjoy her own religious opinions, and worship God according to the dictates of her own reason and conscience; and not to molest or restrain her in this respect, provided she does not in her zeal disturb the public peace, nor rebel against his lawful authority. Such is the equality and dignity which our laws confer upon the female character; and such the relation in which the husband and wife stand to one another." Poor v Poor (1836) 8 NH 307, 29 AD 664, 670 (Richardson,CJ)
13 See supra §211
14 See supra §212
A man's wives have claims upon his support in the order of their acquisition by him. Boyce v Boyce (1935?) —— NYSup.Ct. —— (Wenzel,J) where it appeared that a man was paying alimony of $1,000 a month to two ex-wives and was about to marry a third time. And see Ex. 21:10
15 Lister's Case (1721) 8 Mod. 22, saying a wife is entitled to reasonable liberty "if her behavior is not very bad."
16 1 Cor. 7:4 ("The wife hath not power of her own body, but the husband: and likewise also the husband hath not power of his own body, but the wife")

17 Poor v Poor (1836) 8 NH 307, 29 AD 664, 669 (Richardson,CJ)
18 Titus 2:4
19 Est. 1:20
20 Eph. 5:33
"An honest woman will reverence her husband." Ecclesiasticus 26:24
21 Titus 2:5
"Women are commanded to be under obedience." 1 Cor. 14:34
Tribute to a virtuous wife: Prov. 31:10-31
22 Est. 1:20 (decree of king Ahasuerus: "all wives shall give to their husbands honour, both to great and small")
23 1 Pet. 3:6
24 1 Cor. 7:3
"She that is married careth . . . how she may please her husband." 1 Cor. 7:34
25 "Wives, submit yourselves unto your own husbands." Eph. 5:22; Col. 3:18
"Let her submit to the authority of her husband, and remember that the dignity of a wife can not be violated by such submission." Poor v Poor (1836) 8 NH 307, 29 AD 664, 673 (Richardson,CJ)
26 1 Pet. 3:1
". . . in the old time the holy women also" were "in subjection unto their own husbands." 1 Pet. 3:5
27 Eph. 5:24
28 Poor v Poor (1836) 8 NH 307, 29 AD 664, 669 (Richardson,CJ) observing that a wife is wisely made subject in many things to the authority of her husband, as he is subject to the laws under which he lives.

church is subject unto Christ."[29] A woman who goes out in
open rebellion against her husband may not properly complain of ill treatment which she has wantonly provoked.[30]

[§216] —— In the case of Queen Vashti the rule was
established throughout the kingdom of the Medes and Persians that "every man should bear rule in his own house."[31]
It appears that when king Ahasuerus "was merry with wine,
he commanded . . . the seven chamberlains . . . to bring
Vashti the queen before the king with the crown royal, to
shew the people and the princes her beauty: for she was
fair to look on."

"But the queen Vashti refused to come at the king's commandment
by his chamberlains: therefore was the king very wroth, and his anger
burned in him.
"Then the king said to the wise men, which knew the times . . .
"What shall we do unto the queen Vashti according to law, because
she hath not performed the commandment of the king, Ahasuerus, by
the chamberlains?
"And Memucan answered before the king and the princes, Vashti the
queen hath not done wrong to the king only, but also to all the princes,
and to all the people that are in all the provinces of the king Ahasuerus.
"For this deed of the queen shall come abroad unto all women, so
that they shall despise their husbands in their eyes, when it shall be
reported, The king Ahasuerus commanded Vashti the queen to be
brought in before him, but she came not.
"Likewise shall the ladies of Persia and Media say this day unto all
the king's princes, which have heard of the deed of the queen. Thus
shall there arise too much contempt and wrath.
"If it please the king, let there go a royal commandment from him,
and let it be written among the laws of the Persians and the Medes,
that it be not altered, That Vashti come no more before king Ahasuerus;
and let the king give her royal estate unto another that is better than
she.
"And the saying pleased the king and the princes; and the king did
according to the word of Memucan."[32]

[§217] Mosaic law provides for an "ordeal" or "trial
of jealousy" that was to be had "when a wife goeth aside
to another instead of her husband, and is defiled, or when
the spirit of jealousy cometh upon him, and he be jealous
over his wife."[33] If it happens that the prescribed test dis-
closes that the woman is guilty, she "shall be a curse among

29 Eph. 5:24
30 Poor v Poor (1836) 8 NH 307, 29
AD 664, 666 (Richardson,CJ) saying:
"if a wife chooses so to act and to
talk as to raise a storm in the temper
of an irritable husband, it is doing her
no injustice to say to her, when it has
come attended only with harsh and
abusive language, that she has had in
its peltings her just and merited reward. However reprehensible his conduct may have been in this respect, she
is not to be heard, when she would
complain of it."
31 See supra §211
32 Est. 1:10-21
33 Num. 5:29,30; 14 Harv. LR (1901)
511 (Thayer)
  Husband not to be jealous, see supra
§211

her people,"[34] but if she "be not defiled, but clean; then she shall be free."[35]

CHAPTER 32

PARENT AND CHILD

[§218]   The law recognizes a relationship between parent and child,[36] implying certain mutual rights and duties[37] not only during the period of infancy but also after the child has attained its majority and ceased to be a minor.[38] This relationship may arise as a result of the natural birth of the child[39] or through its adoption.[40]

Though Biblical law admits of the "correction"[41] of children and requires that they be "obedient,"[42] yet it is solicitous of their welfare.   Thus it appears that Jesus commanded his hearers to "suffer little children, and forbid them not, to come unto me,"[43] and that he warned them to "take heed that ye despise not one of these little ones."[44]

[§219]   Adoption is a ceremony by which one makes another his legal child and heir.[45]   The practice seems to have originated in Babylon and "to have taken root in Egypt."[46]

34 Num. 5:27
35 Num. 5:28
36 As to the parent and child relation in the patriarchal days, see the story of the sacrifice of Jephthah's daughter. Judges 11:34-40
Proceeding for establishment of paternity, see infra §220
37 See infra §222 et seq.
38 The Talmud (see §15) divided minority into three periods: (1) infancy, from birth until six years of age; (2) impubescence, from the seventh to the thirteenth year, and (3) adolescence, from the thirteenth to the twentieth year. It may be inferred that one attained his majority at the age of twenty. 38 Case & Comment (1932) No. 2, p 4
39 Legitimacy of child born to wife's handmaid, see supra §210
40 See infra §219
41 See infra §222

42 See infra §228
43 Matt. 19:14; Mark 10:14; Luke 18:16; White v Richeson (1906) 94 SW (Tex. Civ.App.) 202, 204 (Neill,J)
44 Matt. 18:10
45 Hehr's Adm'r. v Hehr (1941) 157 SW2d (Ky.) 111, 113 (Stanley,C)
The person adopted was probably taken into the family that had no children, for the purpose of keeping the family alive and providing an heir. 14 Gr.B. (1902) 493 (Amram)
The adoptor and the person adopted may or may not be related by blood. It is immaterial.
46 Hockaday v Lynn (1906) 200 Mo. 456, 98 SW 585, 118 ASR 672 (Lamm,J) observing further that the Babylonian code of Hammurabi, compiled from 2285 to 2242 B.C., section 185, provided, "If a man has taken a young child 'from his waters' to sonship, and has reared him up, no one has any possible claim against that nursling."

Adoptions undoubtedly were of rather frequent occurrence among the ancient Hebrews,[47] and were familiar to the writers of the Bible.[48]

Abram seems to have adopted Eliezer as his heir **apparent**, and he occupied that position until the birth of Isaac.[49] Jacob adopted Ephraim and Manasseh, sons of Joseph, saying "And now thy two sons . . . are mine; as Reuben and Simeon, they shall be mine."[50] Pharaoh's daughter adopted Moses; it is said that the child Moses grew and his mother brought him unto Pharaoh's daughter, "and he became her son."[1] And Mordecai, who appears to have been childless, seems to have adopted Esther, his uncle's daughter. "When her father and mother were dead," he took her "for his own daughter."[2]

[§220]   The paternity of children may be legally determined in suits brought for that purpose.[3]   Thus Biblical law provides that when a wife "hath . . . brought children by another man (than her own husband), she shall be brought out into the congregation, and inquisition shall be made of her children."[4]   But suit may be brought not alone to adjudge whether a certain man, though he deny it, is a child's father; it may also be brought to determine which of two women, where both claim it, is a child's mother.[5]

[§221] ——— The Case of the Two Harlots was tried before king Solomon. It is related that "two women, that were harlots came unto the king and stood before him."

"And this one woman said, O my lord, I and this woman dwell in one house; and I was delivered of a child with her in the house.

47 14 Gr.B. (1902) 493 (Amram)

48 "Paul assumed the doctrine of adoption to be well known to his readers, and borrows the use of the doctrine as a hammer to clinch nails driven by him on matters of faith." Hockaday v Lynn (1906) 200 Mo. 456, 98 SW 585, 118 ASR 672 (Lamm,J) citing Rom. 8:16,17
  But the English law did not recognize adoption. Vidal v Commagere (1858) 13 La.Ann. 516 (Merrick,CJ); Morrison v Sessions' Estate (1888) 70 Mich. 297, 38 NW 249, 14 ASR 500 (Champlin,J)

49 Gen. 15:2,3; 14 Gr.B. (1902) 493 (Amram)

50 Gen. 48:5

1 Ex. 2:10
  The adoption of Moses was doubtless in conformity with Primitive law. His mother "took for him an ark of bulrushes, and daubed it with slime and with pitch, and put the child therein; and she laid it in the flags by the river's brink." Her action constituted an abandonment of the child or a public offer of the child for adoption. "And the daughter of Pharaoh came down to wash herself at the river . . . and when she saw the ark among the flags, she sent her maid to fetch it. And when she had opened it, she saw the child: and, behold, the babe wept. And she had compassion on him . . . And the maid went and called the child's mother. And Pharaoh's daughter said unto her, Take this child away, and nurse it for me, and I will give thee thy wages. And the woman took the child and nursed it. And the child grew, and she brought him unto Pharaoh's daughter, and he became her son. And she called his name Moses: and she said, Because I drew him out of the water. Ex. 2:3, 5,6,8-10

2 Est. 2:7,15; 14 Gr.B. (1902) 493 (Amram)

3 See 3 RCL 750

4 Ecclesiasticus 23:23,24

5 See infra §221

"And it came to pass the third day after that I was delivered, that this woman was delivered also; and we were together; there was no stranger with us in the house, save we two in the house.

"And this woman's child died in the night; because she overlaid it.

"And she arose at midnight, and took my son from beside me, while thine handmaid slept, and laid it in her bosom, and laid her dead child in my bosom.

"And when I rose in the morning to give my child suck, behold it was dead: but when I had considered it in the morning, behold, it was not my son, which I did bear.

"And the other woman said, Nay; but the living is my son, and the dead is thy son. And this said, No; but the dead is thy son, and the living is my son. Thus they spake before the king.

"Then said the king, The one saith, This is my son that liveth, and thy son is the dead; and the other saith, Nay; but thy son is the dead, and my son is the living.

"And the king said, Bring me a sword. And they brought a sword before the king.

"And the king said, Divide the living child in two, and give half to the one, and half to the other.

"Then spake the woman whose the living child was unto the king, for her bowels yearned upon her son, and she said, O my lord, give her the living child, and in no wise slay it. But the other said, Let it be neither mine nor thine, but divide it.

"Then the king answered and said, Give her the living child, and in no wise slay it: she is the mother thereof.

"And all Israel heard of the judgment which the king had judged; and they feared the king: for they saw that the wisdom of God was in him, to do judgment."[6]

[§222] According to Biblical law, a father and mother are entitled to receive "honour"[7] and "obedience"[8] from their children.[9] And it is not only their natural and legal right, but also their express and positive duty to chasten,[10] correct[11] and reprove[12] their children,[13] to command or teach them to observe the law,[14] and to instruct[15] and train them "in the way" they "should go."[16]

6　1 Kings 3:16-28
"King Solomon's philosophy was apparently . . . that the interests of the child . . . could best be entrusted to the woman who bore the child most affection." 46 Case & Comment (1941) No. 4, p 10 (Taylor,J, Kings County [N.Y.] Court)

7　Ecclesiasticus 3:2 ("the Lord hath given the father honour over the children")

8　Ecclesiasticus 3:2 ("the Lord . . . hath confirmed the authority of the mother over the sons")

9　See infra §229

10　Prov. 19:18; Heb. 12:7,8

11　Prov. 22:15, 23:13,14 29:17; Ecclesiasticus 42:15

12　Prov. 29:15

13　Two Ways 4:9 ("Thou shalt not remove thy hand from thy son, or from thy daughter, but from youth up shall teach them the fear of God")

14　Deut. 32:46

15　Ecclesiasticus 7:23

16　"Train up a child in the way he should go: and when he is old, he will not depart from it." Prov. 22:6, quoted in 14 Or. LR (1934-1935) 454, and in In re Schein (1937) 156 Or. 661, 668, 69 P2d 298 (Campbell,J)
"It is common knowledge that those who are taught to respect parental authority in their early years also conform to the laws of the land and the conventions of society throughout their adult life." In re Schein, supra

[§223] —— In Primitive law, a father was regarded as the owner of his children. He had absolute control of them,[17] even the power of life and death.[18] They were his property,[19] and he could sell them as though they were cattle,[20] or they might be seized and sold by his creditor to satisfy a debt.[21]

Vestiges of the ancient law have survived to modern times,[22] for a father still has legal control over his children[23] within reasonable limits. He is ordinarily entitled to their custody[24] and services.[25] But they are no longer considered property[26] and cannot be made the subject of a contract.[27] And Biblical law forbids a father to "provoke" his children to anger, "lest they be discouraged."[28]

[§224] —— More specific instructions are given in Ecclesiasticus with respect to the care and training of children. As to sons it is said:

"He that loveth his son causeth him oft to feel the rod, that he may have joy in him in the end."[29]

"He that maketh too much of his son shall bind up his wounds; and his bowels will be troubled at every cry.

". . . a child left to himself will be wilful.[30]

"Give him no liberty in his youth, and wink not at his follies.[31]

17 A father had control of his daughters after they were married if they remained in his house. Gen. 31:43; 14 Gr.B. (1902) 232 (Amram)

And even when they left their father's household, it seems that he had power to take them from their husbands. So Samson's father-in-law took Sampson's wife from him and gave her to a companion (Judges 15:2), and king Saul took his daughter Michal from David and gave her to another man (1 Sam. 25:44).

18 Gen. 22:10 ("And Abraham stretched forth his hand, and took the knife to slay his son [Isaac]"); Judges 11:39 (Jephthah offered up his daughter for a burnt offering)

19 14 Gr. B. (1902) 232 (Amram)

20 "It was common for the father to sell his daughter as a wife or as a bondwoman." 14 Gr. B. (1902) 232 (Amram)

Laban sold his daughters, Leah and Rachel, for seven years' labor for each of them. Gen. 29:18-29. See supra §§148, 192

21 2 Kings 4:1 ("the creditor is come to take unto him my two sons to be bondmen"); Matt. 18:25 ("forasmuch as he had not to pay, his lord commanded him to be sold, and his wife, and children, and all that he had, and payment to be made")

22 Maine's Anc. L. p 133

23 Control of children is parental. Harfst v Hoegen (1942) 163 SW2d (Mo.) 609, 613, 141 ALR 1136 (Douglas,J)

24 But "it is universally recognized that the mother is the natural custodian of her young . . . In the case of girls it is obvious that they are particularly in need of the sympathy, affection, consideration and tender care which only a mother can give—and so normally they should be in her custody." Washburn v Washburn (1942) 49 Cal.App. 2d 581, 588, 122 P2d 96 (Hanson,J pro tem)

25 "The father is entitled to the services of his sons while they live with him, but however strange it may appear, the mother has no such right." Commonwealth v Murray (1812) 4 Binney (Pa.) 487, 494 (Yeates,J)

26 In suits involving children, courts are no longer governed by the so-called natural rights of the parents. In such a case the supposed welfare of the child is the chief consideration. See 17 Am Jur 517

27 White v Richardson (1906) 94 SW (Tex.Civ.App.) 202, 204 (Neill,J)

28 Col. 3:21

"Provoke not your children to wrath: but bring them up in the nurture and admonition of the Lord." Eph. 6:4

29 Ecclesiasticus 30:1

30 Ecclesiasticus 30:7,8

31 Ecclesiasticus 30:11

"Chastise thy son, and hold him to labour, lest his lewd behavior be an offence unto thee."[32]

And concerning daughters, it is directed to "have a care of their body, and shew not thyself cheerful toward them."[33]

"If thy daughter be shameless, keep her in straitly, lest she abuse herself through overmuch liberty.[34]

"Keep a sure watch over a shameless daughter."[35]

[§225]　——　A natural and moral obligation rests upon a father to support his child,[36] even though its mother is not his lawful wife and the child is therefore called illegitimate.[37] Indeed it has been said that "the duty of a father to support and care for his helpless minor offspring is enjoined by the law of God."[38] And St. Paul intimates that parents ought to "lay up," that is, make financial provision, for their children.[39]

[§226]　——　Under Biblical law, one of the duties of parents is to see that their children are suitably married. It is incumbent upon them to take wives for their sons, and give their daughters to husbands.[40] As to the marriage of daughters, it is directed to "marry (off) thy daughter, and so shalt thou have performed a weighty matter; but give her to a man of understanding."[41] And upon the marriage of a daughter, it is customary and proper that her parents make her a suitable gift.[42]

[§227]　Children are entitled, no doubt, to receive maintenance[43] and protection from their parents.[44] On the other hand, as regards the duties of children, the so-called "first commandment with promise"[45] is to "fear"[46] or "honour thy

---

32 Ecclesiasticus 30:13
33 Ecclesiasticius 7:24
34 Ecclesiasticus 26:10
35 Ecclesiasticus 42:11
36 "The duty of parents to provide for the maintenance of their children, is a principle of natural law; an obligation . . . laid on them not only by nature itself, but by their own proper act, in bringing them into the world: for they would be in the highest manner injurious to their issue, if they only gave their children life, that they might afterwards see them perish." 1 Bl. Com. 447
Duty to support wife, see supra §212
37 Hehr's Admr. v Hehr (1941) 157 SW2d (Ky.) 111, 113 (Stanley,C)
A bastard has a right of support from his natural father. 14 Harv.LR (1901) 23 (Ayer)
38 Forbes v Jennings (1928) 124 Or. 497, 264 P 856 (McBride,J)
But no passage has been noticed that

expresses the father's duty in this regard. It was doubtless taken for granted.
39 2 Cor. 12:14
40 Jer. 29:6
41 Ecclesiasticus 7:25
42 See Gen. 29:24,29
Dowry, see supra §192
43 Duty of parent to support children, see supra §225
Blackstone said that children have "a perfect right of receiving maintenance from their parents." 1 Bl.Com. 447
44 "The arm" of a father "should protect" his child. Stanton v Willson's Executors (1808) 3 Day (Conn.) 37, 3 AD 225, 259
And under modern statutes, a parent is authorized to use "any necessary force" to protect a child "from wrongful injury." See Cal.Civ.Code (1872) §50
45 Eph. 6:2
46 Lev. 19:3

father and mother"[47] "both in word and deed"[48] and "with thy whole heart,"[49] "all the days of thy life,"[50] "that it may be well with thee[1] and thou mayest live long on the earth."[2] This commandment extends to the wife of a son, who is bound to honour her father-in-law and mother-in-law who, by the marriage, become her parents in the sight of the law.[3]

[§228] —— The duty of "honouring" father and mother[4] includes the obligation of rendering them due obedience.[5] Moreover it is expressly commanded that children obey their parents[6] "in all things"[7]—"for this is right."[8] According to this commandment, Esther the adopted daughter of Mordecai, even after she had become the wife of the king, "did the commandment" of her foster father "like as when she was brought up with him."[9] Also the sons of Jonadab obeyed the voice of their father "to drink no wine . . . nor to build houses . . . to dwell in."[10]

But "protection and obedience are relative duties"[11] and it has been said that—

"When the wisdom that should guide the infant is lost in delirium, and the arm that should protect, and the hand that should feed him is lifted for his destruction, obedience is no longer a duty, and the child cannot, with any propriety, be said to be under the government of a father."[12]

On the other hand, children are commanded not to curse,[13] mock,[14] or rob their parents,[15] nor to "set light by"[16] or "smite" them.[17] But a child, as well as an adult, is entitled to rest on the Sabbath day.[18]

---

47 Ex. 20:12; Deut. 5:16; Matt. 15:4, 19:19; Mark 7:10, 10:19; Luke 18:20; Eph. 6:2
48 Ecclesiasticus 3:8
49 Ecclesiasticus 7:27
50 Tobit 4:3
1 Eph. 6:5
". . . that it may go well with thee . . ." Deut. 5:16
2 Eph. 6:3
". . . that thy days may be long upon the land which the Lord thy God giveth thee." Ex. 20:12
". . . that thy days may be prolonged." Deut. 5:16
3 Tobit 10:12. See supra §187, n 10
4 See supra §227
5 Respect as including obedience, see §109
6 Eph. 6:1
"My son, keep thy father's commandment, and forsake not the law of thy mother." Prov. 6:20

7 Col. 3:20
8 Eph. 6:1
". . . for this is well pleasing unto the Lord." Col. 3:20
9 Est. 2:20
10 Jer. 35:8,9
11 Rights and duties as correlative, see supra §126
12 Stanton v Willson's Executors (1808) 3 Day (Conn.) 37, 3 AD 255, 259
13 Ex. 21:17; Lev. 20:9; Prov. 20:20; Matt. 15:4; Mark 7:10
14 Prov. 30:17
15 Prov. 28:24 ("Whoso robbeth his father or his mother, and saith, It is no transgression, the same is the companion of a destroyer")
16 Deut. 27:16; Ezek. 22:7
17 Ex. 21:15
18 See infra §319

[§229] —— It is incumbent upon children, whatever their age or maturity, to "recompense" their father and mother, in some measure, "the things that they have done" for them.[19] Thus, it is the duty of a child to "hearken" unto his father,[20] to help him "in his age,"[21] and not to "despise him . . . when thou are in thy full strength,"[22] nor "grieve him . . . as long as he liveth,"[23] nor "forsake him.[24] Similarly, it is a child's duty to "do that which shall please" his mother,[25] and not to anger her,[26] nor "despise" her "when she is old,"[27] nor grieve her,[28] nor forget her "sorrows."[29]

[§230] —— Under Primitive law it was considered a duty of the surviving son or sons to attend to the burial of a deceased father or mother, and several instances of the performance of this last duty are mentioned. Thus, it is said that Isaac and Ishmael buried Abraham, though Abraham had long previously banished Ishmael and his mother;[30] Esau and Jacob buried their father Isaac;[31] Joseph and his brethren buried their father Jacob;[32] and the sons of Mattathias buried him "in the sepulchres of his fathers."[33] Tobit commanded his son Tobias, "when I am dead, bury me, . . . and when she (thy mother) is dead, bury her by me in one grave."[34] And Tobias "honourably" buried his father and mother, and also his father-in-law and mother-in-law.[35]

[§231] —— According to a Jewish custom or "tradition" prevalent at the beginning of the Christian era, a son might "emancipate" or free himself from any further obligation to his parents. The rule was that—

"Whosoever shall say to his father or his mother, It is a gift, by whatsoever thou mightest be profited by me;
"And honour not his father or his mother, he shall be free . . ."[36]

And being emancipated, the son was entitled to receive "the

---

19 Ecclesiasticus 7:28 ("how canst thou recompense them . . . ?")
"Remember thy father and thy mother when thou sittest among great men." Ecclesiasticus 23:14
20 Prov. 23:33
21 Ecclesiasticus 3:12
22 Ecclesiasticus 3:13
23 Ecclesiasticus 3:12
24 Ecclesiasticus 3:16 ("He that forsaketh his father is as a blasphemer")
25 Tobit 4:3
26 Ecclesiasticus 3:16 ("he that angereth his mother is cursed of God")
27 Prov. 23:22; Tobit 4:3
When "she that hath (had) many children is waxed feeble." 1 Sam. 2:5

28 Tobit 4:3
29 Ecclesiasticus 7:27
30 Gen. 25:9
31 Gen. 35:29
32 Gen. 50:6,12,13
33 1 Mac. 2:70
34 Tobit 4:3,4
35 Tobit 14:11-13
36 Matt. 15:5,6; Mark 7:11,12
In modern law, a child may be emancipated by permanent departure from the family home with the consent of the father, but not by a mere departure from home to obtain employment. See 1 Jones' Bl.Com. (1916) 639 n.

portion of goods" that should come to him out of his father's property.[37]

Jesus disapproved of the emancipation rule as being a transgression of the commandment that a child honor his father and mother.[38]

CHAPTER 33

MASTER AND SERVANT

[§232]   In Biblical law, the topic of "master and servant" deals with the ancient relation of the master of the household and his domestic servants or slaves, who labored about the house or homestead and were recognized as members of the master's family—occupying a position somewhat inferior, no doubt, to that of his wife or wives and his children.[39]   The rules pertaining to "free" or "hired" servants are given attention in a subsequent chapter.[40]

It is a self-evident truth in the law of servants—whether they be bond or free—that "no man can serve two masters:[41] for either he will hate the one, and love the other; or else he will hold to the one, and despise the other."[42]   And it is forbidden to "accuse . . . a servant unto his master, lest he curse thee, and thou be found guilty."[43]

[§233]   Among the ancients, "bond-service" and "slavery" were not ordinarily regarded as improper or unlawful.[44]   But

---

37   Luke 15:12
Receiving his portion cut him off from further sharing in his father's property. See Luke 15:31, where the father said to the son who had remained at home, "all that I have is thine."
"If a son says to his father and his mother, 'Thou art not my father nor my mother' he shall abandon the house, field, plantation, and other property, but his own full portion shall be delivered to him by his father. His father and his mother shall say to him, 'Thou are not our son'; and he shall go out from the place." Sumerian Code, ¶4

38   Matt. 15:3,6; Mark 7:13

39   But it has been said that a child "differeth nothing from a servant." Gal. 4:1

40   See infra §§251-260

41   Matt. 6:24; Century Indemnity Co. v Carnes (1940) 138 SW2d (Tex.Civ. App.) 555, 560 (Speer,J)
"No servant can serve two masters." Luke 16:13; McAllister v Marshall (1814) 6 Binney (Pa.) 338, 6 AD 458, 464 (Brackenridge,J)

42   Matt. 6:24
"The voice of divinity, speaking from within the sublimest incarnation known to all history, proclaimed and emphasized the maxim nearly two thousand years ago on occasions of infinite sacredness."   Stockton Plumbing Co. v Wheeler (1924) 68 Cal.App. 592, 229 P 1020, 1024 (Hart,J)

43   Prov. 30:10

44   Isaac had a "great store of servants." Gen. 26:14
Joseph was sold for a servant: Gen. 37:28; Ps. 105:17

it was not intended that Israelites should be bond-servants.[45] Mosaic law provided that—

". . . my servants, which I brought forth out of the land of Egypt . . . shall not be sold as bondmen.

"Both thy bondmen, and thy bondmaids, which thou shalt have, shall be of the heathen that are round about you; of them shall ye buy bondmen and bondmaids.

"Moreover, of the children of the strangers that do sojourn among you, of them shall ye buy, and of their families that are with you, which they begat in your land: and they shall be your possession.

"And ye shall take them as an inheritance for your children after you, to inherit them for a possession; they shall be your bondmen for ever; but over your brethren the children of Israel, ye shall not rule one over another with rigor."[46]

Formerly a man might renounce his liberty and make himself a slave.[47] But this is seemingly forbidden by Christian law. It is said to be not "the servant of men"[48] nor "entangled again with the yoke of bondage."[49]

[§234] Though the holding of Israelites as bond-servants was forbidden,[50] Mosaic law nevertheless placed a limitation upon the length of service of a "Hebrew manservant," declaring that—

"If thou buy a Hebrew servant, six years he shall serve: and in the seventh he shall go out free for nothing.

"If he came in by himself, he shall go out by himself; if he were married, then his wife shall go out with him.

"If his master have given him a wife, and she have born him sons or daughters; the wife and her children shall be her master's, and he shall go out by himself.

"And if the servant shall plainly say, I love my master, my wife, and my children; I will not go out free;

"Then his master shall bring him unto the judges; he shall also bring him to the door, or unto the door post; and his master shall bore his ear through with an awl; and he shall serve him for ever."[1]

But the law forbade one, when freeing such a servant, to "let him go empty,"[2] providing to the contrary that "Thou shalt furnish him liberally out of thy flock, and out of thy floor, and out of thy winepress."[3]

[§235] —— Concerning a daughter that had been sold as a maidservant, Mosaic law provided that—

---

45 1 Kings 9:22 (saying that Solomon made no bondmen of the children of Israel); and see Judith 16:23 (stating that Judith "made her maid free" before she died)

And "the air of England has long been too pure for a slave, and every man is free who breathes it." Lord Mansfield (48 YaleLJ [1939] 495

46 Lev. 25:42,44-46

47 22 Geo. LJ (1934) 430
48 1 Cor. 7:23
49 Gal. 5:1
50 See supra §233

1 Ex. 21:2-6; and see Deut. 15:12, 16-18

Length of service by hired servant, see infra §256

2 Deut. 15:13
3 Deut. 15:14

". . . if a man sell his daughter to be a maidservant, she shall not go out as the menservants do.

"If she please not her master, who hath betrothed her to himself, then shall he let her be redeemed: to sell her unto a strange nation he shall have no power, seeing he hath dealt deceitfully with her.

"And if he have betrothed her unto his son, he shall deal with her after the manner of daughters.

"If he take him another wife; her food, her raiment, and her duty of marriage, shall he not diminish.

"And if he do not these three unto her, then shall she go out free without money."[4]

[§236] —— Mosaic law provided that liberty should be "proclaimed throughout all the land unto all the inhabitants thereof" on the fiftieth year[5]—the year of jubilee.[6] And king Zedekiah "made a covenant with all the people which were at Jerusalem, to proclaim liberty unto them."[7]

"That every man should let his manservant, and every man his maidservant, being an Hebrew or an Hebrewess, go free; that none should serve himself of them, to wit, of a Jew his brother."[8]

But it appears that "when all the princes, and all the people" had obeyed the covenant and let their Hebrew servants go, "they turned, and caused the servants and the handmaids, whom they had let go free, to return, and brought them into subjection for servants and for handmaids."[9] And because of their repudiation of the covenant, Jeremiah condemned Zedekiah, the princes, priests and people, to be given "unto the hands of their enemies."[10]

[§237] —— With respect to the redemption of "a poor Hebrew" who had sold himself to "a rich sojourner or stranger," Mosaic law prescribed that—

". . . one of his brethren may redeem him:

"Either his uncle, or his uncle's son, may redeem him, or any that is nigh of kin unto him of his family may redeem him; or if he be able, he may redeem himself.

"And he shall reckon with him that bought him from the year that he was sold to him unto the year of jubilee: and the price of his sale shall be according unto the number of years, according to the time of a hired servant shall it be with him.

"If there be yet many years behind, according unto them he shall give again the price of his redemption out of the money that he was bought for.

"And if there remain but few years unto the year of jubilee, then he shall count with him, and according unto his years shall he give him again the price of his redemption.

---

4 Ex. 21:7-11
5 Lev. 25:10
6 See infra §269
7 Jer. 34:8

8 Jer. 34:9
9 Jer. 34:10,11
10 Jer. 34:19-21

"And as a yearly hired servant shall he be with him: and the other shall not rule with rigor over him in thy sight.

"And if he be not redeemed in these years, then he shall go out in the year of jubilee, both he, and his children with him."[11]

[§238] —— Though Mosaic law permitted bond-service, it forbade the forcible return of a fugitive servant to his master. In this connection it is expressly provided that

"Thou shalt not deliver unto his master the servant which is escaped from his master unto thee; He shall dwell with thee, even among you, in that place which he shall choose in one of thy gates, where it liketh him best: thou shalt not oppress him."[12]

Under this rule it was incumbent upon a master to guard against the escape of his servant, for if he broke away from his master, as many did at times,[13] the law afforded no relief.

[§239] Broadly speaking, the master could do as he pleased with his servant.[14] At least, he might correct him and make him work.

". . . bread, correction and work, (are) for a servant.

"If thou set thy servant to labour, thou shalt find rest: but if thou let him go idle, he shall seek liberty.

"A yoke and a collar do bow the neck: so are tortures and torments for an evil servant.[15]

"Send him to labour, that he be not idle; for idleness teacheth much evil.

"Set him to work, as is fit for him: if he be not obedient, put on more heavy fetters."[16]

But a master ought to give his servant "that which is just and equal;"[17] he should not "defraud him of liberty"[18] or threaten him;[19] nor should a master evilly "entreat" a servant that "worketh truly."[20] On the contrary, it is directed to—

". . . be not excessive toward any; and without discretion do nothing.

"If thou have a servant, let him be unto thee as thyself, because thou hast bought him with a price.

"If thou have a servant, entreat him as a brother: for thou hast need of him, as of thine own soul: if thou entreat him evil, and he run from thee, which way wilt thou go to seek him?"[21]

---

11 Lev. 25:47-54

12 Deut. 23:15,16

13 ". . . there be many servants nowadays that break away every man from his master." 1 Sam. 25:10

14 Gen. 16:6 ("Abram said unto Sarai, Behold, thy maid is in thy hand; do to her as it pleaseth thee," and Sarai "dealt hardly" with Hagar, so that "she fled from her face")

15 Ecclesiasticus 42:1,5 ("be not thou ashamed . . . to make the side of an evil servant to bleed")

16 Ecclesiasticus 33:24-28

17 Col. 4:1

18 Ecclesiasticus 7:21 ("Let thy soul love a good servant, and defraud him not of liberty")

19 Eph. 6:9 ("And, ye masters . . . forbear . . .threatening")

20 Ecclesiasticus 7:20

21 Ecclesiastcius 33:29-31

"Thou shalt not command thy servant or thy handmaiden, who hope on the same God, in thy bitterness, lest they fear not the God who is over both." Two Ways 4:10

[§240] —— Though a master might "correct" his servant,[22] he had no right to kill or seriously injure him. To the contrary, it is provided that

". . . if a man smite his servant, or his maid, with a rod, and he die under his hand: he shall be surely punished.

"Notwithstanding, if he continue a day or two, he shall not be punished: for he is his money."[23]

"And if a man smite the eye of his servant, or the eye of his maid, that it perish; he shall let him go free for his eye's sake.

"And if he smite out his manservant's tooth, or his maidservant's tooth; he shall let him go free for his tooth's sake."[24]

A master was entitled to damages for injury to his servant by the wrongful act of another. Thus, in case a manservant or maidservant was gored by an ox belonging to another, the latter was required to pay the master 30 shekels of silver.[25]

[§241] The law recognized that a servant had certain rights. Thus as between several servants, in the same household, the eldest was entitled to the rank of seniority—the "eldest servant" of Abraham's house "ruled over all that he had."[26] And in some cases, a servant might achieve the status of a son—"a wise servant shall have rule over a son that causeth shame, and shall have part of the inheritance among the brethren."[27] A servant was entitled also to rest on the Sabbath.[28] And when the master mistreated or threatened a servant, he might flee to save himself from death or serious injury.[29] If the master maimed him,[30] so as to cause the loss of an eye or tooth, he was entitled to his freedom.[31] On the other hand, a servant was bound to honour,[32] obey[33] and please his master in all things;[34] to subject[35] or submit himself to the master;[36] to render him faithful,[37] hearty[38] and willing service;[39] and not to "answer"[40] or despise him;[41] nor purloin

22 See supra §239
23 Ex. 21:20,21
24 Ex. 21:26,27
25 Ex. 21:32
26 Gen. 24:2
27 Prov. 17:2
"Thou art no more a servant but a son." Gal. 4:7
28 See infra §319
29 See Gen. 16:6 (stating that Hagar fled when Sarai dealt hardly with her)
30 See infra §362
31 See supra §240
32 1 Tim. 6:1 ("Let . . . servants . . . count their own masters worthy of all honour . . .")
33 Eph. 6:5; Col. 3:22; Titus 2:9
34 Titus 2:9 ("Exhort servants . . . to please them [their masters] well in all things")

35 1 Pet. 2:18 ("Servants, be subject to your masters with all fear; not only to the good and gentle, but also to the froward")
"And ye, servants, shall be subject to your masters, as to a type of God, in modesty and fear." Two Ways 4:11
36 Gen. 16:7,9 ("And the angel of the Lord found her [Hagar] . . . and said unto her, Return to thy mistress, and submit thyself unto her hands")
37 Titus 2:10 ("shewing all good fidelity")
38 Col. 3:23 ("And whatsoever ye do, do it heartily, as to the Lord, and not unto men")
39 Eph. 6:7 ("With good will doing service, as to the Lord, and not to men")
40 Titus 2:9
41 1 Tim. 6:2

from him.[42] In particular, it was required of a steward that he be "faithful,"[43] and that he give an account of his stewardship when he may be no longer steward.[44] And a servant might not take advantage of his position by secretly receiving for himself gifts from one who had received benefits at the hands of his master.[45]

CHAPTER 34

HOST AND GUEST

242 In general   243 Duties of the host   244 Rights and duties of the guest

[§242] In former times, it was considered that one should "receive" a stranger[46]or traveller, lest he be obliged to lodge in the street.[47] So Abraham set food before three men who "appeared unto him in the plains of Mamre," as "he sat in the tent door in the heat of the day," and "he stood by them under the tree" as "they did eat."[48] And Lot, sitting "at even . . . in the gate of Sodom" and seeing two strangers, "rose up to meet them: and he bowed himself with his face toward the ground;"

"And he said, Behold now, my lords, turn in, I pray you, into your servant's house, and tarry all night, and wash your feet, and ye shall rise up early, and go on your ways. And they said, Nay; but we will abide in the street all night.

"And he pressed upon them greatly; and they turned in unto him, and entered into his house."[49]

Much later, Publius, the chief man of the island of Melita, received St. Paul and others and lodged them three days,[50] and St. Paul, when dwelling in his hired house at Rome, received all that came in unto him."[1] On the other hand Diotrephes, being a malicious man, did not receive the brethren, and forbade them that would.[2]

But, though it was customary to open one's door to strangers or travellers[3] if there was room for them,[4] it was not ex-

---

42 Titus 2:10
43 1 Cor. 4:2
44 Luke 16:2, quoted in McAllister v Marshall (1814) 6 Binney (Pa.) 338, 6 AD 458, 463 (Brackenridge,J)
45 2 Kings 5:20-27 (where Gehazi, servant of Elisha, was condemned to suffer leprosy); State v Buswell (1894) 40 Neb. 158, 58 NW 728, 24 LRA 68 (Ryan, C)

46 Heb. 13:2 ("Be not forgetful to entertain strangers")
47 Job 31:32
48 Gen. 18:2-8
49 Gen. 19:1-3; see also Judges 19:16-21
50 Acts 28:7
1 Acts 28:30
2 3 John v 10
3 Job 31:32
4 Mark 2:2

pected that one should bring "every man" into his house.[5] Thus it was thought proper not to receive a deceitful or mischievous man,[6] or one who came with false doctrine.[7]

[§243] One who was taken into another's house as a guest became, for the time being, a member of the host's family.[8] It was the duty of the host to treat his guest "courteously"[9] and to care for all of his wants,[10] that is, to furnish a "guest-chamber"[11] or "room to lodge in,"[12] to provide "bread and wine" for the guest and his servant[13] and water with which to wash their feet,[14] and to supply "straw and provender" for their beasts of burden.[15] It was also incumbent upon the host to protect his guest against those who would molest him. Thus it appears that Lot endeavored to protect two men who "came under the shadow of his roof" at Sodom against evil men of the city.[16] Rahab, the harlot, hid two of Joshua's spies who had lodged in her house, and helped them to escape from their pursuers.[17] And the "old man" who "sojourned in Gibeah" sought, like Lot, to protect a wayfaring man that he had brought into his house from "men of the city" who "beset the house round about."[18] This ancient duty of a host to guard his guest is recognized in modern laws which authorize one to use "any necessary force" to protect a guest from "wrongful injury."[19]

[§244] A guest, in turn was expected to "eat such things" as were set before him,[20] that is, to accept the accommodations that were offered by his host "without murmurings."[21] The rule, as given by St. Paul, is that—

"If any . . . bid you to a feast, and ye be disposed to go, whatsoever is set before you, eat, asking no questions."[22]

And upon his departure, it seems that custom demanded of a guest that he give a present to his host, or confer some benefit or favor upon him.[23] But it is not clear how long a guest might properly remain with his host. He may doubtless pause

5 Ecclesiasticus 11:29
"A man that hath no house, and lodgeth wheresoever the night taketh him" is as a thief "that skippeth from city to city." Ecclesiasticus 36:26
6 Ecclesiasticus 11:29-33
7 2 John v 10
8 13 Gr.B. (1901) 72 (Amram)
9 Acts 28:7
10 Judges 19:20 ("let all thy wants lie upon me")
11 In Jerusalem at the time of Jesus it was seemingly customary among householders to have a "guestchamber" in which visitors might "eat the pass-

over." See Mark 14:14-16; Luke 22:11-13
12 Gen. 24:23,25
13 Judges 19:19
14 Gen. 18:4, 24:32
15 Gen. 24:32; Judges 19:21
16 Gen. 19:1-11
17 Josh. 2:1-16
18 Judges 19:16-25
19 See Cal.Civ.Code (1872) §50
20 Luke 10:8
21 Phil. 2:14
22 1 Cor. 10:27
23 See Gen. 18:9-14, 19:10-16

to rest and refresh himself in the heat of the day,[24] or, arriving in the evening, he may tarry all night.[25] Again, he may "tarry with him a few days."[26] Thus, a guest may lodge three days with his host,[27] and being urged he may tarry a day or two more and depart on the fourth or fifth day,[28] or he may tarry with him seven days.[29] On the other hand, a guest should "give place" or depart when a "brother" of the host "cometh to be lodged" and he has need of his house.[30]

24 Gen. 18:1
25 Gen. 19:2. And see Num. 22:8,19;
Josh. 4:3; Jer. 14.8
26 Gen. 27:44

27 Acts 28:7
28 Judges 19:4-10
29 1 Sam. 10:8; Acts 28:14
30 Ecclesiasticus 29:27

PART IV

ECONOMICS AND WELFARE

CHAPTER 35

INTRODUCTION

[§245]　The economic system of the Bible is agrarian;[31] it is based upon the supposition that nearly all of the people live upon the land and engage in agricultural pursuits.[32]　It was intended that there should be neither poverty[33] nor riches[34]—neither beggary[35] nor great wealth—in the land, but that every man should be economically independent and self-supporting, possessing his habitation and means of livelihood and enjoying the products of his labor; in short, that each should sit "under his vine and fig tree"[36] and "eat the fruit thereof."[37]

According to Biblical law, it is elemental that every man should "bear his own burden,"[38]—maintain himself and his family[39]—and should "labour,"[40] plant his garden[41] and till his land.[42]　On the other hand, the law recognizes that "the

---

31　See Cauley's "Agrarianism' (1935)

32　When God created man and woman —a human pair—he built no city for them and their children. On the contrary, "the Lord God planted a garden . . . and there he put the man (and woman) whom he had formed." Gen. 2:8

The first city was built by Cain, who did not do well as a tiller of the ground, whose offering therefrom was unacceptable to the Lord, and who, in a jealous rage killed his brother Abel. Gen. 4:2-17

33　Prov. 11:4 ("Riches profit not in the day of wrath")

34　Prov. 30:8 ("give me neither poverty nor riches")

35　Ecclesiasticus 40:28 (" . . . lead not a beggar's life; for better it is to die than to beg. The life of him that dependeth on another man's table is not to be counted for a life; for he polluteth himself with other men's meat")

36　1 Mac. 14:11,12 ("He [Simon] made peace in the land, and Israel rejoiced with great joy; for every man sat under his vine and his fig tree, and there was none to fray them")

37　Prov. 27:18

" . . . eat ye every one of his vine, and every one of his fig tree, and drink ye every one the waters of his own cistern." Isa. 36:16

38　Gal. 6:5

39　One ought to maintain himself that he may say, "in all things I have kept myself from being burdensome unto you, and so will I keep myself." 2 Cor. 11:9

40　Ecclesiasticus 40:18

41　Jer. 29:5 ("plant gardens, and eat the fruit of them")

42　Prov. 28:19 ("He that tilleth his land shall have plenty of bread")

profit of the earth is for all;"[43] that "every man should . . .
enjoy the good of all his labour,"[44] and "the husbandman that
laboreth must be first partaker of the fruits."[45]　Finally, the
Scriptures teach that one should be content with such things
as he has[46]—with "food and raiment"[47] or "water, and bread,
and clothing, and an house to cover shame"[48]—or with his
"wages,"[49] and should "labour not to be rich"[50] nor set his
heart upon gold[1] or goods.[2]

[§246]　——　The desire to possess, instead of serve—to
avoid productive labor and instead, by such evil devices as
human ingenuity can contrive, to lay hands upon the products
and possessions of others, whether of lands[3] or money,[4] "silver, or gold, or apparel,"[5]—has been a curse of man since
long before the children of Israel were taken into captivity by
the Assyrians.[6]　The gratification of this cupidity is detrimental to the general welfare, nor is it a thing that the law
should encourage or satisfy.　To the contrary it is said that
"there is not a more wicked thing than a covetous man,"[7] and
Jesus especially cautioned to "take heed and beware of covetousness," observing that "a man's life consisteth not in the
abundance of the things which he possesseth."[8]

Many Scriptural passages condemn and forbid covetous-
ness[9] and envy,[10] as well as deceit,[11] extortion,[12] fraud[13] and
greed,[14] the oppression,[15] robbery[16] and spoiling of others,[17]

43　Ecclesiasticus 5:9
44　Ecclesiasticus 3:13
". . . thou shalt eat the labor of
thine hands: happy shalt thou be, and
it shall be well with thee." Ps. 128:2
". . . it is good and comely for one
. . . to enjoy the good of all his labour
that he taketh under the sun all the
days of his life, which God giveth him:
for it is his portion." Ecclesiastes
5:18
45　2 Tim. 2:6
46　Heb. 13:5; and see Ecclesiasticus
40:18 ("To labour, and to be content
with that a man hath, is a sweet life")
47　1 Tim. 6:7,8 ("For we brought nothing into this world, and it is certain
we can carry nothing out. And having
food and raiment let us be therewith
content")
48　Ecclesiasticus 29:21
49　Luke 3:14
50　Prov. 23:4
1　Tobit 12:8 ("It is better to give
alms than to lay up gold")
"He that loveth gold shall not be
justified . . . Gold hath been the ruin
of many, and their destruction was
present. It is a stumblingblock unto
them that sacrifice unto it, and every

fool shall be taken therewith." Ecclesiasticus 31:5-7
2　Ecclesiasticus 5:1,8
3　Micah 2:1,2 ("fields")
4　Tobit 5:18
5　Acts 20:33
6　See infra §250
7　Ecclesiasticus 10:9
8　Luke 12:15
9　Jer. 22:17; Micah 2:1,2; Hab. 2:9;
Acts 20:33; Eph. 5:3; Col. 3:5; Heb. 13:5
10　Gal. 5:21
11　Jer. 5:27; Ecclesiasticus 10:8
12　Ezek. 22:12
13　See supra §153
14　Tobit 5:18 ("Be not greedy to add
money to money")
"Woe unto them that join house to
house, that lay field to field, till there
be no place, that they may be placed
alone in the midst of the earth." Isa.
5:8
15　Jer. 22:17; Ezek. 22:29; Ecclesiasticus 36:9; Micah 2:1,2
16　Micah 2:1,2 ("Woe to them that
. . . take . . . [fields] by violence")
17　Isa. 33:1 ("Woe to thee that spoil-
est")

and all unrighteous dealings by which riches may be gotten.[18] The law is summarized in the commandment that "Thou shalt not covet"[19]—

"Thou shalt not covet thy neighbour's house, thou shalt not covet thy neighbour's wife, nor his manservant, nor his maidservant, nor his ox, nor his ass, nor anything that is thy neighbour's."[20]

[§247] —— The "pursuit of riches" therefore is unlawful[21]—"he that maketh haste to be rich shall not be innocent"[22]—and one who troubles himself and others in seeking wealth is an offender against the law.[23] "Better is a little with righteousness," it is said, "than great revenues without right,"[24] and "the love of money is the root of all evil."[25]

Commercial enterprises can scarcely be profitably conducted, nor riches acquired, without trespass upon the rights of others.[26] "As a nail sticketh fast between the joinings of the stones; so doth sin stick close between buying and selling."[27] Hence, "a merchant shall hardly keep himself from doing wrong"[28] and "a rich man shall hardly enter into the kingdom of heaven."[29] Indeed, "rich men" are generally condemned throughout the Scriptures[30] as having "eaten up the poor."[31] For example, in the Old Testament it is said:

"Hear this, O ye that swallow up the needy, even to make the poor of the land to fail,

"Saying, When will the new moon be gone, that we may sell corn? and the sabbath, that we may set forth wheat, making the ephah small, and the shekel great, and falsifying the balances by deceit?

---

18 Jer. 17:11, 22:13, Amos 5:11; Ecclesiasticus 10:8
"He that getteth riches, and not by right, shall leave them in the midst of his days, and at his end shall be a fool." Jer. 17:11
19 Rom. 13:9
20 Ex. 20:17
"Neither shalt thou desire thy neighbour's wife, neither shalt thou covet thy neighbour's house, his field, or his manservant, or his maidservant, his ox, or his ass, or any thing that is thy neighbour's." Deut. 5:21
"Thou shalt not covet thy neighbour's goods." Two Ways 2:2
21 Meaning that it does not accord with the spirit of the law. And see Hab. 2:6 ("Woe to him that increaseth that which is not his")
22 Prov. 28:20; Wilt v Franklin (1809) 1 Binney (Pa.) 502, 526 (Brackenridge,J)
"He that hasteth to be rich hath an evil eye, and considereth not that poverty shall come upon him." Prov. 28:22
"They that will be rich fall into temptation and a snare, and into many foolish and hurtful lusts." 1 Tim. 6:9
23 Prov. 15:16 ("Better is a little with the fear of the Lord, than great treasure and trouble therewith")

24 Prov. 16:8
"A little with righteousness is better than much with unrighteousness." Tobit 12:8
25 1 Tim. 6:10
26 The business and pursuits of the present day are incompatible with the customs of primitive Christians. Schriber v Rapp (1836) 5 Watts (Pa.) 351, 30 AD 327, 329 (Gibson,CJ, saying this "may be true")
27 Ecclesiasticus 27:2
28 Ecclesiasticus 26:29 (". . . and an huckster shall not be freed from sin")
"He is a merchant, the balances of deceit are in his hand: he loveth to oppress." Hosea 12:7
29 Matt. 19:23
30 Jer. 5:26-29; Hosea 4:7; Tim. 6:9
"I will . . . punish the men that are settled on their lees: that say in their heart, the Lord will not do good, neither will he do evil. Therefore, their goods shall become a booty, and their houses a desolation: they shall also build houses, but not inhabit them; and they shall plant vineyards, but not drink the wine thereof." Zeph. 1:12,13
31 Ecclesiasticus 13:19 ("As the wild ass is the lion's prey in the wilderness: so the rich eat up the poor")

"That we may buy the poor for silver, and the needy for a pair of shoes; yea, and sell the refuse of the wheat?

"The Lord hath sworn by the excellency of Jacob, Surely I will never forget any of their works.

"Shall not the land tremble for this, and every one mourn that dwelleth therein? and it shall rise up wholly as a flood; and it shall be cast out and drowned, as by the flood of Egypt.

"And it shall come to pass in that day, saith the Lord God, that I will cause the sun to go down at noon, and I will darken the earth in the clear day:

"And I will turn your feasts into mourning, and all your songs into lamentation; and I will bring up sackcloth upon all loins, and baldness upon every head; and I will make it as the mourning of an only son, and the end thereof as a bitter day."[32]

Again, in the New Testament, James addresses "rich men," saying:

"Go to now, ye rich men, weep and howl for your miseries that shall come upon you.

"Your riches are corrupted, and your garments are moth-eaten.

"Your gold and silver is cankered; and the rust of them shall be a witness against you, and shall eat your flesh as it were fire. Ye have heaped treasure together for the last days.

"Behold, the hire of the laborers who have reaped down your fields, which is of you kept back by fraud, crieth: and the cries of them which have reaped are entered into the ears of the Lord of Sabaoth.

"Ye have lived in pleasure on the earth, and been wanton; ye have nourished your hearts, as in a day of slaughter.

"Ye have condemned and killed the just; and he doth not resist you."[33]

Jesus advised those who would be "perfect" to "go and sell that thou hast, and give to the poor."[34] Nevertheless, it is said that "Riches are good unto him that hath no sin"[35] and that the rich man is blessed "that is found without blemish, and hath not gone after gold."[36]

[§248] A community of goods—or communism—appears to have been practiced among the early Christian churches or communities.[37] Apparently it did not arise from a divine command[38] but was ordained by the Apostles[39]—perhaps as a special and temporary appointment.[40]

---

32 Amos 8:4-10

33 James 5:1-6

34 Matt. 19:21; Mark 10:21; Luke 18:22
"He that hath two coats, let him impart to him that hath none; and he that hath meat, let him do likewise." Luke 3:11

35 Ecclesiasticus 13:24

36 Ecclesiasticus 31:8

37 The early Church was "an organized community, having its laws, its magistrates, its discipline." 28 Unit. Rev. 293

38 The community of goods did not arise from a divine command; it was merely a practical demonstration of the brotherly love existing among the early Christians. Hurst's Short History of the Early Church (1886) 4
But see Two Ways 4:8 ("Thou . . . shalt share all things with thy brother . . .")

39 Schriber v Rapp (1836) 5 Watts (Pa.) 351, 30 AD 327, 333 (Gibson,CJ); State v Amana Society (1906) 132 Iowa 304, 109 NW 894, 11 AnnCas 231, 8 LRANS 909, 913 (Ladd,J)

40 See infra §249

According to the Pentecostal ideal, a church "was intended to be but a single family, upon a large scale, with only one purse, where self was to be abjured, and the general good alone considered."[41] It is related in the Acts of the Apostles that—

". . . all that believed were together, and had all things in common. "And sold their possessions and goods, and parted them to all men, as every man had need."[42]
". . . the multitude of them that believed were of one heart and of one soul: neither said any of them that ought of the things which he possessed was his own: but they had all things common.
". . . and great grace was upon them all.
"Neither was there any among them that lacked: for as many as were possessors of lands or houses sold them, and brought the prices of the things that were sold,
"And laid them down at the apostles' feet: and distribution was made unto every man according as he had need."[43]

In particular, it is recorded that "Joses . . . a Levite, and of the country of Cyprus, having land, sold it, and brought the money, and laid it at the apostles' feet."[44] But Ananias and Sapphira, having sold a possession, deceitfully withheld a portion of the price, for which they were condemned by Peter.[45]

[§249] —— It is generally thought that the early Christian community of property was intended as a temporary expedient.[46] But many groups, some even in modern times, have adhered to the contrary view and have adopted tenets inculcating communistic features.[47] The doctrine finds some

41 Burt v Oneida Community (1893) 137 NY 346, 33 NE 307, 19 LRA 297 (Maynard,J)

42 Acts 2:44,45; Ruse v Williams (1913) 14 Ariz. 445, 130 P 887, 45 LRANS 923, 925 (Franklin,CJ)

43 Acts 4:32-35; Schriber v Rapp (1836) 5 Watts (Pa.) 351, 30 AD 327, 332 (Gibson, CJ); Ruse v Williams (1913) 14 Ariz. 445, 130 P 887, 45 LRANS 923, 925 (Franklin,CJ)

44 Acts 4:36,37

45 Acts 5:1-11. And see supra §163

46 "A vast majority of Christians, undoubtedly, think that the community of property . . . was of special and temporary appointment." Schriber v Rapp (1836) 5 Watts (Pa.) 351, 30 AD 327, 333 (Gibson,CJ)

"Possibly a majority of Christians have concluded that community ownership of property . . . was merely temporary." State v Amana Society (1906) 132 Iowa 304, 109 NW 893, 11 AnnCas 231, 8 LRANS 909, 913 (Ladd,J)

47 For cases involving religious organizations with communistic features, see—

Amana Society: State v Amana Society (1906) 132 Iowa 304, 109 NW 894, 11 Ann Cas 231, 8 LRANS 909

Faithists: Ellis v Newbrough (1891) 6 NM 181, 27 P 490

Harmony Society: Schriber v Rapp (1836) 5 Watts (Pa.) 351, 30 AD 327; Baker v Nachtrieb (1856) 19 How. (US) 126, 15 L ed 528; Speidel v Henrici (1886) 120 US 377, 30 L ed 718; Schwartz v Duss (1902) 187 US 10, 47 L ed 53

Oneida Community: Burt v Oneida Community (1893) 137 NY 346, 19 LRA 297

Separatists: Goesele v Bimeler (1852) 14 How. (US) 590, 14 L ed 554

Shakers: Waite v Merrill (1826) 4 Me. 102, 16 AD 238; Gass v Wilhite (1834) 2 Dana (Ky.) 170, 26 AD 446

Spiritual Class: Ruse v Williams (1913) 14 Ariz. 445, 130 P 887, 45 LRANS 923

support in the Scriptures, and it may be urged that "the awful fate of Ananias and Sapphira for concealing a part of the price of their property" should "be accepted as proof that communal life was enjoined."[48]

[§250] The Biblical principles of economics have never been generally observed, for they run counter to the innate and natural covetousness of man[49]—his desire to reap what he did not sow[50] "and to gather where he has not strawed."[1] They can become fully operative, it seems, only in a righteous society—one in which righteous people are predominant and in which their government curbs every manifestation of covetousness.[2]

But there has long been hope of a "new earth"[3] or a "new order"[4]—a "kingdom" of God upon earth"[5]—when man shall be a "new creature,"[6] with a "new spirit,"[7] clad with "new garments,"[8] dwelling in a "new house"[9] and singing a "new song."[10] The new order is foretold in the book of Isaiah:

". . . behold, I create new heavens and a new earth . . .

". . . they shall build houses, and inhabit them; and they shall plant vineyards, and eat the fruit of them.

"They shall not build and another inhabit; they shall not plant and another eat . . .

"They shall not labour in vain, nor bring forth for trouble . . ."[11]

The hoped-for "new order" is doubtless intended to be a unified world, governing itself by the rules of Biblical law— a universal cooperative Christian society wherein each sustains himself by his own efforts and all cooperate for the common good. In this society, men will "dwell together in unity,"[12] "bearing one another's burdens"[13] helping "every

---

48 Doctrines of righteousness are too frequently forgotten in the ordinary pursuits of life, and contests for wealth in some circles are waged with the rapacity of beasts of prey. Surely, a scheme of life designed to obviate such results, and, by removing temptations and inducements of ambition and avarice, to nurture the virtues of unselfishness, patience, love, and service, ought not to be denounced. See State v Amana Society (1906) 132 Iowa 304, 109 NW 894, 11 Ann Cas 231, 8 LRANS 909, 914 (Ladd,J)

49 See supra §246

50 Luke 19:21

1 Matt. 25:26

2 See supra §246

3 Isa. 65:17, 66:22; 2 Pet. 3:13; Rev. 21:1

4 "The needy shall not always be for-

gotten; the expectation of the poor shall not perish for ever." Ps. 9:18

"Every valley shall be exalted, and every mountain and hill shall be made low." Isa. 40:4

5 Meaning a rule of right and reason

6 2 Cor. 5:17; Gal. 6:15

7 Ezek. 11:19, 18:31, 36:26

8 1 Kings 11:29

9 Deut. 20:5

10 Ps. 33:3, 96:1, 98:1, 144:9, 149:1; Ida. 42:10; Rev. 5:9, 14:3

Meaning, no doubt, embracing a (to them) new philosophy—that of brotherly love and mutual helpfulness.

11 Isa. 65:17, 21-23

12 Ps. 133:1

13 Gal. 6:2 (and so fulfilling "the law of Christ")

one his neighbor,"[14] and none seeking wealth for himself.[15] The husbandman will eat the fruits of his labors;[16] and he that hath earned wages will not "put them into a bag with holes,"[17] he will not spend his money "for that which is not bread" or his "labour for that which satisfieth not."[18] But there will be "opportunity for leisure," whereby cometh "the wisdom of a learned man."[19]

CHAPTER 36

LABOR—THE LAW OF EMPLOYMENT

251 In general   252 Legal attitude toward labor   253 Duty and right to work
254 Contract of employment   255 Employment of women   256 Length of service
257 The six-day week   258 Treatment of hirelings   259 Wages   260 Bonus

[§251]   In modern times the bond-servant or slave[20] has generally given place to the "hireling" or servant who works for wages. Such servants or employees were known even to Primitive law, but it is only in recent years—as society has turned from agriculture to industry and commerce—that the notion of full-time and life-long employment as a hireling has come into vogue, and that the legal relation of employer and employee—as distinguished from that of master and servant —has arisen. This should be kept in mind in considering Biblical rules concerning labor.

[§252]   Biblical law expressly approves of labor[21]—whether it be for one's self or another[22]—and commends diligence[23] and industry.[24] It is said that there is profit in all labour,[25] even if one works for nothing,[26] and that "he that laboureth,

---

14 Isa. 41:6 ("They helped every one his neighbor; and every one said to his brother, Be of good courage")

15 1 Cor. 10:24 ("Let no man seek his own, but every man another's wealth")

16 Prov. 27:18

17 Haggai 1:6

18 Isa. 55:2; and see Luke 15:13

19 Ecclesiasticus 38:24 ("he that hath little business shall become wise")

20 See supra §232 et seq.

21 Prov. 13:11 ("he that gathereth by labor shall increase"); Ecclesiasticus 7:15 ("Hate not laborious work") 51:30 ("Work your work betimes")

"The habit of work is what men most need." 14 Or.LR (1934-1935) 450

22 In either case, "he that laboreth, laboreth for himself." Prov. 16:26

23 Prov. 12:24 ("The hand of the diligent shall bear rule"), 13:4 ("the soul of the diligent shall be made fat"), 22:29 ("he shall stand before kings")

24 Ecclesiasticus 9:10 ("Whatsoever thy hand findeth to do, do it with thy might")

25 Prov. 14:23 ("but the talk of the lips tendeth only to penury")

26 Powell v Augusta R. Co. (1886) 77 Ga. 192, 200 (Bleckley,CJ), saying that "It is better for happiness, as well as for virtue, to work for nothing than to be idle."

and aboundeth in all things" is better "than he that boasteth himself, and wanteth bread."[27] On the other hand, the law frowns upon slothfulness[28] and the slothful person[29] or sluggard,[30] saying:

"Go to the ant thou sluggard; consider her ways, and be wise:
"Which having no guide, overseer, or ruler,
"Provideth her meat in the summer, and gathereth her food in the harvest.
"How long wilt thou sleep, O sluggard? when wilt thou arise out of thy sleep?
"Yet a little sleep, a little slumber, a little folding of the hands to sleep:
"So shall thy poverty come as one that travelleth, and thy want as an armed man."[31]

[§253] But Biblical law does not stop with mere commendations of labor;[32] the rule, as laid upon Adam, is that "In the sweat of thy face shalt thou eat bread."[33] The duty of working is imposed upon all men in order that each may "bear his own burden"[34] and "eat his own bread,"[35] but not for the purpose of acquiring riches.[36] The rule is that "if any would (will) not work, neither should (shall) he eat."[37] This does not mean, however, that one must work as a hireling or servant,[38] but that he should do "whatsoever" his "hand findeth to do"[39]—whether for himself or others[40]—and "walk

27 Ecclesiasticus 10:27

28 Prov. 19:15 ("Slothfulness casteth into a deep sleep and an idle soul shall suffer hunger")

29 Prov. 12:24 ("the slothful shall be under tribute"), 15:19 ("The way of a slothful man is as a hedge of thorns"), 18:9 ("He . . . is brother to him that is a great waster"), 31:25 ("The desire of the slothful killeth him; for his hands refuse to labor")

30 Prov. 13:4 ("the sluggard desireth, and hath nothing"), 20:4 (he "will not plow by reason of the cold; therefore shall he beg in harvest, and have nothing")

31 Prov. 6:6-11
"I went by the field of the slothful, and by the vineyard of the man void of understanding;
"And, lo, it was all grown over with thorns, and nettles had covered the face thereof, and the stone wall thereof was broken down.
"Then I saw, and considered it well; I looked upon it and received instruction.
"Yet a little sleep, a little slumber, a little folding of the hands to sleep:
"So shall thy poverty come as one that travelleth; and thy want as an armed man." Prov. 24:30-34

32 See supra §252

33 Gen. 3:19; 42 Wash.L.Rep. (1914) 772 (Barnard)

34 Gal. 6:5

35 2 Thess. 3:12
Modern laws and police regulations seem to recognize this principle. Idleness, in the sense of mere inaction is not a crime and perhaps may not be made so. In re McCue (1908) 7 Cal.App. 765, 766, 96 P 110 (Allen, PJ)
But one who is idle and who loiters or wanders about without any employment, occupation or visible means of support, is subject to punishment as a "vagrant." See Cal.Pen.Code (1872) §647; 42 Wash.L.Rep. (1914) 772 (Barnard)

36 See supra §245
"Let him that stole steal no more: but rather let him labour, working with his hands." Eph. 4:28

37 2 Thess. 3:10
"An idle soul shall suffer hunger." Prov. 19:15
The rule was enforced in the Virginia colony by Capt. John Smith in 1607-8.

38 See supra §251

39 Ecclesiasticus 9:10

40 See supra §252

worthy" of his "vocation."[41]   The requirement is merely to "do your own business" and work, not merely with the hands of others, but "with your own hands,"[42] to the end "that ye may walk honestly toward them that are without, and that ye may have lack of nothing."[43]   And if one is a servant it is his duty to do "all those things which are commanded" by his master.[44]

Obviously, since it is incumbent upon one to work, he has a right to do so. Rights and duties being correlative,[45] one must necessarily be free to do that which he is bound to do. But this is not to say that one may demand employment of another.

[§254]   The relationship of "master and hireling"—or employer and employee—arises out of a contract of "hiring" or employment, which may be made in words or by conduct,[46] and by the year[47] or the day,[48] the laborer agreeing to work and the master to pay a wage.[49]

The first of such contracts mentioned in the Scriptures were those wherein Laban employed Jacob. In their initial contract, Jacob offered to work for Laban, saying: "I will serve thee seven years for Rachel thy younger daughter."[50] Laban accepted the offer, saying: "It is better that I give her to thee, than that I should give her to another man: abide with me."[1]   When Jacob had served Laban seven years,[2] and the agreed time of payment arrived, Laban substituted Leah in place of Rachel, contending that custom required the elder daughter to be first given in marriage.[3]   Jacob accepted the substitution and made a second contract to serve seven more years for Rachel but exacted his wage—that is, delivery of Rachel—in advance.[4]   At the end of this period he made a third contract to serve Laban for a share of his livestock, "the speckled and spotted cattle, and all the brown cattle among the sheep, and the spotted and speckled among the goats."[5]

---

41 Eph. 4:1 ("I . . . beseech you that ye walk worthy of the vocation wherewith ye are called")
"St.Paul calls upon every one to exert himself to do his duty in the class in which he finds himself placed." 27 Harv.LR (1914) 607 (Pound) citing Eph. 5:22, 6:1-5
42 1 Thess. 4:11; and see 2 Thess. 3:12 ("we command . . . that with quietness they work")
43 1 Thess. 4:12
44 Luke 17:10
45 See supra §126
46 18 RCL 493 (Davids)
47 Lev. 25:53

48 Matt. 20:2
49 Ex. 2:9
50 Gen. 29:18
1 Gen. 29:19
2 Gen. 29:20
3 Gen. 29:26
4 Gen. 29:27-30
5 Gen. 30:32
Jacob took advantage of his master Laban, by artificially increasing his share of the stock at the latter's expense; but this seems to have been regarded as justified by prior acts of Laban.

Pharaoh's daughter made a contract with the natural mother of Moses, saying: "Take this child (Moses) away, and nurse it for me, and I will give thee thy wages. And the woman took the child, and nursed it."[6] Long afterward, Tobit made a contract to hire Raphael, who represented himself as Azarias, and to pay him "a drachm a day, and things necessary."[7] Contracts for the hiring of laborers are also mentioned in a parable of Jesus.[8]

[§255] In primitive society "maidservants" were sold by the head of one family to that of another, often, no doubt, with a view to the marriage of the "maid" to her master or his son.[9] But there seems to have been no notion of any general employment of women as "hirelings," nor did they engage in business or the professions, until recent times.[9a] It was recognized, however, that a married woman might properly do "women's works" for others for hire in case of necessity, as when her husband was poor and incapacitated. Thus in the book of Tobit it is said, "my wife Anna did take women's works to do. And when she had sent them home to the owners, they paid her wages, and gave her also . . . a gift more than the wages."[10]

[§256] The Lord directed Adam to labor "till thou return unto the ground," that is, till death. But the Scriptures prescribe neither a minimum nor a maximum age for labor, and it is probable that no occasion for such regulations existed in ancient times.[12] It was doubtless considered proper that within reasonable limits, children should aid their parents and the aged should care for themselves. But neither were "employed" in the modern sense as "hirelings." The direction to "wax old in thy work"[13] may be taken to mean merely that one should remain active so long as he is able.[14] But a provision of Mosaic law in reference to the Levites suggests the

---

6 Ex. 2:9

7 Tobit 5:3-14

8 See Matt. 20:1-15

9 See supra §235

9a Keller v Downey (1942) 161 SW2d (Tex.Civ.App.) 803, 811 (Combs,J, dissenting)

The harmony of the family "is repugnant to the idea of a woman adopting a distinct and independent career from that of her husband. . . . The paramount destiny and mission of woman are to fulfill the noble and benign offices of wife and mother. This is the law of the Creator." Bradwell v Illinois (1872) 16 Wall. (US) 130, 21 L ed 442 (Bradley,J)

10 Tobit 2:11,12,14

11 Gen. 3:19

12 Limitation upon bond-servant, see supra §234

13 Ecclesiasticus 11:20

14 For it is common knowledge that one soon dies after retirement following many years of active service, especially where the retirement is sudden and complete.

fixing of the span of active or at least public service at 25 years—from the ages of 25 to 50.

". . . from twenty and five years old and upward they (the Levites) shall go in to wait upon the service of the tabernacle of the congregation;

"And from the age of fifty years they shall cease waiting upon the service thereof, and shall serve no more:

"But shall minister with their brethren in the tabernacle of the congregation, to keep the charge, and shall do no service . . ."[15]

[§257] The week has always consisted of "six working days"[16] and the Sabbath of rest,[17] for it appears even in the story of the creation that God created "the heavens and the earth . . . and all the host of them" in six days, and that "he rested on the seventh day."[18] The commandments regarding work are—"Six days shall work be done,"[19] "Six days thou shalt do thy work,"[20] and "Six days thou shalt work."[21] And it has been said that "There are six days when men ought to work."[22] But inasmuch as the work commandments are associated with others relating to Sabbath observance[23] the view has been taken that the direction to work six days is merely permissive[24]—that one may work or not for six days, but that he must "rest" on the seventh.[25] This interpretation, however, violates plain Scriptural language and ignores the legal duty and right to labor[26] except upon the Sabbath and other appointed holidays.[27]

But the law is not to be understood as requiring an employee to work a six-day week for his employer. His employment may be for less than six days if he does other work when not employed. Biblical law does not sanction idleness[28] and the "folding of hands."[29]

[§258] A hired servant is doubtless entitled to fair and just treatment by his master. So it is said to "entreat . . . not evil . . . the hireling that bestoweth himself wholly for

---

15   Num. 8:24-26

16   Ezek. 46:1

17   See infra §319

18   Gen. 1;31, 2:1,2

19   Ex. 35:2; Lev. 23:3
"Six days may work be done." Ex. 31:15

20   Ex. 23:12

21   Ex. 34:21
"Six days shalt thou labour, and do all thy work." Ex. 20:9; Deut. 5:13

22   Luke 13:14
Jesus did not question these words of the "ruler of the synagogue." His response pertained only to the lawful-

ness of healing the sick on the Sabbath day. Luke 13:15,16

23   See infra §319

24   And so it is in Ex. 31:15

25   See City Council v Benjamin (1846) 2 Strob. (S.C.) 508, 49 AD 608, 614 (O'Neall,J)

26   See supra §253

27   See infra §319
Rules of interpretation, see supra §41 et seq.

28   Prov. 19:15
"Why stand ye here all the day idle?" Matt. 20:6

29   Prov. 6:10, 24:33; and see supra §252

thee,"[30] and to oppress not "an hired servant that is poor and needy, whether he be of thy brethren, or of thy strangers that are in thy land within thy gates."[31]

The privacy of an employee should not be unnecessarily violated, as by inquiring into personal matters that do not properly concern the employer. Raphael, pretending to be Azarias, objected even to inquiry as to his tribe or family, saying: "Dost thou seek for a tribe or family, or an hired man to go with thy son?"[32]

[§259] The employment contract may properly fix the amount of wages to be paid the laborer, as for example, "a penny a day"[33] or "a drachm a day, and things necessary."[34] If no definite wage is agreed upon, as where the employer merely says "I will give thee thy wages,"[35] the laborer is entitled to receive "whatsoever is right"[36] "according to his own labour."[37] But, under the old law, when a definite wage is contracted for, he may not complain that another laborer is given the same wage for less work.[38]

A hired servant ought not to be defrauded[39] or oppressed in respect of his wages.[40] "The labourer is worthy of his hire"[41] or "reward,"[42] meaning that he is entitled to his wages, not "as a matter of bounty"[43] or grace, "but of debt"[44] or right.[45] Also it is said that "the workman is worthy of his meat."[46]

The law expressly requires that the hire of a servant be given him "out of hand"[47] at the end of the day: "the wages of him that is hired shall not abide with thee all night until the morning"[48] and "the sun (shall not) go down" before pay-

30 Ecclesiasticus 7:20
31 Deut. 24:14; Moore v Indian Spring Channel Gold Mining Co. (1918) 37 Cal. App. 370, 371, 174 P 378 (Chipman,PJ)
32 Tobit 5:11
33 Matt. 20:2
34 Tobit 5:14
35 Ex. 2:9
36 Matt. 20:7
37 1 Cor. 3:8 ("every man shall receive his own reward according to his own labour")
38 Matt. 20:1-15
Nor, of course, that another labourer is given a greater wage for the same work.
The parable (Matt. 20:1-16), which is one of the earliest references to labor disputes, indicates that inequality of wages has always been a source of complaint.
39 Ecclesiasticus 34:22 ("he that de-

fraudeth the labourer of his hire is as a bloodshedder")
40 Jer. 22:13 ("Woe unto him . . . that useth his neighbour's service without wages, and giveth him not for his work";) Mal. 3:5 ("I will be a swift witness . . . against those that oppress the hireling in his **wages")**
41 Luke 10:7
42 1 Tim. 5:18
43 2 Cor. 9:5
44 Rom. 4:4 ("Now to him that worketh is the reward not reckoned of grace, but of debt")
45 "The recompense of a man's hands shall be rendered unto him." Prov. 12:14
46 Matt. 10:10
47 Tobit 4:14 ("Let not the wages of any man, which hath wrought for thee, tarry with thee, but give him it out of hand")
48 Lev. 19:13

ment of the wage of a servant that is poor and needy.[49] But where a servant is employed to make a journey in behalf of the master, his wages may properly be paid upon his return.[50]

[§260] A bonus may properly be given a "profitable" servant, who has rendered meritorious and valuable service for his master[1]—who has done more perhaps than that which it was his duty to do.[2] Thus the employers of Anna paid her wages and gave her "a gift more than the wages,"[3] and Tobit agreed to "add something" to the wages of Azarias (Raphael) upon his safe return.[4]

CHAPTER 37

MONEY AND LENDING

[§261] From the earliest period of history, money—in the form of pieces of gold and silver—has been used.[5] Money was already "current" among merchants at the time of Abraham, who paid "four hundred shekels of silver, current money with the merchant"—about 1860 B.C.—for the field containing the cave of Machpelah.[6] Money is frequently mentioned in the

49 Deut. 24:15 ("At his day thou shalt give him his hire, neither shall the sun go down upon it; for he is poor, and setteth his heart upon it: lest he cry against thee unto the Lord, and it be sin unto thee"); Moore v Indian Spring Channel Gold Mining Co. (1918) 37 Cal. App. 370, 381; 174 P 378 (Chipman,PJ)

50 Tobit 12:1

1 "It is due unto him." Tobit 12:4

2 Luke 17:10

3 Tobit 2:12,14

4 Tobit 5:15; and see Tobit 12:1-5 saying: "Then Tobit called upon his son Tobias, and said unto him, My son, see that the man have his wages, which went with thee, and thou must give him more. And Tobias said unto him, O father, it is no harm to me to give him half of those things which I have brought; for he hath brought me again to thee in safety, and made whole my wife, and brought me the money, and likewise healed thee. Then the old man said, It is due unto him. So he called the angel, and he said unto him, Take half of all that he have brought, and go away in safety."

5 "These metals are scattered over the world in small quantities; they are sus-ceptible of division, capable of easy impression, have more value in proportion to weight and size, and are less subject to loss by wear and abrasion than any other material possessing these qualities. It requires labor to obtain them; they are not dependent upon legislation or the caprices of the multitude; they cannot be manufactured or decreed into existence, and they do not perish by lapse of time. They have, therefore, naturally, if not necessarily, become throughout the world a standard of value. In exchange for pieces of them, products requiring an equal amount of labor, are readily given. When the product and the piece of metal represent the same labor, or an approximation to it, they are freely exchanged. There can be no adequate substitute for these metals." Juilliard v Greenman (1884) 110 US 421-470, 28 L ed 204, 219 (Field,J, dissenting)

6 Gen. 23:16

It is thought that money at this time (around 1860 B.C.) was made in the form of rings, probably of silver. Later it was made in the shape of discs or coins. In 700 B.C., coins of gold, silver, and a mixture of gold and silver, were in use in Asia Minor. Bronze coins came into use about 600 B.C.

Scriptures.[7] Thus it appears that during a famine in Canaan, about 1707 B.C., the sons of Jacob took "bundles of money" into Egypt to buy corn.[8] But the first Scriptural reference to coinage is the authority given by king Antiochus to Simon the high priest and prince of Jews to "coin money for thy country with thine own stamp."[9]

In the absence of money, the people exchanged commodities or other property, as they no doubt did before it came into use. Thus, on failure of money among the Egyptians in the time of Joseph, they exchanged their cattle and lands for food.[10]

[§262]   The law disapproves of unnecessary borrowing. It is commanded that "thou shalt not borrow."[11] In particular, it is reprehensible to "banquet upon borrowing"[12] or to build one's house "with other men's money."[13] It is reasoned that "the borrower is servant to the lender."[14]

On the other hand a lender of money ought not to be reproached,[15] for it is not improper to lend to another,[16] and in some circumstances it is one's duty to do so.[17] Jesus commanded that one turn not away "from him that would borrow of thee."[18] And doubtless it is better to lend money to a brother or friend, and lose it, than to let it "rust under a stone to be lost."[19] But one should not lend "unto him that is mightier than thyself; for is thou lendest him, count it but lost."[20]

[§263]   "Usury" originally meant any charge for the use of money[21] or property loaned to another, and not—as the word has erroneously come to mean in modern parlance—merely an excessive charge for a loan.[22] From primitive days

---

7 See for example Lev. 25:37; Deut. 23:19; 2 Kings 5:26; Ecclesiastes 7:12, 10:19; Isa. 52:3, 55:1; Micah 3:11; Matt. 17:24, 22:19, 25:18; Mark 6:8; Luke 9:3; Acts 8:20, 24:26
   Not money, but "the love of money" —covetousness—is "the root of all evil." 1 Tim. 6:10

8 Gen. 42:2,35

9 1 Mac. 15:6

10 Gen. 47:17,20; and see supra §§100, 165

11 Deut. 15:6

12 Ecclesiasticus 18:33 ("Be not a beggar by banqueting upon borrowing, when thou hast nothing in thy purse")

13 Ecclesiasticus 21:8 ("He that buildeth his house with other men's money is like one that gathereth himself stones for the tomb of his burial")

14 Prov. 22:7; Daly v Maitland (1879) 88 Penn. St. 384, 32 AR 457, 459 (Sharswood,CJ)

15 Ecclesiasticus 29:28

16 Deut. 15:6 ("thou shalt lend unto many nations")

17 See supra §157, and infra §273

18 Matt. 5:42

19 Ecclesiasticus 29:10

20 Ecclesiasticus 8:12

21 4 Tex.LR (1926) 519 (Hughes) saying that "such charges were in themselves deemed immoral."

22 See 27 RCL 203
   In early times, "usury" and "interest" were synonymous, but later interest came to signify a moderate and lawful charge, and usury an excessive and unlawful charge, for the use of money. 4 Jn. Marshall LQ (1939) 489 (Schneider)

the taking of interest or usury was regarded with abhorrence,[23] and in many nations it was formerly prohibited by law.[24] According to an ancient dictum—

"Money is naturally barren; and to make it breed money is preposterous, and a perversion of the end of its institution, which was only to secure the purpose of exchange and not of profit."[25]

[§264] —— Biblical law condemns interest, except when exacted of "strangers,"[26] commanding that

"If thou lend money to any of my people that is poor by thee, thou shalt not be to him as an usurer, neither shalt thou lay upon him usury."[27]

"Thou shalt not lend upon usury to thy brother; usury of money, usury of victuals, usury of any thing that is lent upon usury:

"Unto a stranger thou mayest lend upon usury; but unto thy brother thou shalt not lend upon usury: that the Lord thy God may bless thee in all that thou settest thine hand to in the land whither thou goest to possess it."[28]

It has been said that the prohibition against usury was intended—

"First, to obviate that avaricious disposition so observable in that people, and to prevent it from running out into oppression of one another; and second, thereby to cement them into a closer bond of amity to each other. Third, to secure and strengthen that democratical government Moses intended to institute, by preserving some kind of equality in property. Upon which principle, the laws of Jubilee, and against alienating land for ever, were also instituted."[29]

But like many other wise provisions, these against usury were violated even by the nobles, priests and rulers, who found the charging of usury a convenient method of acquiring more wealth without labor. Thus it is related that Nehemiah rebuked the nobles and rulers of his time for the exaction of usury, and took an oath of the priests to leave off usury.[30]

---

23 4 Jn. Marshall LQ (1939) 489 (Schneider)

24 "Usury seems to have been always condemned by the ancient laws of England, though an usurer was only punishable by ecclesiastical censures in his lifetime. But if it was found by twelve men after his death, that he died an usurer, he was compared to a thief, his goods were forfeited to the King, and his lands escheated." Anderson v Winston (1736) Jefferson's (Va.) Rep. 24, 27

Early laws of the Chinese and Hindus prohibited usury. 4 Jn Marshall LQ (1939) 489 (Schneider)

25 Hill v George (1849) 5 Tex. 87, 90 Cravens, Spec.J) saying that "The right to recover interest does not seem to be one of those incidents that naturally follow upon parting with the use of money," and quoting the Aristotelian dictum.

Usury as being not against natural justice, see Puffendorf's Law of Nature, B. 5, c. 7, s. 8 ad finem, and Barbeyrac's notes thereupon

26 Ps. 15:5; Prov. 28:8; Jer. 15:10; Ezek. 22:12

Under the law of Moses, the Jewish nation were "permitted to take usury of strangers, though not of one another." Anderson v Winston (1736) Jefferson's (Va.) Rep 24

27 Ex. 22:25; 42 Wash.L. Rep. (1914) 771 (Bernard); and see Lev. 25:36,37

28 Deut. 23:19,20

He that "hath given forth upon usury, and hath taken increase . . . shall surely die." Ezek. 18:13

29 Anderson v Winston (1736) Jefferson's (Va.) Rep. 24

30 Neh. 5:1-12

In a parable of Jesus, the master reproved his servant for not having put his money to the exchangers so that he should later receive his money with usury.[31] But this is to be understood as teaching that a servant should bestir himself to promote the interests of his master, and not as divine approval of the forbidden practice of usury.

[§265] —— Out of respect for Mosaic law, primitive Christians took no interest.[32] And "the common law of England proscribed the taking of any, the least interest for the loan of money as being a mortal sin."[33] But since the Sixteenth Century[34] nearly all countries have departed from the old rule by allowing the collection of interest at stipulated rates.[35] It has been reasoned that money is now loaned to facilitate commerce rather than, as formerly, to relieve the distress of the poor,[36] and it is commonly thought that, under modern conditions, lending upon interest is necessary—that it is "of great use in all trading countries."[37]

CHAPTER 38

DEBT, RELEASE AND RESTITUTION

[§266] The law looks with disfavor upon the incurring of debt. The general rule is to "owe no man any thing"[38] and thus to be "chargeable to no man."[39] Credit should not be

31 Matt. 25:27

32 Anderson v Winston (1736) Jefferson's (Va.) Rep. 24, 27
The early Christian church forbade interest. St.Augustine denounced agreements for interest as an unjust appropriation. Epist. 43, 25

33 Hill v George (1849) 3 Tex. 87, 91 (Cravens, Spec.J)
The taking of interest was spoken of a "grinding the faces of the poor." Isa. 3:15

34 Interest was first sanctioned in England in 1545, the rate being set at 10 per cent.

35 Hill v George (1849) 5 Tex. 87, 91 (Cravens, Spec. J)

36 18 Ore. LR (1938) 59
But modern laws generally make no distinction as between commercial and distress loans. In practice, when commercial loans bear six per cent interest, the poor are usually obliged to pay interest at 12, 18 or even 60 per cent.

37 Anderson v Winston (1736) Jefferson's (Va.) Rep. 24, 28
But this view is by no means universal. Some have concluded that modern laws allowing interest but limiting the rate thereof have produced more harm than good—that they have caused excessive private and public debts and have resulted in periodic economic depressions or panics. The question is probably insoluable at present. The modern economic structure rests on interest-bearing debt. But one may venture to say the structure would have been sounder had Biblical law been adhered to.

38 Rom. 13:8

39 2 Cor. 11:9

given hastily,[40] but when it has been given the debtor should do justice to the creditor.[41] In other words he should pay the debt,[42] and he should doubtless pay it promptly, for it is said to "Let not thine hand be stretched out to receive, and shut when thou shouldst repay."[43] But if one cannot pay his debt, then according to the Christian law, it should be forgiven him.[44]

[§267] —— Under the old law, a debtor who failed or was unable to pay his debt—like a thief unable to make restitution[45]—could be seized and sold into bondage.[46] Even his wife and children, and all of his possessions could be taken and sold if necessary to pay the debt.[47] Moreover a creditor could seize a defaulting debtor "and cast him into prison till he should pay the debt."[48]

But the sale or imprisonment of a debtor is inconsistent with the doctrines of Christian law, under which the debt should be forgiven[49] at least where the debtor asks for patience and promises to pay.[50] And whereas debtors were formerly imprisoned both in England and the American states, that practice has been generally abolished except in cases of fraud.[1]

[§268] Mosaic law—though not demanding the "forgiveness" of debt—provided for the release or discharge of all indebtedness,[2]—other than that owing by "strangers"—at the time of the seven-year sabbath, when the law was publicly read to the people.[3]

"At the end of every seven years thou shalt make a release.

"And this is the manner of the release: Every creditor that lendeth ought unto his neighbour shall release it; he shall not exact it of his neighbour, or of his brother; because it is called the Lord's release.

---

40 Ecclesiasticus 19:4 ("He that is hasty to give credit is lightminded")
41 McAllister v Marshall (1814) 6 Binney (Pa.) 338, 6 AD 458, 465 (Brackenridge,J) saying "I say to the debtor do justice to the creditor; love, mercy and this, is the language of the scripture."

The claims of creditors rest on legal obligations higher than the demands of affection or generosity. "A man must be just before he is generous." Kahre v McCourtney (1942) 162 SW2d (Ark.) 41, 43 (Mehaffy,J)
42 2 Kings 4:7 ("pay thy debt")
43 Ecclesiasticus 4:31
44 Matt. 18:27
"And forgive us our debts, as we forgive our debtors." Matt. 6:12
"And forgive us our sins; for we also forgive every one that is indebted to us." Luke 11:4

45 Ex. 22:3
46 See supra §233
47 See Isa. 50:1 ("which of my creditors is it to whom I have sold you?"); Matt. 18:25 ("But forasmuch as he [a servant who owed a certain king ten thousand talents] had not to pay, his lord commanded him to be sold, and his wife, and children and all that he had, and payment to be made")
48 Matt. 18:30
49 See supra §266
50 Matt. 18:26,29 ("Have patience with me, and I will pay thee all")

1 "No person shall be imprisoned for debt . . . unless in cases of fraud." See for example, Cal.Const. (1879) art. I, §15
2 Neh. 10:31
3 Deut. 31:10

"Of a foreigner thou mayest exact it again: but that which is thine with thy brother thine hand shall release;

"Save when there shall be no poor among you; for the Lord shall greatly bless thee in the land which the Lord thy God giveth thee for an inheritance to possess it."[4]

Modern statutes of limitation and bankruptcy acts fulfill the purpose of the ancient law of sabbatical release—the former by forbidding the bringing of an action upon a debt after a certain number of years[5] and the latter enabling a debtor to turn over his property in satisfaction of his debts.[6]

[§269] Mosaic law further provided for a "fifty-year jubilee," which was intended to check a tendency that had arisen to dispose of family inheritances to strangers,[7] and also to preserve "some kind of equality in property."[8] This law required that—

". . . thou shalt number seven sabbaths of years unto thee, seven times seven years; and the space of seven sabbaths of years shall be unto thee forty and nine years.

"Then shalt thou cause the trumpet of the jubilee to sound on the tenth day of the seventh month; in the day of atonement shall ye make the trumpet sound throughout all your land.

"And ye shall hallow the fiftieth year, and proclaim liberty throughout all the land unto all the inhabitants thereof: it shall be a jubilee unto you; and ye shall return every man unto his possession, and ye shall return every man unto his family.

"A jubilee shall that fiftieth year be unto you: ye shall not sow, neither reap that which groweth of itself in it, nor gather the grapes in it of thy vine undressed.

"For it is the jubilee; it shall be holy unto you: ye shall eat the increase thereof out of the field.

"In the year of this jubilee ye shall return every man unto his possession

"And if thou sell ought unto thy neighbour, or buyest ought of thy neighbour's hand, ye shall not oppress one another:

"According to the number of years after the jubilee thou shalt buy of thy neighbour, and according unto the number of years of the fruits he shall sell unto thee:

"According to the multitude of years thou shalt increase the price thereof, and according to the fewness of years thou shalt diminish the price of it: for according to the number of years of the fruits doth he sell unto thee.[9]

"And if a man purchase of the Levites, then the house that was sold, and the city of his possession, shall go out in the year of jubilee: for the houses of the cities of the Levites are their possession among the children of Israel."[10]

---

4   Deut. 15:1-4
5   34 Am Jur 13
6   6 Am Jur 516
7   14 Gr.B. (1902) 85 (Amram)

8   Anderson v Winston (1736) Jefferson's (Va.) Rep. 24
9   Lev. 25:8-16
10   Lev. 25:33

CHAPTER 39

INCOMPETENTS AND INDIGENTS

270 In general   271 The afflicted   272 The aged   273 The poor   274 —— Harvest
rules   275 —— Public aid   276 Widows and orphans

[§270]   That the afflicted must be cared for, the hungry fed, and the naked clothed, has long been accepted by the civilized social conscience the world over.[11]   According to Biblical law, the burden of caring for an afflicted or incompetent person rests upon the head of the family to which he belongs,[12] that is, the husband[13] or father.[14]   But the law also makes it a universal duty, resting upon everyone according to his ability, to "comfort the feeble-minded,"[15] "give alms,"[16] "relieve the oppressed"[17] and "support the weak."[18]

[§271]   The law not only forbids "oppression" generally,[19] but it more specifically condemns the "oppression" of those who are afflicted,[20] that is "the maimed, and the halt, and the blind."[21]   With reference to the blind and the deaf, it is provided that "thou shalt not . . . put a stumblingblock before the blind"[22] nor make him "to wander out of the way,"[23] and that "thou shalt not curse the deaf."[24]

[§272]   The duty of caring for an aged and decrepit father or mother is one which rests upon a child, and in particular upon a son.   Though a son may properly "leave" his parents and "cleave" unto his wife,[25] he has no right to neglect them. On the contrary, the child is bound to "honour" his father and mother.[26]

"Honour thy father and mother in word and deed . . ."
". . . help thy father in his age, and grieve him not as long as he liveth.

---

11 Powers v First Nat. Bank (1942) 161 SW2d (Tex.Com.App.) 273, 278 (Brewster,C)

12 See supra §207

13 See supra §212

14 See supra §225

15 1 Thess. 5:14 (and "warn them that are unruly")

16 Tobit 4:7,8 ("Give alms of thy substance; . . . If thou hast abundance, give alms accordingly: if thou have but a little, be not afraid to give according to that little")

17 Isa. 1:17

18 1 Thess. 5:14
"Strengthen ye the weak hands, and confirm the feeble knees." Isa. 35:3

19 See supra §246

20 Prov. 22:22 ("oppress [not] the afflicted in the gate")

21 Luke 14:21

22 Lev. 19:14

23 Deut. 27:18 ("cursed be he that maketh the blind to wander out of the way")

24 Lev. 19:14

25 See supra §197

26 See supra §227

"And if his understanding fail, have patience with him, and despise him not when thou art in thy full strength."[27]

Generally, one should not "dishonour . . . a man in his old age,"[28] nor should one "rebuke . . . an elder, but entreat him as a father"[29] and "the elder women as mothers."[30]   And in Leviticus it is directed to "rise up before the hoary head, and honour the face of the old man."[31]

But the law also places certain duties upon the aged, as regards their behavior—

"That the aged men be sober, grave, temperate, sound in faith, in charity, in patience.
"The aged women likewise, that they be in behavior as becometh holiness, not false accusers, not given to much wine, teachers of good things."[32]

[§273]   According to the Scriptures "the poor shall never cease out of the land"[33]—"ye have the poor always with you."[34]   The law forbids the oppression,[35] robbery[36] and vexation[37] of the poor.   On the other hand it demands that they be given consideration[38] and mercy[39]—that they be helped or "relieved."[40]   Thus it is commanded

". . . Thou shalt open thine hand wide unto thy brother, to thy poor, to thy needy, in thy land."[41]
". . . thou . . . shalt surely lend him sufficient for his need, in that which he wanteth."[42]
"Take thou no usury of him, or increase:
"Thou shalt not give him thy money upon usury, nor lend him thy victuals for increase."[43]

27 Ecclesiasticus 3:8,12,13
28 Ecclesiasticus 8:6
29 1 Tim. 5:1
30 1 Tim. 5:2
31 Lev. 19:32
    "The faces of elders were not honoured." Lam. 5:12
32 Titus 2:2,3
    "The hoary head is a crown of glory, if it be found in the way of righteousness." Prov. 16:31
33 Deut. 15:11
34 Matt. 26:11; Mark 14:7; John 12:8
    This has often been recognized. See 1 Ore.LR (1921) No. 2, p. 1; Dodge v Williams (1879) 46 Wis. 70, 50 NW 1103, 1105 (Ryan,CJ); Rummens v Evans (1932) 168 Wash. 527, 13 P2d 26, 28 (Holcomb, J); State v Hutchinson (1933) 173 Wash. 72, 21 P2d 514, 515 (Holcomb,J, dissenting)
    But the law pertaining to the seven-year release intimates that there may be occasions "when there shall be no poor among you." See supra §268

35 Zech. 7:10; Prov. 22:16
    "He that oppresseth the poor reproacheth his Maker." Prov. 14:31
    He that "hath oppressed the poor and needy . . . shall surely die." Ezek. 18:12,13
36 Prov. 22:22
37 Ezek. 22:29
    "Whoso mocketh the poor reproacheth his maker." Prov. 17:5
38 Ps. 41:1 ("Blessed is he that considereth the poor")
39 Prov. 14:31 ("he that honoreth" his Maker "hath mercy on the poor")
40 Lev. 25:35 ("if thy brother be waxen poor, and fallen into decay with thee; then thou shalt relieve him: yea, though he be a stranger, or a sojourner, that he may live with thee")
41 Deut. 15:11
    "Thou shalt not turn away from him that hath need." Two Ways 4:8
42 Deut. 15:8
43 Lev. 25:36,37

"And if thy brother that dwelleth by thee be waxen poor, and be sold unto thee; thou shalt not compel him to serve as a bondservant:

"But as an hired servant, and as a sojourner, he shall be with thee, and shall serve thee unto the year of jubilee:[44]

"And then shall he depart from thee, both he and his children with him, and shall return unto his own family, and unto the possession of his fathers shall he return.[45]

"Thou shalt not rule over him with rigour."[46]

Nevertheless it is recognized that poverty often results from "slothfulness" or "unrighteousness,"[47] and the law requires neither that the slothful be fed[48] nor the wicked helped.[49]

[§274] —— Mosaic law sets forth several "harvest rules" which were designed as a "poor law" for the benefit of "the needy and the passing stranger."[50]

". . . when ye reap the harvest of your land, thou shalt not wholly reap the corners of thy field, neither shalt thou gather the gleanings of thy harvest.

"And thou shalt not glean thy vineyard, neither shalt thou gather every grape of thy vineyard; thou shalt leave them for the poor and stranger."[1]

"When thou cuttest down thine harvest in thy field, and hast forgot a sheaf in the field, thou shalt not go again to fetch it: it shall be for the stranger, for the fatherless, and for the widow . . .

"When thou beatest thine olive tree, thou shalt not go over the boughs again: it shall be for the stranger, for the fatherless and for the widow.

"When thou gatherest the grapes of thy vineyard, thou shalt not glean it afterward: it shall be for the stranger, for the fatherless, and for the widow."[2]

Under this law the poor and unfortunate—like Naomi and Ruth[3]—were able to subsist without begging alms.[4]

[§275] —— According to Biblical law charity is a personal and private duty.[5] There is nothing to suggest that a

---

44 See supra §269

45 Lev. 25:39-41

46 Lev. 25:43

47 "I have been young and now am old, yet have I not seen the righteous forsaken, nor his seed begging bread." Ps. 37:25; McAllister v Marshal (1814) 6 Binney (Pa.) 338, 6 AD 458, 466 (Brackenridge,J)

48 2 Thess. 3:10

49 See supra §162

"Insolvency in itself carries with it the presumption of dishonesty; for it is oftener the result of imprudence, than of misfortune; and I cannot call the man who makes use of the property of others, even imprudently, a perfectly honest man; and the man, who runs in debt, makes use of the property of

others." Wilt v Franklin (1809) 1 Binney (Pa.) 502, 526 (Brackenridge,J)

50 See 5 Cal.Jur. 28; Hull's Estate (1894) 3 Coffey's Cal.Prob. Dec. 378; Fontain v Ravenel (1855) 17 How. (US) 369, 15 L ed 80; Dodge v Williams (1879) 46 Wis. 70, 50 NW 1103, 1107

1 Lev. 19:9,10

"And when ye reap the harvest of your land, thou shalt not make clean riddance of the corners of thy field when thou reapest, neither shalt thou gather any gleaning of thy harvest: thou shalt leave them unto the poor, and to the stranger." Lev. 23:22

2 Deut. 24:19-21

3 See Ruth, ch. 2

4 13 Gr.B. (1901) 313 (Amram)

5 See supra §18

government—except in times of public calamity like the famine in Egypt[6]—should be an agency for the care of the afflicted, the aged, or the poor. On the contrary it appears that government fulfills its appointed purposes when it keeps the peace and administers justice,[7] leaving it to the heads of families and to the various communities to care for their own members. But "the pauper is not to be left starving" when those who ought to maintain him fail of their duty.[8] For some time and in many countries the care of the afflicted and the feeding and clothing of the poor have been recognized "as an obligation attaching to government itself to be discharged by public taxation. It is a duty that enlightened countries make every reasonable effort to perform."[9]

[§276] Various passages are to be found in reference to the protection and welfare of "the widow and the fatherless."[10] It is said that "The Lord . . . relieveth the fatherless and widow,"[11] and it appears that trusts were sometimes established by "rich men" for their relief.[12] It is commanded that one "judge,"[13] "plead for"[14] and "visit" widows and orphans,[15] and that the corners of the field, the forgotten sheaf and the gleanings be left for them.[16] On the other hand, it is forbidden to "afflict,"[17] oppress[18] or vex[19] "any widow, or fatherless child,"[20] or to take a widow's "raiment" in pledge.[21] But it is recognized that some widows are not entitled to relief. So although St. Paul says to "Honour widows that are widows indeed," he observes that

". . . if any widow have children or nephews, let them . . . requite their parents . . .
"If any man or woman . . . have widows. let them relieve them.[22]

---

6 See supra §100
7 See supra §77
It may be argued that when government adequately performs its legitimate functions, and thus protects its people against oppression, there will be little need for public or organized charity.
8 Overseers v Overseers (1810) 3 Binney (Pa.) 22, 25 (Tilghman,CJ)
9 Powers v First Nat. Bank (1942) 161 SW2d (Tex.Com.App.) 273, 278 (Brewster,C)
10 Mal. 3:5
"The orphan has always presented a strong appeal to charitable impulse." Powers v First Nat. Bank (1942) 161 SW2d (Tex.Com.App.) 273, 280 (Brewster,C)
11 Ps. 146:9
12 2 Mac. 3:10,11 (noting that in the reign of Seleucus, certain rich men had deposited money in the temple at Jerusalem for the relief of widows and fatherless children)

13 Isa. 1:7
14 Isa. 1:17
15 James 1:27 ("Pure religion and undefiled before God and the Father is this, to visit the fatherless and widows in their affliction, and to keep himself unspotted from the world")
"Be as a father unto the fatherless, and instead of an husband unto their mother." Ecclesiasticus 4:10
16 See supra §275
17 Ex. 22:22-24 ("Ye shall not afflict any widow, or fatherless child. If thou afflict them in any wise, and they cry at all unto me . . . I will kill you with the sword")
18 Zech. 7:10 ("oppress not the widow, nor the fatherless"); Mal. 3:5 ("I will be a swift witness against . . . those that oppress . . . the widow, and the fatherless")
19 Ezek. 22:7
20 Ex. 22:22
21 See supra §158
22 1 Tim. 5:3,4,16

PART V

GENERAL LAWS

CHAPTER 40

MISCELLANEOUS PROVISIONS

277 Buildings   278 Clothing   279 Cutting of hair and beard, and marking or mutilating body   280 Giving and changing names

[§277]   In the beginning, men usually dwelt in tents.[23] But they began at a very early time to erect buildings: it appears that Cain built a city.[24]   It is doubtless lawful and proper to build houses and dwell in them,[25] for God made houses for some.[26]   But one should not build a house with another's money.[27]   Before starting to build, he should count the cost "whether he have sufficient to finish it."[28]

The Scriptures contain specifications for the ark built by Noah,[29] the altar,[30] ark[31] and tabernacle constructed under the direction of Moses in the wilderness,[32] and the temple and palace of Solomon.[33]   And a building regulation—similar to modern building regulations in force in cities[34]—is found in Mosaic law.   The provision is that—

"When thou buildest a new house, then thou shalt make a battlement for thy roof, that thou bring not blood upon thine house, if any man fall from thence."[35]

This regulation indicates a duty on the part of a property owner to guard against injury to others by reason of the construction or condition of his property.[36]

23 Gen. 4:20 (those who had cattle)
24 Gen. 4:17
25 The prophet Jeremiah commanded the captives who were carried away to Babylon to "Build ye houses, and dwell in them." Jer. 29:5
But Jonadab commanded his sons not to build houses to dwell in, but to dwell in tents, and they obeyed him. Jer. 35:7-10
26 God made houses for the Hebrew midwives in Egypt who feared him. Ex. 1:21
27 See supra §262

28 Luke 14:28
29 Gen. 6:14-16
30 Ex. 27:1-8
31 Ex. 25:10-22
32 Ex., chaps. 25-27
33 1 Kings, chaps. 6,7
34 42 Wash. L. Rep. (1914) 772 (Barnard)
35 Deut. 22:8
36 Benton v St.Louis (1913) 248 Mo. 108, 154 SW 473 (Lamm, J) saying that Deut. 22:8 is authority for requiring guard rails on sidewalks along deep excavations or on stairways.

[§278] Nakedness is natural to man, no doubt.[37] At first, Adam and Eve "were both naked, the man and his wife, and were not ashamed."[38] But when they had eaten the forbidden fruit, their "eyes . . . were opened" and they clothed themselves in aprons of fig leaves sewed together.[39] And afterwards the Lord clothed them in "coats of skins."[40] In the course of time, other materials came to be used for clothing.[41] Mosaic law prescribes that clothing shall be made of a single, unmixed material, such as wool or linen; the rule being that "thou shalt not wear a garment of divers sorts, as of woolen and linen together."[42] And to prevent one from masquerading in clothing of the opposite sex, the law requires that—

"The woman shall not wear that which pertaineth unto a man, neither shall a man put on a woman's garment: for all that do so are abomination unto the Lord thy God."[43]

[§279] Mosaic law forbade the cutting of the hair and beard in imitation of others who indulged in such practices out of superstition. It provides that "Ye shall not round the corners of your heads, neither shalt thou mar the corners of thy beard,[44] also that "ye shall not make any baldness between your eyes for the dead."[45] According to the New Testament, a man should have short, and a woman long, hair. It is said that "if a man have long hair, it is a shame unto him, but if a woman have long hair, it is a glory to her."[46]

Mosaic law also forbide the marking or mutilation of the body.

"Ye shall not make any cuttings in your flesh for the dead,[47] nor print any marks upon you."[48]

[§280] According to the primitive custom, a child was ordinarily given its name by its father,[49] as the head of the family.[50] But sometimes the name was given by the child's

---

37 Rule as to apparel of women, see infra §332
38 Gen. 2:25
39 Gen. 3:7
40 Gen. 3:21
"The lambs are for thy clothing." Prov. 27:28
41 The Israelites were required to "make fringes upon the four quarters" of their garments, that they might look upon them "and remember all the commandments of the Lord, and do them." Num. 15:38,39; Deut. 22:12
42 Deut. 22:11
". . . neither shall a garment mingled of linen and woolen come upon thee." Lev. 19:19

43 Deut. 22:5
44 Lev. 19:27
The law further provided as to priests that "They shall not make baldness upon their head, neither shall they shave off the corner of their beard." Lev. 21:5
45 Deut. 14:1
46 1 Cor. 11:14,15
47 ". . . ye shall not cut yourselves . . . for the dead." Deut. 14:1
Priests were forbidden to "make any cuttings in their flesh." Lev. 21:5
48 Lev. 19:28
49 See for example Gen. 4:26, 5:28,29, 16:15, 21:3
50 See supra §211

mother,[1] though a name so given might subsequently be changed by the father.[2] Also, some persons were known by two names, a proper name and an alias.[3]

A name may be changed by legal authority as well as by the father or the person himself. Thus, it appears that the Lord changed Abram's name to Abraham,[4] Sarai's to Sarah,[5] and Jacob's to Israel;[6] Jesus changed Simon's name to Cephas,[7] and Saul's name was changed to Paul.[8] Joash gave his son Gideon a new name,[9] though he continued to be called Gideon as before. And Jeremiah changed Pashur's name to Magor-missabib.[10] The Bible also furnishes a precedent for changing the name of one who has gone to dwell in a foreign country, so as to conform to the tongue of the land. Thus, it is said that Pharaoh changed Joseph's name to Zaphnath-paaneah,[11] and that the prince of the eunuchs of Nebuchadnezzar "gave unto Daniel the name of Belteshazzar; and to Hananiah, of Shadrach; and to Mishael, of Meshach; and to Azariah, of Abednego."[12]

CHAPTER 41

AGRICULTURE—HUSBANDRY

281 In general   282 Rules governing agriculture   283 The sabbatical rest

[§281] Agriculture or "husbandry" includes horticulture and stock raising, as well as the ordinary cultivation of the soil for food. This occupation is regarded with particular esteem.[13] It is said that "the most High hath ordained husbandry,"[14] and that they are "blessed" who "sow beside all waters, that send forth thither the feet of the ox and the ass."[15] But from earliest times, some tilled the soil while

---

1 See for example Gen. 4:25, 30:11, 13,18,20

2 See Gen. 35:18 (where Rachael, dying in childbirth, named the child Ben-oni, but his father Jacob changed the name to Benjamin)

3 See Gen. 36:1,8 (that "Esau" was also called "Edom"); Judges 7:1 (referring to "Jerubbaal, who is Gideon"); Acts 13:9 (noting that Saul "is also called Paul")

4 Gen. 17:5

5 Gen. 17:15

6 Gen. 32:28, 35:10

7 John 1:42 ("Thou art Simon the son of Jona: thou shalt be called Cephas,

which is by interpretation, A stone")

8 Acts 13:9

9 Judges 6:32

10 Jer. 20:3

11 Gen. 41:45

12 Dan. 1:7

13 "He that tilleth his land shall be satisfied with bread" (Prov. 12:11), that is to say, he "shall have plenty of bread" (Prov. 28:19). "He . . . shall increase his heap" (Ecclesiasticus 20:28).

14 Ecclesiasticus 7:15
The Lord sent forth Adam from the garden of Eden, "to till the ground from whence he was taken." Gen. 3:23

15 Isa. 32:20

others dwelt in tents and had cattle.[16] "Cain was a tiller of the ground," but "Abel was a keeper of sheep."[17] "Abram was very rich in cattle"[18] and "Lot also . . . had flocks, and herds, and tents."[19] Isaac "sowed" in the land,[20] but also "had possession of flocks, and possession of herds."[21] On the other hand, Jonadab commanded his sons to have no vineyard, nor field, nor seed, and Jeremiah commended them for their filial obedience.[22]

[§282] The duties of a tiller of the soil are to plow and sow his land,[23] plant his garden[24] and prune his vineyard, and gather in the fruits thereof,[25] without observance of the wind or regard to the clouds.[26]

"He that observeth the wind shall not sow; and he that regardeth the clouds shall not reap.

"In the morning sow thy seed, and in the evening withhold not thine hand: for thou knowest not whether shall prosper, either this or that, or whether they both shall be alike good."[27]

The plowman "should plow in hope,"[28] not stopping "by reason of the cold."[29] But he may not use "an ox and an ass together."[30]

With respect to seed, it is commanded that "thou shalt not sow thy field with mingled seed"[31] and "thou shalt not sow thy vineyard with divers seeds."[32] Nor should one sow too sparingly. "He which soweth sparingly shall reap also sparingly, and he which soweth bountifully shall reap also bountifully."[33]

One should "hedge" his "possession about with thorns,"[34]

---

16 Gen. 4:20 (saying that "Jubal . . . was the father of such as dwell in tents, and of such as have cattle")

17 Gen. 4:2

18 Gen. 13:2

19 Gen. 13:5

20 Gen. 26:12

21 Gen. 26:14 ("and the Philistines envied him")

"Jacob was a plain man, dwelling in tents," but "Esau was a cunning hunter, a man of the field." Gen. 25:27

22 Jer. 35:7,18,19; and see supra §277

23 Gen. 47:23 ("ye shall sow the land")

24 Jer. 29:5

25 Lev. 25:3

But it is forbidden to reap the corners of the field, to go a second time over the boughs of the olive tree, or to gather the gleanings. See supra §274

And doubtless it is better to "leave a few . . . noxious branches to their luxuriant growth, than, by pruning them away, to injure the vigour of those yielding . . . proper fruits." Report on Virginia Resolutions, 4 Madison's Works 544

26 Ecclesiastes 11:4

27 Ecclesiastes 11:4,6

28 1 Cor. 9:10

29 Prov. 20:4 ("The sluggard will not plow by reason of the cold; therefore shall he beg in harvest, and have nothing")

30 Deut. 22:10

This requirement suggests the law against cruelty to animals. 42 Wash. L.Rep. (1914) 772 (Barnard)

31 Lev. 19:19

32 Deut. 22:9 ("lest the fruit of thy seed which thou has sown, and the fruit of thy vineyard, be defiled")

33 2 Cor. 9:6

34 Ecclesiasticus 28:24

for "where no hedge is, there the possession is spoiled."[35]
And if he has cattle, he should know the state of his flocks
and look well to his herds.[36]

[§283]   Mosaic law further enjoins the observance of a
seventh year of rest for land, "that the poor of thy people . . .
and . . . the beasts of the field" may eat.[37]

"Six years thou shalt sow thy field, and six years thou shalt prune
thy vineyard, and gather in the fruit thereof;
"But in the seventh year shall be a sabbath of rest unto the land,
. . . thou shalt neither sow thy field, nor prune thy vineyard.
"That which groweth of its own accord of thy harvest thou shalt
not reap, neither gather the grapes of thy vine undressed: for it is a
year of rest unto the land.
"And the sabbath of the land shall be meat for you; for thee, and
for thy servant, and for thy maid, and for thy hired servant, and for
thy stranger that sojourneth with thee.
"And for thy cattle, and for the beast that are in thy land, shall
all the increase thereof be meat."[38]

CHAPTER 42

ANIMALS AND BIRDS

284 In general   285 Giving assistance to animals in distress   286 Estrays   287
Injuries and trespasses by animals   288 Injuries to animals   289 Birds

[§284]   The Scriptures make many references to animals
and birds, both wild and domestic.[39]   Concerning the breeding of animals, it is commanded that "thou shalt not let thy
cattle gender with a diverse kind."[40]   And with respect to the
treatment of work animals, the law prescribes that "thou
shalt not muzzle the ox when he treadeth out the corn."[41]   On

---

35 Ecclesiasticus 36:25
36 Prov. 27:23
"Hast thou cattle? have an eye to
them: if they be for thy profit, keep
them with thee." Ecclesiasticus 7:22
37 Ex. 23:10,11 ("And six years thou
shalt sow thy land, and shalt gather
in the fruits thereof: but the seventh
year thou shalt let it rest and lie
still; that the poor of thy people may
eat; and what they leave the beasts
of the field shall eat. In like manner
thou shalt deal with thy vineyard,
and with thy oliveyard")
38 Lev. 25:3-7
"And if ye shall say, What shall we
eat the seventh year? behold, we shall
not sow, nor gather in our increase:

"Then I will command my blessing
upon you in the sixth year, and it
shall bring forth fruit for three years.
"And ye shall sow the eighth year,
and eat yet of old fruit until the ninth
year; until her fruits come in ye shall
eat of the old store." Lev. 25:20-22
39 Rules as to animals delivered to
another for keeping, see supra §155
Punishment of animals as for crime,
see infra §341
40 Lev. 19:19
41 Deut. 25:4; 1 Tim. 5:18
But see 1 Cor. 9:9,10, saying "Doth
God take care for oxen? . . . For our
sakes, no doubt, this is written."
As to working an ox and an ass together, see supra §282

the Sabbath day, domestic animals should be permitted to rest:[42] and during the Sabbatical year also the cattle and beasts of the field should be permitted to rest and eat of the increase of the land.[43]

[§285] "A righteous man regardeth the life of his beast,"[44] and "the good shepherd giveth his life for the sheep."[45] The law imposes the duty of giving assistance when an animal is in distress, whoever its owner may be. It is prescribed, in Mosaic law, that—

"If thou see the ass of him that hateth thee lying under his burden, . . . thou shalt surely help with him."[46]

And if—

"Thou shalt . . . see thy brother's ass or his ox fall down by the way . . . thou shalt surely help him to lift them up again."[47]

[§286] With respect to stray animals, Mosaic law declares that "if thou meet thine enemy's ox or his ass going astray, thou shalt surely bring it back to him again."[48]

"Thou shalt not see thy brother's ox or his sheep go astray, and hide thyself from them: thou shalt in any case bring them again unto thy brother.

"And if thy brother be not nigh unto thee, or if thou know him not, then thou shalt bring it unto thine house, and it shall be with thee until thy brother seek after it, and thou shalt restore it to him again. "In like manner shalt thou do with his ass . . ."[49]

[§287] Mosaic law contains rules which govern when an animal kills a person other than its owner, when it kills another animal, or when it trespasses upon lands.[50] Concerning the killing of a person by an animal, the law is that—

"If an ox gore a man or a woman, that they die; then the ox shall be surely stoned, and his flesh shall not be eaten; but the owner of the ox shall be quit.

"But if the ox were wont to push with his horn in time past, and it hath been testified to his owner, and he hath not kept him in, but that he hath killed a man or a woman; the ox shall be stoned, and his owner also shall be put to death.

"If there be laid on him a sum of money, then he shall give for the ransom of his life whatsoever is laid upon him.

42　See infra §319
43　See supra §283
44　Prov. 12:10
45　John 10:11
46　Ex. 23:5
47　Deut. 22:4

48　Ex. 23:4
49　Deut. 22:1-3
　　Generally as to lost property, see supra §133
50　Liability in primitive law for harm caused by animals, see 7 Harv. LR (1894) 325, 449 (Wigmore)

"Whether he have gored a son, or have gored a daughter, according to this judgment shall it be done unto him.

"If the ox shall push a manservant or a maidservant; he shall give unto their master thirty shekels of silver, and the ox shall be stoned."[1]

And as regards the killing of one animal by another, the law says:

". . . if one man's ox hurt another's that he die; then they shall sell the live ox, and divide the money of it; and the dead ox also they shall divide.

"Or if it be known that the ox hath used to push in time past, and his owner hath not kept him in; he shall surely pay ox for ox, and the dead shall be his own."[2]

Under Biblical law, as under modern law, the owner's liability for an injury done by an animal depends on his knowledge of its viciousness[3]—whether "the ox were wont to push with his horn in time past,[4] and it hath been testified to his owner,"—and on the failure of the owner to take precautions against his committing injury.[5]

In case of the trespass of an animal upon lands of one other than his owner, Mosaic law provides that—

"If a man shall cause a field or vineyard to be eaten, and shall put in his beast, and shall feed in another man's field; of the best of his own field, and of the best of his own vineyard, shall he make restitution."[6]

[§288] The law concerning the infliction of fatal injuries upon another's animal is that "he that killeth a beast . . . shall restore it,"[7] "he . . . shall make it good; beast for beast."[8] And in respect of animals which are injured or killed by falling into an excavation, it is provided that—

". . . if a man shall open a pit, or if a man shall dig a pit, and not cover it, and an ox or an ass fall therein; the owner of the pit shall make it good, and give money unto the owner of them, and the dead beast shall be his."[9]

---

1 Ex. 21:28-32
2 Ex. 21:35,36
3 It is necessary to show that the owner knew the animal (dog) was vicious. Shelby v Seung (1927) 144 Wash. 317, 257 P 838 (Main,J)
4 31 Harv. LR (1918) 965 (Isaacs); 42 Wash. L Rep. (1914) 771 (Barnard)
5 Ex. 21:29,36

In modern law "if any man has a dangerous domestic animal, and knows it to be such, he is in duty bound to keep it shut up, or in some way to guard his neighbor from injury by reason of its dangerous character; and if

he fails to do this, he will be liable in damages for any loss sustained by the neighbour, caused by such animal." 42 Wash. L.Rep. (1914) 771 (Barnard)

If a dog is vicious and the owner knows it, he keeps the dog at his peril and is liable to any person—even a trespasser—who, without fault, is injured by it. Brewer v Furtwangler (1933) 171 Wash. 617, 18 P2d 837 (Millard,J)

6 Ex. 22:5; and see infra §341
7 Lev. 24:21
8 Lev. 24:18
9 Ex. 21:33,34

[§289] Mosaic law contains a requirement—somewhat like those of modern laws—for the protection of birds.[10]

"If a bird's nest chance to be before thee in the way in any tree, or on the ground, whether they be young ones, or eggs, and the dam sitting upon the young, or upon the eggs, thou shalt not take the dam with the young:

"But thou shalt in any wise let the dam go, and take the young to thee; that it may be well with thee, and that thou mayest prolong thy days."[11]

In later times, birds were bought and sold. Thus it appears that doves were sold in the temple until Jesus "cast out all them that sold and bought;"[12] also that sparrows were sold "two for a farthing"[13] or "five for two farthings."[14]

CHAPTER 43

DEATH AND BURIAL

290 In general　　291 Burial places　　292 Markers

[§290] According to the primitive custom, a mourning period of seven days was observed upon the death of a neighbour or relative.[15] So, on the death of Judith "the house of Israel lamented for seven days."[16] And it is said that one should—

"let tears fall down over the dead, and begin to lament, as if thou hadst suffered great harm thyself; and then cover his body according to the custom and neglect not his burial."[17]

It was customary, among those who were able, to wrap or "wind up" the corpse in clean linen cloths,[18] with "spices,"[19] "a mixture of myrrh and aloes, about a hundred pound weight."[20] And it was considered the duty of a surviving husband to bury his deceased wife,[21] and of a surviving son to bury his deceased father or mother.[22]

---

10 See Wash.L.Rep. (1914) 772 (Barnard)

11 Deut. 22:6

12 Matt. 21:12; Mark 11:15; John 2:13-16

13 Matt. 10:29

14 Luke 12:6

15 Ecclesiasticus 22:12 ("Seven days do men mourn for him that is dead")
"Abraham came to mourn for Sarah, and to weep for her." Gen. 23:2

16 Judith 16:24; and see infra §333

17 Ecclesiasticus 38:16

18 Matt. 27:59; Mark 15:46; Luke 23:53; Acts 5:6

19 John 19:40

20 John 19:39
As to the embalming of Israel and Joseph in Egypt, see Gen. 50:2,26

21 See supra §213

22 See supra §230

[§291] In former times, burials were made in caves,[23] sepulchres,[24] or tombs,[25] and among all tribes and nations, savage and civilized, the resting places of the dead were regarded as sacred.[26] The remains of members of a family were customarily buried together—the body of a man with those of his fathers[27] and the body of a widowed husband or wife with that of the spouse who had first died.[28] For this purpose permanent family burying places were required,[29] such as the cave of Macpelah that Abraham purchased.[30]

[§292] Custom also sanctions the marking of burial places by pillars or monuments. It appears that Jacob "set a pillar" upon Rachael's grave,[31] and that Simon "built a monument upon the sepulchre of his father and his brethren, and raised it aloft to the sight, with hewn stone behind and before."[32] But it is supposed that one year should be allowed to elapse between the date of death and the time of the erection of any memorial structure.[33]

23 Gen. 23:19, 25:9,10; 29:31, 50:13 and Josh. 24:32 (all referring to burials in the cave of Machpelah); Judith 16:23
"Decency, as well as regard to the public health, point out the necessity of consigning the dead body to its original earth." 5 Binney (Pa. 1812) 179 (Yeates,J)

24 2 Chron. 16:14 ("they buried him [Asa] in his own sepulchres, which he had made for himself in the city of David, and laid him in the bed which was filled with sweet odours and divers kinds of spices prepared by the apothecaries' art: and they made a very great burning for him"); 1 Mac. 2:70 (the sons of Mattathias "buried him in the sepulchres of his fathers at Modin, and all Israel made great lamentation for him")

25 Matt. 27:60; Mark 6:29
26 Craig v Presbyterian Church (1879) 88 Pa. St. 42, 32 AR 417, 425 (Agnew, CJ,dissenting)
27 1 Mac. 2:70
28 Tobit 4:4 ("when she [thy mother] is dead, bury her by me in one grave"), 14:12 (when Anna the mother of Tobias was dead "he buried her with his father")
". . . they buried" Judith "in the cave of her husband Manasses." Judith 16:23
The young men buried Sapphira "by (beside) her husband" Ananias. Acts 5:10

29 Gen. 25:10, 49:31
30 Gen. 23:3-19; and see supra §170

"When Abraham, standing by the dead body of Sarah, addressed the sons of Heth, saying 'I am a stranger and sojourner with you, give me a possession of a burying place with you, that I may bury my dead out of my sight,' they offered him a choice of their sepulchres; but Abraham, intent upon a possession of his own, where the remains of her he had loved might repose in security, purchased the field of Macpelah of Ephron, the Hittite, for four hundred shekels of silver. Even more touching is the reference to Jacob, who, dying in Egypt, surrounded by his children, charged them and said unto them, 'I am to be gathered unto my people, bury me with my fathers in the cave that is in the field of Macpelah.' There they buried Abraham and Sarah, his wife, there they buried Isaac and Rebecca, his wife, and there I buried Leah.' Tradition has preserved to this day the identity of the cave and the tombs of those ancient worthies, undisturbed even by the Moslem, whose mosque covers and protects their resting place." Craig v Presbyterian Church (1879) 88 Pa. St. 42, 32 AR 417, 425 (Agnew, CJ,dissenting)

31 Gen. 35:20
The place was known for many centuries. See 1 Sam. 10:2
32 1 Mac. 13:27,28 ("Moreover he set up seven pyramids, one against another, for his father and his mother, and his four brethren")
33 Loeb v McCaughn (1927) 20 Fed. 2d 1002 (Dickinson,J) saying that this has the force of an obligation among "people of the Jewish faith."

CHAPTER 44

EDUCATION—SCHOOLS

[§293]   The Sacred Writings declare the desirability of instruction[34] and knowledge,[35] to the end that men—like the children of Isachar[36]—may have wisdom[37] and understanding,[38] and that they may walk uprightly.[39] Sons are admonished to "gather instruction from thy youth up: so shalt thou find wisdom till thine old age."[40] On the other hand the Scriptures caution that "much study is a weariness of the flesh,"[41] that "he that increaseth knowledge increaseth sorrow"[42] and that evil shall come upon those who are "perverted" by wisdom and knowledge.[43]

"The true benefit of . . . education is not to clothe the man with power to accumulate or display fine parts among his fellow men by employing himself about philosophic syllogisms or sophistical argument, but rather to uproot prejudices and give a broad tolerance for the rights and opinions of others, dropping the readiness to be offended and to hate, but to commiserate and pity rather."[44]

[§294]   In Mosaic law it is directed to teach "the things which thine eyes have seen" to "thy sons and thy sons' sons"[45] but this relates "to the statutes and . . . the judgments."[46] No provision was made for any formal or public education of

---

34 Prov. 8:10 ("Receive my instruction, and not silver; and knowledge rather than choice gold"), 19:20 ("Hear counsel, and receive instruction, that thou mayest be wise in thy latter end"), 23:12 ("Apply thine heart unto instruction, and thine ears to the words of knowledge")

35 Prov. 19:2 (". . . that the soul be without knowledge, it is not good"), 24:4 (". . . by knowledge shall the chambers of the mind be filled with all precious and pleasant riches")

". . . the Lord is a God of knowledge. 1 Sam. 2:3

"My people are destroyed for lack of knowledge." Hosea 4:6

36 1 Chron. 12:32

37 "Wisdom is the principal thing; therefore get wisdom . . ." Prov. 4:7

38 Deut. 4:6

". . . the Lord give thee wisdom and understanding." 1 Chron. 22:12

39 Prov. 15:21 ("a man of understanding walketh uprightly")

40 Ecclesiasticus 6:18

41 Ecclesiastes 12:12

42 Ecclesiasticus 1:18

43 "Thy wisdom and thy knowledge, it hath perverted thee, and thou hast said in thine heart, I am, and none else beside me. Therefore shall evil come upon thee . . ." Isa. 47:10,11

44 Ruse v Williams (1913) 14 Ariz. 445, 130 P 887, 45 LRANS 923, 927 (Franklin,CJ)

It has been said to be a "self-evident truth" that "an uneducated man, not qualified for any service other than manual labor, is as good as an educated man." Texas Employers' Ins. Assn. v McNorton (1936) 92 SW2d (Tex.Civ. App.) 562, 570 (Looney,J)

45 Deut. 4:9

46 Deut. 4:1

Provision for reading and expounding the law to all the people, including children, see supra §65

the young. It was doubtless contemplated that there should be a class of "learned men"[47] and there were colleges or schools for those who were intended to be priests, prophets[48] or singers,[49] or to occupy civil offices. Among other classes, it was expected merely that each man should be "wise in his work."[50] Generally it seems to have been thought that such education as children had they were to receive from their parents, who are admonished to "instruct"[1] "teach"[2] and "train" their children, who, in turn, are counselled to "hear the instruction of thy father, and forsake not the law of thy mother."[3] But St. Paul states that "the aged women" should "teach the young women to be sober, to love their husbands, to love their children, to be discreet, chaste, keepers at home, good, obedient to their own husbands . . ."[4]

In modern times the education of the young is considered an important function of government,[5] and the father of a child is regarded as having delegated part of his parental authority to the tutor or school-master.[6]

"The general theory of our educational system is that every child in the state, without regard to race, creed, or wealth, shall have the facilities for a free education."[7]

[§295] Formerly it was customary in American schools to conduct a morning exercise consisting in the reading aloud of a portion of the Bible, saying the Lord's prayer, and singing religious and patriotic songs.[8] It has often been decided that the Bible may properly be read in schools and the fact that Christianity is the prevailing religion may otherwise be

47 Ecclesiasticus 38:24

48 2 Chron. 34:22 (referring to Huldah, the prophetess who "dwelt in Jerusalem in the college")

49 1 Chron. 25:7 ("the number of them . . . that were instructed in the songs of the Lord . . . was two hundred four-score and eight")

50 Ecclesiasticus 38:31

1 Ecclesiasticus 7:23

2 See History of Susanna, v. 3, saying that the parents of Susanna "were righteous and taught their daughter according to the law of Moses."

3 Prov. 1:8, 4:1

4 Titus 2:3-5; and see infra §332

5 Herold v School Directors (1915) 136 La. 1034, 68 So. 116, LRA1915D 941, 945 (Sommerville,J)

In America, the education of the people is regarded as so much a matter of public concern, and of such paramount importance, that the constitutions of the various states have imposed on their legislatures the duty to make suitable provisions for the support and maintenance of public schools. "A general diffusion of the advantages of education" has been declared to be "essential to the preservation of the rights and liberties of the people." Donahoe v Richards (1854) 38 Me. 379, 61 AD 256, 257 (Appleton,J)

The desirability of academic freedom is recognized. But "academic freedom does not mean academic license. It is the freedom to do good and not to teach evil." Kay v Board of Higher Education—The Bertrand Russell Case (1940) 173 Misc. (NY) 943, 18 NYS2d 829 (McGeehan,J) criticized in YaleLJ (1941) 778 (Hamilton)

6 Harfst v Hoegen (1942) 163 SW2d (Mo.) 609, 613 (Douglas,J) citing 1 Bl. Com. 452

7 State v Smith (1942) 127 P2d (Kan.) 518, 522 (Harvey,J)

8 See Annotation, "Sectarianism in schools." 5 ALR 841, 20 ALR 1334, 31 ALR 1121, 57 ALR 185

recognized.[9]   In several jurisdictions it has been held that the King James' Version of the Bible is not a sectarian publication,[10] and that the mere reading of selections therefrom, without comment by the teachers, does not violate religious freedom.[11]   But in some states the law forbids Bible-reading in public schools,[12] on the theory that such reading is a preference given to Christians and a discrimination against non-Christians.[13]

[§296]   In recent times also, regulations have been adopted which require pupils to pledge allegiance and salute the American flag.[14]   According to a certain religious belief "the flag is a graven image" and a salute of the flag constitutes a worship of "other gods."[15]   But the courts have generally held

[9] 9 Cal. LR (1921) 264 (Radin) reviewing Zollman's American Civil Church Law (1917)
    Religious liberty is not infringed by repeating the Lord's prayer: Knowlton v Baumhover (1918) 182 Iowa 691, 166 NW 202, 5 ALR 841 (Weaver,J); Billard v Board of Education (1904) 69 Kan. 53, 76 P 442, 105 ASR 148; Church v Bullock (1907) 100 SW (Tex.Civ.App.) 1025, affirmed in 109 SW 115
    Nor by teaching the Ten Commandments: Commonwealth v Cooke (1859) 7 Am.L.Reg. (Mass.) 417
    Nor by singing hymns: People v Board of Education (1910) 245 Ill. 334, 29 LRANS 442, 92 NE 251 (Dunn,J)

[10] Evans v Selmas School Dist. (1924) 193 Cal. 54, 222 P 801, 31 ALR 1121

[11] 11 Cal. LR (1923) 185; Donahoe v Richards (1854) 38 Me. 379, 61 AD 256; Freeman v Scheve (1902) 65 Neb. 853, 59 LRA 927, 91 NW 846; Hackett v Brookville School Dist. (1905) 120 Ky. 608, 87 SW 792, 69 LRA 592; Wilkerson v City of Rome (1922) 152 Ga. 762, 110 SE 895, 20 ALR 1334

[12] 9 Cal. LR (1921) 264 (Radin) quoting Zollman's American Civil Church Law, p 33, to the effect that such a law "harks back to a conception of religious liberty that is Jacobinical rather than American."
    Reading the King James version of the Bible, repeating the Lord's prayer, and singing hymns, as a part of the exercises of a public school, violates constitutional provisions forbidding appropriation of public money in aid of sectarian purposes, and providing for "the free exercise and enjoyment of religious profession and worship, without discrimination." People v Board of Education (1910) 245 Ill. 334, 92 NE 251, 29 LRANS 442 (Dunn,J)
    At one time Illinois was the only state which put a "constitutional padlock on the Bible in the public schools." Wilkerson v City of Rome (1922) 152 Ga. 762, 110 SE 895, 20 ALR 1334, 1346 (Gilbert,J) quoting Schofield
    Giving credits for Bible study done outside of school violates the constitution of Washington. State v Frazier (1918) 102 Wash. 369, 173 P 35, LRA 1918 F 1056

[13] Herold v School Directors (1915) 136 La. 1034, 68 So. 116, LRA1915D 941 (Sommerville,J)

[14] Power of a legislature or school authorities to prescribe and enforce an oath of allegiance, flag salute, or other ritual of a patriotic character, see note, 110 ALR 383
    APPROVED PRACTICE IN SCHOOLS IN PLEDGING ALLEGIANCE AND SALUTING THE FLAG
    "Standing with the right hand over the heart, all repeat together the following pledge:
    "I pledge allegiance to the Flag of the United States of America and to the Republic for which it stands: One Nation, indivisible, with liberty and justice for all.
    "At the words 'to the flag,' the right hand is extended, palm upward, toward the flag and this position is held until the end, when the hand, after the words 'justice for all,' drops to the side."
    State v Smith (1942) 127 P2d (Kan.) 518, 519 (Harvey,J) quoting Manual of Patriotic Instruction, p 17

[15] State v Smith (1942) 127 P2d (Kan.) 518, 520 (Harvey,J) referring to Jehovah's Witnesses
    A school regulation requiring dancing as a part of the curriculum held inapplicable to the children of taxpayers whose religious convictions were offended thereby. See Hardwick v Fruitridge School Dist. (1921) 54 Cal. App. 696, 205 P 49

that the pledge of allegiance and flag salute do not relate to religion.[16]

"The salute and pledge do not go beyond that which, according to generally recognized principles, is due to government. There is nothing in the salute or the pledge of allegiance which constitutes an act of idolatry, or which approaches to any religious observance. It does not in any reasonable sense hurt, molest, or restrain a human being in respect to "worshipping God.""[17]

CHAPTER 45

FOOD AND DRINK—RULES OF ETIQUETTE

[§297] The Scriptures contain many provisions relating to food and drink, some of which are noticed in this chapter. Among other things, it has been said that "every man should eat and drink, and enjoy the good of all his labor."[18]

[§298] But in eating, as in other things, one should observe discretion,[19] moderation[20] and temperance.[21] Thus it is said that one should "have a care of his meat and diet"[22] and "be not unsatiable in any dainty thing, nor too greedy upon meats,"[23] and that "every man that striveth for the mastery is temperate in all things."[23a]

"For excess of meats bringeth sickness, and surfeiting will turn into choler.

"By surfeiting have many perished; but he that taketh heed prolongeth his life."[24]

---

16 Case of Three Children sentenced to reform school for refusal to salute the flag, see 4 Jn. Marshall LQ (1939) 586

17 Nichols v Mayor and School Committee of Lynn (1937) 297 Mass. 65, 110 ALR 377, 7 NE2d 577 (Rugg,J) dismissing petition for writ of mandamus to compel the reinstatement of a pupil
But in Kansas, it has been held that a child may not be expelled from school for failure to salute the flag, where such failure was based on sincere religious beliefs of the child or his parents. State v Smith (1942) 127 P2d (Kan.) 518 (Harvey,J)

18 Ecclesiastes 3:13, 5:18
"There is nothing better for a man,

than that he should eat and drink, and that he should make his soul enjoy good in his labor. This also I saw, that it was from the hand of God." Ecclesiastes 2:24

19 Ps. 112:5

20 Phil. 4:5
Sound sleep cometh of moderate eating: he riseth early, and his wits are with him." Ecclesiasticus 31:20

21 Gal. 5:23

21 Gal. 5:23

22 Ecclesiasticus 30:25

23 Ecclesiasticus 37:29

23a 1 Cor. 9:25

24 Ecclesiasticus 37:30,31

[§299] In the beginning, the prescribed diet of man consisted of "fruit and herbs."

". . . God said, Behold, I have given you every herb bearing seed, which is upon the face of all the earth, and every tree, in the which is the fruit of a tree yielding seed; to you it shall be for meat."[25]

But in the course of time it was considered proper to eat "all food that is (can be) eaten,"[26] including the flesh of animals.[27]

"Every moving thing that liveth shall be meat for you; even as the green herb have I given you all things."[28]

". . . thou mayest kill and eat flesh in all thy gates, whatsoever thy soul lusteth after, . . . as of the roebuck, and as of the hart."[29]

On the other hand, it is commanded that "Thou shalt not eat any abominable thing."[30] Even before Moses, the distinction seems to have been made between "clean" and "unclean" beasts,[31] and under Mosaic law "clean" things may be eaten, while "unclean" beasts, fishes, fowls and creeping things may not.[32] The law further prescribes that—

"Ye shall not eat of anything that dieth of itself; thou shalt give it unto the stranger that is in thy gates, that he may eat it; or thou mayest sell it unto an alien."[33]

". . . neither shall ye eat any flesh that is torn of beasts in the field; ye shall cast it to the dogs."[34]

[§300] —— It is expressly and repeatedly forbidden to "eat . . . blood"[35] or anything "with the blood."[36]

". . . ye shall eat no manner of blood, whether it be of fowl or of beast, in any of your dwellings.[37]

"And whatsoever man there be of the house of Israel, or of the

---

25 Gen. 1:29
"Of every tree of the garden thou mayest freely eat: But of the tree of knowledge of good and evil, thou shalt not eat of it." Gen. 2:16,17
"Thou shalt eat the herb of the field." Gen. 3:18

26 Gen. 6:21 (stating that God said unto Noah, "take thou unto thee of all food that is eaten, and thou shalt gather it to thee; and it shall be for food for thee, and for them")

27 But "it is good" not "to eat flesh" if thereby "thy brother stumbleth, or is offended, or is made weak." Rom. 14:21

28 Gen. 9:3
"Every creature of God is good, and nothing to be refused, if it be received with thanksgiving." 1 Tim. 4:4

29 Deut. 12:15
"When the Lord thy God shall enlarge thy border . . . thou mayest eat flesh, whatsoever thy soul lusteth after." Deut. 12:20

30 Deut. 14:3

31 Gen. 7:2 (commandment to Noah, "Of every clean beast thou shalt take to thee by sevens, the male and his female: and of beasts that are not clean by two, the male and his female")

32 Lev., Chap. 11; Deut., chap. 14 (in which chapters are set forth the beasts which are clean and those which are unclean)

33 Deut. 14:21

34 Ex. 22:31

35 Gen. 9:4; Deut. 12:16,23,24; 15:23
"Thou shalt pour it upon the ground as water." Deut. 12:16,24, 15:23

36 Lev. 19:26; Ezek. 33:25

37 Lev. 7:26
This provision is the basis of a Jewish dietary law forbidding the eating of blood-spotted eggs.

strangers that sojourn among you, that eateth any manner of blood; I . . . will cut him off from among his people."[38]

". . . No soul of you shall eat blood, neither shall any stranger that sojourneth among you eat blood."[39]

". . . Ye shall eat the blood of no manner of flesh: . . . whosoever eateth it shall be cut off."[40]

[§301] —— The use of certain kinds of fats for food is also forbidden. The rule is that—

". . . Ye shall eat no manner of fat, of ox, or of sheep, or of goat."[41]

"And the fat of the beast that dieth of itself, and the fat of that which is torn with beasts, may be used in any other use: but ye shall in no wise eat of it."[42]

But it was considered that fats other than those expressly forbidden might lawfully be used. Thus it appears that after the reading of the law to the people[43] Nehemiah said to them, "Go your way, eat the fat, and drink the sweet, and send portions unto them for whom nothing is prepared."[44] It seems that fats such as that of the goose or of vegetable origin may properly be eaten.

[§302] —— Honey was recognized as a proper and useful food at a very early period, and it is thought to have been man's only sweetening material for thousands of years. In the Scriptures it appears that the sons of Israel took "a little honey" as a gift to their brother Joseph in Egypt;[45] Samson and his father and mother ate honey taken out of the carcass of a lion;[46] and John the Baptist subsisted upon a diet of locusts and wild honey.[47] It is recommended to "eat thou honey, because it is good; and the honeycomb, which is sweet to thy taste."[48] But honey should nevertheless be eaten moderately: "It is not good to eat much honey."[49]

[§303] —— Milk and the products thereof—butter[50] and cheese[1]—have also been used for food since primitive times.[2]

---

38 Lev. 17:10

39 Lev. 17:12

40 Lev. 17:14
And see 1 Sam. 14:31-34, where it appears that the people killed and ate with the blood animals captured from the Philistines.

41 Lev. 7:23

42 Lev. 7:24
"It shall be a perpetual statute for your generations throughout all your dwellings, that ye eat neither fat nor blood." Lev. 3:17

43 See supra §65

44 Neh. 8:10

45 Gen. 43:11,15,26

46 Judges 14:8,9

47 Matt. 3:4; Mark 1:6

48 Prov. 24:13

49 Prov. 25:27

50 Gen. 18:8; Deut. 32:14 (butter of kine); Judges 5:25; 2 Sam. 17:29; Job 20:17, 29:6; Ps. 55:21; Isa. 7:15,22
"Surely the churning of milk bringeth forth butter." Prov. 30:33

1 1 Sam. 17:18; 2 Sam. 17:29

2 Milk of sheep (Deut. 32:14) and goats (Prov 27:27), as well as that of kine, was used. It was kept in bottles (Judges 4:18—Jael "opened a bottle of milk"), and was sometimes drunk with wine (Solomon's Song 5:1).

Thus it appears that the meal which Abraham prepared for three strangers who visited him in the plains of Mamre included butter and milk,[3] and that Jesse sent David his son with "ten cheeses" to the camp where his brothers were serving in the army of Saul against the Philistines.[4]

[§304]   Biblical law allows a moderate use of wine[5] or "wine mingled with water."[6] It is said that "wine maketh the heart glad"[7] and that "wine is as good as life to a man, if it be drunk moderately;"[8] and St. Paul recommended that Timothy "drink no longer water, but use a little wine for thy stomach's sake and thine often infirmity.[9] But it is improper to "tarry long at the wine"[10] or to drink "mixed" or "sparkling" wine.[11] And it is wrongful for kings to drink wine or for princes to drink strong drink, lest they forget the law and pervert judgment.[12]

[§305]   "Table manners" are governed by rules given in the Book of Ecclesiasticus.

"If thou sit at a bountiful table, be not greedy upon it, and say not, There is much meat on it.

"Stretch not thine hand withersoever it (thine eye) looketh, and thrust it not with him (another) into the dish.

"Eat, as it becometh a man, those things which are set before thee:[13] and devour not, lest thou be hated.

---

3 Gen. 18:8

4 1 Sam. 17:18

See also 2 Sam. 17:29, saying that Shobi, Machir and Barzillai brought butter "and cheese of kine" for David, "and for the people that were with him, to eat."

5 Accordingly where the Bible has been regarded as a rule of political government, it has never been considered to contain any absolute prohibition of the use and sale of intoxicating liquors as a beverage. Appeal of Allyn (1909) 81 Conn. 534, 71 A 794, 23 LRANS 630 (Baldwin,CJ)

"Wine has been thought good for man from the time of the Apostles until recent years." Tyson v Banton (1927) 273 US 418, 446, 71 L ed 718, 729 (Holmes,J, dissenting)

But the sons of Jonadab were commended because they obeyed the commandment of their father to drink no wine all their days. Jer. 35:8

6 2 Mac. 15:39 ("wine mingled with water is pleasant, and delighteth the taste")

Drunkenness, see infra §359

7 Ps. 104:15; 4 Binney (Pa. 1812) 351 (Brackenridge,J)

"Give strong drink unto him that is ready to perish, and wine unto those that be of heavy hearts. Let him drink, and forget his poverty, and remember his misery no more." Prov. 31:6,7

8 Ecclesiasticus 31:27

9 1 Tim. 5:23

"It is hurtful to drink wine or water alone." 2 Mac. 15:39

10 See infra §359

Nor is it "good" to drink wine if thereby "thy brother stumbleth, or is offended, or is made weak." Rom. 14:21

11 Prov. 23:29-32 ("Who hath woe? who hath sorrow? who hath contentions? who hath babbling? who hath wounds without cause? who hath redness of eyes? They that tarry long at the wine; they that go to seek mixed wine. Look not thou upon the wine when it is red, when it giveth his colour in the cup, when it moveth itself aright. At the last it biteth like a serpent, and stingeth like an adder")

"Various intoxicating drinks should not be mixed. "The court . . . concurs" with defendant Harris, "as to the mistake he made in the mixing of drinks. Rum, fruit juice, whiskey, and beer! What a potent mixture! It is not surprising that Harris had a sudden and complete 'blackout.' " Willoughby v Driscoll (1942) 120 P2d (Ore.) 768, 772 (Belt,J)

12 Prov. 31:4,5

13 See also Luke 10:8

"Leave off first for manners' sake; and be not unsatiable, lest thou offend.

"When thou sittest among many, reach not thine hand out first of all.

"A very little is sufficient for a man well nurtured . . ."[14]

CHAPTER 46

HEALTH, HEALING AND PHYSICIANS

306 In general   307 Health regulations   308 Cleanliness   309 Quarantine   310 Healing   311 Medicines   312 Physicians

[§306]   The subjects of health, healing and physicians are dealt with in many passages of the Scriptures.

Biblical law is properly concerned as to the health of the people. So it is said:

"Better is the poor, being sound and strong of constitution, than a rich man that is afflicted in his body.

"Health and good estate of body are above all gold, and a strong body above infinite wealth."[15]

In modern law also the public health is considered as being a vital concern of the state.[16]

[§307]   Health or sanitary regulations are found in Mosaic law.[17]   Thus there are rules as to leprosy[18] and the "cleansing" of lepers,[19] and as to "unclean issues and their cleansing."[20]   And warning is given to "take heed in the plague of leprosy, that thou observe diligently, and do according to all that the priests the Levites shall teach you: as I commanded them, so ye shall observe to do."[21]

Under Mosaic law, health regulations were administered and enforced by the priests, who were thus the forerunners of modern health officers and boards of health.[22]

14 Ecclesiasticus 31:12-19
Rules at feasts, see Ecclesiasticus 32:1-11

15 Ecclesiasticus 30:14,15
"Beloved, I wish above all things thous mayest . . . be in health." 3 John v 2

16 Pacific Coast Dairy v Agricultural Department (1942) 19 Cal. 2d 818, 123 P2d 442 (Traynor,J)

17 Military regulations, see supra §121

18 Lev., chap. 13

19 Lev., chap. 14

20 Lev., chap. 15

21 Deut. 24:8

22 "The republic of Venice . . . established the first board of health. It consisted of three nobles, and was called the 'Council of Health.' It was ordered to investigate the best means of preserving health, and of preventing the introduction of disease from abroad. Its efforts not having been entirely successful, its powers were enlarged in 1504, so as to grant it 'the power of life and death over those who violated the regulations for health.' No appeal was allowed from the sentence of this tribunal." 91 North Am. Rev. 442

"During the plague in London in 1665, the magistrates consulted to devise means for stopping, or at least impeding, the progress of the disease, and the result of their deliberations was a series of orders which appointed commissioners, searchers, chirurgeons, and buriers to each district. . . . every house which was visited, as it was called, was by those orders marked with a red cross of a foot long in the middle of the door, evident to be seen. See 22 Littell's Living Age 227

"The law has not yet conferred upon boards of health the old-time custom of the Samnites, of examining . . . the young people for the discovery of venereal disease." Rock v Carney (1921) 216 Mich. 280, 185 NW 798, 22 ALR 1178, 1181 (Wiest,J)

[§308] One of the ancient health requirements is that of personal cleanliness,[23] and not only physical but also moral or spiritual cleanliness.[24] The Scriptures mention the washing of the face,[25] the hands,[26] and the feet,[27] and the washing of clothes.[28] The rule seems to be to "wash thyself"[29] "with water"[30] and "be clean,"[31] and to "touch no unclean thing."[32] It is traditional to wash before eating[33]—it was said of "the Pharisees and all the Jews" that "except they wash, they eat not."[34] And there are provisions in Mosaic law as to bathing after copulation,[35] concerning the purification of women after childbirth,[36] and regarding the uncleanness and purification of persons who come in contact with the dead.[37]

[§309] Measures to prevent the spread of dangerous communicable diseases, and to provide for the isolation and segregation of those diseased, are practically as old as history.[38] Mosaic law provided for the quarantining of those who were afflicted with communicable disease or who had handled or touched the dead. It required "every leper, and every one that hath an issue, and whosoever is defiled by the dead" to be "put out of the camp."[39]

"Both male and female shall ye put out, without the camp shall ye put them; that they defile not their camps . . ."[40]
"And the leper in whom the plague is, his clothes shall be rent, and his head bare, and he shall put a covering upon his upper lip, and shall cry Unclean, unclean.[41]
"All the days wherein the plague shall be in him . . . he shall dwell alone; without the camp shall his habitation be."[42]

---

23 See for example Matt. 23:25; Luke 11:39; Gal. 5:19; Col. 3:5
24 "O Jerusalem, wash thine heart from wickedness." Jer. 4:14
"Let us cleanse ourselves from all filthiness of the flesh and spirit." 2 Cor. 7:1
25 Gen. 43:31; Matt. 6:17
26 Deut. 21:6; Ps. 26:6; Matt. 27:24
27 Gen. 18:4, 19:2, 24:32, 43:24; Judges 19:21; 1 Sam. 25:41; 2 Sam. 11:8; Luke 7:38; John 13:5,6,8,14; 1 Tim. 5:10
28 Lev. 14:8,9
29 Ruth 3:3; Isa. 1:16
30 Lev. 14:8; Ezek. 16:4; Eph. 5:26
"And the daughter of Pharaoh came down to wash herself at the river." Ex. 2:5
31 2 Kings 5:13; Isa. 1:16; Mark 1:41
". . . be ye clean that bear the vessels of the Lord." Isa. 52:11
Jacob commanded his household and all that were with him to "be clean, and change your garments." Gen. 35:2
32 Isa. 52:11; 2 Cor. 6:17

33 Matt. 15:2
34 Mark 7:4
But Jesus considered this unimportant. See Mark 7:5-9
35 Lev. 15:16-18; People v Angier (1941) 44 Cal.App.2d 417, 419, 112 P2d 659 (Moore,PJ)
36 Lev. chap. 12
37 Num. 19:11-22
38 Rock v Carney (1921) 216 Mich. 280, 185 NW 798, 22 ALR 1178, 1181 (Wiest,J)
39 Num. 5:2
40 Num. 5:3
41 Lev. 13:45
The forced cry of "unclean, unclean" was the forerunner of the modern warning placard. Rock v Carney (1921) 216 Mich. 280, 185 NW 798, 22 ALR 1178, 1181 (Wiest,J)
42 Lev. 13:46
But these measures were not sufficient to stamp out leprosy. It appears that there were "many lepers in Israel in the time of Eliseus (Elisha) the prophet." Luke 4:27

In ancient Greece and Rome those who were infected with leprosy were separated from the well. In 1448, a code of quarantine was adopted in Venice, and in 1603 an act was passed in England for shutting up all such houses as appeared to contain any infected person.[43]

[§310] Instances of divine or miraculous healing have occurred, no doubt, throughout the ages, and a particular "gift of healing" has long been recognized.[44] The Scriptures teach that all diseases may be divinely healed,[45] to the end that the righteous may not be taken away in the midst of their days[46] nor die before their time,[47] but that they may fulfill the number of their days—formerly three score years and ten[48] but now being increased[48a]—until the Lord in the fullness of time takes "away their breath" and "they die, and return to their dust.[49]

Nevertheless even in Biblical times divine healings were exceptional.[50] Ordinarily diseases were treated by spiritual and physical measures—the rule being that a sick person should pray, live righteously, consult a physician, and take medicine.

". . . in thy sickness be not negligent: but pray unto the Lord, and he will make thee whole.

"Leave off from sin, and order thine hands aright, and cleanse thy heart from all wickedness.

"Then give place to the physician, for the Lord hath created him: let him not go from thee, for thou hast need of him.

---

43 This act was enforced during the plague of London in 1665. Rock v Carney (1921) 216 Mich. 280, 185 NW 798, 22 ALR 1178, 1181 (Wiest,J) citing 22 Littell's Living Age, p 227

Orders by the Lord Mayor and Aldermen of the City of London concerning the infection of the plague, 1665, see Daniel Defoe's "A Journal of the Plague Year"

44 1 Cor. 12:9

45 Ps. 103:3

"He sent his word, and healed them." Ps. 107:20

". .. if thou wilt, thou canst make me clean." Matt. 8:2

Christ also "is the Savior of the body." Eph. 5:23

46 Ps. 102:24

". . . bloody and deceitful men shall not live out half their days." Ps. 55:23

47 "Be not over much wicked, neither be thou foolish: why shouldest thou die before thy time?" Ecclesiastes 7:17

48 "The days of our years are three-score years and ten; and if by reason of strength they be fourscore years, yet is their strength labour and sorrow; for it is soon cut off, and we fly away." Ps. 90:10

But originally the span of life was greater. "And the Lord said, My Spirit shall not always strive with man, for that he also is flesh: yet his days shall be a hundred and twenty years." Gen. 6:3

48a "There shall be no more thence an infant of days, nor an old man that hath not filled his days: for the child shall die a hundred years old; but the sinner being a hundred years old shall be accursed." Isa. 65:20

49 Ps. 104:29

In every account of the raising of the dead it will be noted that the person restored to life was young.

50 "And many lepers were in Israel in the time of Eliseus (Elisha) the prophet; and none of them was cleansed, saving Naaman the Syrian." Luke 4:27

"There is a time when in their hands there is good success.[1]
"For they shall also pray unto the Lord, that he would prosper that, which they give for ease and remedy to prolong life."[2]

Prayer as a means of treating disease is given more emphasis in the New Testament, where it is said:

"Is any sick among you? let him call for the elders of the church, and let them pray over him, anointing him with oil in the name of the Lord;
"And the prayer of faith shall save the sick, and the Lord shall raise him up; and if he have committed sins, they shall be forgiven him.
"Confess your faults one to another, and pray one for another, that ye may be healed. The effectual fervent prayer of a righteous man availeth much."[3]

[§311] The use of an anaesthetic in a surgical operation has a Scriptural basis, for it is said that "the Lord God caused a deep sleep to fall upon Adam, and he slept; and he took one of his ribs, and closed up the flesh instead thereof."[4]

Moreover it has always been the custom to use "healing medicines" in sickness,[5] nor is this against the Scriptures, for it is recommended that one "use physick or ever thou be sick"[6] and it is said that "The Lord hath created medicines out of the earth; and he that is wise will not abhor them."[7]

The Scriptural and natural medicine consists in herbs— "the fruit" of the tree "shall be for meat, and the leaf thereof for medicine."[8] But in a case of boils the prescription was to "let them take a lump of figs, and lay it for a plaster (poultics) upon the boil, and he shall recover."[9]

[§312] Physicians are of a most ancient and honorable profession. They were found in Egypt during the sojourn of the Israelites in that land, and in Palestine at the time of Jesus. It is related that "Joseph commanded his servants the physicians to embalm his father: and the physicians embalmed Israel."[10] And Luke is mentioned in the New Testament as "the beloved physician."[11]

---

1 Ecclesiasticus 38:9,10,12,13
But king Asa "in his disease . . . sought the physicians. And Asa slept with his fathers, and died." 2 Chron. 16:12,13
Tobit says: "I went to the physicians, but they helped me not." Tobit 2:10
And it is said of "a certain woman" that she "had suffered many things of many physicians, and had spent all that she had, and was nothing bettered, but rather grew worse." Mark 5:26; Luke 8:22
2 Ecclesiasticus 38:14
3 James 5:14-16
4 Gen. 2:21
5 Jer. 30:13

"A merry heart doeth good like a medicine." Prov 17:22
6 Ecclesiasticus 18:19
7 Ecclesiasticus 38:4
8 Ezek. 47:12
"The leaves of the tree were for the healing of the nations." Rev. 22:2
9 Isa. 38:21
10 Gen. 50:2
There were also midwives in Egypt before the exodus. The Hebrew midwives. of whom two are mentioned by name (Shiphrah and Puah), feared God and God dealt well with them. See Ex. 1:15-21
11 Col. 4:14

A physician—or at any rate one who prays "unto the Lord"[12]—is entitled to confidence and respect. Thus in Ecclesiasticus it is said:

"Honour a physician with the honour due unto him for the uses which ye may have of him: for the Lord hath created him.
"For of the most High cometh healing, and he shall receive honour of the king.
"The skill of the physician shall lift up his head: and in the sight of great men he shall be in admiration."[13]

But one should resort to the services of a physician only when he is sick, and after he has first performed his prescribed duties to "pray" and "leave off from sin."[14] It is said that "they that are whole need not a physician,"[15] and the conduct of Asa was condemned in that "in his disease he sought not to the Lord, but to the physicians."[16]

The taking of a reward for being instrumental in a divine healing seems to have been regarded as improper. So Elisha refused to "take a blessing" from Naaman when he had been healed of his leprosy,[17] and Elisha condemned his servant Gehazi to be a leper for following after Naaman and receiving "gifts" from him.[18] But a physician who treats diseases by physical means is doubtless entitled to a fee, depending upon the severity of the disease and the ability of the patient or his family to pay.[19]

---

12 Ecclesiasticus 38:14
13 Ecclesiasticus 38:1-3
14 See supra §310
15 Matt. 9:12; Mark 2:17; Luke 5:31
16 2 Chron. 16:12
17 2 Kings 5:15,16
18 2 Kings 5:20-27; State v Buswell (1894) 40 Neb. 158, 58 NW 728, 24 LRA 68 (Ryan,C)
19 This was the rule under the Code of Hammurabi (see supra § 13, n 2) which provided as follows:
"215 If a doctor has treated a gentleman for a severe wound with a bronze lancet and has cured the man, or has opened an abcess of the eye for a gentleman with a bronze lancet and has cured the eye of the gentleman, he shall take ten shekels of silver.
"216 If he (the patient) be the son of a poor man, he shall take five shekels of silver.
"217 If he be a gentleman's servant, the master of the servant shall give two shekels of silver to the doctor.

"218 If the doctor has treated a gentleman for a severe wound with a lancet of bronze and has caused the gentleman to die, or has opened an abcess of the eye for a gentleman with a bronze lancet and has caused the loss of the gentleman's eye, one shall cut off his hands.
"219 If a doctor has treated the severe wound of a slave of a poor man with a bronze lancet and has caused his death, he shall render slave for slave.
"220 If he has opened his abcess with a bronze lancet and has made him lose his eye, he shall pay money, half his price.
"221 If a doctor has cured the shattered limb of a gentleman, or has cured the diseased bowel, the patient shall give five shekels of silver to the doctor.
"222 If it is the son of a poor man, he shall give three shekels of silver.
"223 If a gentleman's servant, the master of the slave shall give two shekels of silver to the doctor.
Hughes v Medical Examiners (1926) 162 Ga. 246, 134 SE 42, 49 (Hill,J)

CHAPTER 47

PROSTITUTION

[§313] Prostitution—the granting of sexual indulgence for "gifts"[20] or "hire"[21]—was practiced in remote antiquity, and many Scriptural passages refer to "harlots"[22] or "whores,"[23] and to "whoremongers"[24] and "whoredom."[25]

In ancient times, the prostitute covered her face with a "veil"[26] and "sat in an open place . . . by the way,"[27] that she might be seen by passing men,[28] or dwelt in a house in the city where men lodged[29] or assembled.[30] Then as now she was ordinarily a woman whose family ties had been broken, an orphan or outcast—a "stranger" or wanderer. The law expressly forbade the prostitution of a "daughter," "to cause her to be a whore; lest the land (thereby) fall to whoredom . . . and become full of wickedness,"[31] and prescribed that there should be "no whore of the daughters of Israel."[32]

[§314] The usual punishment for prostitution was social ostracism—a "cutting off" from polite society.[33] It is said that "an harlot shall be accounted as spittle"[34] and "a shameless woman . . . as a dog."[35] Though she increased "the transgressors among men,"[36] she was not treated as a criminal unless she brought shame upon her father or upon the priesthood. Mosaic law declared that if the daughter of a priest "profane herself by playing the whore . . . she shall be burnt with fire."[37] And while the death penalty may have been

---

20 Ezek. 16:33 ("They give gifts to all whores"

21 Gen. 38:16,17 (Tamar said to Judah, "What wilt thou give me, that thou mayest come in unto me? And he said, I will send thee a kid from the flock. And she said, Wilt thou give me a pledge, till thou send it?")

22 See for example Prov. 7:10, 29:3; Jer. 2:20; Hosea 4:13,14; Ecclesiasticus 26:22

23 "The Bible talks bluntly of harlots and whores, but it does not incite to immorality." People v Wendling (1932) 258 NY 451, 180 NE 169, 81 ALR 799, 800 (Pound,J)
Hire of whore as payment of vow, see infra §326

24 Eph. 5:51; 1 Tim. 1:10; Heb. 13:4; Rev. 21:8; Ecclesiasticus 23:17

25 Hosea 4:11; Tobit 4:12

26 Gen. 38:14,15

27 Gen. 38:14
"She . . . lieth in wait as for a prey." Prov. 23:28

28 Gen. 38:15

29 Josh. 2:1

30 Jer. 5:7

31 Lev. 19:29

32 Deut. 23:17; see also Hosea 3:3 ("thou shalt not play the harlot")

33 "At one time, not so greatly remote, prostitution was not regarded as immoral and in some countries is not even now banned by the law." State v Malusky (1930) 59 ND 501, 230 NW 735, 71 ALR 190, 193 (Nuessle,J)

34 Ecclesiasticus 26:22

35 Ecclesiasticus 26:25

36 Prov. 23:28

37 Lev. 21:9

imposed in some other cases, it was seemingly thought that a woman should not be burned for prostitution—not for a single act at least—where she could show some reasonable excuse for her fault.   Thus although Judah commanded that Tamar be brought forth and burnt, the sentence was not executed because he had failed to give her to his son Shelah when the latter was grown.[38]

[§315]   It is doubtless reprehensible—and so in a measure unlawful—to frequent the society of prostitutes.[39]   In various passages of the Scriptures admonishments are given that one keep from the "evil"[40] or "strange" woman,[41] and that one "meet not with an harlot"[42] nor give his "soul" unto them.[43] It is cautioned to "beware of all whoredom,"[44] and the consequences of this evil are stated.[45]   Nevertheless it appears that some otherwise worthy biblical characters, such as Samson,[46] "went in unto harlots;" and it seems not to have been regarded as a legal offense.   Thus in the case of Judah and Tamar, Judah admitted no wrong for having "come in unto" Tamar, supposing her to be a harlot, but only "because that I gave her not to Shelah my son."[47]

CHAPTER 48

RELIGION

316 False prophecy   317 Idol worship—Making images and likenesses   318 Holidays   319 Sabbath—Biblical law   320 —— The Christian Sunday   321 Sanctuary —Altar, tabernacle and temple   322 "Service" of God—"Other Gods"   323 Sorcery —Fortune telling   324 Swearing—Profanity   325 The Priesthood—Tithing   326 Vows and their redemption

[§316]   "False prophets" are they who "speak lies in the name of the Lord."[48]   They are denounced in the Scriptures.

---

38 Gen. 38:24-26
Reputation alone is not sufficient to prove that a woman is a prostitute. There must be evidence of illicit acts. Gibson v State (1942) 162 SW2d (Tex. Crim.App.) 703, 704 (Davidson,J)

39 Ecclesiasticus 41:17 ("Be ashamed of whoredom before father and mother"), 41:20 (Be ashamed "to look upon an harlot")

40 Prov. 6:24
41 Prov. 7:5
42 Ecclesiasticus 9:3 ("lest thou fall into her snares")
43 Ecclesiasticus 9:6 ("that thou lose not thine inheritance")
44 Tobit 4:12

45 Prov. 6:26 ("by means of a whorish woman a man is brought to a piece of bread"), 7:26 ("many strong men have been slain by her"), 23:27 ("a whore is a deep ditch; and a strange woman is a narrow pit.") ; Ecclesiasticus 19:2,3 ("he that cleaveth to harlots will become impudent; Moths and worms shall have him to heritage")

46 Judges 16:1
47 Gen. 38:26
48 Zech. 13:3 ("it shall come to pass, that when any shall yet prophesy, then his father and his mother that begat him shall say unto him, Thou shalt not live; for thou speakest lies in the name of the Lord: and his father and his mother that begat him shall thrust him through when he prophesieth")

". . . Let not your prophets and your diviners, that be in the midst of you, deceive you, neither hearken to your dreams which ye cause to be dreamed. For they prophesy falsely . . ."[49]

Jesus warned his hearers to "Beware of false prophets, which come to you in sheep's clothing, but inwardly they are ravening wolves,"[50] saying that "Ye shall know them by their fruits."[1]

[§317] Mosaic law forbids the worship of idols,[2] characterizing this practice as an "abomination"[3] or "spiritual fornication."[4] It is commanded that "thou shalt not bow down thyself" to idols, "nor serve them;"[5] "neither shalt thou set thee up any image,"[6] nor "turn . . . unto idols,"[7] nor "worship the work of thine hands."[8]

The law further prohibited the making of images and likenesses, providing that—

"Thou shalt not make unto thee any graven image, or any likeness of any thing that is in heaven above, or that is in the earth beneath, or that is in the water under the earth."[9]

"Ye shall not make with me gods of silver, neither shall ye make unto you gods of gold."[10]

"Thou shalt make thee no molten gods."[11]

And it was prescribed that the man should be "cursed,"

---

49 Jer. 29:8.9

Punishment of false prophets, see infra §385

50 Matt. 7:15

1 Matt. 7:16

St. Paul caused Elymas the sorcerer to become temporarily blind. Acts 13:11

2 Ezek. 33:25; 1 Cor. 10:7; Gal. 5:20

3 1 Kings 21:26 (saying that Ahab "did very abominably in following idols")

But because he humbled himself upon being reproved by the prophet Elijah, the punishment of "evil upon his house" was postponed until after his death. 1 Kings 21:29

4 Wisdom of Solomon 14:12

5 Ex. 20:5; Deut. 5:9; State v Smith (1942) 127 P2d (Kan.) 518, 520 (Harvey,J)

Flag salute in schools, see supra §296

6 Deut. 16:22

Graven images were not permitted to be brought into Jerusalem. Even Roman standards, with their eagles, were kept outside. 1 Wells' Outline 572

7 Lev. 19:4

8 ". . . they were no gods, but the work of men's hands, wood and stone: therefore they have destroyed them." Isa. 37:19

"Thy graven images also will I cut off, and thy standing images out of the midst of thee; and thou shalt no more worship the work of thine hands." Micah 5:13

9 Ex. 20:4; Deut. 5:8; State v Smith (1942) 127 P2d (Kan.) 518,520 (Harvey,J)

"Ye shall make no idols nor graven image, neither rear you up a standing image, neither shall ye set up any image of stone in your land, to bow down unto it." Lev. 26:1

"Take ye therefore good heed . . . lest ye . . . make you a graven image, the similitude of any figure, the likeness of male or female; the likeness of any beast that is on the earth, the likeness of any winged fowl that flieth in the air; the likeness of any thing that creepeth on the ground, the likeness of any fish that is in the waters beneath the earth." Deut. 4:15-19

10 Ex. 20:23

11 Ex. 34:17; and see Lev. 19:4

"Molten images are wind and confusion." Isa. 41:29

that is, punished, "that maketh any graven or molten image
. . . and putteth it in a secret place."[12]

[§318] Mosaic law provided for the observance of certain
days as "high" or "holy" days,[13] in addition to the observance of the Sabbath.[14] The Israelites were commanded to
keep three stated feasts,[15] and to refrain from work on
stated days.[16]

The American Thanksgiving Day, which is a holiday when
proclaimed by the President, is said to be founded on the
provision of Mosaic law requiring the keeping of—

". . . the feast of harvest, the first fruits of thy labors, which thou
hast sown in the field: and the feast of ingathering, which is in the
end of the year, when thou hast gathered thy labors out of the field."[17]

[§319] Mosaic law requires the keeping of "sabbath
days."[18]

"Remember the sabbath day, to keep it holy.[19]
"Six days shalt thou labour, and do all thy work.
"But the seventh day is the sabbath of the Lord thy God; in it thou
shalt not do any work, thou, nor thy son, nor thy daughter, thy manservant, nor thy maidservant, nor thy cattle, nor thy stranger that
is within thy gates."[20]

The Sabbath is said to have been "blessed" and "hallowed"
because "in six days the Lord made heaven and earth, the
sea, and all that in them is, and rested the seventh day,"[21]
and the keeping of the Sabbath is said to have been commanded as a memorial that the Lord brought the Israelites

---

12 Deut. 27:15
"And now they sin more and more,
and have made them molten images
of their silver, and idols according to
their own understanding, all of it the
work of the craftsmen: they say of
them, Let the men that sacrifice kiss
the calves. Therefore they shall be as
the morning cloud, and as the early
dew that passeth away, as the chaff
that is driven with the whirlwind out
of the floor, and as the smoke out of
the chimney." Hosea 13:2,3

13 Ecclesiasticus 33:9 ("Some . . .
[days] hath he [the Lord] made high
days, and some of them hath he made
ordinary days")

14 See infra §319

15 Ex., chaps. 12, 23 and 34; Lev.,
chaps. 16 and 23; Num., chaps. 9, 28
and 29; Deut., chap. 16

16 Lev. 16:29, 23:25,28,31,35,36; Num.
28:18,25,26, 29:7,12,35

17 Ex. 23:16; 42 Wash. L.Rep. (1914)
771 (Barnard)

18 Ex. 20:8, 31:13 ("Verily my sabbaths ye shall keep"); Lev. 19:3,30,

26:2; Deut. 5:12 ("Keep the sabbath
day to sanctify it"); Isa. 56:2 ("Blessed
is the man that . . . keepeth the sabbath from polluting it"); Ezek. 44:24
("they [the priests] shall hallow my
sabbaths")

Among the Babylonians and also, it is
thought, among the Hebrews in very
early times, the Sabbath was the fifteenth day of the month. Certain feast
days were also called Sabbaths. See
Lev. 23:24,32,39. It is not known when
the sabbath of the fifteenth day of
the month was changed to the weekly
or seventh-day sabbath.

The annual or ceremonial sabbaths
are referred to in Col. 2:16

19 See supra §257

20 Ex. 20:8-10; Deut. 5:12-14; Ex parte
Newman (1858) 9 Cal. 502, 522, (Field,J,
dissenting)

"Six days ye shall gather it (manna);
but on the seventh day, which is the
sabbath, in it there shall be none."
Ex. 16:26

Punishment for sabbath breaking,
see infra §§387, 388

21 Ex. 20:11

out of bondage in Egypt "through a mighty hand and by a stretched out arm."[22] It is a day set apart for "an holy convocation,[23] and also for rest[24] and refreshment;[25] it is to be observed "in earing time and in harvest" as well as at other seasons.[26] But it is not to be observed as a day for "doing thine own ways, nor finding thine own pleasures, nor speaking thine own words."[27]

The general rule is that no work should be done on the Sabbath.[28] "The gates should be shut"[29] and every man should "abide . . . in his place."[30] No asses should be laden,[31] no burdens bourne,[32] no fires kindled,[33] no sheaves brought in,[34] no sticks gathered,[35] no victuals or wares bought[36] or sold,[37] and no wine tread in the presses.[38] But it is lawful to save life on the Sabbath,[39] that is, to heal the sick[40] or to rescue an animal that has fallen into a pit.[41] Nor is it improper for one who is hungry to "pluck and eat corn" on the Sabbath,[42] nor for one who has an ox or an ass in a stall to loose it and lead it to water.[43] Moreover it was not considered wrongful in time of war to fight against those who "make battle with us on the sabbath day."[44]

[§320] —— Originally the Christians—most of whom at first were Jews—observed the Sabbath in accordance with Mosaic law,[45] and they also observed Sunday, or the first

22 Deut. 5:15

23 Lev. 23:3 ("the seventh day is . . . an holy convocation; ye shall do no work therein")

24 Ex. 34:21 ("on the seventh day thou shalt rest"); Deut. 5:14 ("the seventh day is the sabbath . . . that thy manservant and thy maidservant may rest as well as thou")

25 Ex. 23:12 ("on the seventh day thou shalt rest: that thine ox and thine ass may rest, and the son of thy handmaid, and the stranger, may be refreshed")

26 Ex. 34:21

27 Isa. 58:13

28 Ex. 20:10; Lev. 23:3; Deut. 5:14; Jer. 17:22

29 Neh. 13:19

30 Ex. 16:29 (". . . abide ye every man in his place, let no man go out of his place on the seventh day")

31 Neh. 13:15

32 Jer. 17:21,22 ("bear no burden on the sabbath day, nor bring it in by the gates of Jerusalem; neither carry forth a burden out of your house on the sabbath day")

33 Ex. 35:3 ("Ye shall kindle no fire throughout your habitations upon the sabbath day")
Electricity is considered as fire. Under a strict interpretation, the turning on of an electric switch is the kindling of a fire.

34 Neh. 13:15

35 Num. 15:32-35
The Stick-gatherer's Case, see infra §388

36 Neh. 10:31

37 Neh. 13:15

38 Neh. 13:15

39 Mark 3:4; Luke 6:9

40 Matt. 12:10-13; Mark 3:1-5; Luke 14:3,4, 6:8-10, 13:14-16; John 7:23

41 Matt. 12:11 (sheep); Luke 14:5 (ass or ox)

42 Matt. 12:1-8; Mark 2:23-28; Luke 6:1-5

43 Luke 13:15

44 1 Mac. 2:41

45 See supra §319
Jesus kept the Sabbath. See Luke 4:16,31
And so did the Apostles. See Acts 13:14-26, 16:11,13, 17:2,3, 18:1,11

day of the week, in honor of the resurrection of Christ.[46] But it appears that when the Jews as a whole had rejected Christianity—which was then "taken" to the "gentiles"— and when the number of non-Jewish Christians had greatly increased, Sunday became the more prominent day[47] and eventually the observance of the seventh day by Christians was entirely discontinued.[48]

"By common consent Sunday is a day set apart for cessation from all secular employment by the Christian world. It is among the first and most sacred institutions of that religion. Viewed merely from a legal standpoint, it is a day of rest. Sunday legislation is more than 15 centuries old. It originated in Rome, A.D. 321, when Constantine the Great passed an edict commanding all judges and inhabitants of cities to rest on the venerable day of the Sun."[49]

The observance of Sunday as the Sabbath—the application of the commandments concerning the Sabbath to the first instead of the seventh day of the week—does not accord with the letter of Mosaic law,[50] nor is such observance commanded in the New Testament,[1] but it is generally thought to satisfy the spirit of the law[2] as requiring the observance of one day in seven—a rule founded in experience and sustained by science.[3]

---

[46] "The cessation from all secular employment on Sunday is one of the earliest observances of the Christian world." People v Mantel (1929) 134 NY Misc Rep 529, 236 NYS 122 (Turk,J), stating further that "Sunday means a calendar day, which consists of 24 hours, and commences and ends at midnight."
In the New Testament, the first day of the week is mentioned in Matt. 28:1; Mark 16:1,2,9; Luke 24:1; John 20:1,19; Acts 20:6-8; 1 Cor. 16:1,2
The Sabbath is mentioned in Matt. 12:1,5,8,10,11,12; 24:20; 28:1; Mark 1:21; 2:23,24,27,28; 3:2,4; 6:2; 15:42; 16:1; Luke 4:16,31; 6:1,2,5,6,7,9; 13:10,14,15,16; 14:1,3,5; 23:54,56; John 5:9,10,16,18; 7:22,23; 9:14,16; 19:31; Acts 1:12; 13:14, 27,42,44; 15:21; 16:13; 17:2; 18:4

[47] Sunday, as the name implies, was a pagan day, sacred to the sun god and derived from the Mithraic religion. It had been observed by the Greeks, Romans, and others who were converted to Christianity and who had not been accustomed to observance of the Mosaic Sabbath. That the resurrection had occurred on Sunday, and that the non-Jewish Christians had previously regarded it as a sacred day, doubtless seemed sufficient reasons for transferring the Sabbath to Sunday, which has since been almost universally observed.

[48] By the fourth century Sunday observance was required by church law, and the Emperor Constantine confirmed it by law of the state.

[49] People v Ramsay (1926) 128 (NY) Misc Rep 39, 217 NYS 799 (Heffernan,J); People v Mantel (1929) 134 (NY) Misc Rep 529, 236 NYS 122 (Turk,J)
Sunday laws are not based on the Fourth Commandment. 46 Va. St. Bar Proceedings (1934) 199 (Hunter)

[50] See supra §42

[1] There is no record of Sunday being appointed as a sabbath, nor of any sacredness being attached to it.

[2] See supra §42

[3] Ex parte Newman (1858) 9 Cal. 502, 520 (Field,J,dissenting) saying "There is no nation, possessing any degree of civilization, where the rule is not observed, either from the sanctions of law or the sanctions of religion."
If it were now to be decided as to whether the seventh or the first day should be observed as the weekly sabbath, there could scarcely be doubt as to the required answer. But the almost uniform practice of Christian peoples for more than sixteen centuries cannot be lightly ignored. It must be presumed that the early Christians, in observing the first rather than the seventh day, were actuated by some reason or reasons which to them seemed good and sufficient, if only to distinguish themselves from the Jews and afford some public evidence that Christianity was not merely a new Jewish sect.

Sunday laws were passed at an early day in England and they became the pattern of similar laws in America.[4] In these laws, Sunday is regarded merely as a civil day, which is a convenient one for the suspension of business because of its general observance as a holy day by most of the people.[5]

[§321] Many passages of the Scriptures pertain to places of worship. In general it is provided that "ye shall . . . reverence my sanctuary,"[6] meaning that ordinarily it should not be violated even to seize a criminal who has taken refuge therein.[7] And concerning the "altar" it was provided that—

"An altar of earth thou shalt make unto me . . .
"And if thou wilt make me an altar of stone, thou shalt not built it of hewn stone: for it thou lift up thy tool upon it, thou hast polluted it.
"Neither shalt thou go up by steps unto my altar, that thy nakedness be not discovered thereon."[8]

It was forbidden to plant any grove or tree "near the altar of the Lord."[9] Nor was any stranger permitted to come near the tabernacle—"the stranger that cometh nigh shall be put to death."[10] Jesus forbade the transaction of any business in the temple, saying, "make not my Father's house an house of merchandise."[11]

[§322] Biblical law demands that one "love"[12] and "serve"[13] the Lord. Jesus asserted that "the first and great commandment"[14] is that "thou shalt love the Lord thy God with all thine heart, and with all thy soul, and with all thy might (mind)."[15] Also "it is written" that "Thou shalt worship the Lord thy God, and Him only shalt thou serve."[16] It is not permissible to worship a "fellow-servant" even though he (or she) be an angel.[17]

---

4 People v Ramsey (1926) 128 (NY) Misc Rep 39, 217 NYS 799 (Heffernan,J)
"Sunday laws are enacted, so that we, and all others, may have the benefit of rest and quiet, and an opportunity for worship, and religious reading and meditation, at least one day out of seven." 42 Wash. L.Rep. (1914) 770 (Bernard)

5 Under American Constitutions, the law may not enforce religious observances. But a state may establish a day of rest as a civil institution. Donahoe v Richards (1854) 38 Me. 379, 61 AD 256, 273 (Appleton,J)

6 Lev. 19:30, 26:2

7 See infra §430

8 Ex. 20:24-26

9 Deut. 16:21

10 Num. 1:51

11 John 2:16

12 Deut. 6:5, 10:12, 11:1, 19:9, 30:6; Matt. 22:37; Mark 12:30; Luke 10:27

13 Deut. 6:13, 10:2, 11:13, 13:4; Josh. 22:5; 1 Sam. 7:3; Matt. 4:10; Luke 4:8

14 Matt. 22:38; and see Mark 12:29
As to the second "of all the commandments," see supra §19

15 Deut. 6:5; Matt. 22:37

16 Matt. 4:10; Luke 4:8

17 The angel before whom John fell down to worship said, "See thou do it not: for I am thy fellow-servant, and of thy brethren the prophets." Rev. 22:9
But it can scarcely be called an act of worship, within the inhibition "him only shalt thou serve," to pledge allegiance to one's country and to salute the flag thereof. See supra §296

Mosaic law forbids the service or worship of other gods.[18] The commandments are that "Thou shalt have no other gods before me"[19] and that "thou shalt worship no other god."[20] Nor may the "heavenly bodies" be worshipped, for it is said to—

"take . . . good heed unto yourselves . . . lest thou lift up thine eyes unto heaven, and when thou seest the sun, and the moon, and the stars, even all the host of heaven, shouldest be driven to worship them."[21]

In Rome, the Twelve Tables originally forbade adherence to foreign faiths, but the rule was later relaxed so as to allow the peoples of conquered provinces to practice their own religions, thus permitting the spread of Christianity among the provinces and ultimately resulting in its official adoption. And in modern law, matters of worship are generally left to each individual to decide for himself.[22] So in America all religions are now tolerated and given equal protection.[23] No distinction is recognized as between the several sects, Christian or otherwise.[24]

[§323] Sorcery has assumed many forms through the ages, and has been known by various names, such as astrology, augury, divination, enchantment, fortune-telling, magic, necromancy, soothsaying and witchcraft.[25] It is not merely a wrongful exploitation of human frailty—deceiving and misleading many[26]—but is also considered as an encroachment upon religion in that it diverts the people from seeking "unto their God"[27] and "guideth to idolatry."[28] Accordingly it is provided in Mosaic law that "ye shall not . . . use enchantment, nor observe times,"[29] nor "regard . . . them that have familiar spirits, neither seek after wizards, to be defiled by them."[30]

18 Punishment for the worship of other gods, see infra §§390-392

19 Ex. 20:3; Deut. 5:7
"Jacob said unto his household, and to all that were with him, Put away the strange gods that are among you." Gen. 35:2

20 Ex. 34:14; and see Deut. 6:14; Josh. 23:16; Judges 3:7,8; Ps. 81:9; Jer. 25:6

21 Deut. 4:15,19
Sun worship is called "heliolatry."

22 Wash. L.Rep. (1914) 770 (Barnard)

23 Baptist Church v Witherell (1832) 3 Paige Ch. (NY) 296, 24 AD 223, 229

24 Powers v First Nat. Bank (1942) 161 SW2d (Tex.Com.App.) 273, 279 (Brewster,C)

25 Witchcraft as a crime, see infra §394

26 "Divinations, and soothsayings, and dreams, are vain; . . . dreams have deceived many, and they have failed that put their trust in them." Ecclesiasticus 34:5,7

27 "And when they shall say unto you, Seek unto them that have familiar spirits, and unto wizards that peep, and that mutter: should not a people seek unto their God?" Isa. 8:19

28 My child, be not an augur, for it guideth to idolatry; nor an enchanter, nor an astrologer, nor a purifier, nor do thou consent to look on these things, for from all these things idolatry is begotten. Two Ways, 3:4

29 Lev. 19:26

30 Lev. 19:31
"Thou shalt not use magic, thou shalt not practice sorcery" Two Ways 2:2

". . . the soul that turneth after such as have familiar spirits, and after wizards, to go a whoring after them, I will even set my face against that soul, and will cut him off from among his people."[31]

"There shall not be found among you any one that . . . useth divination, or an observer of times, or an enchanter, or a witch, or a charmer, or a consulter with familiar spirits, or a wizard, or a necromancer."[32]

But notwithstanding the law, the use of divination and enchantments persisted to some extent in Biblical times,[33] and even to the present day. On at least two occasions the "workers with familiar spirits" were "put away" out of the land.[34]

[§324] Mosaic law commands that "Thou shalt not take the name of the Lord thy God in vain,"[35] "neither shalt thou profane the name of thy God."[36] But it was formerly regarded as proper to use the name of the Lord in taking a solemn oath.[37] The evil of profanity consisted in naming the Lord in intemperate and needless swearing, as appears by the admonition to—

"Accustom not thy mouth to swearing; neither use thyself to the naming of the Holy One.

"Use not thy mouth to intemperate swearing, for therein is the word of sin."[38]

Christian law forbids all swearing,[39] and any use of the Lord's name by way of an oath is therefore profanity. The offense of blasphemy, which is related to profanity, is discussed in a later section.[40]

[325] The priesthood is the subject of many provisions of Mosaic law, some of which are noticed at appropriate places in this book, while others are considered as being of no present importance. In general it was commanded to "reverence" the priests.[41]

". . . honour the priest; and give him his portion, as it is commanded thee, the first-fruits, and the trespass offering, and the gift of the shoulders, and the sacrifice of sanctification, and the first-fruits of the holy things."[42]

Tithing was ordained for the support of the priesthood.

31 Lev. 20:6
32 Deut. 18:10,11
33 See 2 Kings 17:17
34 1 Sam. 28:3-10 (Saul "put away those that had familiar spirits, and the wizards, out of the land," but nevertheless sought out and consulted a woman with a familiar spirit [the witch of Endor], promising that she should not be punished); 2 Kings 23:24 (Josiah "put away . . . the workers with familiar spirits, and the wizards . . . . that were spied in the land of Judah and Jerusalem")

35 Ex. 20:7; Deut. 5:11
36 Lev. 18:21, 19:12, 22:32
   Addiction to obscene or disgusting language — called "Coprolalia" — is a symptom of insanity. State v Wallace (1942) 35 Ore.Adv.Sh. 273, 299 (Brand,J)
37 See supra §151
38 Ecclesiasticus 23:9,13
39 See supra §151
40 See infra §379
41 Ecclesiasticus 7:29
42 Ecclesiasticus 7:31

Mosaic law provided for setting apart a tenth of such things as annually increased or rendered an annual crop.[43]

". . . all the tithe of the land, whether of the seed of the land, or of the fruit of the tree, is the Lord's."[44]

"And, behold, I have given the children of Levi all the tenth in Israel for an inheritance, for their service which they serve, even the service of the tabernacle of the congregation."[45]

But in former times the duties of the priesthood were not confined to religious matters. They were the governing class, and performed many political and social functions. Provisions for their support, including tithing, therefore, took the place of taxes.[46]

The tithing system was adopted into the Christian church, and has survived to some extent and in a modified form, to the present time. But generally in modern law no tithes are required nor public taxes levied for religious purposes.[47]

[§326] Vows were sometimes made by the ancients for the purpose of invoking divine favor.[48] Thus it is related that—

". . . Jacob vowed a vow, saying, If God will be with me, and will keep me in this way that I go, and will give me bread to eat, and raiment to put on,

"So that I come again to my father's house in peace; then shall the Lord be my God;

"And this stone, which I have set for a pillar, shall be God's house: and of all that thou shalt give me I will surely give the tenth unto thee."[49]

Mosaic law provided for the making and redemption of vows.[50] In particular it was required that a vow, having been made, should be paid or performed.[1]

"When thou shalt vow a vow unto the Lord thy God, thou shalt not slack to pay it . . .

"But if thou shalt forbear to vow, it shall be no sin in thee.

"That which is gone out of thy lips thou shalt keep and perform; even

---

43 The term was applied to predial tithes, such as grain and fruit; mixed tithes, such as the young of animals, milk, etc.; and personal tithes, such as the products of labor.

44 Lev. 27:30

45 Num. 18:21

46 See supra §101

For many centuries the tithe constituted the usual tax or assessment.

47 42 Wash.L.Rep. (1914) 770 (Bernard)

48 A vow was like a contract between its maker and the Lord, by which some sacrifice or service was promised for a divine favor. It was made with solemn fromality and was considered as absolutely binding. See 13 Gr.B. (1901) 37(Amram)

49 Gen. 28:20-22

50 Lev. 27:2-29

1 Ecclesiastes 5:4,5 ("When thou vowest a vow unto God, defer not to pay it; . . . better is it that thou shouldest not vow, than that thou shouldest vow and not pay")

But it was expressly forbidden to "bring the hire of a whore . . . into the house of the Lord thy God for any vow." Deut. 23:18

a freewill offering, according as thou hast vowed unto the Lord thy God, which thou hast promised with thy mouth."[2]

But a vow improvidently made could be commuted or redeemed.[3] So it appears that Jephthah might have redeemed his vow to offer up for a burnt offering "whatsoever cometh forth of the doors of my house to meet me, when I return in peace from the children of Ammon,"[4] thus avoiding the sacrifice of his only daughter, by paying to the priest the estimation of her value according to her age.[5]

CHAPTER 49

"STRANGERS"—ALIENS

[§327] Under Primitive law, a stranger or alien—a member of another family or tribe—was an enemy, who might be robbed or even killed as though he were a wild animal.[6] So Cain greatly feared to be banished for killing his brother Abel because, as "a fugitive and a vagabond" he would be an "outlaw" and liable to be killed on sight by anyone whom he might meet.[7]

This rule had changed by the time of Moses, for Mosaic law at first was solicitous of the welfare of strangers.[8] It provided that "the stranger that dwelleth with you shall be unto you as one born among you, and thou shalt love him as thyself."[9] But later it was recognized that the presence of many strangers was detrimental, even dangerous, to the nation—that "they shall be snares and traps unto you, and scourges in your sides, and thorns in your eyes, until ye perish from off this good land which the Lord your God hath given you."[10] And it is further said that—

---

2 Deut. 23:21-23
"Let nothing hinder thee to pay thy vow in due time." Ecclesiasticus 18:22
3 Lev. 27:1-25; 13 Gr.B. (1901) 39 (Amram)
4 Judges 11:30,31
5 Lev. 27:4,5
6 13 Gr.B. (1901) 594 (Amram); 14 Harv.LR (1901) 514, 515 (Thayer); Maine's Early History of Institutions, p 65; 28 Yale LJ (1919) 782
7 Gen. 4:14 ("everyone that findeth me shall slay me")
8 See Ps. 146:9 ("The Lord preserveth the strangers")

9 Lev. 19:34; and see Deut. 10:19 ("Love ye therefore the stranger: for ye were strangers in the land of Egypt")
This originally referred to a stranger in a process of conversion into an Israelite. 14 Harv.LR (1901) 516 (Thayer)
10 Josh. 23:13
"Receive a stranger into thine house, and he will disturb thee, and turn thee out of thine own." Ecclesiasticus 11:34

". . . the sons of the stranger shall not (eat thy corn nor) drink thy wine, for the which thou hast labored:

"But they that have gathered it shall eat it, . . . and they that have brought it together shall drink it . . ."[11]

[§328] Discrimination against strangers was generally forbidden by Mosaic law. Thus, as we have seen, it was commanded that there should be "one law" for the native born and the stranger.[12] Other provisions required that the law be read to the "stranger that is within thy gates," as well as to the native born.[13] that he should not eat blood or flesh with blood,[14] that he should not do any work on the Sabbath,[15] and that he should not be oppressed,[16] vexed,[17] nor turned aside from his right.[18]

[§329] ——— But under Primitive law, an alien—when permitted to live in the land—could not buy a "possession" without the consent of the people. This can be seen by the account of the purchase of the cave of Machpelah, in that Abraham, being "a stranger and a sojourner" first addressed "the sons of Heth," entreating them to "give" him—that is, permit him to buy—a "possession of a burying place."[19] And in Mosaic law, it was not deemed improper to exclude strangers from participating in religious affairs,[20] to exempt them from the benefits of the seven-year release,[21] to give or sell to them meat of animals dying of themselves,[22] nor upon occasion to segregate[23] and enumerate them.[24] Thus "David commanded to gather together the strangers that were in the land of Israel,"[25] and Solomon "numbered" all the strangers that were in the land.[26]

[§330] Though the law required that strangers be fairly treated,[27] it was not intended that they should "devour" the land[28] or the strength of the people,[29] nor that they should fill themselves with the wealth of the people through exploitation.[30] On the contrary, it was evidently supposed that

11　Isa. 62:8,9
12　See supra §50
13　See supra §65
14　See supra §300
15　See supra §319
16　Ex. 22:21, 23:9; Ezek. 22:7,29; Zech. 7:10
17　Ex. 22:21; Lev. 19:33 ("And if a stranger sojourn with thee in your land, ye shall not vex him")
18　Mal. 3:5 ("and I will be a swift witness . . . against those that . . . turn aside the stranger from his right")
19　Ex. 23:3,4

20　See supra §51
21　See supra §268
22　See supra §299
23　See Neh. 13:3 ("Now it came to pass, when they had heard the law, that they separated from Israel all the mixed multitude")
24　See supra §99
25　1 Chron. 22:2
26　2 Chron. 2:17
27　See supra §328
28　Isa. 1:7
29　Hosea 7:9
30　Prov. 5:10

the strangers, with some exceptions, should constitute a sub-servient class, from whose ranks bondmen[31] and hired serv-ants[32] might be obtained, and prostitutes recruited.[33] In Isaiah it is said that "strangers shall stand and feed your flocks, . . . the sons of the alien shall be your plowmen and your vine-dressers,"[34] and "the sons of the strangers shall build up thy walls." Solomon, in building the "house of the Lord" and the "house for his kingdom," set the strangers apart, some to be bearers of burdens, others to be hewers in the mountain, and others to be overseers.[36]

CHAPTER 50

WOMEN

331 In general   332 Apparel and conduct   333 Status in modern times

[§331]   The Scriptures contain many provisions pertain-ing to women,[37] both married[38] and unmarried,[39] and relating, among other things, to the treatment of females captured in warfare,[40] the status and rights of a wife,[41] the employment of women,[42] the care of widows,[43] and the practice and pun-ishment of prostitution.[44]

According to the doctrines of Biblical law it appears that a woman was nearly always subject to masculine authority. As a daughter she was bound to obey her father,[45] and as a wife she became subject to the domination of her husband.[46] If she was divorced by her husband it seems that she went or was sent back to her own family or became another man's wife.[47]   But if her husband died and she became a widow, she passed, along with the rest of the family property, into the hands of his successor.[48]

31 See supra §233
32 See supra §251 et seq.
33 See supra §313
34 Isa. 61:5
35 Isa. 60:10
36 2 Chron. 2:17,18
37 Reading of the law to women, see supra §65
38 Slander of wife by husband, see supra §184
   Responsibility of wife for crime, see infra §339
   Interference by wife in combat be-tween husband and another, see infra §364

39 Case of the Daughters of Zelophe-had, see supra §139
   Right of marriage and remarriage, see supra §189
   Maidservants, see supra §235
40 See supra §123
41 See supra §214 et seq.
42 See supra §255
43 See supra §279
44 See supra §§313, 314
45 See supra §228
46 See supra §215
47 See supra §203
48 14 Gr.B. (1902) 343 (Amram); and see supra §186

[§332]　Christian law prescribes that women shall "adorn themselves in modest apparel"[49]—that they shall not wear "gold,[50] or pearls, or costly array,"[1] and that they shall not "braid"[2] or "plait" their hair.[3]　Women are not to be suffered to "teach men,"[4] nor to "usurp authority" over them.[5] On the other hand they are to be taught "to be sober, to love their husbands, to love their children, to be discreet, chaste, keepers at home, good, obedient to their own husbands."[6] Women are held to a higher standard of conduct than men,[6a] for it is said that "all wickedness is but little to the wickedness of a woman."[7]　She is expected to exercise "discretion,"[8] and especially to avoid being "drunken"[9] and a "gadder about."[10]

[§333]　Though the Biblical rules concerning women now seem harsh and perhaps unjust, they were suited, no doubt, to the conditions and standards of former times.[11]　Also it is to be noted that the authority of a father over his daughter, or that of a husband over his wife, carried with it the duties of protecting and supporting her.[12]　And in ancient society,[13] as in more recent times, women occasionally attained important positions.[14]　Thus it is related that Deborah became a judge of Israel,[15] and that "Judith . . . was in her time

49 1 Tim. 2:9
Woman not to wear man's clothing, see supra §278

50 1 Pet. 3:3

1 1 Tim. 2:9

2 1 Tim. 2:9

3 1 Pet. 3:3-5 ("For after this manner in the old time the holy women also, who trusted in God, adorned themselves")

4 1 Tim. 2:12
"I have a few things against thee, because thou sufferest that woman Jezebel . . . to teach." Rev. 2:20
But "aged women" may teach "young women." Titus 2:3,4
"Let your women keep silence in the churches: for it is not permitted unto them to speak; but they are commanded to be under obedience, as also saith the law. And if they will learn any thing, let them ask their husbands at home: for it is a shame for women to speak in the church." 1 Cor. 14:34,35

5 1 Tim. 2:12

6 Titus 2:4,5; and see supra §294

6a Texas law, for example, "seems to accept the validity of a separate standard of conduct for men and women since a man who seduces a married woman is treated as a proper subject for death at the hand of the husband but a woman who leads a husband astray is not regarded as equally deserving of death at the hand of the wife." 21 Tex. LR (1942) 20 (Stumberg)

7 Ecclesiasticus 25:19

8 Prov. 11:22 ("As a jewel of gold in a swine's snout, so is a fair woman who is without discretion")

9 See infra §359

10 Ecclesiasticus 26:8
A "wicked woman" should not be given "liberty to gad about." Ecclesiasticus 25:25

11 Gill v Board of Commissioners (1912) 160 NC 176, 76 SE 203, 43 LRANS 293, 302 (Clark,CJ,dissenting) saying that the former "status of women" was "rejected by the common sense and sense of justice of our race."

12 See supra §§212, 225

13 See for example 2 Kings 4:8, saying that there was "a great woman" in Shunem.

14 Women have "held the highest office in England and Russia, as for instance Elizabeth and Victoria in England, Isabella of Spain, and Catherine of Russia, who were among the most able sovereigns of those countries." Gill v Board of Commissioners (1912) 160 NC 176, 76 SE 203, 43 LRANS 293, 302 (Clark,CJ,dissenting)

15 Judges 4:4

honourable in all the country," so that when she died "the house of Israel lamented her seven days."[15a]

Under modern law, women are generally accorded the same rights as men, save that the husband remains nominally the head of the family."[16] In several states property acquired by either the husband or the wife after the marriage is held to be the common or community property of both.[17] And in many countries women are now competent to vote and to hold office.[18]

15a Judith 16:21,24
16 See supra §211
17 See 5 Cal. Jur. 282, 23 Tex Jur 100
18 Gill v Board of Commissioners (1912) 160 NC 176, 76 SE 203, 43 LRANS 293, 302 (Clark,CJ,dissenting)
Women have been made eligible as jurists and jurors. 36 Case & Comment (1930) No. 2, p 8 (Dynes)

PART VI

PENAL LAW—CRIMES AND PUNISHMENTS

CHAPTER 51

INTRODUCTORY

334 In general   335 Inevitability of offenses   336 License to commit offense

[§334]   A crime is ordinarily regarded as some act or omission which is forbidden by law and punished by society in its own name or behalf.[19]   But it may also consist in "a general course of conduct or mode of life" that is prejudicial to the public,[20] such as being a drunkard[21] or a vagrant,[22] or an habitual criminal.[23]   In either case, the existence of "law" is essential,[24] for a crime is an offense against the law itself—not merely a wrong to an individual.[25]   When there is no law, "sin is not imputed"[26] and "there is no transgression."[27]

Modern criminal law is said to have been inspired by the Scriptual commandments which say "thou shalt not."[28]   But

---

19   See 8 RCL 51
A criminal is a man who has done some act which in popular estimation is particularly harmful, such as treason, murder, robbery or theft. See 14 Ore. LR (1934-1935) 98 (Radin)

But criminal law and procedure are also used for the enforcement of mere regulations of convenience and order, wholly without relation to any moral qualities. Burgess v State (1931) 161 Md. 162, 155 A 153, 75 ALR 1471, 1477 (Digges,J)

20   See 8 RCL 52

21   See infra §359

22   See Morgan v Virginia (1937) 168 Va. 731, 191 SE 791, 111 ALR 62 (Gregory,J) referring to vagrancy as an offense that "does not consist in particular affirmative acts of a person but of his mode of life, habits, and character."

23   One charged with being an habitual criminal is charged merely with a status, which, if substantiated, calls for increased punishment for the latest crime of which he has been convicted. In re Towne (1942) 114 Wash. Dec. 513, 129 P2d 230 (Steinert,J)

24   And in criminal cases, "the greatest caution must be used not to stretch the principles of the law beyond their established limits." Commonwealth v Snelling (1812) 4 Binney (Pa.) 379, 383 (Tilghman,CJ)

25   See 8 RCL 51
But the criminal act usually constitutes a wrong against a person, that is, a "trespass" (see supra § 176), as well as a transgression of the law.

26   Rom. 5:13

27   Rom. 4:15

28   42 Wash.L.Rep. (1914) 770 (Barnard)

present-day statutes have largely substituted mere declaratory statements for prohibitory commands in reference to crimes.[29]   So the statutes generally do not say "thou shalt not" do certain things, but they define and classify various acts, and specify punishments to be inflicted if such acts are committed.[30]

[§335]   Crimes, like death, are seemingly inevitable, for all men are fallible[31]—"there is no man that sinneth not,"[32] and it is impossible but that offences will come."[33]

"Woe unto the world because of offenses! for it must needs be that offences come; but woe to that man by whom the offence cometh.

"Wherefore if thy hand or thy foot offend thee, cut them off, and cast them from thee: it is better for thee to enter into life halt or maimed, rather than having two hands or two feet to be cast into everlasting fire.

"And if thine eye offend thee, pluck it out, and cast it from thee: it is better for thee to enter into life with one eye, rather than having two eyes to be cast into hell fire."[34]

Hunger will doubtless drive a man to wrongdoing, as it caused Esau to sell his birthright.[35]   But it is not the hungry or poverty stricken alone who resort to crime,[36] for material abundance or prosperity seems to yield certain kinds of offenses.[37]   Thus it was said that—

". . . thy children have forsaken me, and sworn by them that are no gods: when I had fed them to the full, they then committed adultery, and assembled themselves by troops in the harlots' houses.

"They were as fed horses in the morning: every one neighed after his neighbour's wife."[38]

[§336]   Biblical law does not tolerate criminality[39] nor "justify the wicked."[40]   Saul swore to the witch of Endor that no punishment would "happen" to her if she would "divine" unto him "by the familiar spirit."[41]   But he was a wicked man, from whom the Lord had departed,[42] and his

29 "It has frequently occurred to me that it would have been better and certainly much more simple and effective, had the federal and state governments in enacting criminal laws and other regulatory measures followed the model of the decalogue, and simply said 'Thou shalt not' do this, that, or the other thing desired to be prohibited; and then prescribed penalties according to the magnitude of the offense."   14 Or.LR (1934-1935) 456 (Moody)

30 See 14 Ore.LR (1934-1935) 90 et seq. (Radin)

31 "All men are fallible; none are perfect, we perceive, even though we have the Divine command of 'Be ye therefore perfect, even as your Father which is in Heaven is perfect'."   Century In-

demnity Co. v Carnes (1940) 138 SW2d (Tex.Civ.App.) 555, 560 (Speer,J) quoting Matt. 5:48

32 1 Kings 8:46; 2 Chron. 6:36

33 Luke 17:1

34 Matt. 18:7-9

35 Gen. 25:29-34; and see supra §165

36 Allen v State (1913) 23 Idaho 772, 131 P 1112 (Ailshie,CJ)

37 Prov. 1:32 ("The prosperity of fools shall destroy them")

38 Jer. 5:7,8

39 Ecclesiasticus 15:20 ("The Lord hath commanded no man to do wickedly")

40 Ex. 23:7

41 1 Sam. 28:10

42 1 Sam. 28:15,16

oath is no authority for granting a license or indulgence to commit crime or immunity from punishment therefor.[43] To the contrary, it is said that the Lord hath given no man "license to sin."[44]

In modern law, an offense which is unlawful in itself, as being against the law of nature, or clearly against the public good, cannot be made dispunishable by any previous license.[44a] Nor does constitutional liberty of conscience authorize acts of licentiousness or justify practices inconsistent with the peace and safety of the state.[45]

CHAPTER 52

CRIMINAL RESPONSIBILITY

[§337]   Under Primitive law, when family and tribal solidarity was very strong,[46] an act of one member of a family was considered the act of all,[47] and the family as a whole was regarded as being responsible for a crime committed by any of its members.[48]   Accordingly—death being the punishment for crime[49]—it was the law that a father might be put to death for a crime of his child, or that a child might be put to death for a crime of his father.[50]

[§338]   By Mosaic law, each person was made responsible for his own crime.[1]   It established the general rule that "every man shall be put to death (that is, suffer punishment) for his own sin,"[2] and that "the fathers shall not be put to

---

43   See supra §6
44   Ecclesiasticus 15:20
44a   Ex parte Wells (1855) 18 How. (US) 307, 15 L ed 421, 424 (Wayne,J) saying that "a grant of this kind would be against reason and the common good, and therefore void."
45   Ruse v Williams (1913) 14 Ariz. 445, 130 P 887, 45 LRANS 923, 927 (Franklin,CJ)
   It does not authorize one to teach that abduction, adultery and fornication are lawful, proper, and good for the community. See Kay v Board of Higher Education—The Bertrand Russell Case (1940) 173 Misc. (NY) 943, 18 NYS2d 821, 829 (McGeehan,J) criticized in 50 Yale LJ (1941) 778 (Hamilton)
46   See supra §186
47   14 Gr.B. (1902) 84 (Amram)
48   12 Gr.B. (1900) 198 (Amram); Maine's Anc. L. 122
   Criminal responsibility means punishability. One is punished for an act for

which he is considered responsible. See State v Wallace (1942) 131 P2d (Or.) 222, 229 (Brand,J)
49   See infra §421
50   14 Gr.B. (1902) 84, 490 (Amram)
   The rule of Deut. 24:16, that "the fathers shall not be put to death for the children," presupposes that before its promulgation fathers were put to death for their children, and children for their fathers. 14 Gr.B. (1902) 490, 491 (Amram)
1   Thus changing the Primitive rule under which one member of a family might be slain for the crime of another. See supra §337
2   Deut. 24:16; Jer. 31:30 ("every one shall die for his own iniquity")
   And this rule is now followed in all civilized countries, that the guilty—not the innocent—should be punished. 11 Harv.LR (1897) 298 (Lowell)
   "Where the offence is, let the great axe fall." Hamlet, Act IV, sc. 5, L. 218

death for the children, neither shall the children be put to death for the fathers."[3] But a father might still be required to deliver up his son for punishment.[3a]

According to this rule, as soon as the kingdom had been confirmed in the hands of Amaziah,

". . . he slew his servants which had slain the king his father. "But the children of the murderers he slew not: according unto that which is written in the book of the law of Moses, wherein the Lord commanded, saying, 'The fathers shall not be put to death for the children, nor the children be put to death for the fathers; but every man shall be put to death for his own sin'."[4]

[§339] In Biblical law it seems that a married woman was responsible for a crime even though it was committed by both the husband and the wife, and it might therefore have been supposed that she acted in obedience to him.[5] Thus in the Case of Adam, and Eve, and the Serpent, Eve was condemned to sorrow and subjection to her husband[6] though the commandment concerning the eating of the fruit was given to Adam alone and not to her.[7] And in the Case of Ananias and Sapphira,[8] the wife was held equally responsible with her husband for an offense which they had agreed together to commit.[9]

At common law, during the continuance of the union the husband alone is responsible for crimes committed by his wife in his presence—the law not considering her, in such a case, as acting by her own will, but by his compulsion.[10]

[§340] Children were made responsible by Mosaic law for the crimes which they committed, but not for the crimes of their fathers.[11] It was thought that "children should not bear the iniquity of the fathers."[12] But in several instances both before and after Moses, punishment for crimes or wrongs committed by a father was inflicted upon an innocent

---

3 Deut. 24:16
3a See Judges 6:30
4 2 Kings 14:5,6; 2 Chron. 25:3,4
5 See supra §215
6 Gen. 3:16
7 Gen. 2:16,17; 13 Gr.B. (1901) 200 (Amram)
Or it may be considered that Eve was punished for having caused Adam to break the command concerning the eating of fruit.
8 See supra §163
9 Acts 5:9
10 Poor v Poor (1836) 8 NH 307, 29 AD 664, 669 (Richardson,J)
"Each of the woman defendants (convicted of treason), though knowing the seriousness and evil nature of her actions, undoubtedly followed the leadership of her husband. This being true, the Court recognizes a distinction between the husbands' and wives' degree of guilt . . ." United States v Haupt (1942) 47 F Supp 836, 842 (Campbell,DJ)
11 See supra §338
12 Ezek. 18:17 ("he shall not die for the iniquity of his father"); Wallach v Van Riswick (1876) 92 US 202, 210, 23 L ed 473, 476 (Strong,J)
But an illegitimate child did suffer for the iniquity of his natural parents. See supra §136
And the Lord visited "the iniquity of the fathers upon the third and fourth generation." Ex. 20:5; 34:7; Num. 14:18; Deut. 5:9

son. Thus, after "Ham, the father of Canaan, saw the nakedness of his father (Noah), and told his two brethren without,"
Noah said "Cursed be Canaan; a servant of servants shall
he be unto his brethren."[13] The "firstborn" of Egypt were
punished for the refusal of Pharaoh to permit the Israelites
to depart from the land.[14] And "the child that Uriah's wife
(Bath-sheba) bare unto David" was condemned to die because David caused Uriah to be killed "with the sword" and
took his wife.[15] Because of "abominations" committed by
Solomon in his old age, his son Rehoboam was condemned to
be deprived of the greater part of the kingdom.

". . . the Lord said unto Solomon, Forasmuch as this is done of thee,
and thou hast not kept my covenant and my statutes, which I have commanded thee, I will surely rend the kingdom from thee, and will give it
to thy servant.
"Notwithstanding in thy days I will not do it for David thy father's
sake: but I will rend it out of the hand of thy son."[16]

And in the case of Ahab, after his reproval by Elijah for
having taken possession of Naboth's vineyard and having
done "very abominably in following idols"[17]—

" . . . the word of the Lord came to Elijah the Tishbite, saying,
"Seest thou how Ahab humbleth himself before me? because he
humbleth himself before me, I will not bring the evil in his days: but
in his son's days will I bring the evil upon his house."[18]

Biblical law does not specify the age at which a child became responsible for crime.[19] But according to the Talmud[20]
it appears that liability to capital punishment began at the
age of 20.[21] At common law, a child under the age of seven
was considered incapable of committing a crime, a child
between the ages of seven and 14 was presumed to be incapable but his capacity could be shown, and a child more than
14 years old was presumed to be capable but this presumption could be overcome by proof.[22]

13 Gen. 9:22,25
14 Ex. 12:29 ("And it came to pass,
that at midnight the Lord smote all the
firstborn in the land of Egypt, from
the firstborn of Pharaoh that sat on
his throne unto the firstborn of the
captive that was in the dungeon; and
all the firstborn of cattle")
15 2 Sam. 12:14
16 1 Kings 11:12
17 1 Kings 21:1-26
18 1 Kings 21:28,29
19 Minimum ages for contracting marriage, see supra §190
"From time immemorial the status of
a minor of tender years has been recognized in law to be different from that
of one of more mature years." Wal-

green Co. v Industrial Com. (1926) 323
Ill. 194, 153 NE 831, 832 (Heard,J)
The law has refused to hold children
to the same accountability as adults.
Artukovich v Astendorf (1942) 21 AC
343, 350, 131 P2d 831 (Edmonds,J, dissenting)
20 See supra §15
21 38 Case & Comment (1932) No. 2, p 4
22 4 Bl.Com. 23
In England in the early eighteenth
century, a nine year old child was
found guilty of murder and was
hanged; a 13 year old girl was burned
to death for the crime of murder; and
an eight year old boy was executed for
committing arson. See 26 Marquette
LR (1942) 175 (McKenna & Grossman)

[§341] In Primitive law,[23] and even under Mosaic law,[24] animals were sometimes formally condemned and punished for acts of a criminal nature,[25] and particularly for acts causing the death of a person.[26] Thus in the Case of Adam, and Eve, and the Serpent, the Lord cursed the serpent "above all cattle," for having beguiled Eve to eat of the forbidden fruit.[27] And it was decreed that any "beast" which should touch mount Sinai, when the Lord had "come down in the sight of all the people" upon it, "shall surely be stoned, or shot through."[28] But it is recognized that herbivorous animals, such as cows and mules, are attracted by a field of growing corn, and no sort of blame can be laid against such an animal for attempting to gratify its taste.[29]

CHAPTER 53

DEFENSES

[§342] In Primitive law, an act was judged by its effect. If it caused death or otherwise harmed another, the actor was punishable though it was done accidentally or unintentionally.[30] Even after the establishment of Mosaic law, one was considered as being responsible for accidental or unintentioned wrongs. Thus in the Case of Ussah it is related that "God smote him there for his error" in that he "put forth his hand to the ark of God, and took hold of it, for the oxen shook it."[31] But ordinarily an offense committed unintentionally or "ignorantly"[32] was either left unpunished

23 Gen. 9:5 ("And surely your blood of your lives will I require: at the hand of every beast will I require it . . .")
Primitive law did not distinguish between human and animal causes of harm. 36 Case & Comment (1930) No. 2, p 11 (Dox)

24 Ex. 21:28 ("If an ox gore a man or a woman, that they die: then the ox shall be surely stoned . . .")

25 Liability for injuries and trespasses by animals, see supra §287

26 "Even an inanimate object which had caused bloodshed was deemed liable for blood-guilt and was subject to solemn process of condemnation." 28 Cal. LR (1940) 424, n 11

In modern times, also, animals have been tried and punished as for crime. In 1857, Chinese at Auburn, California, solemnly tried and convicted a horse which had killed a Chinese man. They took it to their burying ground for execution, but it was rescued by a party of white citizens. See Oakland Tribune, "The Knave," vol. CXXXVII, No. 3, Jan. 3, 1943, quoting Placer Press

27 Gen. 3:14,15
28 Ex. 19:11-13
29 Barnett v State (1931) 117 Tex.Crim. Rep. 358, 35 SW2d 441 (Lattimore,J)
30 36 Case & Comment (1930) No. 2 p 11 (Dox)
31 2 Sam. 6:6,7
32 See Heb. 5:2 ("have compassion on the ignorant")

—the killer, for example, being permitted to flee to a city of refuge[33]—or was punished less severely.[34]

Under modern law, an act accidentally or unintentionally committed is not ordinarily punished as a crime.[35] It has been reasoned that human actions can hardly be considered as culpable, either in law or morals, unless an intelligent consent goes with them,[36] and that conduct flowing from an honest judgment, though uninformed and mistaken, ought not to be condemned.[37]

[§343] But it is no defense that one was encouraged or caused by another to commit an offense.[38] This plea was first interposed unsuccessfully by Adam, who asserted that "The woman whom thou gavest to be with me, she gave me of the tree, and I did eat,"[39] and then by Eve, who said "The serpent beguiled me, and I did eat."[40]

That one was enticed to commit a crime may be considered, however, when the penalty is imposed.[41] Thus in Adam's case, though the law prescribed the death penalty, he was sentenced merely to work for a living. It has been suggested that the judge took into consideration the fact that there was a strong inducement for the breach of the law, inasmuch as Eve had already eaten of the fruit; and it was through her persuasion that Adam ate of it also.[42]

[§344] In Mosaic law a clear distinction was made as between those who committed offenses "through ignorance" and those who offended "presumptuously."[43] The law provided that—

". . . if any soul sin (commit an offense) through ignorance, then he shall bring a she goat of the first year for a sin offering.

"And the priest shall make an atonement for the soul that sinneth ignorantly, when he sinneth by ignorance before the Lord, to make an atonement for him; and it shall be forgiven him.

"Ye shall have one law for him that sinneth through ignorance, both for him that is born among the children of Israel, and for the stranger that sojourneth among them.

---

33 Deut. 19:4,5; and see infra §431

34 See infra §344

According to the Talmud, duress was a good excuse for the commission of a crime other than murder; deafness if accompanied by dumbness was a complete excuse; and idiocy, lunacy or extreme intoxication was a good defense except when the crime was committed during a lucid interval or when the defendant was sober. 38 Case & Comment (1932) No. 2, p 4 (Goldberg)

35 See 7 Cal. Jur. 851

36 State v Brown (1888) 38 Kan. 390, 16 P 259, 260 (Valentine,J)

37 Zebach's Lessee v Smith (1810) 3 Binney (Pa.) 69, 73 (Yeates,J)

38 Tucker v State (1912) 7 Okla.Crim. Rep. 634, 125 P 1089, 1093

39 Gen. 3:12

40 Gen. 3:13

41 Matters affecting imposition of punishment, see infra §§ 423-427

42 13 Gr.B. (1901) 201 (Amram)

43 Knowledge as affecting legal responsibility, see supra §§48, 49

"But the soul that doeth ought presumptuously, whether he be born in the land, or a stranger, the same reproacheth the Lord; and that soul shall be cut off from among his people.
"Because he hath despised the word of the Lord, and hath broken his commandment, that soul shall utterly be cut off; his iniquity shall be upon him."[44]

But under Christian law, one who committed an offense through ignorance of the law was not altogether blameless,[45] the rule being that—

"He that knoweth his master's will, and doeth it not, shall be beaten with many stripes, but he that knoweth it not, with few."[46]

St. Paul, however, is said to have "obtained mercy" for offenses committed before his conversion because he "did it ignorantly."[47] And when charged with speaking evil of the chief priest, he justified himself by saying he did not know the man was the chief priest.[48]

Generally, under modern law, ignorance of the law is no excuse for a criminal act[49]—"not that all men know the law, but because it is an excuse every man will plead and no man can tell how to refute him."[50]

CHAPTER 54

OFFENSES AGAINST THE GOVERNMENT, LAW AND ORDER

[§345] The law requires that one "seek peace"[1] and "walk orderly."[2] Among other things, it is commanded to "be at peace among yourselves,"[3] to "follow peace[4] with all men,"[5] to "follow after the things which make for peace,"[6] and "if

---

44 Num. 15:27-31
"Under the Talmud unless the defendant had been warned immediately before he committed a crime that his intended act was a punishable offense and unless he had clearly declared his willingness to bear the punishment, he could not be penalized. Furthermore if any time elapsed between the warning and the commission of the offence the culprit could not be punished, even if the crime were a capital one. These requirements have no equal in ancient or modern law. The Rabbis who administered the law were very loath to pronounce the capital penalty and they took every opportunity to avoid doing it." 38 Case & Comment (1932) No. 2, p 3 (Goldberg)
45 See supra §48
46 Hall v State (1912) 7 Okla.Crim. Rep. 126, 122 P 729 (Doyle,J); and see Luke 12:47,48

47 1 Tim. 1:13
But not in ignorance of the law. St. Paul was well versed in the law. See supra §98
48 Acts 23:3-5
49 See 8 RCL 123
50 John Selden (1584-1654) English statesman and political writer
1 Ps. 34:14 ("seek peace, and pursue it"); Jer. 29:7 ("seek the peace of the city whither I have caused you to be carried away captives"); 1 Pet. 3:11 ("seek peace and ensue it")
2 Acts 21:24
3 1 Thess. 5:13
4 2 Tim. 2:22
5 Heb. 12:14
"Be in peace with many: nevertheless have but one counsellor of a thousand." Ecclesiasticus 6:6
6 Rom. 14:19

it be possible, as much as lieth in you," to "live peaceably with all men."[7] Conversely, the Scriptures direct that one "abstain from strife,"[8] "strive not with a man without cause, if he have done thee no harm,"[9] and "strive not in a matter that concerneth thee not."[10] So, although no punishment is specifically prescribed therefor, it is doubtless an offense to disturb or commit a breach of the peace, as by engaging in a riot,[11] fighting[12] or "striving"[13]—except in self-defense[14] or to protect a member of one's family[15] or a guest[16]—or following a "multitude to do evil."[17]

[§346] It is likewise an offense to "raise a false report"[18] or to "go up and down as a talebearer,"[19] for these things are calculated to disturb the peace and order of the people. "The words of a talebearer," it has been observed, "are as wounds,"[20] and "where there is no talebearer, the strife ceaseth."[21] Canaan, son of Ham, was condemned to servitude merely because of his father's delinquency in telling his brothers of the drunkenness and nakedness of their father.[22]

In Ecclesiasticus it is warned to "be not called a whisperer"[23]—meaning no doubt a "tale-bearer"—for "a whisperer separateth chief friends,"[24] and a "curse" is pronounced against "the whisperer and double-tongued: for such have destroyed many that were at peace."[25]

[§347] The law forbids meddling,[26] murmuring[27] and sedition,[28] since acts of this character are calculated to cause

---

7 Rom. 12:18
8 Ecclesiasticus 28:8
"Go not forth hastily to strive." Prov. 25:8
9 Prov. 3:30
10 Ecclesiasticus 11:9
11 Rom. 13:13 ("Let us walk . . . not in rioting")
12 See supra §177
13 2 Tim. 2:24 ("the servant of the Lord must not strive")
14 ". . . that thou mayest save thy own life . . ." 1 Kings 1:12
15 ". . . and the life of thy son . . ." 1 Kings 1:12   See supra §222
16 See supra §243
17 Ex. 23:2
18 Ex. 23:1
19 Lev. 19:16
"A talebearer revealeth secrets." Prov. 11:13, 20:19
He "separateth very friends." Prov. 17:9
"Rehearse not unto another that which is told unto thee." Ecclesiasticus 19:7

"Be ashamed . . . of . . speaking again that which thou hast heard." Ecclesiasticus 41:17,23
20 Prov. 18:8, 26:22
21 Prov. 26:20
22 Gen. 9:22-27
As to the responsibility of a child for the misdeeds of his father, see supra §§337, 340
23 Ecclesiasticus 5:14
24 Prov. 16:28
25 Ecclesiasticus 28:13
26 Prov. 24:21 ("meddle not with them that are given to change"); Ecclesticus 11:10 ("meddle not with many matters: for if thou meddle much, thou shalt not be innocent")
27 Wisdom of Solomon 1:10,11 ("the noise of murmuring is not hid. Therefore beware of murmuring, which is unprofitable")
"My child, be not a murmurer, for it guideth to blasphemy; nor self-willed, nor evil-minded, for from all these things blasphemies are begotten." Two Ways, 3:6
28 Gal. 5:20

"the righteous to go astray in an evil way"[29] and to sow "discord among brethren."[30] St. Paul counselled the Corinthians that they should not "murmur . . . as some of them (of whom it is written) also murmured, and were destroyed of the destroyer."[31]

[§348] The extreme offense against government is "treason." In the Bible, as in old English law, two kinds of treason are recognized, namely "high" and "petty" treason, the former being committed against the king or the state,[32] and the latter against a parent.[33]

[§349] —— The Biblical law of high treason is that "whosoever he be that doth rebel" against the leader of the nation, or who in time of warfare, "will not hearken unto [his] words in all that [he] commandest him, he shall be put to death."[34] The law also prescribed the death penalty for one who would not "hearken . . . unto the judge."[35] Under American law, treason consists in levying war against one's own country or in adhering to its enemies, giving them aid and comfort.[36]

The Case of Bigthan and Teresh was one in which the defendants were tried and convicted for treason. It is related that—

" . . . while Mordecai sat in the king's gate, two of the king's chamberlains, Bigthan and Teresh, of those which kept the door, were wroth, and sought to lay hand on the king Ahasuerus.

"And the thing was known to Mordecai, who told it unto Esther the queen; and Esther certified the king thereof in Mordecai's name.

"And when inquisition was made of the matter, it was found out; therefore they were both hanged on a tree . . ."[37]

Other treasons were committed in the time of the Maccabees. It is stated that Maccabeus accused certain men who had taken money and let enemies escape, "so he slew those that were found traitors,"[38] and that "Rhodocus, who was in the Jews' host, disclosed the secrets to the enemies; therefore he was sought out, and when they had gotten him, they put him in prison."[39]

---

29 Prov. 28:10 ("Who causeth the righteous to go astray in an evil way, he shall fall himself into his own pit")
30 Prov. 6:16,19 ("These . . . things doth the Lord hate: . . . he that soweth discord among brethren")
31 1 Cor. 10:10
32 See infra §349
33 See infra §350
34 Josh. 1:18

35 Deut. 17:12 ("And the man that will do presumptuously, and will not harken . . . unto the judge, even that man shall die")
36 U.S. Const. (1789) Art. III, §3
37 Est. 2:21-23
See also Est. 12:3,2 (referring to "Gabatha and Tharra")
38 2 Mac. 10:21,22
39 2 Mac. 13:21

[§350] —— Petty treason consisted in the killing of the head of the family, or even in the "cursing" or "smiting" of one's father or mother. Mosaic law provided that "he that curseth his father, or his mother, shall surely be put to death,"[40] and also that "he that smiteth his father, or his mother, shall be surely put to death."[41] This offense was not condoned by Jesus, who observed that "God commanded . . . He that curseth father or mother, let him die the death,"[42] and reproved the Jews for having "made the commandment of God of none effect by your tradition."[43]

[§351] —— —— Mosaic law further provided for the summary trial and execution of an incorrigible son.

"If a man have a stubborn and rebellious son, which will not obey the voice of his father, or the voice of his mother, and that, when they have chastened him, will not hearken unto them:
"Then shall his father and his mother lay hold on him, and bring him out unto the elders of his city, and unto the gate of his place:
"And they shall say unto the elders of his city, This our son is stubborn and rebellious, he will not obey our voice; he is a glutton, and a drunkard.
"And all the men of his city shall stone him with stones, that he die: so shalt thou put evil away from among you; and all Israel shall hear, and fear."[44]

CHAPTER 55

OFFENSES AGAINST JUSTICE

[§352] Bribery, according to the old writers, is the crime of "taking or giving a reward to influence the actions of a person 'in judicial place'."[45] Though it is likely that this offense was seldom punished in ancient times, the Scriptures recognize the impropriety of accepting a bribe,[46] taking a

---

40 Ex. 21:17
"For every one that curseth his father or his mother shall be surely put to death: he hath cursed his father or his mother; his blood shall be upon him."
"Whoso curseth his father or his mother, his lamp shall be put out in obscure darkness." Prov. 20:20
41 Ex. 21:15
42 Matt. 15:4
See also Mark 7:10 "For Moses said, . . . Whoso curseth father or mother, let him die the death."

43 Matt. 15:6; Mark 7:13
44 Deut. 21:18-21
45 See 4 RCL 177
46 Ps. 26:9,10 ("Gather not my soul with sinners, . . . their right hand is full of bribes") ; Isa. 33:15,16 ("He that . . . shaketh his hands from holding of bribes . . . shall dwell on high") ; Amos 5:12 ("For I know your manifold transgressions . . . they take a bribe") ; Ecclesiasticus 40:12 ("All bribery shall be blotted out")

gift,[47] or asking[48] or taking a reward[49] to pervert justice.[50] Particularly as regards taking gifts, it is expressly commanded in Mosaic law that "thou shalt take no gift: for the gift blindeth the wise, and perverteth the words of the righteous."[1]

[§353] —— Samuel, when "old and graybearded," sought to free himself from suspicion of bribery, fraud, and oppression.[2] It is related that after Saul had been made king[3]—

"Samuel said unto all Israel . . .
"Behold, here I am: witness against me before the Lord, and before his anointed: whose ox have I taken? or whose ass have I taken? or whom have I defrauded? whom have I oppressed? or whose hand have I received any bribe to blind mine eyes therewith? and I will restore it to you.
"And they said, Thou has not defrauded us, nor oppressed us, neither hast thou taken aught of any man's hand.
"And he said unto them, The Lord is witness against you, and his anointed is witness this day, that ye have not found aught in my hand. And they answered, he is witness."[4]

[§354] —— Judas Iscariot took a reward to "betray innocent blood." According to the account of this matter in the book of Matthew:

". . . one of the twelve, called Judas Iscariot, went unto the chief priests.
"And said unto them, What will ye give me, and I will deliver him (Jesus) unto you? And they covenanted with him for thirty pieces of silver.
"And from that time he sought opportunity to betray him.
"And . . . Judas . . . came, and with him a great multitude with swords and staves, from the chief priests and elders of the people.
"And forthwith he came to Jesus, and said Hail master; and kissed him.
"And Jesus said unto him, Friend, wherefore art thou come? Then came they, and laid hands on Jesus, and took him."[5]

. . . .
"Then Judas, . . . when he saw that he (Jesus) was condemned, repented himself, and brought again the thirty pieces of silver to the chief priests and elders,
"Saying, I have sinned in that I have betrayed the innocent blood. And they said, What is that to us? see thou to that.
"And he cast down the pieces of silver in the temple, and departed, and went and hanged himself.

---

47 Prov. 17:23 ("A wicked man taketh a gift . . . to pervert . . . judgment"), 29:4 ("he that receiveth gifts overthroweth the land") And see supra §161
48 Micah 7:3
49 Micah 3:11
50 See infra §434
"He that . . . taketh (no) reward against the innocent . . . shall never be moved." Ps. 15:5
1 Ex. 23:8; to same effect Deut. 16:19

"All bribery . . . shall be blotted out." Ecclesiasticus 40:12
2 It is not enough for justice or the public morals that an innocent man be saved from the actual penalty of a crime. He ought, if possible, to be freed from all suspicion. 11 Harv.L.R (1897) 298 (Lowell)
3 See supra §90
4 1 Sam. 12:1-5
5 Matt. 26:14,15,16,47,49,50

"And the chief priests took the silver pieces, and said, It is not lawful for to put them in the treasury, because it is the price of blood.

"And they took counsel, and bought with them the potter's field, to bury strangers in."[6]

[§355] "False swearing"[7] or "giving false testimony,"[8] is repeatedly condemned—thus signifying, no doubt, that this offense was prevalent in ancient as it is in modern, times.[9] It is commanded that "ye shall not swear by my name falsely,"[10] that "thou shalt not bear false witness against thy neighbour,"[12] and that "thou shalt . . . put not thine hand with the wicked to be an unrighteous witness."[13]

[§356] —— Punishment of perjury is mandatory. It is prescribed that "a false witness shall not be unpunished."[14]

"If a false witness rise up against any man to testify against him that which is wrong;

"Then both the men, between whom the controversy is, shall stand before the Lord, before the priests and the judges, which shall be in those days;

"And the judges shall make diligent inquisition: and, behold, if the witness be a false witness, and hath testified falsely against his brother;

"Then shall ye do unto him, as he had thought to have done unto his brother: so shalt thou put the evil away from among you."[15]

[§357] —— The Case of the "Two Judges" arose in the trial of Susanna, and the facts concerning the perjuries committed by the judges are set out in the discussion of that case.[16] With regard to the trial and punishment of the perjured judges, it is related that when Daniel had separately examined them and disclosed their perjury—

". . . all the assembly cried out with a loud voice, and praised God, who saveth them that trust in him.

6 Matt. 27:3-7; see also Mark 14:10,11, 43-46; Luke 22:3-6, 47,48,54; John 18:1-5
7 Zech. 8:17 ("love no false oath; for all these are things that I hate, saith the Lord"); Mal. 3:5 ("I will be a swift witness . . . against false swearers")
8 Prov. 6:16,19 ("These . . . things doth the Lord hate: A false witness that speaketh lies"), 21:28 ("A false witness shall perish"), 24:28 ("Be not a witness against thy neighbour without cause")
9 See supra §43, n 42
"There will be perjury, where there are oaths, but this does not prove that all oaths are useless." Vanatta v Anderson (1811) 3 Binney (Pa.) 417, 423, (Tilghman,CJ)
10 Lev. 19:12
11 Matt. 19:18; Rom. 13:9; Two Ways 2:3
"Do not bear false witness." Mark 10:19; Luke 18:20

12 Ex. 20:16
"Neither shalt thou bear false witness against thy neighbour." Deut. 5:20
"A man that beareth false witness against his neighbour is a maul, and a sword, and a sharp arrow." Prov. 25:18
The injunction—"Thou shalt not bear false witness against thy neighbour"—comes from the Most High. Ex parte Newman (1858) 9 Cal. 502, 522 (Field,J, dissenting)
Modern criminal laws against perjury are based upon it. 42 Wash.LR (1914) 770 (Barnard)
13 Ex. 23:1
"The law shall be found perfect without lies." Ecclesiasticus 34:8
14 Prov. 19:5,9
15 Deut. 19:16-19
In Texas law, when perjury is committed on a trial of a capital felony, the punishment of the perjury shall be death. See 32 Tex Jur 825, § 40.
16 See infra §399

"And they arose against the two elders, for Daniel had convicted them of false witness by their own mouth.

"And according to the law of Moses they did unto them in such sort as they maliciously intended to do to their neighbour: and they put them to death. Thus the innocent blood was saved the same day."[17]

CHAPTER 56

OFFENSES AGAINST MORALS

358 In general   359 Drunkenness   360 Association with drunkards, and causing others to drink

[§358] Generally speaking, "offenses against morals" means all those offenses against common decency and social propriety. The term will include adultery, fornication, incest, rape and sodomy, but these and similar offenses are considered in the chapter dealing with "sexual offenses."[18] The topic of "prostitution" is also discussed elsewhere.[19]

Nor is morality concerned merely with sex. There is no aspect of life in which nonconformity with customary standards cannot be challenged as immoral.[19a] The law demands that "all things be done decently and in order."[20] Anything otherwise done is an offense against good morals, though no one is directly injured. Lewdness,[21] lasciviousness,[22] and indecent exposure[23] are doubtless offenses of this character, as well as drunkenness,—a subject next considered.

[§359] Drunkenness[24] is an offense against decency and morals,[25] except in the possible case where one becomes intoxicated without appreciating the nature of the beverage or the

---

17 History of Susanna (Dan.13) v. 60-62

18 See infra §396 et seq.

19 See supra §§313-315

19a See 50 Yale LJ (1941) 781 (Hamilton)

20 1 Cor. 14:40

21 Ezek. 22:9, 24:47-49
". . . in lewdness is decay and great want: for lewdness is the mother of famine." Tobit 4:13

22 Gal. 5:19

23 Gen. 9:21 (Noah, being drunken with wine, "was uncovered within his tent")

24 "Intoxication tends to lessen and sometimes destroy the powers of observation and the element of caution. As said by Scotland's bard: 'Inspiring bold John Barleycorn, What dangers thou canst make us scorn'." Southern Traction Co. v Kirksey (1920) 222 SW (Tex.Civ.App.) 702, 704 (Jenkins,J)

One is drunk or intoxicated "when he is under the influence of an intoxicating liquor to such an extent as to tend to prevent him from exercising the care and caution which a sober and prudent person would have exercised under the same circumstances." Willoughby v Driscoll (1942) 120 P2d (Ore.) 768, 772 (Belt,J)

25 "Voluntary intoxication (i.e., drunkenness) is an offense not only malum prohibitum but malum in se, condemned as wrong in and of itself by every sense of common decency and good morals from the time that Noah in his drunkenness brought shame to his sons so that they backed in to cover his nakedness, and Lot's daughters employed it for incestuous purposes. Drunkenness was declared wrong in and of itself and punishment provided by the Israelites." People v Townsend (1921) 214 Mich. 267, 183 NW 177, 179, 16 ALR 902 (Wiest,J)

effects of its use.[26] Biblical law demands sobriety[27] and temperance,[28] not merely in drinking but in all things.[29] Contrariwise, it forbids drunkenness,[30] and excessive[31] and habitual drinking,[32] or intemperance.[33] Drunkenness in judges, priests, prophets[34] and bishops,[35] and in women,[36] and laboring men[37] is particularly denounced.

Drunkenness was forbidden and punished in ancient China and India, while in Rome the censors turned drunken members out of the Senate and branded them with infamy. Drunkenness in a public place was always a misdemeanor at common law.[38] In England drunkenness was formerly pilloried as the root and foundation of many sins, such as bloodshed, stabbing, murder, swearing and such like.[39] In Massachusetts Bay Colony in 1633-34, one (Robte Coles) who was convicted of drunkenness was disfranchised and sentenced to wear a red letter D for a year. Modern statutes generally declare drunkards to be disorderly persons and make it an offense for one to be drunk in any public place.[40]

[§360] According to Biblical law, it is improper for one to associate with winebibbers,[41] or to urge[42] or compel another to drink so as to make "him drunken also."[43] So it is said that in Babylon—

---

26 Gen. 9:21

27 Titus 1:8; 1 Pet. 1:13, 4:7, 5:8

28 See supra §298

29 Gal. 5:23, saying that "there is no law" against "temperance."

30 Gal. 5:21; Eph. 5:18 ("be not drunk with wine")
"Drink not wine to make thee drunken: neither let drunkenness go with thee in thy journey." Tobit 4:15
"Drunkenness increaseth the rage of a fool till he offend; it diminisheth strength, and maketh wounds." Ecclesiasticus 31:30

31 Eph. 5:18
"Wine drunken with excess maketh bitterness of the mind, with brawling and quarrelling." Ecclesiasticus 31:29

32 "Woe unto them that rise up early in the morning that they may follow strong drink; that continue till night, till wine inflame them!" Isa. 5:11

33 Prov. 23:29 et seq.
"Shew not thy valiantness in wine; for wine hath destroyed many." Ecclesiasticus 31:25

34 "The priest and the prophet have erred through strong drink, they are swallowed up of wine, they are out of the way through strong drink; they err in vision, they stumble in judgment." Isa 28:7

35 1 Tim. 3:2

36 Ecclesiasticus 26:8
Women should "adorn themselves" with "sobriety." 1 Tim. 2:9; and see supra §332

37 Ecclesiasticus 19:1 ("A labouring man that is given to drunkenness shall not be rich")

38 State v Brown (1888) 38 Kan. 390, 16 P 259
Bacon, in his abridgment of the common law, lists drunkenness as one of the sins of heresy.

39 4 Jac. i, cap. 5
Ecclesiastical judges and officers were given power to censure and punish drunkards.
Dunstan is said to have labored in the cause of temperance in England to the end that King Edgar at his instance restricted the number of taverns and the quality of intoxicants that might be sold.

40 See Mich. Comp. Laws (1915) §§7774, 15530; People v Townsend (1921) 214 Mich. 267, 183 NW 177, 179, 16 ALR 902 (Wiest,J); State v Boag (1936) 154 Ore. 354, 59 P2d 396 (Kelly,J)

41 Prov. 23:20 ("Be not among winebibbers")

42 Ecclesiasticus 31:31 ("press not upon him [thy neighbour] with urging him [to drink]")

43 Hab. 2:15 ("Woe unto him that giveth his neighbour drink, that puttest the bottle to him, and makest him drunken also")

". . . the drinking was according to the law; none did compel: for so the king (Ahasuerus, king of the Medes and Persians) had appointed to all the officers of his house, that they should do according to every man's pleasure."[44]

Under modern law, it is generally a crime to give or sell intoxicants to an habitual drunkard or to a minor.[45]

CHAPTER 57

OFFENSES AGAINST THE PERSON

[§361] "Children are a heritage of the Lord,"[46] and it is doubtless a crime to procure an abortion or kill a new-born child.[47] Under Mosaic law, if a woman with child be hurt so as to cause a miscarriage, without other "mischief," the person responsible is required to be punished "according as the woman's husband will lay upon him."[48]

[§362] An assault—in the sense of a beating or striking of another—is not merely a trespass[49] for which the law will allow damages to the injured person,[50] but it is also—in some cases at least—a crime which the state will punish.[1] If the wrongful act results in the maiming of the victim—the loss or "perishing"[2] of some bodily member, such as an ear,[3] eye[4] or tooth[5]—it constitutes mayhem,[6] and this is a more serious offense because it impairs the victim's ability to defend himself and to make his livelihood.

[§363] —— Concerning the punishment for assault or mayhem, Mosaic law provides that "If men strive . . . and . . . any mischief follow, then thou shalt give life for life; eye for eye, tooth for tooth, hand for hand, foot for foot; burning

---

44 Est. 1:8
45 See 30 Am Jur 423
46 Ps. 127:3
47 Two Ways 2:2
48 Ex. 21:22 ("he shall pay as the judges determine")
49 See supra §177
50 See infra §456 et seq.
1 See infra §363

2 Ex. 21:26
3 See infra §365
4 The Philistines committed mayhem upon Samson. They "put out his eyes." Judges 16:21
5 Smiting of eye or tooth of servant as entitling him to freedom, see supra §240
6 See 8 RCL 304

for burning, wound for wound, stripe for stripe."[7]   In other words, "if a man cause a blemish in his neighbour; as he hath done, so shall it be done to him; breach for breach, eye for eye, tooth for tooth: as he hath caused a blemish in a man, so shall it be done to him again."[8]

[§364] —— A wife who interferes in "strife" between her husband and another man does so at her peril.   The rule of Mosaic law in such cases is that—

"When men strive together one with another, and the wife of the one draweth near for to deliver her husband out of the hand of him that smiteth him, and putteth forth her hand, and taketh him by the secrets:
"Then thou shalt cut off her hand, thine eyes shall not pity her."[9]

[§365] —— Peter committed mayhem upon Malchus, a servant of the high priest, at the time of the betrayal of Jesus. It is related that—

". . . Simon Peter having a sword drew it, and smote the high priest's servant, and cut off his right ear. The servant's name was Malchus.
"Then said Jesus unto Peter, Put up thy sword into the sheath . . ."[10]

It does not appear that this offense was prosecuted or punished, for the reason, no doubt, that Jesus, according to the account in Luke, "touched" the ear of the wounded man, "and healed him."[11]

[§366]   Homicide is the killing of a human being.[12]   Beginning with the first rule[13] and the first cases mentioned in Genesis,[14] the Scriptures contain many denunciations of this ancient crime;[15] thus indicating that mankilling has been of frequent occurrence through the ages.[16]   The general rule is "Thou shalt not kill"[17] or "Do not kill."[18]   More particularly it is commanded that thou shalt not slay "the innocent and right-

---

7   Ex. 21:22-25

8   Lev. 24:19,20; see also Deut 19:21

9   Deut. 25:11,12

10   John 18:10,11; see also Matt. 26:51, 52; Mark 14:47; Luke 22:50

11   Luke 22:51

12   See 26 Am Jur 157

A slingshot is a dangerous weapon, within a statute making it a crime to carry such a weapon. State v Loew (Mich. 1942) The Recorder (S.F.), vol. 83, no. 27, p 1, citing Sam. 1:17 (David and Goliath)

13   Gen. 9:6 ("Whoso sheddeth man's blood, by man shall his blood be shed")

14   See infra §§369, 370

15   See Ezek. 33:25; Hosea 4:2; Gal. 5:21; and other citations infra, this section.

Instances of conspiracy to kill are also referred to. See Gen. 37:18, 28, 36 (Joseph's brethren conspired to kill him, but instead sold him for twenty pieces of silver to merchantmen who took him to Egypt and sold him into slavery); 2 Chron. 24:21 (Zabad and Jehozabad conspired against Zechariah, son of Jehoiada the priest, and stoned him with stones at the commandment of the king)

16   See supra §43, n 42

17   Ex. 20:13; Deut. 5:17; Matt. 5:21; Rom. 13:9; Two Ways 2:2

The divine command is "thou shalt do no murder." Matt. 19:18; Ex parte Newman (1858) 9 Cal. 502, 522 (Field,J, dissenting)

The various modern statutes against murder, assault, mayhem, etc., are based on this commandment. 42 Wash.L.Rep. (1914) 770 (Bernard,J)

18   Mark 10:19; Luke 18:20

eous."[19]   And it is further enjoined that "thou (shalt not) stand against the blood of thy neighbour,"[20] nor take a reward "to slay an innocent person."[21]

[§367] —— "At one time the wilful killing of another was not considered evil in itself,"[22] and it was not considered unlawful for anyone to kill a "fugitive" or "vagabond" who bore no mark of divine protection.[23] But the Cain case established the unlawfulness of the killing of a brother.[24] The commandment "thou shalt not kill" originally meant "thou shalt not kill a member of another family belonging to the same tribe or nation."[25]   Later it came to be understood as forbidding the killing of any person whatsoever.[26]   But it presupposes that there is no just cause for taking life,[27] for there are circumstances in which killing is not unlawful,[27a] as where it is done as a punishment for crime[28] or in warfare.[29]

It has been urged that the merciful killing of persons suffering from painful and incurable diseases should be legalized.[30]   But it will be noted that after Saul had been "sore

19 Ex. 23:7 ("the innocent and righteous slay thou not: for I will not justify the wicked"); Prov. 6:16,17 ("These . . . things doth the Lord hate: . . . hands that shed innocent blood")
20 Lev. 19:16
21 Deut. 27:25 ("Cursed be he that taketh reward to slay an innocent person")
Judas Iscariot took a reward to betray innocent blood. See supra §354
22 State v Malusky (1930) 59 ND 501, 230 NW 735, 71 ALR 190, 193 (Nuessle,J) saying that this is so among some savage peoples today.
23 Gen. 4:14
Such a person, being a "stranger," was regarded as a wild beast, more dangerous than others because of his greater intelligence.
24 See infra §369
But it did not disturb the power of the patriarch or father over the members of his family. See supra §223
25 14 Gr.B. (1902) 231 (Amram)
This "taboo" has been said to represent "the very essence of social necessity, if internal cohesion and order are to be maintained." 28 Yale LJ (1919) 782 (Keller)
At one time, it was thought that honor might be vindicated or that guilt or innocence might be determined by mortal combat between individuals or factions. State v Malusky (1930) 59 ND 501, 230 NW 735, 71 ALR 190, 193 (Nuessle,J)
26 See supra §44
27 22 Geo.LJ (1934) 428 (Scott)
27a In some states (Georgia, New Mexico and Texas), a husband has the privilege of killing his wife's paramour. He

is the paramour's executioner and the killing is not a crime. In other states, the killing of the paramour is manslaughter. But the husband is not permitted in any state to kill his wife, though she is likely to be an equal partner in guilt with the paramour. 21 Tex.LR (1942) 17-20 (Stumberg)
28 See infra §§421, 472
29 See supra §116; State v Malusky (1930) 59 ND 501, 230 NW 735, 71 ALR 190, 193 (Nuessle,J) saying that "Even now killing is justified in time of war."
Under the ancient common law of England (around 1200 A.D.) the only justifiable killing was one done in the enforcement of the law. It was no defense that one killed by accident, in self-defense, or while insane. The killer was spared only by royal pardon. See 43 Yale LJ (1934) 539, 540 (Perkins)
30 Such killing is called "euthanasia," meaning "easy death." It may not be said to violate the spirit of the commandment against killing, which was doubtless intended to prohibit merciless or willful killings.
The Hippocratian oath says: "If any shall ask me for a drug to produce death I will not give it, nor will I suggest such council." But some physicians have assumed a "right to kill" in the case of infants born imbecile or doomed to a life of pain.
The case of a husband who, at the request of his wife suffering from an incurable illness, prepared a cup of poison and placed it on a chair beside her bed, see People v Roberts (1920) 211 Mich. 187, 178 NW 690, affirming his conviction of first degree murder.

wounded of the archers" in a battle with the Philistines, his armourbearer refused to kill him to prevent his falling alive into the hands of his enemies and being abused by them.[31] Also that David ordered the execution of a young man of the Amalekites who reported that he had killed Saul at his request because he was "sure that he could not live after that he was fallen."[32]

[§368] —— Punishment by banishment or exile was imposed in the first Scriptural case of murder,[33] and according to tradition the death penalty for murder was not formally enunciated until after the flood.[34] Under Mosaic law the punishment for mankilling is that the killer "shall surely be put to death."[35]

"He that smiteth a man so that he die, shall be surely put to death.[36]

"And if a man lie not in wait, but God deliver him (the victim) into his hand; then I will appoint thee a place whither he shall flee.[37]

"But if a man come presumptuously upon his neighbour, to slay him with guile; thou shalt (even) take him from mine altar, that he may die.[38]

"If a man smite his servant, or his maid, with a rod, and he die under his hand; he shall be surely punished.[39]

"If a thief be found breaking up, and be smitten that he die, there shall no blood be shed for him.[40]

"If the sun be risen upon him, there shall be blood shed for him; for he should make full restitution: if he have nothing, then he shall be sold for his theft."[41]

In justification of the imposition of the death penalty upon a murderer, it was reasoned that "the voice" of the victim's blood "crieth out from the ground."[42] Therefore the "shedder of blood" must "surely die."[43] This ancient notion is recognized in modern law,[44] for in many states Mosaic law is literally followed—the life of a murderer is taken to expiate for the killing of his victim.[45]

---

31 1 Sam. 31:4

32 2 Sam. 1:2-15
"And David said unto him, Thy blood be upon thy head: for thy mouth hath testified against thee, saying I have slain the Lord's anointed." 2 Sam. 1:16

33 See infra §369

34 13 Gr.B. (1901) 592 (Amram)

35 Num. 35:16-18, 21, 30; 12 Gr.B. (1900) 386 (Amram); 42 Wash.L.Rep. (1916) 770 (Barnard)
". . . he that killeth any man shall surely be put to death." Lev. 24:17
". . . and he that killeth a man, he shall be put to death." Lev. 24:21

36 Ex. 21:12

37 Ex. 21:13; and see infra §431

38 Ex. 21:14

39 Ex. 21:20; and see supra §240

40 Ex. 22:2
The Twelve Tables of Rome provided that "If a theft be committed at night and the thief be killed, let his death be deemed lawful; if in the daytime, only if he defends himself with a weapon." St.Augustine, T. 8,12,13

41 Ex. 22:3; and see infra §§375, 419

42 Gen. 4:10; and see infra §369

43 Ezek. 18:10,13

44 See infra §421

45 42 Wash.L.Rep. (1914) 770 (Barnard)

[§369] —— The Cain Case is the first Scriptural account of murder. It is related that Cain, a farmer, "talked with Abel his brother," who was a sheepman,[46] "and it came to pass, when they were in the field, that Cain rose up against his brother, and slew him,"[47] "because his own works were evil and his brother's righteous."[48]

The record then shows the following proceedings:

1 **Accusation** (Thou hast killed thy brother Abel)—"Where is Abel thy brother?"

2 **Plea** (Not guilty)—"I know not. Am I my brother's keeper?"[49]

3 **Evidence**—"the voice of thy brother's blood crieth unto me from the ground."[50]

4 **Judgment**—Thou shalt be "a fugitive and a vagabond in the earth."[1]

5 **Petition for clemency**—"My punishment is greater than I can bear," for "everyone that findeth me shall slay me."[2]

6 **Judgment modified**—"the Lord set a mark upon Cain, lest any finding him should kill him," and decreed that "whosoever slayeth Cain, vengeance shall be taken on him sevenfold."[3]

Thus it appears that Cain was outlawed for his offense—sentenced not to death but to perpetual banishment or exile.[4] And so he went "and dwelt in the land of Nod, on the east of Eden,"[5] where his wife bore a son named Enoch and Cain built a city of the same name.[6]

[§370] —— Many other killings are related in the Scriptures—too many for all to be enumerated here. The second killer was Lamech, who declared to his wives, "I have slain a man to my wounding, and a young man to my hurt."[7] Simeon and Levi slew a man in their anger,[8] and Moses slew an Egyptian and hid him in the sand.[9] Rechab and Baanah slew Ishbosheth as he lay on his bed.[10] David killed Uriah the Hittite "with the sword of the children of Ammon,"[11] and "ten young

---

46 Gen. 4:2

47 Gen. 4:8

48 1 John 3:12

49 Gen. 4:9

50 Gen. 4:10

1 Gen. 4:12
Note that at the time this offense was committed the rule prescribing the death penalty for homicide had not been pronounced. See supra §368

2 Gen. 4:13,14
See supra §368

3 Gen. 4:15
The "Mark of Cain" was not a brand indicating that Cain was a condemned murderer, but was to show that he was under God's protection and that his life was to be spared. See 13 Gr.B. (1901) 594 (Amram)

4 See 13 Gr.B. (1901) 592 et seq. (Amram)

5 Gen. 4:16

6 Gen. 4:17

7 Gen. 4:23
"If Cain shall be avenged sevenfold, truly Lamech seventy and sevenfold." Gen. 4:24
According to Hebrew tradition, Lamech slew Cain, mistaking him for a wild beast, and subsequently beat to death a youth who caused him to make the mistake.

8 Gen. 49:6

9 Ex. 2:12

10 2 Sam. 4:5-12

11 2 Sam. 12:9

men that bare Joab's armour compassed about and smote Absalom and slew him."[12]   Joab also slew Abner and Amasa.[13] Shallum the son of Jabesh slew Zechariah the son of Jeroboam,[14] and Menahem the son of Gadi slew Shallum.[15] Jehoram "slew all his brethren with the sword, and divers also of the princes of Israel."[16]   His own servants slew Joash "on his bed,"[17] and Amon's servants "slew him in his own house."[18] Ishmael the son of Nethaniah smote Gedaliah and slew him.[19] The Jews killed Jesus,[20] and Herod the king killed James.[21]

[§371]   Kidnaping is an offense, under Biblical law, which is punishable by death.[22]   It is declared that "he that stealeth a man, and selleth him, or if he be found in his hand, he shall surely be put to death,"[23] and that "If a man be found stealing any of his brethren of the children of Israel, and maketh merchandise of him, or selleth him; then that thief shall die; and thou shalt put evil away from among you."[24]

Before the adoption of the foregoing rules, the sons of Jacob kidnaped and sold their brother Joseph to passing merchants.[25]   For this offense they were never legally punished.

CHAPTER 58

OFFENSES AGAINST PROPERTY

[§372]   The removal of landmarks was prohibited by Mosaic law, in order that the established boundaries of lands might be preserved.   The law provided that—

"Thou shalt not remove thy neighbour's landmark, which they of old time have set."[26]

And in a later passage, a curse is pronounced against him "that removeth his neighbour's landmark."[27]   Nevertheless it

---

12   2 Sam. 18:15
13   1 Kings 2:5,6,28-34
14   2 Kings 15:10   15   2 Kings 15:14
16   2 Chron. 21:18,19
17   2 Chron. 24:25
18   2 Chron. 33:24   19   Jer. 41:2
20   1 Thess. 2:15   21   Acts 12:1,2
James was the first of the twelve disciples to be murdered.

22   See infra §421
23   Ex. 21:16
24   Deut. 24:7
25   Gen. 37:28
26   Deut. 19:14
27   "Cursed be he that removeth his neighbour's landmark. And all the people shall say Amen." Deut. 27-17; 14 Harv.LR (1900) 510 (Thayer)

appears that landmarks were sometimes removed,[28] and the rule against their removal is repeated in subsequent writings.[29]

[§373] Robbery is the taking of property "away by violence" from the person or possession of another.[30] The Scriptures contain numerous passages in reference to robbery[31] and robbers,[32] but the term seems ordinarily to be used merely in the sense of "cheating" or "stealing."[33]

The general rule concerning "robbery" is that, "Thou shalt not . . . rob" thy neighbour.[34] More particularly it is commanded to rob not "the poor,"[35] nor "the fatherless,"[36] nor one's "father or his mother."[37] The punishment for robbery is death,[38] and the law also prescribes that one who takes "a thing . . . away by violence" shall "restore that which he took" and "add the fifth part more thereto."[39]

Barabbas "a notable prisoner"[40] who was released at the time of the trial of Jesus, is said to have been a robber.[41] And St. Paul speaks of having been "in perils of robbers."[42]

[§374] Theft—or stealing—is an offense repeatedly denounced in the Scriptures,[43] and the term "thief" has been an opprobrious one throughout the ages and in every country.[44] The law governing theft is that "Thou shalt not steal"[45]—a

28 Job 24:2 ("Some remove the landmarks")

29 Prov. 22:28 ("Remove not the ancient landmark, which thy fathers have set"), 23:10 ("Remove not the old landmark")

30 Lev. 6:2; and see 23 RCL 1139

31 Lev. 19:13, 26:22; 1 Sam. 23:1; Ps. 62:10; Prov. 21:7, 22:22, 28:24; Isa. 10:2, 17:14, 61:8; Ezek. 22:29, 39:10; Amos 3:10; Nahum 3:1; Mal. 3:8; Phil. 2:6

32 Job 5:5, 12:6, 18:9; Isa. 42:24; Jer. 7:11; Ezek. 7:22, 18:10; Dan. 11:14; Hosea 6:9, 7:1; Obad. v 5; John 10:8, 18:40; Acts 19:37; 2 Cor. 11:26

33 See John 10:1 ("He that entereth not by the door . . . but climbeth up some other way, the same is a thief and a robber")

34 Lev. 19:13

35 Prov. 22:22

36 Isa. 10:1,2 ("Woe unto them that . . . rob the fatherless")

37 Prov. 28:24 ("Whoso robbeth his father or his mother, and saith, It is no transgression; the same is the companion of a destroyer")

38 Ezek. 18:10,12,13

39 Lev. 6:2-5

40 Matt. 27:16

41 John 18:40. But see Mark 15:7 (saying that Barabbas had committed murder in insurrection) and Luke 23:19 (stating that he was cast into prison for sedition and murder)

42 2 Cor. 11:26; Ruse v Williams (1913) 14 Ariz. 445, 130 P 887, 45 LRANS 923, 927 (Franklin,J)

43 Prov. 29:24; Hosea 4:2; Zech. 5:3; Tobit 2:13; Ecclesiasticus 41:17,19
    "Larceny became an offense only as property rights were defined and society sought to benefit itself and protect the individual by penalizing the appropriation of property by those who could not justify such appropriation by the prescribed rules." State v Malusky (1930) 59 ND 501, 230 NW 735, 71 ALR 190, 193 (Nuessle,J)

44 State v Malusky (1930) 59 ND 501, 230 NW 735, 71 ALR 190, 214 (Christianson,J)
    But it is observed that "Men do not despise a thief, if he steal to satisfy his soul when he is hungry." Prov. 6:30

45 20:15; Lev. 19:11 ("Ye shall not steal"); Deut. 5:19 ("Neither shalt thou steal"); Matt. 19:18; Mark 10:19 ("Do not steal"); Luke 18:20; Rom. 13:9; Two Ways 2:2

commandment given to mankind by a higher authority than human law-makers,[46] and one which "applies with equal force and propriety to the industrialist of a complex civilization as to the simple herdsman of ancient Israel."[47]   On this commandment the various modern statutes against theft, embezzlement, forgery, false pretenses, and deceits, are said to be based.[48]

[§375] —— A thief was doubtless subject to punishment by death,[49] but ordinarily under Mosaic law it seems that he was required merely to "make full restitution"[50] or, if he had nothing, he was "sold for his theft."[1]   But it is declared that if a thief is found who has stolen to satisfy hunger, "he shall restore sevenfold; he shall give all the substance of his house."[2]   On the other hand, if a man steals an animal, that is, an ox or ass or sheep, and it "be certainly found in his hands alive . . . he shall restore double;"[3] but "if a man shall steal an ox, or a sheep, and kill it, or sell it; he shall restore five oxen for an ox, and four sheep for a sheep."[4]   In case of the theft of "money or stuff" delivered unto another to keep, the rule is, "if the thief be found, let him pay double."[5]

[§376] —— Theft may be committed by borrowing from another without intention to repay or return the loan.[6]   The historic example of this offense is in the "spoiling" of the Egyptians by the Israelites before the exodus.   It is related that—

"the children of Israel did according to the word of Moses: and they borrowed of the Egyptians jewels of silver, and jewels of gold, and raiment: And the Lord gave the people favour in the sight of the Egyptians, so that they lent unto them such things as they required. And they spoiled the Egyptians."[7]

It has been asserted that the Israelites expected to return and did not design to deceive the Egyptians, but the narrative does not support this view. The offense seems to have been justified on the ground that the Israelites had long been

46 State v Malusky (1930) 59 ND 501, 230 NW 735, 71 ALR 190, 214 (Christianson,J)
47 Hollywood Motion Picture Equipment Co. v Furer (1940) 16 Cal. 2d 184, 105 P2d 299 (Moore,J pro tem.)
48 42 Wash.L.Rep. (1914) 770 (Barnard,J)
49 Two thieves were crucified with Jesus. Matt. 27:38; Mark 15:27; and see infra §421

50 See infra §456 et seq.
1 Ex. 22:3; and see infra §419
2 Prov. 6:31; and see infra §459
3 Ex. 22:4; and see infra §458
4 Ex. 22:1; and see infra §459
5 Ex. 22:7; and see infra §458
6 See 32 Am Jur 922
7 Ex. 12:35,36

held in bondage to the Egyptians, and would otherwise have left the country empty-handed.

[§377] —— The Case of Rachel is also one in which a theft was committed and not punished.[8] It is related that—

"Jacob rose up, and set his sons and his wives upon camels;
"And he carried away all his cattle and all his goods which he had gotten, . . .
". . . and Rachel (his wife) had stolen the images that were her father's (Laban's)[9]
". . . And it was told Laban on the third day, that Jacob had fled.
"And he took his brethren with him, and pursued after him . . . and overtook him in the mount of Gilead.
"And Laban said to Jacob . . .
". . . wherefore hast thou stolen my gods?
And Jacob answered . . .
"With whomsoever thou findest thy gods, let him not live . . .
"And Laban went into Jacob's tent, and into Leah's tent, and into the two maidservants' tents; but he found them not. Then he . . . entered Rachael's tent.
". . . And Laban searched all the tent, but found them not."

And after making a covenant with Jacob[10] "Laban departed, and returned unto his place."[11]

[§378] —— The Case of the "Little Ewe Lamb" was a hypothetical one, propounded by Nathan to king David. It is said that—

". . . the Lord sent Nathan unto David. And he came unto him, and said unto him, There were two men in one city; the one rich and the other poor.
"The rich man had exceeding many flocks and herds:
"But the poor man had nothing, save one little ewe lamb, which he had bought and nourished up: and it grew up together with him, and with his children; it did eat of his own meat, and drank of his own cup, and lay in his bosom, and was unto him as a daughter.
"And there came a traveller unto the rich man, and he spared to take of his own flock and of his own herd, to dress for the wayfaring man that was come unto him; but took the poor man's lamb, and dressed it for the man that was come to him.
"And David's anger was greatly kindled against the man; and he said to Nathan, As the Lord liveth, the man that hath done this thing shall surely die:
"And he shall restore the lamb fourfold . . ."[12]

8 See 13 Gr.B. (1901) 406 (Amram)
9 They are believed to have been the images of Laban's ancestors. 14 Harv. LR (1900) 522 (Thayer)
10 See supra §148
11 Gen. 31:17-55
12 2 Sam. 12:1-6; and see 28 Ky.LJ (1940) 118-120 (Vold)

CHAPTER 59

OFFENSES AGAINST RELIGION

[§379]   Blasphemy is an offense consisting in cursing[13] or reviling God,[14] or in "making" oneself God,[15] "equal with God,"[16] or the "son of God."[17]   But it was seemingly no offense under Mosaic law for a stranger to blaspheme his own gods.[18]   The punishment for unlawful blasphemy was death,[19] which was originally inflicted by stoning.[20]

". . . he that blasphemeth the name of the Lord, he shall surely be put to death, and all the congregation shall certainly stone him: as well the stranger, as he that is born in the land, when he blasphemeth in the name of the Lord, shall be put to death."[21]

[§380]   —— The case of the Son of Shelomith was the first prosecution for blasphemy under Mosaic law.

". . . the son of an Israelitish woman, whose father was an Egyptian, went out among the children of Israel: and this son of the Israelitish woman and a man of Israel strove together in the camp.
"And the Israelitish woman's son blasphemed the name of the Lord, and cursed. And they brought him unto Moses:
"And they put him in ward, that the mind of the Lord might be shewed them.
"And the Lord spoke unto Moses, saying:
"Bring forth him that hath cursed without the camp; and let all that heard him lay their hands upon his head, and let all the congregation stone him."[22]
"And Moses spake to the children of Israel, that they should bring forth him that had cursed out of the camp, and stone him with stones. And the children of Israel did as the Lord commanded Moses."[23]

[§381]   —— Naboth was falsely prosecuted for blasphemy in order that king Ahab might obtain possession of his vine-

13 Lev. 24:15
14 Ex. 22:28 ("Thou shalt not revile the gods")
   Profanity, see supra §324
15 John 10:33
16 John 5:18
17 John 19:7
18 See infra §385
19 Lev. 24:15 ("Whosoever curseth his God shall bear his sin")
20 See infra §421
21 Lev. 24:16
22 Lev. 24:10-14
23 Lev. 24:23

yard, which Naboth had refused to sell.[24]   It is related that
Jezebel, Ahab's wife—

". . . wrote letters in Ahab's name, and sealed them with his seal, and
sent the letters unto the elders and to the nobles that were in his city,
dwelling with Naboth.

"And she wrote in the letters, saying, Proclaim a fast, and set Naboth
on high among the people:

"And set two men, sons of Belial, before him, to bear witness against
him, saying, Thou didst blaspheme God and the king. And then carry
him out, and stone him, that he may die.

"And the men of his city, even the elders and the nobles who were the
inhabitants in his city, did as Jezebel had sent unto them, and as it was
written in the letters which she had sent unto them.

"They proclaimed a fast and set Naboth on high among the people.

"And there came in two men, children of Belial, and sat before him:
and the men of Belial witnessed against him, even against Naboth, in
the presence of the people, saying, Naboth did blaspheme God and the
king. Then they carried him forth out of the city, and stoned him with
stones, that he died."[25]

[§382]   —— Daniel's Case is recorded in the History of
the Destruction of Bel and the Dragon.   It is said that king
Cyrus of Persia decreed that Daniel should die for having
"spoken blasphemy against Bel," an idol of the Babylonians,
in that he had stated that the idol was "but clay within, and
brass without, and did never eat or drink any thing." But
the judgment was conditioned that the priests of Bel should
certify (prove) that Bel devoured the daily measures of flour,
carcasses of sheep and vessels of wine which the king caused
to be set before him. By secretly strewing ashes throughout
the temple, Daniel convinced the king that the daily offerings
were consumed by the priests and their wives and children,
and the king caused them instead to be slain for their deceit.[26]

[§383]   —— The Case of Jesus—doubtless the most noted
of all prosecutions—was ostensibly one of blasphemy. He was
condemned by the chief priests and elders, and all the council,
for this offense, though the real complaint against him was
that he was "perverting the nation."[27]   The record, as found
in the Gospel of Matthew, shows that—

". . . they that had laid hold of Jesus led him away to Caiaphas the
high priest, where the scribes and the elders were assembled.

24 See supra §168
25 1 Kings 21:8-13
   Naboth was avenged by Jehu. See 2
Kings 9:22-26

26 Dan. 14:1-21
27 Luke 23:2

"Now the chief priests, and elders, and all the council, sought false witness against Jesus, to put him to death:

"But found none: yea, though many false witnesses came, yet found they none.[28]

"At the last came two false witnesses,

"And said, This fellow said, I am able to destroy the temple of God, and to build it in three days.

"And the high priest arose, and said unto him, Answerest thou nothing? what is it which these witness against thee?

"But Jesus held his peace. And the high priest answered and said unto him, I adjure thee by the living God, that thou tell us whether thou be the Christ, the son of God.

"Jesus saith unto him, Thou hast said: nevertheless I say unto you, Hereafter shall ye see the Son of man sitting on the right hand of power, and coming in the clouds of heaven.

"Then the high priest rent his clothes, saying, He hath spoken blasphemy; what further need have we of witnesses? Behold, now ye have heard his blasphemy.

"What think ye? They answered and said, He is guilty of death."[29]

[§384] —— Stephen's Case is the last of the blasphemy prosecutions mentioned in the Scriptures.[30] It is related that—

". . . there arose certain of the synagogue of the Libertines, and Cyrenians, and Alexandrians, and of them of Cilicia and of Asia, disputing with Stephen.

"And they were not able to resist the wisdom and the spirit by which he spake.

"Then they suborned men, which said, We have heard him speak blasphemous words against Moses, and against God.

"And they stirred up the people, and the elders, and the scribes, and came upon him, and caught him, and brought him to the council,

"And set up false witnesses, which said, This man ceaseth not to speak blasphemous words against this holy place, and the law:

"For we have heard him say, that this Jesus of Nazareth shall destroy this place, and shall change the customs which Moses delivered us."[31]

Stephen was permitted to answer the accusation, after which "all that sat in the council,"[32]—

". . . cried out with a loud voice, and stopped their ears, and ran upon him with one accord,

"And cast him out of the city, and stoned him . . .

"And he kneeled down, and cried with a loud voice, Lord, lay not this sin to their charge. And when he had said this, he fell asleep."[33]

28 Mark 14:56 ("many bare false witness against him, but their witness agreed not together")

29 Matt. 26:57-66; see also Mark 14:53-64; Luke 22:66-71; John 19:7

30 There were doubtless many other prosecutions for blasphemy of which we have no Scriptural record.

31 Acts 6:9-14

32 Acts 6:15

33 Acts 7:57,58,60

[§385]   False prophecy, as we have seen, consists in speaking "lies in the name of the Lord."[34] This offense is punishable by death."[35] The law provides that—

". . . the prophet, which shall presume to speak a word in my name, which I have not commanded him to speak, or that shall speak in the name of other gods, even that prophet shall die."[36]

[§386]   —— The best evidence of false prophecy is that the thing prophesied has not come to pass.

"When a prophet speaketh in the name of the Lord, if the thing follow not, nor come to pass, that is the thing which the Lord hath not spoken, but the prophet hath spoken it presumptuously: thou shalt not be afraid of him."[37]

[§387]   Sabbath-breaking consists in the doing of forbidden things on the Sabbath[38] or—according to the ordinary Christian view—on Sunday.[39] Under Mosaic law, the offense of "breaking" or "defiling" the Sabbath was punishable by death. The rule was that "every one that defileth it (the Sabbath) shall be put to death:[40]

". . . Whosoever doeth any work in the sabbath day, he shall surely be put to death."[41]

[§388]   —— The "Stick-gatherer's Case" is one of the earliest recorded cases in which punishment was inflicted for a violation of law. It is related that—

". . . while the children of Israel were in the wilderness, they found a man that gathered sticks upon the sabbath day.
"And they that found him gathering sticks brought him unto Moses and Aaron, and unto all the congregation.
"And they put him in ward, because it was not declared what should be done to him.
"And the Lord said unto Moses, The man shall be surely put to death: all the congregation shall stone him with stones without the camp.
"And all the congregation brought him without the camp, and stoned him with stones, and he died; as the Lord commanded Moses."[42]

---

34 See supra §316
35 See infra §421
36 Deut. 18:20
   "Woe unto the foolish prophets, that follow their own spirit, and have seen nothing! . . . mine hand shall be upon the prophets that see vanity and that divine lies." See Ezek. 13:3,9; also Ezek. 22:28; Micah 3:5-11
   Jeremiah was accused of being a false prophet. See Jer. 26:8-24

37 Deut. 18:22
38 See supra §319
39 See supra §320
40 Ex. 31:14
41 Ex. 31:15, 35:2
42 Num. 15:32-36
   See also John 5:5-18, where it appears that the Jews sought to kill Jesus because he had broken the sabbath by healing an infirm man.

[§389] The making of sacrifices to "other gods" is an offense against Mosaic law.[43] The rule as to the punishment of this offense is that—

"He that sacrificeth unto any god, save unto the Lord only, he shall be utterly destroyed."[44]

And more particularly as to the worship of Moloch, "the abomination of the children of Ammon,"[45] it is forbidden to "let any of thy seed pass through the fire."[46] The law declares that "There shall not be found among you any one that maketh his son or his daughter to pass through the fire."[47] This offense also was punishable by death.

". . . Whosoever he be of the children of Israel, or of the strangers that sojourn in Israel, that giveth any of his seed unto Molech; he shall surely be put to death: the people of the land shall stone him with stones."[48]

Notwithstanding these provisions, it appears that Ahaz "made his son to pass through the fire,"[49] and that others "sacrificed their sons and their daughters . . . unto the idols of Canaan."[50]

[§390] Serving "other gods" was also an offense punishable by death.[1] It is declared that he that "hath lifted up his eyes to the idols . . . shall surely die."[2] And concerning the trial and execution of one who has worshipped any heavenly body, it is prescribed that—

"If there be found among you, . . . man or woman, that hath . . . gone and served other gods, and worshipped them, either the sun, or moon, or any of the host of heaven, . . . and it be told thee, and thou hast heard of it, and inquired diligently, and behold, it be true, and the thing certain, . . . then thou shalt bring forth that man or that woman, . . . unto thy gates, . . . and shalt stone them with stones, till they die."[3]

[§391] —— Advocating the worship of "other gods" was likewise a capital offense under Mosaic law. The law provided that—

"If there arise among you a prophet, or a dreamer of dreams, . . . saying, Let us go after other gods, . . . that prophet, or that dreamer of dreams, shall be put to death."[4]

43 See supra §322	49 2 Kings 16:3
44 Ex. 22:20	50 Ps. 106:37,38
45 1 Kings 11:7	1 See supra §322
46 Lev. 18:21	2 Ezek. 18:12,13
47 Deut. 18:10	3 Deut. 17:2-5
48 Lev. 20:2	4 Deut. 13:1-5

"If thy brother, the son of thy mother, or thy son, or thy daughter, or the wife of thy bosom, or thy friend, which is as thine own soul, entice thee secretly, saying, Let us go and serve other gods, . . . thou shalt surely kill him; thine hand shall be first upon him to put him to death, and afterwards the hand of all the people. And thou shalt stone him with stones, that he die."[5]

[§392] —— Solomon, though a king of much wisdom,[6] was drawn into idolatry in his old age.

"For it came to pass, when Solomon was old, that his wives turned away his heart after other gods: and his heart was not perfect with the Lord his God, as was the heart of David his father.

"For Solomon went after Ashtoreth the goddess of the Zidonians, and after Milcom the abomination of the Ammonites.

"Then did Solomon build a high place for Chemosh, the abomination of Boab, . . . and for Molech, the abomination of the children of Ammon.

"And likewise did he for all his strange wives, which burnt incense and sacrificed unto their gods.

"Wherefore the Lord said unto Solomon, Forasmuch as this is done of thee, and thou hast not kept my covenant and my statutes, which I have commanded thee, I will surely rend the kingdom from thee and give it to thy servant.

"Notwithstanding, in thy days I will not do it for David thy father's sake: but I will rend it out of the hand of thy son.

"Howbeit I will not rend away all the kingdom; but will give one tribe to thy son for David my servant's sake, and for Jerusalem's sake which I have chosen."[7]

At a later time, king Ahaziah was condemned to die of an injury because he sent messengers to inquire of Baal-zebub the god of Ekron.[8]

[§393] The violation of a sacred place, such as an altar or temple,[9] or a burial place,[10] was doubtless an offense under Mosaic law. Mount Sinai was considered a sacred place when "the Lord descended upon it" prior to the giving of the Ten Commandments."[11] It was decreed that—

". . . whosoever toucheth the mount shall be surely put to death .

"There shall not a hand touch it, but he shall surely be stoned, or shot through; whether it be beast or man, it shall not live . . ."[12]

But it was not a crime to destroy the "high places" of "other gods," who were expected themselves to deal with anyone who

---

5 Deut. 13:6-10

6 See 1 Kings 10:6-8, for the testimony of the queen of Sheba concerning the wisdom of Solomon. And see supra §27

7 1 Kings 11:4-8, 11-13; and see supra §340

8 2 Kings 1:1-17

9 See supra §321
The Jews, "which were of Asia," cried out against Paul, saying "This is the man" that "hath polluted this holy place," i.e., the temple. See Acts 21:28

10 See supra §291

11 See supra §13

12 Ex. 19:12,13

offended them. Thus in the case of Gideon, who cast down the altar of Baal and cut down the grove that was by it,[13] his father Joash, in refusing to surrender him to the people of the city for punishment, said to them:

"Will ye plead for Baal? will ye save him? he that will plead for him, let him be put to death whilst it is yet morning: if he be a god, let him plead for himself, because someone hath cast down his altar."[14]

[§394]   The use and practice of sorcery, as we have seen, is against the law.[15] "Witchcraft" is condemned as a "work of the flesh."[16] "Soothsayers"[17] or "sorcerers"[18] are criminals: the possession of a "familiar spirit"[19] or the practice of "witchcraft" is a capital offense.[20] The law directs that "Thou shalt not suffer a witch to live"[21] and that "A man also or woman that hath a familiar spirit, or that is a wizard, shall surely be put to death: they shall stone them with stones: their blood shall be upon them."[22]

[§395] —— The Twelve Tables of Rome[23] are said to have prescribed the death penalty for one who bewitched another's hanging fruit or spirited away a crop from his fields.[24] And during the Dark Ages the belief in witches was widespread.[25] Nine millions of men and women are said to have been burned or otherwise executed for witchcraft.[26] The doctrine of witchcraft also was taught in American Christian churches in the early colonial days,[27] and alleged witches were tried and sentenced to death at Salem in 1692.[28]

But while a belief in witchcraft is not considered as evidence of insanity,[29] there is no such thing as a witch known in modern law.[30]

13 Judges 6:25-27
14 Judges 6:31; and see 13 Gr.B. (1901) 493 et seq. (Amram)
15 See supra §323
16 Gal. 5:20
"I will cut off witchcrafts out of thine hand." Micah 5:12
17 Micah 5:12 ("thou shalt have no more soothsayers")
18 Mal. 3:5 ("I will be a swift witness against the sorcerers")
19 Lev. 20:27
20 Micah 5:12
21 Ex. 22:18
22 Lev. 20:27
23 See supra §13, n 2
24 Muirhead's Roman Law, 2d ed., 140
25 "Belief in witches, as well as in many superstitions, was prevalent in olden times, and the law recognized them." 42 Wash.L.Rep. (1914) 771 (Barnard)
26 Psychic phenomena and the law: 24 Harv.LR (1911) 625 (Lee)
27 First Baptist Church v Witherell (1832) 3 Paige Ch. (NY) 296, 24 AD 223, 229
28 The charge of witchcraft, like an accusation of rape (22 RCL 1229 ¶ 66), was doubtless one easily made and readily proved to those who believed in the doctrine of witchcraft, but was difficult or impossible to refute.
29 Addington v Wilson (1854) 5 Ind. 137, 139, 61 AD 81 (Perkins,J); Hotema v United States (1902) 186 US 413, 421, 46 L ed 1225 (Peckam,J)
30 42 Wash.L.Rep. (1914) 771 (Barnard)

"Witch-hunting is no longer sanctioned. The suspicions and hatreds of Salem have ceased. Neighbor no longer inveighs against neighbor through fear of the evil eye."[31]

CHAPTER 60

SEXUAL OFFENSES

396 Adultery   397 —— Punishment   398 —— David's Case   399 —— Susanna's Case   400 —— Case of "A Woman Taken in Adultery"   401 Bestiality   402 Fornication   403 Incest   404 —— Punishment   405 —— The Lot Case   406 Onanism   407 Rape   408 Amnon's Case   409 Relation with "Unclean Woman"   410 Sodomy

[§396]   Adultery is denounced in many Scriptural passages.[32]   An adulterer is "a man that breaketh wedlock"[33] by "defiling"[34] or committing "abomination"[35] or "adultery" with his neighbour's wife;[37] an adultress is a wife that "taketh strangers instead of her husband"[37] or "that leaveth her husband, and bringeth in an heir by another."[38]

The commandment is: "Thou shalt not commit adultery"[39] —"thou shalt not lie carnally with thy neighbour's wife to defile thyself with her."[40]   And not only does the law condemn adultery; it even disapproves of "gazing" upon another man's wife[41] or looking "on a woman to lust after her."[42]

"Sit not at all with another man's wife, nor sit down with her in thine arms, and spend not thy money with her at the wine; lest thine heart incline unto her, and so through thy desire thou fall unto destruction."[43]

---

31 Johnson v State (1942) 163 SW2d (Ark.) 153, 158 (Smith,CJ, dissenting)

32 See notes, infra this section

33 Ecclesiasticus 23:18

34 Ezek. 18:6, 33:26

35 Ezek. 22:11

36 Hosea 4:2; Gal. 5:19
". . . I will be a swift witness against . . . the adulterers." Malachi 3:5
"Adulterers God will judge." Heb. 13:4

37 Ezek. 16:33

38 Ecclesiasticus 23:22

39 Ex. 20:14; Deut. 5:18; Matt. 5:27, 19:18; Mark 10:19; Luke 18:20; Rom. 13:9; Two Ways 2:2
On this commandment, modern criminal laws against adultery are based.

42 Wash.L.Rep. (1914) 770 (Barnard)
"So he that goeth in to his neighbour's wife; whosoever toucheth her shall not be innocent. . . . But whoso committeth adultery with a woman lacketh understanding: he that doeth it destroyeth his own soul. A wound and dishonour shall he get and his reproach shall not be wiped away. For jealousy is the rage of a man: therefore he will not spare in the day of vengeance. He will not regard any ransom; neither will he rest content, though thou givest many gifts." Prov. 6:29, 32-35

40 Lev. 18:20

41 Ecclesiasticus 41:17,21,22 ("Be ashamed . . . to gaze upon another man's wife; or to be overbusy with his maid, and come not near her bed")

42 Matt. 5:27,28 ("Ye have heard that it was said by them of old time, Thou shalt not commit adultery: But I say unto you, That whosoever looketh on a woman to lust after her hath committed adultery with her already in his heart")

43 Ecclesiasticus 9:9

[§397] ——— The punishment for adultery, under Mosaic law, was death.[44]

". . . the man that committeth adultery with another man's wife, even he that committeth adultery with his neighbour's wife, the aulterer and the adultress shall surely be put to death."[45]

"If a man be found lying with a woman married to an husband, then they shall both of them die, both the man that lay with the woman, and the woman: so shalt thou put away evil from Israel.

"If a damsel that is a virgin be betrothed unto an husband, and a man find her in the city, and lie with her;

"Then ye shall bring them both out unto the gate of that city, and ye shall stone them with stones that they die; the damsel, because she cried not, being in the city; and the man, because he hath humbled his neighbour's wife: so thou shalt put away evil from among you."[46]

But the death penalty was not inflicted where the woman was a bondmaid. In such a case the rule was that—

". . . whosoever lieth carnally with a woman, that is a bondmaid, betrothed to a husband, and not at all redeemed, nor freedom given her; she shall be scourged: they shall not be put to death, because she was not free."[47]

In modern law, adultery is punished but little, if at all.[48] The law seems to have more sympathy for the adulterer than the thief, though the adulterer's crime is more harmful to society. But—

"the people . . . exhibit their moral sense in a higher degree than is expressed in their laws; for they justify the avenging of wrong by a father, husband, brother, son, or the victim herself upon the life of a wrongdoer, and they seldom will clothe a known libertine with office, notwithstanding great ability and mental fitness therefor. With the people a known adulterer is an enemy of society, who forfeits his life if caught in the act by one who suffers by his lawlessness; and the adulteress becomes an outcast, shunned and despised, as though she wore on her breast the scarlet letter of her shame—a punishment far more terrible than confinement in prison."[49]

[§398] ——— David's Case was one of adultery and murder, thus showing that illicit love has been a source of murder from the most ancient days.[50] It is related that—

---

44 Ezek. 18:11,13 (He that "defileth his neighbor's wife . . . shall surely die"); Moore v Strickling (1899) 46 W.Va. 515, 33 SE 274, 50 LRA 279, 283 (Dent,P)

45 Lev. 20:10

46 Deut. 22:22-24

47 Lev. 19:20

48 At common law, adultery is not punishable unless it is open and notorious. See 4 Bl. Com. 65; White v White (1890) 82 Cal. 427, 449, 7 LRA 799, 23 P 276, 283 (Thornton,J)

But "the evil became so grave a menace to the welfare of the early Saxon state in Britain that our rude forebears made adultery a capital offense." In re Maki (1943) 56 ACA 692, 697, 133 P2d —— (Moore, PJ)

49 Moore v Strickling (1899) 46 W.Va. 515, 33 SE 274, 50 LRA 279, 283 (Dent,P)

50 Ex parte Harkins (1912) 7 Okla. Crim.Rep. 464, 124 P 931, 940 (Furman,J)

". . . it came to pass in an evening-tide, that David arose from off his bed, and walked upon the roof of the king's house: and from the roof he saw a woman washing herself; and the woman was very beautiful to look upon.

"And David sent and enquired after the woman. And one said, Is not this Bath-sheba, the daughter of Eliam, the wife of Uriah the Hittite?

"And David sent messengers, and took her; and she came in unto him, and he lay with her; for she was purified from her uncleanness: and she returned unto her house.

"And the woman conceived, and sent and told David, and said, I am with child.

"And David sent to Joab, saying, "Send me Uriah the Hittite. And Joab sent Uriah to David."[1]

"And it came to pass . . . that David wrote a letter to Joab, and sent it by the hand of Uriah.

"And he wrote in the letter saying, Set ye Uriah in the forefront of the hottest battle, and retire ye from him, that he may be smitten, and die.

"And it came to pass, when Joab observed the city, that he assigned Uriah unto a place where he knew that valiant men were.

"And the men of the city went out, and fought with Joab: and there fell some of the people of the servants of David; and Uriah the Hittite died also."[2]

"And when the wife of Uriah heard that Uriah her husband was dead, she mourned for her husband.

"And when the mourning was past, David sent and fetched her to his house, and she became his wife, and bare him a son. But the thing that David had done displeased the Lord."[3]

"And the Lord sent Nathan unto David . . .

"And Nathan said to David . . .

"Wherefore hast thou despised the commandment of the Lord, to do evil in his sight? thou hast killed Uriah the Hittite with the sword, and hast taken his wife to be thy wife, and hast slain him with the sword of the children of Ammon.

"Now therefore the sword shall never depart from thine house . . .

". . . I will raise up evil against thee out of thine own house, and I will take thy wives before thine eyes, and give them unto thy neighbour . . ."[4]

"And David said unto Nathan, I have sinned against the Lord. And Nathan said unto David, The Lord also hath put away thy sin; thou shalt not die.

"Howbeit . . . the child . . . that is born unto thee shall surely die.

"And Nathan departed unto his house. And the Lord struck the child that Uriah's wife bare unto David, and it was very sick.

"And it came to pass on the seventh day, that the child died."[5]

[§399] —— In Susanna's Case, it appears that "two old judges" who lodged at the house of Susanna and her husband accused her of adultery with "a young man," and upon their testimony she was found guilty and condemned to death.

1   2 Sam. 11:2-6
2   2 Sam. 11:14-17
3   2 Sam. 11:26,27

4   2 Sam. 12:1,7,9-11
5   2 Sam. 12:13-15,18

When she had been led out to be stoned, Daniel refused to participate in the execution, charging that the judges had testified falsely and demanding a re-examination. Execution of the sentence upon Susanna was stayed, and the people returned to the place of judgment, where the judges were separately examined and the falsity of their testimony demonstrated. The original sentence of Susanna was doubtless regarded as vacated, and the two old judges were sentenced to suffer the same punishment they had intended to bring upon her, that is, death by stoning.[6]

[§400] ⸺ The Case of "A Woman Taken in Adultery" is recorded in the Gospel of John.

"And the scribes and Pharisees brought unto him (Jesus) a woman taken in adultery; and when they had set her in the midst,

"They say unto him, Master, this woman was taken in adultery, in the very act.

"Now Moses in the law commanded us, that such should be stoned: but what sayest thou?

"This they said, tempting him, that they might have to accuse him. But Jesus stooped down and with his finger wrote on the ground, as though he heard them not.

"So when they continued asking him, he lifted up himself, and said unto them, He that is without sin among you, let him first cast a stone at her.

"And again he stooped down, and wrote on the ground.

"And they which heard it, being convicted by their own conscience, went out one by one, beginning at the eldest, even unto the last: and Jesus was left alone, and the woman standing in the midst.

"When Jesus had lifted up himself and saw none but the woman, he said unto her, Woman, where are those thine accusers? hath no man condemned thee?

"She said, No man, Lord. And Jesus said unto her, Neither do I condemn thee: go, and sin no more."[7]

[§401] Bestiality is denounced by Mosaic law. The prohibition is that thou shalt not "lie with any beast to defile thyself therewith; neither shall any woman stand before a beast to lie down thereto: it is confusion."[8] The punishment for this offense is death. It is declared that—

". . . if a man lie with a beast, he shall surely be put to death: and ye shall slay the beast.

"And if a woman approach unto any beast, and lie down thereto, thou

6 History of Susanna (Daniel), ch. 13, verses 36-62
7 John 8:3-11
Assuming that the record of this case is genuine Scripture, which many doubt, it is inconsistent with the teachings of the Old and New Testaments as a whole. It should not be regarded as a condonement of adultery or a disapproval of enforcement of criminal laws generally.
8 Lev. 18:23
"Cursed be he that lieth with any manner of beast. And all the people shall say, Amen." Deut. 27:21

shalt kill the woman, and the beast; they shall surely be put to death; their blood shall be upon them."9

[§402] Fornication is referred to but not expressly condemned, in the Old Testament.10 But this offense seems to have been prevalent in the early Christian era,11 for the New Testament contains several passages denouncing it.12 Thus in the First Epistle of St. Paul to the Thessalonians it is said to be "the will of God . . . that ye should abstain from fornication."13 And in his First Epistle to the Corinthians, St. Paul commanded them to "flee fornication,"14 not to commit this offense,15 and to "put away from among yourselves that wicked person" who commits it.16 It was reasoned that "he that committeth fornication sinneth against his own body."17 But no punishment was prescribed, nor is there a record of any one being prosecuted for fornication.

[§403] Incest consists in marriage or sexual relationship between persons near of kin. The rules on the subject are set forth in the Book of Leviticus.

"None of you shall approach to any that is near of kin to him, to uncover their nakedness . . .

"The nakedness of thy father, or the nakedness of thy mother, shalt thou not uncover: she is thy mother; thou shalt not uncover her nakedness.

"The nakedness of thy father's wife shalt thou not uncover: it is thy father's nakedness.18

"The nakedness of thy sister, the daughter of thy father, or daughter of thy mother, whether she be born at home, or born abroad, even their nakedness thou shalt not uncover.19

9 Lev. 20:15,16
"Whosoever lieth with a beast shall surely be put to death." Ex. 22:19

10 See 2 Chron. 21:11; Ezek. 16:15,26,29

11 1 Cor. 5:1 ("It is reported commonly that there is fornication among you")

12 1 Cor. 6:13, 7:2; Gal. 5:19; Eph. 5:3; Rev. 2:14,20
Fornication as ground for divorce, see supra §204

13 1 Thess. 4:3
See also Acts 15:20,29, 21:25

14 1 Cor. 6:18

15 1 Cor. 10:8 ("Neither let us commit fornication as some of them committed, and fell in one day three and twenty thousand")

16 1 Cor. 5:13
See also Two Ways 2:2 ("thou shalt not commit fornication")

17 1 Cor. 6:18

18 Lev. 18:6-8; and see Lev. 20:11 ("And the man that lieth with his father's wife hath uncovered his father's nakedness: both of them shall surely be put to death; their blood shall be upon them"); Deut. 22:20 ("A man shall not take his father's wife, nor discover his father's skirt"); 27:20 ("Cursed be he that lieth with his father's wife; because he uncovereth his father's skirt. And all the people shall say, Amen")
See also Gen. 49:4, where Jacob reproved Reuben, his firstborn, "because thou wentest up to thy father's bed" and lay with Bilhah his father's concubine. (Gen. 35:22)

19 Lev. 18:9, and see Lev. 20:17 ("And if a man shall take his sister, his father's daughter, or his mother's daughter, and see her nakedness, and she see his nakedness, it is a wicked thing: and they shall be cut off in the sight of their people"); Deut. 27:22 ("Cursed be he that lieth with his sister, the daughter of his father, or the daughter of his mother. And all the people shall say, Amen"); Ezek. 22:11 ("another hath humbled his sister")

"The nakedness of thy son's daughter, or of thy daughter's daughter, even their nakedness thou shalt not uncover: for theirs is thine own nakedness.

"The nakedness of thy father's wife's daughter, begotten of thy father, she is thy sister, thou shalt not uncover her nakedness.

"Thou shalt not uncover the nakedness of thy father's sister: she is thy father's near kinswoman.

"Thou shalt not uncover the nakedness of thy mother's sister: for she is thy mother's near kinswoman.[20]

"Thou shalt not uncover the nakedness of thy father's brother, thou shalt not approach to his wife: she is thine aunt.[21]

"Thou shalt not uncover the nakedness of thy daughter in law: she is thy son's wife; thou shalt not uncover her nakedness.[22]

"Thou shalt not uncover the nakedness of thy brother's wife: it is thy brother's nakedness.[23]

"Thou shalt not uncover the nakedness of a woman and her daughter, neither shalt thou take her son's daughter, or her daughter's daughter, to uncover her nakedness; for they are her near kinswomen: it is wickedness.[24]

"Neither shalt thou take a wife to her sister, to vex her, to uncover her nakedness, besides the other in her life time."[25]

[§404] —— The punishment for incest was by "cutting off" or by death. This offense was described as an "abomination," and it was provided in general that—

". . . whosoever shall commit any of these abominations, even the souls that commit them shall be cut off from among their people."[26]

But the law further prescribed, where a man "lieth with his father's wife"[27] or "his daughter in law,"[28] that "both of them shall surely be put to death,"[29] and "if a man take a wife and her mother . . . they shall be burnt with fire, both he and they . . ."[30]

---

20 Lev. 18:10-13; and see Lev. 20:19 ("And thou shalt not uncover the nakedness of thy mother's sister, nor of thy father's sister: for he uncovereth his near kin: they shall bear their iniquity")

21 Lev. 18:14; and see Lev. 20:20 ("And if a man shall lie with his uncle's wife, he hath uncovered his uncle's nakedness: they shall bear their sin; they shall die childless")

22 Lev. 18:15; and see Lev. 20:12 ("And if a man lie with his daughter in law, both of them shall surely be put to death; they have wrought confusion; their blood shall be upon them")

23 Lev. 18:16; and see Lev. 20:21 ("And if a man shall take his brother's wife, it is an unclean thing: he hath uncovered his brother's nakedness; they shall be childless")

". . . John had said unto Herod, It is not lawful for thee to have thy brother's wife." Mark 6:18; and see Matt. 14:4

24 Lev. 18:17; and see Lev. 20:14 ("if a man take a wife and her mother . . . they shall be burnt with fire"); Deut. 27:23 ("Cursed be he that lieth with his mother in law. And all the people shall say, Amen")

25 Lev. 18:18; and see supra §211

26 Lev. 18:29

27 Lev. 20:11

28 Lev. 20:12

29 Lev. 20:11,12

30 Lev. 20:14

[§405] —— In the Lot Case, two incests were committed by Lot with his daughters after the destruction of Sodom and Gomorrah. It is related that—

". . . Lot went up out of Zoar, and dwelt in the mountain, and his two daughters with him; for he feared to dwell in Zoar; and he dwelt in a cave, he and his two daughters.

"And the firstborn said unto the younger, Our father is old, and there is not a man in the earth to come in unto us after the manner of all the earth:

"Come, let us make our father drink wine, and we will lie with him, that we may preserve seed of our father.

"And they made their father drink wine that night: and the firstborn went in, and lay with her father; and he perceived not when she lay down, nor when she arose.

"And it came to pass on the morrow, that the firstborn said unto the younger, Behold I lay yesternight with my father: let us make him drink wine this night also; and go thou in, and lie with him, that we may preserve seed of our father.

"And they made their father drink wine that night also; and the younger arose, and lay with him; and he perceived not when she lay down, nor when she arose.

"Thus were both the daughters of Lot with child by their father."[31]

When these offenses were committed there was no express law against incest, though it was doubtless contrary to custom[32]—otherwise the daughters would not have found it necessary to make their father drunk with wine.[33] For it appears that the offenses were committed without the conscious knowledge of Lot, though for a laudable purpose on the part of his daughters and therefore, perhaps, excusable.

[§406] The offense of Onan was that he violated his duty to marry the widow of his deceased elder brother Er, who had died without issue.[34] It is related that—

". . . Judah said unto Onan, Go in unto thy brother's wife, and marry her, and raise up seed to thy brother.

"And Onan knew that the seed should not be his; and it came to pass, when he went in unto his brother's wife, that he spilled it on the ground, lest that he should give seed to his brother.

"And the thing which he did displeased the Lord: wherefore he slew him . . ."[35]

---

31 Gen. 19:31-38
32 See supra §4
33 Had incest not been against the custom, the daughters would have given their aged father a little wine as a stimulant, but not enough to have made him drunk. The story indicates that he would not have participated in the acts if he had not been intoxicated.

Generally as to the use of wine, see supra §304
34 See supra §191
In common understanding, onanism is self abuse. It is more properly defined as an incomplete sexual act.
35 Gen. 38:8-10

[§407]   Rape is committed when a man has sexual relation with an unwilling woman, not his wife. Bible law makes a distinction between an offense against a "betrothed damsel" and one against an unbetrothed virgin. In the former case, the man is punishable by death; in the latter he is subjected to a penalty and required to marry the girl. The provisions on the subject are that—

". . . if a man find a betrothed damsel in the field, and the man force her, and lie with her: then the man only that lay with her shall die:

"But unto the damsel thou shalt do nothing; there is in the damsel no sin worthy of death: for as when a man riseth against his neighbour, and slayeth him, even so is this matter:

"For he found her in the field, and the betrothed damsel cried and there was none to save her.

"If a man find a damsel that is a virgin, which is not betrothed, and lay hold on her, and lie with her, and they be found;

"Then the man that lay with her shall give unto the damsel's father fifty shekels of silver, and she shall be his wife; because he hath humbled her, he may not put her away all his days."36

[§408]   —— Amnon committed rape upon his half-sister Tamar, and was slain therefor by her brother Absalom. The account of the matter is as follows:

". . . Absalom the son of David had a fair sister, whose name was Tamar; and Amnon the son of David loved her.

"So Amnon lay down, and made himself sick: and when the king was come to see him, Amnon said unto the king: I pray thee, let Tamar my sister come, and make me a couple of cakes in my sight, that I may eat at her hand.

"Then David sent home to Tamah, saying, Go now to thy brother Amnon's house, and dress him meat.

"So Tamar went to her brother Amnon's house; and he was laid down. And she took flour, and kneaded it, and made cakes, in his sight, and did bake the cakes.

"And Amnon said unto Tamar, Bring the meat into the chamber, that I may eat of thine hand. And Tamar took the cakes which she had made, and brought them into the chamber of Amnon her brother.

"And when she had brought them unto him to eat, he took hold of her, and said unto her, Come lie with me, my sister.

"And she answered him, Nay, my brother, do not force me; for no such thing ought to be done in Israel: do not thou this folly.

"Howbeit he would not hearken unto her voice: but, being stronger than she, forced her, and lay with her.

"Then Amnon hated her exceedingly; . . . and Amnon said unto her, Arise, be gone.

"And she said unto him, There is no cause: this evil in sending me away is greater than the other that thou didst unto me. But he would not hearken unto her.

---

36 Deut. 22:25-29
Rape is "an accusation easily to be made and hard . . . to be defended by the party accused, though never so innocent." 1 Pleas of the Crown 634

(Sir Matthew Hale). Therefore, the testimony of the prosecuting witness should be examined with caution. People v Putnam (1942) 20 Cal. 2d 885, 888, 129 P2d 367 (Traynor,J)

"Then he called his servant that ministered unto him, and said, Put now this woman out from me, and bolt the door after her.

". . . when king David heard of all these things, he was very wroth.

"And Absalom . . . hated Amnon, because he had forced his sister Tamar.

"And it came to pass after two full years, that Absalom had sheepshearers in Baal-hazor, . . . and Absalom invited all the king's sons.

". . . And the king . . .

". . . let Amnon and all the king's sons go with him.

"Now Absalom had commanded his servants, saying, Mark ye now when Amnon's heart is merry with wine, and when I say unto you, Smite Amnon; then kill him, fear not; have not I commanded you? be courageous, and be valiant.

"And the servants of Absalom did unto Amnon as Absalom had commanded.

"So Absalom fled, and went to Geshur, and was there three years.

"And the soul of king David longed to go forth unto Absalom: for he was comforted concerning Amnon, seeing he was dead."[37]

[§409]   Under Mosaic law, a woman "sick of her flowers" was regarded as "unclean" for seven days.[38] The law forbade a man to "approach unto a woman to uncover her nakedness, as long as she is put apart for her uncleanness,"[39] or, as it was said, to "come near to a menstruous woman."[40] Violation of this prohibition was punishable by "cutting off"[41] the rule was that "both of them shall be cut off from among their people."[42]

[§410]   Sodomy was so named because of its prevalence among the Sodomites, for which the cities of Sodom and Gomorrah were destroyed.[43] The law of sodomy is that—

"Thou shalt not lie with mankind, as with womankind: it is abomination"[44]

Concerning the punishment of this offense, it was prescribed that—

"If a man also lie with mankind, as he lieth with a woman, both of them have committed an abomination: they shall surely be put to death: their blood shall be upon them."[45]

---

37 2 Sam., chap. 13
38 Lev. 15:19,28
39 Lev. 18:19
40 Ezek. 18:6
41 See infra §417
42 Lev. 20:18
43 Gen. 19:1-25
"That heinous offense (sodomy) derived its name from the tribe of Sodomites in Palestine, which secured universal infamy from the abominable practice of that unnatural vice as a religious rite." People v Battilana (1942) 52 Cal.App.2d 685, 694, 126 P2d 923
44 Lev. 18:22
The offenders "dishonor their own bodies between themselves." Rom. 1:24
See also Two Ways, 2:2 "Thou shalt not corrupt boys."
45 Lev. 20:13

Though it was declared that "there shall be no . . . sodomite of the sons of Israel,"[46] the people were at times given to "vile affections."[47] It is said that "there were sodomites in the land" in the days of Rehoboam the son of Solomon."[48] Nor was this offense unknown in the time of St. Paul, who observed that—

". . . even their women did change the natural use into that which is against nature.

"And likewise also the men, leaving the natural use of the woman, burned in their lust one toward another; men with men working that which is unseemly . . ."[49]

CHAPTER 61

PUNISHMENTS

[§411]   The purpose of punishment, according to Biblical law, is to protect the righteous,[50] whom "the Lord loveth,[1] against the wicked, whom he condemns,[2] by inflicting speedy,[3] severe,[4] and sure punishment[5] upon evildoers,[6] to the end that crime may be suppressed[7] by removing criminals—permanently or temporarily—from the society which they endanger.[8]

"For the upright shall dwell in the land, and the perfect shall remain in it.

---

46 Deut. 23:17
47 1 Rom. 26
48 1 Kings 14:24
49 Rom. 1:26,27
50 See supra §29
1 Ps. 146:8
"A good man obtaineth favor of the Lord." Prov. 12:2
". . . in every nation he that . . . worketh righteousness is accepted" with God. Acts 10:35
2 Prov. 12:2 ("a man of wicked devices" the Lord will condemn)
"The Lord . . . casteth the wicked down to the ground." Ps. 147:6
"The most High hateth sinners, and will repay vengeance unto the ungodly." Ecclesiasticus 12:6

3 See infra §437
4 Kinds of punishment, see infra §417
5 "Though hand join in hand, the wicked shall not be unpunished." Prov. 11:21
6 Duty to enforce the law, see supra §95
7 Punishments are designed to suppress crime. Dickinson v Dickinson (1819) 7 NC (3 Murphey) 327, 330 (Taylor,CJ)
8 14 Ore.LR (1934-1935) 104 (Radin) saying the original purpose of punishment was to reduce the number of criminals by getting rid of those about whose criminal character there could be no doubt.

"But the wicked shall be cut off from the earth, and the transgressors shall be rooted out of it."[9]

So long as there is wickedness in the land, the law must wage continual and uncompromising warfare against the forces of iniquity:[10] otherwise the peace and safety of society will soon be destroyed.[11] Those who "presumptuously" violate the law[12] must be punished, not merely as a deterrent to crime—that the "simple" may be "made wise"[13]—but that evil may be eliminated[14] and the wicked destroyed.[15]

Concerning punishment under modern laws, it has been observed that—

"The morality of our laws is the morality of the Mosaic interpretation of the Ten Commandments, modified only as to the degree or kind of punishment inflicted. In some cases the punishment is less, and in some much severer, yet the underlying morality is the same."[16]

[§412]   The theory of punishment, as disclosed in the Scriptures, is that one should be punished when his conduct shows that he "despises" the law.[17]   The ideas of punishment of a wrongdoer and compensation to one injured by the wrong are quite distinct.[18]   From the standpoint of the victim, the offender should be compelled to make reparation.[19]   But from that of society, his essential fault is willful disobedience of the law.[20]   It is considered that he must be punished, not so much because he has committed some particular offense as that he has become a "transgressor of the law,"[21] and is therefore unworthy to live under it.[22]   Thus it was commanded

9 Prov. 2:21,22

10 White v Williams (1931) 159 Miss. 732, 132 So. 573, 76 ALR 757, 763 (Griffith,J, dissenting)

11 "The peace and safety of civilized society would soon be destroyed if those who violate the criminal laws were not visited with proper retribution therefor." Sanders v Commonwealth (1942) 163 SW2d (Ky.) 493, 496 (Thomas, J)

12 Num. 15:30

13 Prov. 21:11

14 Deut. 17:12,13 ("thou shalt put away the evil from Israel. And all the people shall hear, and fear, and do no more presumptuously"), 19:19 ("so shalt thou put the evil away from among you")

15 Ps. 101:8 ("I will early destroy all the wicked of the land")

16 Moore v Strickling (1899) 46 W.Va. 515, 33 SE 274, 50 LRA 279, 283 (Dent,P)

17 Heb. 10:28
"Improper conduct deserves some punishment. Taggart v Cooper (1810) 3 Binney (Pa.) 34, 35
But one ought not to be punished without cause and without regard of justice. 2 Mac. 4:34, 36
And it is "better that the guilty should sometimes escape, than that every individual should be subject to vexation and oppression." Conner v Commonwealth (1810) 3 Binney (Pa.) 38, 44 (Tilghman,CJ)

18 See infra §456 et seq.

19 See 17 Tex.LR (1938) 3 (Keeton)

20 See 14 Ore.LR (1934-1935) 450

21 James 2:11

22 But the fact that one has suffered punishment does not excuse him from making reparation to his victim. This is made clear in the parable of Nathan to David: "The man that hath done this thing shall surely die" and "he shall restore the lamb fourfold." 2 Sam. 12:5,6; and see supra §378

that "whosoever shall transgress the law . . . shall be punished,"[23] and it is said that—

". . . whosoever shall keep the whole law, and yet offend in one point, he is guilty of all.
"For he that said, Do not commit adultery, also said, Do not kill. Now if thou commit no adultery, yet if thou kill, thou art become a transgressor of the law."[24]

Moreover it was reasoned that one having the mental capacity of distinguishing between right and wrong,[25] has also the power of deciding whether he will do good or evil. If he chooses to do good, society will (or should) insure his safety, but if he chooses to do evil, "his blood," as it is said "shall be upon him."[26] The notion is expressed in the order of Solomon concerning his half-brother Adonijah:

"If he will shew himself a worthy man, there shall not a hair of him fall to the earth: but if wickedness shall be found in him, he shall die."[27]

But the possibility of the reformation of the criminal was recognized in Biblical law where the crime was not such as to call for the death penalty.[28] Thus it is said—

"Have I any pleasure at all that the wicked should die? saith the Lord God; and not that he should return from his ways, and live?"[29]

Even the thief on the cross, it has been noted, was permitted to repent during the hours of his final agony.[30] The rehabilitation or reformation of the criminal is also regarded as an objective of modern criminal justice.[31]

[§413]　　There is nothing in Christian law, when reasonably interpreted,[32] which would deny to a state or other government the right and duty to punish criminals. To the contrary, the principle of punishment is recognized in the New Testament, where it is said that "whatsoever a man soweth, that shall he also reap,"[33] and that "he that leadeth into captivity shall go into captivity: he that killeth with the sword must be killed with the sword."[34] The commandment of Jesus, "that ye resist not evil,"[35] is a rule of individual or personal

23　1 Esdras, 8:24, command of Artaxerxes.
24　James 2:10,11
25　See infra §423
26　See Lev. 20:9
27　1 Kings 1:52
28　See infra §421
29　Ezek. 18:23

30　Melvin v Reid (1931) 112 Cal.App. 285, 292, 297 P 91 (Marks,J)
31　In re Tenner (1942) 20 Cal.2d 670, 673, 128 P2d 338 (Edmonds,J)
32　See supra §41 et seq.
33　Gal. 6:7
34　Rev. 13:10
35　Matt. 5:39

non-resistance[36]—it does not forbid organized society to protect righteous citizens against evil doers.[37]

[§414] But it is an ancient doctrine that an offender should be punished "according to law."[38] Ordinarily there can be no punishment which is not in the statute.[39] So, where the law existing at the time of the commission of an act omits to prescribe punishment therefor, the act—though it may be technically unlawful—is not punishable.[40] And where the law specifies what punishment shall be inflicted, and the manner thereof, the requirements of the statute must be observed[41]— at least the punishment must not be greater nor inflicted in a manner more severe than that which the law says.

[§415] Another time-honored principle is that punishment should be measured according to the fault,[42] or, as it has been expressed, a man should be punished "according to his ways,"[43] "his wickedness,"[44] "his works,"[45] or "the fruit of his doings."[46] It was considered that "every transgression" should thus receive its "just recompense"[47]—a punishment fitting the crime.[48] So under the so-called Lex Talionis rule of Moses—

". . . if a man cause a blemish in his neighbour; as he hath done, so shall it be done to him.[49]
". . . thou shalt give life for life.
"Eye for eye, tooth for tooth, hand for hand, foot for foot.
"Burning for burning, wound for wound, stripe for stripe."[50]

---

36 See supra §18

37 See supra §29

38 See 1 Mac. 15:21
Execution of death sentence, see infra §472

39 See 14 Ore.LR (1934-1935) 103 (Radin) stating that this is a common principle of Anglo-American law.

40 See supra §334
But this rule was not always observed. See for example, The Stickgather's Case (supra §388) where the punishment was prescribed after the offense had been committed.

41 See 15 Am Jur 167

42 Deut. 25:2 (providing that a man shall be beaten "according to his fault")

43 Jer. 17:10 ("every man according to his ways"); Ezek. 33:20 ("every one after his ways")

44 2 Sam. 3:39 ("the Lord shall reward the doer of evil according to his wickedness")

45 See supra §51

46 Jer. 17:10 ("every man . . . according to the fruit of his doings"), 21:14 ("I will punish you according to the fruit of your doings, saith the Lord")

47 Heb. 2:2

48 See 14 Ore.LR (1934-1935) 104 (Radin) saying "we have lost faith in this notion."

49 Lev. 24:19; and see supra §363
"Breach for breach, eye for eye, tooth for tooth; as he hath caused a blemish in a man, so shall it be done to him again." Lev. 24:20

50 Ex. 21:23-25 (announcing the rule in connection with an injury to a pregnant woman); and see supra §§177, 363
". . . thine eye shall not pity; but life shall go for life, eye for eye, tooth for tooth, hand for hand, foot for foot." Deut. 19:21
But this supposedly rigid Mosaic statute was seldom, if ever, interpreted in a literal fashion. See 38 Case & Comment (1932) No. 2, p 2.

[§416] In Primitive law, a family was entitled to redress or avenge offenses against its members.[1] Thus it appears that Simeon and Levi slew Hamor and Shechem because Shechem had dealt with their sister Dinah "as with a harlot."[2] And under early Mosaic law, a kinsman of a slain man had the right and duty—as the avenger of blood—of punishing the slayer[3] if he could catch him before he reached a city of refuge.[4] It was contemplated that the avenger would pursue the slayer, and that he might overtake him and slay him.[5] But the avenger was not allowed to enter a city of refuge.[6] Nor were the elders of a city of refuge permitted to deliver into the hands of an avenger a slayer who had fled to the city after killing his neighbor "unwittingly" and not in hatred.[7] But where one fled to a city of refuge after killing his neighbor in hatred and by lying in wait,

"Then the elders of his city shall send and fetch him thence, and deliver him into the hand of the avenger of blood, that he may die.
"Thine eye shall not pity him, but thou shalt put away the guilt of innocent blood from Israel, that it may go well with thee.[8]

After the settlement of the Israelites in Palestine, it seems that punishment by the avenger was discontinued.[9]

[§417] Various kinds of punishment are mentioned or prescribed in the Scriptures, among them being punishment by beating,[10] bondage or slavery,[11] confiscation of goods,[11a], cutting off or exile,[12] imprisonment[13] and death.[14] Under Mosaic law, it appears that "punishment for offenses against property was restitution from one to five times in amount."[15] But the fact that the law prescribes a certain penalty does not preclude the imposition of a lesser punishment. So in the case

---

1 See 14 Gr.B (1902) 84 (Amram)
Generally as to the family, see supra, §186

2 See Gen., chap. 34; and see supra §182

3 See 12 Gr.B. (1900) 385, 386
The avenger of blood was the nearest relative, to the fifth degree, to any person murdered, whose duty it was to avenge the death. See Gen. 9:5,6
The offender was an outlaw so far as kinsmen of his victim were concerned. 13 Gr.B (1901) 593 (Amram)

4 See infra §431

5 See Deut. 19:6

6 Num. 35:12; Jos. 20:3; and see infra §431

7 Jos. 20:5

8 Deut. 19:11-13

9 See 12 Gr. B. (1900) 197 (Amram)

10 See infra §418

11 See infra §419

11a See Ezra 7:26

12 See supra §§79, 404, 409

13 See infra §420

14 See infra §421
There were five kinds of punishment under ancient Talmudic laws: (1) corporal punishment of flagellation, (2) bondage or slavery, (3) exile, (4) imprisonment, and (5) capital punishment. 38 Case & Comment (1932) No. 2, p 3

15 Moore v Strickling (1899) 46 W.Va. 515, 33 SE 274, 50 LRA 279, 283 (Dent,P) saying that "with us it is usually felony where the amount exceeds twenty dollars."

of Adam, though the prescribed penalty for eating the forbidden fruit was death, he was condemned merely to work for a living."[16]

[§418] —— Beating or corporal punishment was inflicted, it seems, for a minor offense,[16a] such as the troubling of a city by teaching unlawful customs,[17] or for a more serious offense accompanied by extenuating circumstances. Also an offender was sometimes beaten and subjected at the same time to additional or other punishment, such as imprisonment.[18]

Concerning the manner of beating, the law prescribed that—

". . . if the wicked man be worthy to be beaten, . . . the judge shall cause him to lie down, and to be beaten before his face, according to his fault, by a certain number.

"Forty stripes he may give him, and not exceed: lest, if he should exceed, and beat him above these with many stripes, then thy brother should seem vile unto thee."[19]

[§419] —— Bondage or slavery was sometimes decreed as punishment for crime.[20] Mosaic law provided that if a thief have nothing with which to make restitution, "then he shall be sold for his theft."[21] The servitude ceased when labor had been performed equivalent to the amount which would have been required to make restitution, and it is thought to have been limited to six years.[22]

[§420] —— Imprisonment was used from primitive times as punishment for many offenses.[23] Potiphar, "an officer of

---

16 Gen. 3:17-19
16a See Ezra 7:26
17 See Acts 16:20-23
18 See infra §420
19 Deut. 25:2,3

St.Paul, "of the Jews five times received . . . forty stripes save one." 2 Cor. 11:24

Under ancient Talmudic law, corporal punishment or flagellation was inflicted by a quadruple leather strap on the bare back of the offender. More than thirty-nine stripes were never given at any one time. If the prisoner escaped after having been bound or if the lash broke on the second stroke the sentence was considered executed and the prisoner was freed. 38 Case & Comment (1932) No. 2, p 3.

20 See supra §232 et seq.

21 Ex. 22:3; and see supra §375
22 See supra §234; and see 38 Case & Comment (1932) No. 2, p3
23 See Matt. 5:25 ("Agree with thine adversary quickly . . . lest . . . (he) . . . deliver thee to the judge, and the judge deliver thee to the officer, and thou be cast into prison")

Under the ancient Talmudic law, imprisonment was the form of punishment used in four instances: (a) When a murderer could not be legally executed because all the conditions necessary to make the procedure correct were not present; (b) when one procured an assassin; (c) when persons conspired to commit murder and actually assisted in the commission of the crime; (d) when one who had been twice whipped for having twice committed the same offense, committed it a third time. 38 Case & Comment (1932) No. 2, p 4

Pharaoh, captain of the guard," put Joseph in prison, "a place where the king's prisoners were bound,"[24] and Pharaoh put his chief butler and chief baker in the prison where Joseph was bound.[25] King Shalmaneser of Assyria bound king Hosea of Israel in prison for conspiracy.[26] Jeremiah was shut in prison,[27] as was also Zedekiah, "till the day of his death."[28] Herod cast John the Baptist into prison[29] and afterwards caused him to be beheaded there.[30] Barabbas was cast into prison for sedition and murder.[31] The high priest and those with him "laid hands on the apostles and put them in the common prison."[32] Saul (Paul) committed men and women of the church to prison,[33] and later the magistrate cast Paul and Silas into prison, "charging the jailer to keep them safely."[34]

Prisoners were sometimes given only bread and water. King Ahab ordered that the prophet Micaiah be put in prison and fed "with bread of affliction and with water of affliction."[35]

[§421] —— Under ancient law, "almost all things" were "purged with blood,"[36] that is, punished by death.[37] This was true of Mosaic law[38] under which those who committed unmerciful or unnatural offenses were adjudged worthy of death.[39] As to many offenses, the law expressly provided that the offender should die.[40] In particular, murder was punished with death.[41] Blood was demanded for blood,[42] upon the theory, old beyond the memory and records of mankind, that "the land cannot be cleansed of blood that is shed therein, but by the blood of him that shed it."[43]

In England, until comparatively recent times, many crimes

24　Gen. 39:20
25　Gen. 40:3
26　2 Kings 17:4
27　Jer. 32:2
28　Jer. 52:11
29　Matt. 4:12, 14:3
30　Matt. 14:10
31　Luke 23:19
32　Acts 5:17,18
33　Acts 8:3
34　Acts 16:22
35　1 Kings 22:27
36　Heb. 9:22

37　In ancient Greece and Rome, capital punishment was common for even petty crimes. 38 Case & Comment (1932) No. 2, p 2

Execution of the death sentence, see infra §472

38　See for example Deut. 24:16; 1 Mac. 1:50

Under the ancient Talmudic law, capital punishment was theoretically the penalty for 36 offenses: 12 violations of religious precepts, and 24 kinds of wrongs to society. However, in practice this penalty was seldom enforced. 38 Case & Comment (1932) No. 2, p 4

39　Rom. 1:32
40　See supra §349 et seq.
41　See supra §368
42　Pennsylvania v Bell (1793) Addison 156, 1 AD 298, 300, saying that "in all or almost all nations, blood has been demanded for blood."
43　Num. 35:33

were punishable by death[44] unless the offender was able to read.[45] In Blackstone's time more than 150 felonies were so punished.[46] And in America, murderers, kidnapers and rapists are punished capitally in most of the states.[47]

[§422] —— In former times the property of executed offenders—at least of those who were condemned for treason—was subject to confiscation or destruction. The old rule was that "their goods shall become a booty, and their houses a desolation,"[48] thus visiting the penalty, not of death but of attainder and corruption of blood, upon their children by the forfeiture of their inheritances.[49] So in the case of Naboth, who was falsely convicted of blaspheming God and the king,[50] when king Ahab heard that Naboth was dead he went down to Naboth's vineyard and took possession of it.[1] And in Babylonian law it seems that the property of an executed offender was destroyed or forfeited, for it appears that Nebuchadnezzar decreed that those who should speak against God should be cut in pieces and their houses "made a dunghill."[2]

[§423] Under Biblical law, punishment was intended to be imposed "diligently"[3] and equally,[4] that is, upon "every one" according to his "ways" or "works."[5] But an offender whose crime was attended by aggravating circumstances might be punished more severely. So a thief was ordinarily required to make "full restitution" or be "sold for his theft."[6] But where the thief was a rich man and his victim poor, the death penalty might be imposed.[7] On the other hand, it seems

---

44 In 1809 the death penalty was affixed to more than 600 crimes.

45 See 4 Bl. Com. 333

Benefit of clergy was abolished in England in 1827. It seems never to have been recognized in America.

"Till 1487 any one who knew how to read might commit murder as often as he pleased, with no other result than that of being delivered to the ordinary to make his purgation, with the chance of being delivered to him 'absque purgatione.' . . . Even after 1487 a man who could read could commit murder once with no other punishment than that of having M branded on the brawn of his left thumb . . ." 1 Stephen, History of Criminal Law of England (1883) 463,4

46 4 Bl.Com. 18

47 38 Case & Comment (1932) No. 2, p 2

48 Zeph. 1:13

49 See supra §§338, 340

But see 12 Gr.B. (1900) 506, saying there is no "evidence of forfeiture of the estate of the felon who has been convicted and put to death." And see supra §134

50 See supra §381

1 1 Kings 21:16,18

2 Dan. 3:29

3 1 Esd. 8:24

4 See supra §50

5 See supra §415

The law is no respecter of persons. Gould & Co. v Atlanta (1878) 60 Ga. 164 (Bleckley,J) And see supra §50

6 See supra §375

7 2 Sam. 12:5; and see supra §378

probable that a lunatic[8] or insane person[9]—one "not in his right mind,"[10] but, as it was thought, possessed of a devil[11] or unclean spirit[12]—was not punished for crime, save by stripes,[13] though one who committed an offense while drunk was subject to punishment[14] unless he was made drunk against his will.[15]

[§424] —— It was no excuse, as regards punishment for crime, that the offender had theretofore obeyed the law.[16]

". . . The righteousness of the righteous shall not deliver him in the day of his transgression; . . . neither shall the righteous be able to live for his righteousness in the day that he sinneth.

"When I shall say to the righteous, that he shall surely live; if he trust to his own righteousness, and commit iniquity, all his righteousness shall not be remembered; but for his iniquity that he hath committed, he shall die for it.

"When the righteous turneth from his righteousness, and committeth iniquity, he shall even die thereby."[17]

[§425] —— The plain intent of Biblical law is that an offender, whose guilt has been established, shall be punished according to law[18] and "without mercy."[19]

"Thine eye shall not pity him, but thou shalt put away the guilt of innocent blood from Israel, that it may go well with thee."[20]

Mercy is for those who are worthy of it—for those "that receive discipline, and that diligently seek after his (the Lord's) judgments,"[21] and not for those who despise and scorn the law.[22] It is said not to be "a light thing to do wickedly against the laws,"[23] and that "the Lord . . . will not at all

---

8 See Matt. 17:15 ("have mercy on my son; for he is a lunatic, and sore vexed")

9 "The causes of insanity are as varied as the varying circumstances of man.

'Some for love, some for jealousy,
For grim religion some, and some for pride,
Have lost their reason; some for fear of want,
Want all their lives; and others every day,
For fear of dying, suffer worse than death.'
(4 Armstrong on Health, v 84)—
Mutual Life Ins. Co. v Terry (1872) 82 US (15 Wall.) 580, 21 L ed 236, 241 (Hunt,J)

10 Luke 8:35

11 Matt. 9:32, 12:22; Mark 5:15,16,18
"And many of them said, He hath a devil, and is mad." John 10:20

12 Luke 8:29

13 "Stripes" are prepared "for the back of fools." Prov. 19:29

14 "Drunkenness is no excuse for a crime." State v Coleman (1875) 27 La. Ann. 691 (Wyly,J)

15 See supra §405

16 "It had been better for them not to have known the way of righteousness, than after they have known it, to turn" therefrom. 2 Pet. 2:21

17 Ezek. 33:12,13,18

18 See supra §414

19 Heb. 10:28

20 Deut. 19:13,21, 25:12

21 Ecclesiasticus 18:14

22 See supra §412

23 2 Mac. 4:17

acquit the wicked"[24] nor "be slack . . . till he have rendered to every man according to his deeds, and to the works of men according to their devices."[25] More especially, "he shall have judgment without mercy, that hath shewed no mercy."[26]

In modern law also it is recognized that "mercy emboldens sin."[27] Sympathy has no place in a criminal prosecution[28]— it does not justify failure to protect society.[29] But where the law itself is sanguinary—the prescribed punishment being more severe than the offense calls for—the law will be "softened in its application to the case."[30] As the cold, it will be "measured to the shorn lamb."[31]

[§426] —— The reformation of an offender will also be considered, it seems, where—having escaped punishment for a time—he "turns from his evil ways"[32] and by "upright deportment" evinces a sincere departure from his follies.[33] So it has been said that—

". . . as for the wickedness of the wicked, he shall not fall thereby in the day that he turneth from his wickedness . . .

". . . when I say unto the wicked, Thou shalt surely die; if he turn from his sin, and do that which is lawful and right;

"If the wicked restore the pledge, give again that he had robbed, walk in the statutes of life, without committing iniquity; he shall surely live, he shall not die.

"None of his sins that he hath committed shall be mentioned unto him; he hath done that which is lawful and right; he shall surely live.

". . . if the wicked turn from his wickedness, and do that which is lawful and right, he shall live thereby."[34]

[§427] —— Notwithstanding the general rule of equality,[35] it appears that punishment of an offender was sometimes omitted or postponed out of regard for his parent, where the latter had been a righteous man or had occupied a prominent position in society. For example, Solomon was not pun-

24 Nahum 1:3

25 Ecclesiasticus 35:18,19

26 James 2:13

27 Timon of Athens, Act III, sc. 1

28 State v Wallace (1942) 131 P2d (Or.) 222,253 (Kelly,CJ, dissenting)

29 14 Ore.LR (1934-1935) 453

"It is the duty of the courts . . . to mete out justice to all; not to do injustice to the accuser and afford a picnic to the accused." People v Lanigan (1943) 56 ACA 816, 829, 133 P2d —— (Moore, PJ, dissenting)

30 Commonwealth v Snelling (1812) 4 Binney (Pa.) 379, 384 (Brackenridge,J)

31 Henri Estienne (1531-1598) Les Pre-

mices ou le I. livre des Proverbs epigrammatizez, p 47

"But, where the lamb is found carrying, concealed from view, shearing implements of his own, the necessity or wisdom of peculiar solicitude lessens." Pacific Finance Corp v Hendley (1932) 119 Cal.App. 697, 7 P2d 391, 395 (Parker, J pro tem)

32 Ezek. 33:11

33 Moore v Strickling (1899) 46 W.Va. 515, 33 SE 274, 50 LRA 279, 284, (Dent,P) saying that the law will "readily pardon those whose upright deportment evinces a sincere departure from the follies of youth."

34 Ezek. 33:12, 14-16,19

35 See supra §423

ished for taking many strange women as wives and concubines because his father David "kept my commandments and my statutes."[36] Similarly it appears that punishment was deferred or withheld in some cases because of the prominence or social value of the offender. This exception to the rule of equality may be justified where the interests of society itself are better served by permitting the offense to go unpunished, at least for the time being. An example of such action is that of the case of David, wherein it was decreed that he should not die for his offense in causing Uriah to be killed and taking his wife,[37] but that the child born to him of the stolen wife should die[38] and that subsequently his wives should be taken from him and given unto another.[39]

[§428] The Scriptures teach that offenders should not be helped,[40] justified,[41] praised[42] nor shown favor.

"Let favour be shewed to the wicked, yet will he not learn righteousness; in the land of uprightness will he real unjustly, and will not behold the majesty of the Lord."[43]

Nor is the giving of comfort to offenders to be countenanced.

"He that saith unto the wicked, Thou art righteous; him shall the people curse, nations shall abhor him:

"But to them that rebuke him shall be delight, and a good blessing shall come upon them."[44]

It is inexcusable that one have pleasure in those who commit wicked things.[45] And those who teach that evildoers are "good in the sight of the Lord" are condemned.[46]

"Woe unto them that call evil good, and good evil; that put darkness for light, and light for darkness; that put bitter for sweet, and sweet for bitter!"[47]

---

36 1 Kings 11:34
37 2 Sam. 12:13
38 2 Sam. 12:14; and see supra §340
39 2 Sam. 12:11; and see supra §398
"And the king (David) went forth, and all his household after him. And the king left ten women, which were concubines, to keep the house." (2 Sam. 15:16)
". . . Absalom went in unto his father's concubines in the sight of all Israel." (2 Sam. 16:22)
40 2 Chron. 19:2 ("Shouldest thou help the ungodly . . . therefore is wrath upon thee from before the Lord")
41 Prov. 17:15 ("He that justifieth the wicked, and he that condemneth the just, even they both are abomination to the Lord")

42 Prov. 28:4 ("They that forsake the law praise the wicked but such as keep the law contend with them")
43 Isa. 26:10
44 Prov. 24:24,25
45 They are equally guilty who "have pleasure in them that do" evil. Rom. 1:32
"He that biddeth . . . God speed" to a transgressor "is partaker of his evil deeds." 2 John, v. 11
46 Mal. 3:17 ("Ye have wearied the Lord with your words. Yet ye say, Wherein have we wearied him? When ye say, Every one that doeth evil is good in the sight of the Lord, and he delighteth in them; or, Where is the God of judgment?")
47 Isa. 5:20

[§429] Under Primitive law, a murderer could compromise with the kinfolk of his victim by paying blood money.[48] But this was changed by Mosaic law, under which "ransom" may not ordinarily be taken in satisfaction of an offense; that is, the offender may not purchase immunity from punishment. The law provides that—

". . . ye shall take no satisfaction for the life of a murderer, which is guilty of death: but he shall be surely put to death.

"And ye shall take no satisfaction for him that is fled to the city of his refuge, that he should come again to dwell in the land, until the death of the priest."[49]

But in case of the fatal goring of a man or woman by an ox, where the owner had been notified that the ox was wont to push with his horn and had failed to keep the animal up, it is provided that the owner may ransom his life by paying such sum of money as is laid upon him.[50]

[§430] Under Primitive law, a place that had been consecrated by a supposed visitation of God or that was used for worship was considered as being sacred.[1] The law forbade the defilement[2] or pollution of a sacred place or sanctuary,[3] and it was thus ordinarily unlawful for one to enter a sanctuary for the purpose of seizing or slaying another. Accordingly it was customary for those who had committed offenses to take refuge in sacred places in order to escape their pursuers.[4] But one who had slain another "with guile" might be taken from an altar.[5] So it is related that Joab, who had slain Abner and Amasa,[6] "fled unto the tabernacle of the Lord, and caught hold on the horns of the altar."[7]

"And it was told king Solomon that Joab was fled unto the tabernacle of the Lord; and, behold, he is by the altar. Then Solomon sent Benaiah the son of Jehoiada, saying, Go, fall upon him.

"And Benaiah came to the tabernacle of the Lord, and said unto him, Thus saith the king, Come forth. And he said, Nay: but I will die here. And Benaiah brought the king word again, saying, Thus said Joab, and thus he answered me.

"And the king said unto him, Do as he hath said, and fall upon him, and bury him: that thou mayest take away the innocent blood, which Joab shed, from me, and from the house of my father.

48 12 Gr.B. (1900) 386 (Amram)
49 Num. 35:31,32; and see 42 Wash.L. Rep. (1914) 770 (Barnard)
50 Ex. 21:30; and see supra §287
1 See 13 Gr.B. (1901) 70 (Amram)
2 Num. 19:20; Ezek. 5:11, 23:38

3 Zeph. 3:4
Requirement that a sanctuary be reverenced, see supra §321
4 See 12 Gr.B. (1900) 384 (Amram)
5 Ex. 21:14
6 1 Kings 2:5
7 1 Kings 2:28

"So Benaiah the son of Jehoiada went up, and fell upon him, and slew him . . ."8

[§431] —— Mosaic law extended the ancient right of sanctuary by providing for cities of refuge to which slayers that killed "unawares and unwittingly" might flee.9 The law prescribed that—

". . . among the cities which ye shall give unto the Levites there shall be six cities for refuge, which ye shall appoint for the manslayer, that he may flee thither . . .

". . . ye shall appoint you cities to be cities of refuge for you; that the slayer may flee thither, which killeth any person at unawares.

"And they shall be unto you cities for refuge from the avenger; that the manslayer die not, until he stand before the congregation in judgment.

"These six cities shall be a refuge, both for the children of Israel, and for the stranger, and for the sojourner among them: that every one that killeth any person unawares may flee thither.

"And if he smite him with an instrument of iron, so that he die, he is a murderer: the murderer shall surely be put to death.

"And if he smite him with throwing a stone, wherewith he may die, and he die, he is a murderer: the murderer shall surely be put to death.

"Or if he smite him with an hand weapon of wood, wherewith he may die, and he die, he is a murderer: the murderer shall surely be put to death.

". . . if he thrust him of hatred, or hurl at him by laying of wait, that he die:

"Or in enmity smite him with his hand, that he die: he that smote him shall surely be put to death; for he is a murderer: the revenger of blood shall slay the murderer, when he meeteth him.

"But if he thrust him suddenly without enmity, or have cast upon him any thing without laying of wait,

"Or with any stone, wherewith a man may die, seeing him not, and cast it upon him, that he die, and was not his enemy, neither sought his harm:

"Then the congregation shall judge between the slayer and the revenger of blood according to these judgments:

"And the congregation shall deliver the slayer out of the hand of the revenger of blood, and the congregation shall restore him to the city of his refuge, whither he was fled: and he shall abide in it unto the death of the high priest . . .

"But if the slayer shall at any time come without the border of the city of his refuge, whither he was fled;

"And the revenger of blood find him without the borders of the city of his refuge, and the revenger of blood kill the slayer; he shall not be guilty of blood:

---

8 1 Kings 2:29-31,34

9 Josh. 20:3; and see 12 Gr.B. (1900) 385, 13 Gr.B. (1901) 73 (Amram)

"A man that doeth violence to the blood of any person shall flee to the pit; let no man stay him." Prov. 28:17

Roads were prepared so that slayers might quickly reach the cities of refuge. See Deut. 19:3

"Because he should have remained in the city of his refuge until the death of the high priest: but after the death of the high priest the slayer shall return into the land of his possession."[10]

In Roman law, Christian churches were recognized as places of refuge.[11]   And in England, the privilege of sanctuary existed until abolished by statute in 1623.[12]

10   Num. 35:6-28; see also Deut. 4:41-43, 19:1-13; Josh. 20:1-9

11   7 Cal.LR (1918) 102 (Sherman)

12   See 4 Bl. Com. 333
"Houses of worship have been asylums since their very beginning. At one time, the legal privilege of sanctuary attached to churches. And he who entered one of them acquired immunity against the law."   Cain v Universal Pictures Co. (1942) 47 F Supp 1013, 1017 (Yankwich,DJ)

PART VII

PROCEDURE—ADMINISTRATION OF THE LAW

CHAPTER 62

INTRODUCTION

432 In general   433 Lawyers   434 Perversion of justice   435 Place of holding court   436 Proceedings on Sabbath or Sunday   437 Rights to fair trial and speedy justice

[§432] Suits or legal proceedings are primarily a substitute for feuds,[13] and trials are a sort of public ceremony that takes the place of private quarrels—with possible violence—by ending controversies or punishing offenders.[14] It is also the purpose of a trial to enable the judge to do justice between the parties,[15] and, if the facts are disputed, to ascertain the truth in so far as that is humanly possible.[15a]

The Scriptures lend certain encouragement to the settlement of disputes by legal means.[16] It is declared that "If one man sin against another, the judge shall judge him,"[17] and that if one have "a matter against any man, the law is open, and there are deputies" or judges, so that they may "implead one another."[18]

[§433]   Lawyers, or "doctors of the law" as they are called in the New Testament,[19] are men who—being learned in the law, like St. Paul[20]—give counsel to the people in respect of their rights and duties, and aid litigants in the prosecution or defense of their causes.[21] Lawyers obviously render an im-

---

13 Chambers v Baltimore & O.R. Co. (1907) 207 US 142, 148, 52 L ed 143 (Moody,J); In re Barnett (1942) 124 F2d 1005, 1010 (Frank.Cir.J)

"Conflicts in the exercise of rights arise, and the conflicting forces seek adjustments in the courts." Jones v Opelika (1942) 316 US 584, 86 L. ed 1691, 1699 (Reed,J)

14 "The great end of justice is to substitute the notion of right for that of violence." 1 De Tocqueville, Democracy in America (rev.ed 1900) 138

15 2 Sam. 15:4; Laverett v Continental Briar Pipe Co. (1938) 25 F.Supp. 80, 83 (Moscowitz,DJ)

16 See Deut. 16:18-20

17 1 Sam. 2:25

18 Acts 19:38,39 ("Wherefore if Demetrius, and the craftsmen which are with him, have a matter against any man, the law is open, and there are deputies: let them implead one another. But if ye enquire any thing concerning other matters, it shall be determined in a lawful assembly.")

19 Luke 2:46, 5:17; Acts 5:34

20 See supra §98

21 Acts 5:34 (Gamaliel, a doctor of the law, stood up in the council, and defended Peter and other apostles)

portant service to society,[22] and they ought, like Gamaliel, to be held "in reputation among all the people."[23] But through the ages this has not ordinarily been true,[24] for lawyers have generally been employed—not by the poor and oppressed to recover their inheritances and relieve their oppressions—but by the rich and powerful to preserve the existing order of things.[25] So while Jesus, as a child, sat "in the midst of the doctors of law . . . both hearing them, and asking them questions,"[26] in his later life, they "tempted" him,[27] and he denounced or "reproached" them,[28] as having "rejected the counsel of God against themselves."[29]

". . . Woe unto you . . . ye lawyers! for ye lode men with burdens grievous to be borne, and ye yourselves touch not the burden with one of your fingers."[30]

"Woe unto you, lawyers! for ye have taken away the key of knowledge: ye entered not in yourselves, and them that were entering in ye hindered."[31]

In colonial America, there was bitter prejudice against lawyers.[32] Massachusetts barred lawyers from her legislative assembly. Rhode Island had a farmer for chief justice and a

---

22 Even Napoleon, though he feared lawyers, concluded that they were essential in a civilized commonwealth. 14 Cal.St. Bar Jour. (1939) 405 (Duffy)

23 Acts 5:34

24 14 Cal.St. Bar Jour. (1939) 405 (Duffy—"Extremists have always looked with disfavor on lawyers"); 4 Jn. Marshall LQ (1939) 611 ("Through the ages, lawyers have been a popular subject of satire and criticism")

The legal profession "has in all ages been the repository of more of the confidences of mankind than any other, except the ministry, yet it has at times been the object of more distrust and hostility than any of the others." 4 Nev.St. Bar Jour. (1939) 183 (Warren)

"A dislike for lawyers no doubt antedated the ancient legend that when the blind-folded St.Ives walked down the nave among the statues of the saints to select by chance the one who should be the patron of the Bar, he came to that of Saint Michael conquering the devil and embraced the devil." 14 Cal.St. Bar Jour. (1939) 405 (Duffy)

"Solon condemned the law's delays; and the Greek Aristophanes in his play 'The Clouds' proposes the question 'From what class do our lawyers spring?' and the answer is forthcoming, 'Well, from the blackguards.' Jack Cade, the fiery insurgent of the fifteenth century, shouted 'Let's kill all the lawyers' and Shakespeare in the graveyard scene of Hamlet has his hero say 'Why may not that be the skull of the lawyer? Where be his quiddities now, his quillets, his cases, his tenures and his tricks?' " 13 Fla.LJ (1939) 118 (Bentley)

25 "Lawyers as a class are necessarily conservative." 28 Va.LR (1941) 121 (Catterall)

And so are judges, it seems. Where "the experience of mankind for ages affords no example" of a thing, "the courts cannot be expected to look upon it with admiring eyes." Garesche v Levering Inc.Co. (1898) 146 Mo. 436, 48 SW 653, 46 LRA 232,236 (Marshall,J)

26 Luke 2:46; and see supra §98

27 Matt. 22:35 (a lawyer asked Jesus a question for the purpose of "tempting him"); Luke 10:25 ("a certain lawyer stood up, and tempted" Jesus)

28 Luke 11:45

29 Luke 7:30

30 Luke 11:46

31 Luke 11:52

32 13 Fla.LJ (1939) 119 (Bentley)

"The British General Gage insisted that "the lawyers are the source from whence the clamors have flowed in every province." The terrorists of the French Revolution abolished the legal profession . . . John Quincy Adams wrote: 'the mere title of lawyer is sufficient to deprive a man of public confidence.' " 14 Cal.St.Bar Jour. (1939) 405 (Duffy)

blacksmith for his associate.[33]   And in Virginia a law was passed that "none shall plead for recompense."[34]   Yet the legal profession survived, and even from early days lawyers have assumed leadership and attained influence disproportionate to their numbers.[35]

[§434]   Biblical law forbids acts which tend to pervert justice[36]—"to subvert a man in his cause."[37]   It is commanded that—

". . . thou (shalt not) speak in a cause to decline after many to wrest judgment:
"Neither shalt thou countenance a poor man in his cause.
"Thou shalt not wrest the judgment of thy poor in his cause."[38]
"Thou shalt not wrest judgment: thou shalt not respect persons, neither take a gift: for a gift doth blind the eyes of the wise, and pervert the words of the righteous."[39]

In particular, it is commanded to pervert not "the judgment of the stranger, nor of the fatherless,"[40] and a curse is pronounced against one that does so.[41]   Also it is forbidden to "accuse any falsely."[42]

[§435]   In ancient times, court was held at the gate of the city or town,[43] where all public business was transacted before the elders and in the presence of all who came and went.[44] The gate was known as the "judgment place,"[45] and the judge sat there upon the "judgment-seat,"[46] the people standing before him.[47]   During the sojourn of the Israelites in the wilderness, court was held at the door of the tabernacle, and when

---

33 14 Cal. St. Bar Jour. (1939) 405 (Duffy)

34 13 Fla.LJ (1939) 119 (Bentley)

35 Of 56 signers to the Declaration of Independence, 25 were lawyers. Of 55 men who wrote the Constitution, 32 were lawyers. Two-thirds of the American presidents were lawyers. Of 47 secretaries of state, 44 were lawyers. Of 72 cabinet officers, 50 were lawyers. See 4 Jn. Marshall LQ (1939) 612 (Knight)
"Without lawyers, America was a colony, not her own master; with lawyers, and only because of them, America became free.   Under their leadership she has prospered and preserved freedom and opportunity in a far greater degree than the world has ever before seen."   20 Tex.LR (1942) No. 7, p 62 (Carter)

36 Bribery, see supra §§352-354
Perjury, see supra §§355-357

37 Lam. 3:36

38 Ex. 23:2,3,6

39 Deut. 16:19

40 Deut. 24:17

41 Deut. 27:19 ("the judgment of the stranger, fatherless and widow")

42 Luke 3:14 (command of John the Baptist to the soldiers)

43 Deut. 16:18 ("judges . . . shalt thou make thee in all thy gates"); Dan. 2:49 ("Daniel sat in the gate of the king"); Amos 5:15 ("establish judgment in the gate")

44 See for example Ruth 4:1 et seq.

45 Ecclesiastes 3:16; Ex. 18:13; Isa 16:15; Joel 3:12

46 Matt. 27:19; John 19:13; Acts 18:12, 16,17, 25:10,17; Rom. 14:10; 2 Cor. 5:10; James 2:6

47 Ex. 18:13; 1 Kings 3:16

they were settled in Jerusalem, it was held at the door of the temple.[48]   Later judicial proceedings were conducted in a "judgment-hall."[49]

[§436]   Under Mosaic law, it seems that judicial proceedings were not conducted on the Sabbath, though an offender might be arrested on that day and held in "ward."[50]   So in the Stick-gatherer's Case, it appears that the culprit was seized and confined on the Sabbath but that he was subsequently condemned and executed.[1]   But among the early Christians, all days were used alike for hearing causes in the courts, "not sparing, as it seemeth, the Sunday itself."[2]

"It has been said that they had two reasons for this.   One was in opposition to the heathens, who were superstitious about the observance of days and times, conceiving some to be unlucky and others to be lucky, and therefore the Christians laid aside all observance of days.   A second reason was that, by keeping their courts open at all times, they prevented Christians from resorting to heathen courts.   In the year 517, a canon was made in the church by which Sunday was ordered to be dies non juridicus.   This canon of the church was adopted by and incorporated into the common law, and it has been consistently held from that time on that, under the common law, no judicial act ought to be done on the 'Sabbath'."[3]

Under present-day American law, an offender may not be tried and convicted on Sunday.[4]   He may be arrested on Sunday, and the magistrate may commit or discharge him, but he may not try him or pass judgment.[5]

[§437]   It is an ancient doctrine—the observance of which is "essential to the very concept of justice"[6]—that everyone is entitled to a fair trial of his cause.[7]   No matter how repre-

48   12 Gr.B. (1900) 6 (Amram)

49   John 18:28,33, 19:9; Acts 23:35

50   Sabbath rules, see supra §319

1   See supra §388

2   Hellams v Abercrombie (1880) 15 SC 110, 40 AR 684, 686 (Simpson,CJ)

3   People v Mantei (1929) 134 (NY) Misc. 529, 236 NYS 122 (Turk,J) citing Swan v Broome (1764) 3 Burr 1597, 2 Bl. 526 (Lord Mansfield)

"Sunday is stated in all the books to be dies non juridicus; not made so by the statute, but by a canon of the church, incorporated into the common law."   Story v Elliott (1827) 8 Cowen (NY) 27, 18 AD 423 (Savage, CJ)

4   Van Bueren v Commissioners of Wildwood (1931) 153 A (NY) 260

A verdict may be delivered, received and entered on Sunday, but the pronouncement of judgment is a judicial act and is void when performed on Sunday.   People v Ramsey (1926) 129 Misc. (NY) 39, 217 NYS 799 (Heffernan,J)

5   "It is a matter of public policy that no proceedings of the court should be held on Sunday other than those necessary for the preservation of peace and the arrest and detention of those charged with crime.   To hold otherwise would break down and destroy those splendid principles of Sunday observance which have come down to us for many generations long past."   People v Mantei (1929) 134 (NY) Misc. 529, 236 NYS 122 (Turk,J)

6   Lisenba v California (1941) 314 US 219, 236, 86 L ed 166, 180 (Roberts,J)

7   See 11 Am.Jur. 1121

"A litigant is entitled to the honest, unbiased judgment of the judges of those courts before whom his case comes."   Deppe v General Motors Corp. (1942) 131 F2d 379, 382 (Biggs,Cir.J)

hensible his conduct may appear to have been, he has that right,[8] for it is elementary that all men—whether they themselves be just or unjust,[9] or whether they be rich or poor,[10]—stand equally before a court,[11] enjoying the equal protection of the law[12] and receiving justice upon the same terms.[13] Doubtless a judge ought not to give judgment until he has "examined the truth" of the matter,[14] for though he decide justly he cannot be considered just if he decides without hearing both sides.[15] Nor is a trial fair if it is dominated by a mob,[16] as the trial of Jesus appears to have been.[17]

Justice ought also to be dispensed speedily, no doubt, without unduly postponing or prolonging the trial.[18] So it appears that Artaxerxes commanded Ezra to "let judgment be executed speedily" upon "whosoever will not do the law . . . whether it be unto death, or to banishment, or to confiscation of goods, or to imprisonment."[19]

---

8 Garza v State (1942) 160 SW2d (Tex. Crim.App.) 926, 928 (Graves,J) "given . . . by the same law that protects us all."

9 Matt. 5:45

10 See supra §50

11 Safety Casualty Co. v Wright (1942) 160 SW2d (Tex.) 238, 243 (Critz,J) saying that "All litigants stand equally before our courts."

"Equality before the law" is a basic principle. State v Wallace (1942) 131 P2d (Or.) 222,251 (Kelly,CJ, dissenting)

But this means "practical equality." Courts should take care that in achieving theoretical equality they do not produce practical inequality.

12 State v Wallace (1942) 131 P2d (Or.) 222,241 (Brand,J) observing that "Rich and poor should enjoy equal protection of the law."

13 Gould & Co. v Atlanta (1878) 60 Ga. 164 (Bleckley,J) saying that "right is free to all upon the same terms."

14 Ecclesiasticus 11:7 ("Blame not before thou hast examined the truth: understand first and then rebuke")

15 Ex. 22:9 ("the cause of both parties shall come before the judges")

"A litigant is entitled . . . to a full hearing and to full argument in order that the merits of his side of the controversy may be established." Deppe v General Motors Corp. (1942) 131 F2d 379, 382 (Biggs,Cir.J)

16 Moore v Dempsey (1923) 261 US 86, 67 L ed 543 (Holmes,J)

17 See supra §383

A trial may not be said to be fair if the prosecutor knowingly introduces perjured testimony. Mooney v Holohan (1935) 294 US 103, 79 L ed 791, 98 ALR 406

Or if he procures a conviction upon an involuntary confession obtained through coercion or torture. Chambers v Florida (1940) 309 US 227, 84 L ed 716 (Black,J); Brown v Mississippi (1935) 297 US 278, 80 L ed 682 (Hughes,CJ)

Such a trial does not observe "that fundamental fairness essential to the very concept of justice." Lesenba v California (1941) 314 US 219, 236, 86 L ed adv.opns. 166, 180 (Roberts,J)

It is but a pretense. People v Gonzales (1942) 20 Cal.2d 165, 170, 124 P2d 44 (Traynor,J)

18 "The prompt disposition of controversies is calculated to promote justice." Union Cent. Life Ins. Co. v Sobelson (1942) 46 F.Supp. 931, 932 (Byers,DJ)

19 Ezra 7:26

"And whosoever shall transgress against the law of thy God, and of the king, shall be punished diligently, whether it be by death, or other punishment, or by penalty of money, or by imprisonment." 1 Esd. 8:24

CHAPTER 63

THE JUDGES

[§438] The nature of man being such that disputes arise and wrongs are committed from time to time, it is essential to a peaceful society that there be someone to determine who is right and who is wrong[20] and to declare what shall be done.[21] This officer is called a judge, whose function it is to interpret and apply the law,[22] to determine the rights of individuals in particular cases,[23] and to declare the penalties which shall be inflicted upon wrongdoers.[24] The authority of a judge is to be measured by the law with which he deals.[25] So if he administers the law of the land,[26] his authority is confined within the bounds of the state or locality.[27]

[§439] Under Primitive law, the judge was seemingly the chief officer of government[28]—more respected by the people than any other.[29] The Lord was considered as "the Judge of all the earth,"[30] and in the earliest cases mentioned in the Scriptures, it appears that the Lord himself was judge.[31] In later cases, the judge was considered as the representative of God—"the Lord was with the judge"[32] and the judgment was regarded as coming from the Lord.[33] The primitive judge was expected to administer justice directly and swiftly,[34] de-

---

20 Civil suits, see infra §§448-459

21 Internoscia's Internat. L. (1910) xi

22 See supra §41 et seq.

23 See supra §126

24 See supra §411 et seq.
 Criminal prosecutions, see infra §§460-472

25 See supra §5 et seq.

26 See supra §34

27 Pennoyer v Neff (1877) 95 US 714, 720, 24 L ed 565 (Field,J)

28 See 29 Yale LJ (1920) 371 (Green)
 Officers generally, see supra §88 et seq.

29 Respect of officials generally, see supra §109
 The primitive reverence for judges was due, no doubt, to the fact that they were also priests (see infra §440) and though they are no longer selected from

the priesthood, they continue to be regarded, among the people, as sacred personages. Even in modern America, and notwithstanding the almost complete separation of church and state (see supra §86), judges are not usually regarded as being subject to the ordinary human weaknesses or the frailties of old age.

30 Gen. 18:25
 ". . . God is judge himself." Ps. 50:6
 ". . . the Lord the Judge be judge this day between the children of Israel and the children of Ammon." Judges 11:27

31 See supra §§341, 343, 369

32 Judges 2:18

33 Prov. 29:26 ("every man's judgment cometh from the Lord"); and see 12 Gr.B. (1900) 6 (Amram)

34 See 13 Gr.B. (1901) 200 (Amram)

ciding correctly—upon the most inadequate evidence—which of the parties to a controversy was in the right and which in the wrong, or determining the guilt or innocence of one accused of crime and meeting out punishment according to the offense,[35] as did the Lord in the Case of Adam, and Eve, and the Serpent,[36] and in Cain's Case.[37] It was also thought that the wise judge might arrive at the truth of a controversy by some dramatic test, as did Solomon in the Case of the Two Harlots.[38]

[§440] Moses was a judge—the people came to him to inquire of God for the purpose of settling their disputes.[39] But later the law was ordinarily administered by judges, who were usually selected from the priesthood[40] and who served terms of various length. Thus it appears that "Jephthah judged Israel six years,"[41] Ibzan seven years,[42] Abdon eight years,[43] Elon 10 years,[44] Samson 20 years,[45] Jair 22 years,[46] Tola 23 years,[47] and Eli 40 years,[48] and that Samuel, the prophet, "judged Israel all the days of his life."[49] At one time a woman "judged Israel." It is related that—

". . . Deborah, a prophetess, the wife of Lapidoth . . . judged Israel . . . And she dwelt under the palm tree of Deborah, between Ramah and Beth-el in mount Ephraim: and the children of Israel came up to her for judgment."[50]

Under the Talmud there were three classes of courts: (1) The Court of Three, (2) The Lesser Sanhedrin, and (3) The Greater Sanhedrin.[1]

35 See supra §415

36 Gen. 3:1-19; and see supra §§341,343

37 See supra §369

38 See supra §221

39 See 14 Harv.LR (1901) 517 (Thayer), and see infra §442

40 See Ezek. 44:24, stating that "in controversy" the priests "shall stand in judgment."

In Palestine at the present time, Jewish courts are presided over by a rabbi. An appeal lies to the Rabbinical Council.

41 Judges 12:7

42 Judges 12:8,9

43 Judges 12:14

44 Judges 12:11

45 Judges 15:20, 16:31

46 Judges 10:3

47 Judges 10:2

48 1 Sam. 4:18

49 1 Sam. 7:15

50 Judges 4:4,5

1 The Court of Three was a tribunal of three judges who heard civil cases and only minor criminal cases where the penalty was flagellation. The Lesser Sanhedrin was composed of 23 judges. It was established in every town having a male population of 120 or more, and had jurisdiction in civil cases and in criminal cases where the punishment was less than capital. The Great Sanhedrin was the highest court in Judea. Its position was similar to that of the Roman Senate. It was composed of 71 judges and had supreme authority in civil, criminal, religious, political, and social questions. Its decision was final. 38 Case & Comment (1932) No. 2, p 4 (Goldberg)

[§441]   Anciently it was the custom for kings to officiate as judges[2]—to "sit in the throne of judgment"[3]—even though there were ordinary judges appointed for that purpose.[4]   Indeed it was considered as one of the most important functions of a king to "execute judgment and justice"[5]—"not according to the methods of the tiresome lawyers . . . but in the manner of the noble prince, with royal dignity, with worldly wisdom and with swift hand."[6]   Thus it appears that David "executed judgment,"[7] and so did Solomon.[8]   Absalom also assumed to act as a judge, because the king had deputed no one to hear controversies, thereby seeking to win the affection of the people.[9]

In the middle ages not only the king, but every noble, was regarded as being a fountain of justice, though the ordinary work of administering justice was delegated to more learned but usually venal judges.[10]   And in modern times also the executive authority has tended to encroach upon the judiciary,[11] even as the judiciary has encroached upon the legislative authority by assuming the power to determine the validity of laws.

[§442]   After the exodus of the Israelites from Egypt, Moses not only led and governed them, but also heard and determined their private controversies.[12]   But it soon became necessary to appoint other judges to hear minor matters, and it appears that the appointment of such judges was suggested to Moses by his father-in-law.

". . . when Moses' father in law saw all that he did to the people, he said, What is this thing that thou doest to the people? why sitteth thou thyself alone, and all the people stand by thee from morning unto even?

"And Moses said unto his father in law, Because the people come unto me to enquire of God:

"When they have a matter, they come unto me; and I judge between one and another, and I do make them know the statutes of God, and his laws.

2 See supra §94

3 Prov. 20:8

4 Appointment of judges, see infra §444

5 See supra §§94, 95

6 12 Gr.B. (1900) 485, 486 (Amram)

7 1 Sam. 8:15

8 See 1 Kings 3:16-28; and see supra §221

9 2 Sam. 15:1-6

10 3 Ky.St. Bar Jour. (1939) No. 4, p

24 (Lummus) observing further that "Justice was bought and sold, and litigants were expected to make presents to the judges. As late as the time of Lord Bacon, he accepted presents from the parties . . . Only gradually did the bench, even in England, become free from bribery. Personal influence and lobbying continued much longer than bribery."

11 See supra §87 as to the separation of government into three departments

12 Ex. 18:13; and see supra §87

"And Moses' father in law said unto him, The thing that thou doest is not good.

"Thou wilt surely wear away, both thou, and this people that is with thee: for this thing is too heavy for thee; thou art not able to perform it thyself alone.

"Hearken now unto my voice, I will give thee counsel, and God shall be with thee: Be thou for the people to God-ward, that thou mayest bring the causes unto God:

"And thou shalt teach them ordinances and laws, and shalt shew them the way wherein they must walk, and the work that they must do.

"Moreover thou shalt provide out of all the people able men, such as fear God, men of truth, hating covetousness; and place such over them, to be rulers of thousands, and rulers of hundreds, rulers of fifties, and rulers of tens.

"And let them judge the people at all seasons: and it shall be, that every great matter they shall bring unto thee, but every small matter they shall judge: so shall it be easier for thyself, and they shall bear the burden with thee.

"If thou shalt do this thing, and God command thee so, then thou shalt be able to endure, and all this people shall also go to their place in peace.

"So Moses hearkened to the voice of his father in law, and did all that he had said.

"And Moses chose able men out of all Israel, and made them heads over the people, rulers of thousands, rulers of hundreds, rulers of fifties, and rulers of tens.

"And they judged the people at all seasons: the hard causes they brought unto Moses, but every small matter they judged themselves."[13]

By a subsequent provision of Mosaic law, it was commanded that—

"Judges and officers shalt thou make thee in all thy gates, which the Lord thy God giveth thee, throughout thy tribes: and they shall judge the people with just judgment."[14]

Pursuant to this provision, it is related that Jehoshaphat "set judges in the land throughout all the fenced cities of Judah, city by city,"[15] and in Jerusalem he "set of the Levites, and of the priests, and of the chief of the fathers of Israel, for the judgment . . . for controversies."[16] And in the time of Ezra, king Artaxerxes of Persia commanded that "judges and justices" be ordained to judge "all those that know the law."[17]

[§443] In primitive society, when judges were chosen from the priesthood, the qualifications of a judge were doubtless those of a priest—piety and learning.[18] Under ancient

---

13 Ex. 18:14-26; 14 Harv.LR (1901) 509 (Thayer)
14 Deut. 16:18
15 2 Chron. 19:5
16 2 Chron. 19:8
17 1 Esd. 8:23; see also Ezra 7:25
18 See supra §440

Talmudic law, a judge was required to be a worthy man, pious, of good character, and learned in the languages and sciences as well as in the law of his day.[19]   And according to the New Testament a judge must fear God and have due regard for his fellow man. He is an "unjust judge" if he fears not God nor regards man, but gives justice lest he become weary of being troubled by those who seek it.[20]   Also in America it is recognized that a judge ought to be a man of wisdom, uprightness and learning.[21]

Though a judge is doubtless "made of the same stuff as other men,"[22] it is considered that he must be "perfectly and completely independent, with nothing to influence or control him but God and his conscience."[23]   He must be free from all bias or partiality.[23a]

"He cannot be both judge and party, arbiter and advocate in the same cause. Mankind are so agreed in this principle that any departure from it shocks their common sense and sentiment of justice."[24]

[§444]   A judge must be appointed or chosen by some competent authority,[25] such as the king,[26] or a retiring judge,[27] or perhaps by the people themselves.[27a]   It was considered improper for one to judge others in the absence of authority to do so.[28]   Thus it appears that when Moses went out and saw two men of the Hebrews that "strove together," and "said to

19 38 Case & Comment (1932) No. 2, p 5 (Goldberg) observing further that a judge "had to be affable, democratic, and of good appearance. No unmarried man could be a judge. No bribery of judges was ever heard of. Even manifestation of unusual kindness on the part of a judge was frowned upon. Originally the judges were not paid and they made their livelihood at a trade. However those who devoted their entire time to the law were paid."

The Chan Aruch provided: "Each judge shall have the following qualifications: wisdom, humanity, fear of God, be a foe to money, have the love of mankind, he must be loving and truthful, he must love a good name." 44 Case & Comment (1939) No. 6, p 15

20 Luke 18:2-6

21 These are the words used in a commission by the President of the United States appointing a Justice of the Supreme Court: "Know Ye: That reposing special trust and confidence in the Wisdom, Uprightness, and Learning of . . . I have nominated and, by and with the advice and consent of the Senate, do appoint him an Associate Justice

of the Supreme Court of the United States . . ."

22 State v Frazier (1918) 102 Wash. 369, 385, 173 P 35 (Chadwick,J)

23 United States v Manton (1938) 107 Fed.2d 834, 846, quoting Marshall,CJ

23a This was true under ancient Talmudic law. 38 Case & Comment (1932) No. 2, p 5

24 Oakley v Aspinwall (1850) 3 NY 547, 549 (Hurlbut,J)

25 See History of Susanna, v 5 ("The same year were appointed two of the ancients of the people to be judges")

26 Ex. 18:25, 26 ("Moses chose able men out of all Israel . . . and they judged the people")
Or by the chief executive, that is, the governor or president.

27 1 Sam. 8:1 ("when Samuel was old . . . he made his sons judges over Israel")

27a That is, by popular election. But this is of doubtful propriety for the people cannot ordinarily know whether a man is properly qualified to be a judge

28 Matt. 7:1 ("Judge not, that ye be not judged")

him that did the wrong. Wherefore smitest thou thy fellow?" the wrongdoer answered, "Who made thee . . . a judge over us?"[29] Similarly when Jesus was solicited to direct a man to divide his inheritance with his brother, he replied, "Man, who made me a judge or a divider over you?"[30]

[§445] In addition to the local judges who resided in each city and village, it appears that at one time the chief or supreme judge of the land travelled about from place to place to hear the more difficult and important cases and also, no doubt, to instruct and supervise the work of the inferior judges. The first judge who is mentioned in the Scriptures as having travelled in this manner was Samuel. It is said that—

". . . he went from year to year in circuit to Beth-el, and Gilgal, and Mizpeh, and judged Israel in all those places.

"And his return was to Ramah; for there was his house; and there he judged Israel . . ."[31]

[§446] The duties of a judge, according to Biblical law, are summarized in the charge of Moses.

". . . Hear the causes between your brethren, and judge righteously between every man and his brother, and the stranger that is with him.

"Ye shall not respect persons in judgment; but ye shall hear the small as well as the great; ye shall not be afraid of the face of man; for the judgment is God's: and the cause that is too hard for you, bring it unto me (Moses), and I will hear it."[32]

29 Ex. 2:13,14
30 Luke 12:13,14
31 1 Sam. 7:16,17
32 Deut. 1:16,17
"Ye shall do no unrighteousness in judgments: thou shalt not respect the person of the poor, nor honour the person of the mighty: but in righteousness shalt thou judge thy neighbour." Lev. 19:15
". . . Take heed what ye do: for ye judge not for man, but for the Lord, who is with you in the judgment.
"Wherefore now let the fear of the Lord be upon you; take heed and do it: for there is no iniquity with the Lord our God, nor respect of persons, nor taking of gifts.
". . . Thus shall ye do in the fear of the Lord, faithfully, and with a perfect heart.

"And what cause soever shall come to you of your brethren that dwell in their cities, between blood and blood, between law and commandment, statutes and judgments, ye shall even warn them that they trespass not against the Lord, and so wrath come upon you, and upon your brethren; this do, and ye shall not trespass." 2 Chron. 19:6,7,9,10
A judge of a court of the United States is required to take an oath of office which contains, among other things, a declaration that "I will administer justice without respect to persons, and do equal right to the poor and to the rich; and that I will faithfully and impartially discharge and perform all the duties incumbent on me as a judge." 42 Wash.L.Rep. (1914) 770, 771 (Barnard)

A judge is bound to do no "unrighteousness in judgment,"[33] but to "do justice"[34] and "judge righteously,"[35] not "according to the appearance"[36] but according to the law[37] and the facts.[38] It is incumbent upon him to "hold the scales with even hand"[39] and to give judgment without "respect of persons."[40] So he must not yield to the influence of partiality[41] or prejudice[42] or sentiment,[43] nor should he "seek out strained

---

[33] Lev. 19:15,35
"Woe unto them that decree unrighteous decrees, and that write grievousness which they have prescribed. To turn aside the needy from judgment, and to take away the right from the poor of my people, that widows may be their prey, and that they may rob the fatherless!" Isa. 10:1,2

[34] 2 Sam. 15:4; and see supra §§31, 432
"The court seeks to bring all parties before it and to do justice; to protect and care for their interests, even, at times, against themselves." 1 RCL 422 (Davids) referring to admiralty courts.

"Courts, in civilized communities, should do more than decide cases, one way or another, without regard to consideration of justice, merely to prevent private brawls and breaches of the peace. Government . . . through its courts . . . should try, as far as possible, to decide cases correctly—both by ascertaining the actual facts, as near as may be, and then by applying correct legal rules in an effort to do justice to the parties affected by their decisions. And not merely the parties, but the public as well, are interested that justice shall be done." In re Barnett (1942) 124 Fed.2d 1005, 1010 (Frank, Cir.J)

[35] Ps. 72:2 ("He [the king] shall judge thy people with righteousness") Prov. 31:9 ("judge righteously"); Wisdom of Soloman 1:1 ("Love righteousness, ye that be judges of the earth"); Zech. 8:16 ("execute the judgment of truth and peace in your gates")

[36] John 7:24 ("Judge not according to the appearance, but judge righteous judgment")

[37] Ezek. 44:24 ("they shall judge . . . according to my judgments: and they shall keep my laws and my statutes"); John 18:31 ("Then said Pilate . . . judge him according to your law")
"The judges must decide according to the law." Jackson's Lessee v Burns (1810) 3 Binney (Pa.) 75, 85 (Tilghman,CJ)
They may follow the spirit rather than the letter of the law. See supra §42
But they should not pervert the law from its original intention, as federal judges did the Sherman Anti-trust Act,

"which was passed . . . to check the tyranny of the combined money power of the country" but was construed "so as to operate against the freedom and liberty" of laboring men. 29 Va.LR 305 (Boudin) quoting Senator Williams

[38] See supra §46, n 4
"Each case is dependent upon its own factual situation." Willoughby v Driscoll (1942) 120 P2d (Or.) 768, 772 (Belt,J)
It "must be decided upon its own facts." Ulrich v Zimmerman (1942) 163 SW2d (Mo.) 567, 574 (Dalton,C)
"The . . . judge may be mistaken as to what is just and right in the case," but he ought not to be "prevented by any impediment . . . from doing what he believes to be justice." 1 RCL 422 (Davids)

[39] "The ancients often painted Justice as blindfolded, so that parties could not be seen, and holding the scales with even hand. So we should be careful not to know the parties to this suit, and to try the cause as the law and testimony demand." Murphy v Western & A. R. Co. (1885) 23 Fed.637, 21 A&E RR Cases 258, 259 (Key,J)

[40] See supra §50
"We . . . are bound by every tie of religion and duty to see that . . . justice shall flow in her usual and accustomed channels without respect to persons." Respublica v Dennie (1805) 4 Yeates (Pa.) 267, 2 AD 402, 403 (Yeates, J)

[41] See supra §50

[42] "In order to be prepared to decide legal controversies justly, the judge . . . should be careful to avoid the influence of partiality or prejudice." Murphy v Western A. R. Co. (1885) 23 Fed. 637, 21 A&E RR Cases 258 (Key,J)

[43] Ecclesiasticus 4:9 ("be not fainthearted when thou sittest in judgment") ; and see supra §425
"Mere sentiment is not of value in a judicial proceeding." Craig v First Presbyterian Church (1879) 88 Pa. St. 42, 32 AR 417, 424 (Paxson,J
A judge must not suffer his feelings for one party to carry him so far as to do injustice to the other. Willis' Lessee v Bucher (1810) 2 Binney (Pa.) 455, 467 (Tilghman,CJ)

analogies"[44] or "blind himself to realities by a slavish adherence to technicalities."[45]

On the other hand, the law prescribes that the judge shall "justify the righteous, and condemn the wicked;"[46] it is his duty to administer justice to the poor,[47] to "break in pieces the oppressor,"[48] to "deliver him that is spoiled"[49] or "suffereth wrong from the hand of the oppressor,"[50] and to "save the children of the needy."[1]

Doubtless also it is incumbent upon the judge to instruct the people,[2] and to see that the "wicked doth (not) compass about the righteous"[3] in the "place of judgment."[4]

[§447] According to Biblical law, a judge is not merely an oracle,[5] nor is he an umpire presiding over a game[6] of chance or of wits,[7] for it is his duty to uphold the law and not to see justice done only, but to do justice[8]—

". . . requiting the wicked, by recompensing his way upon his own head[9] and . . . justifying the righteous, by giving him according to his righteousness."[10]

His duty is affirmative and positive: it is not adequately performed "by sitting on a bench and watching justice float by."[11] When a trial is being had, the judge should be "a living

---

44 "It is not the province of the courts to seek out strained analogies, or to delve in the debris of a rejected and barbarous legal system, to defeat and set aside steps which the legislature may take in accord with the spirit of an advancing civilization." Gill v Board of Commissioners (1912) 160 NC 176, 76 SE 203, 43 LRANS 293, 302 (Clark,CJ, dissenting)

45 This is not "consonant with justice." Lyons v Brunswick-Balke-Collender Co. (1942) 20 Cal.2d 579, 127 P2d 924 (Carter,J)

46 Deut. 25:1 ("If there be a controversy between men, and they come unto judgment, that the judges may judge them; then they shall justify the righteous, and condemn the wicked")

47 Ps. 72:2,4
"Defend the poor and fatherless: do justice to the afflicted and needy. Deliver the poor and needy: rid them out of the hand of the wicked." Ps. 82:3,4

48 Ps. 72:4

49 Jer. 21:12 ("Execute judgment in the morning, and deliver him that is spoiled out of the hand of the oppressor")

50 Ecclesiasticus 4:9

1 Ps. 72:4

2 Ecclesiasticus 10:1

3 Hab. 1:4 ("the law is slacked, and judgment doth not go forth: for the wicked doth compass about the righteous; therefore wrong judgment proceedeth")

4 Ecclesiastes 3:16 ("I saw . . . the place of judgment, that wickedness was there")

5 Rudd v United States (1909) 173 Fed 912 (Hook,J)

6 3 Wigmore's Evidence (3d ed 1940) §784; In re Barnett (1942) 124 Fed.2d 1005, 1010 (Frank,Cir.J)

7 Laverett v Continental Briar Pipe Co. (1938) 25 F. Supp. 80, 83 (Moscowitz,DJ)

8 See supra §446

9 Crime or iniquity is to be punished by the judge. Job 31:11,28

10 2 Chron. 6:23

11 9 Miss.LJ (1937) 398, quoting Judges and Law Reform (1936) by Warner and Cabot
"If judges are to sit idly by and see justice miscarry because defense is more skillful in practice than offense, then we should, in my opinion, abolish the office of judge. But today, at long last, judges are beginning to renounce the servile status of referee between lawyers and are beginning to reassume the office of dispensers of justice between litigants." 44 Case & Comment (1939) No. 5, p 15 (Humphrey)

participant,"[12] not permitting a party to overcome his adversary by "clever ruses, traps, and surprises,"[13] but himself making "diligent inquisition"[14] so that he may "bring forth judgment unto truth."[15]

CHAPTER 64

CIVIL SUITS

[§448]   The Scriptural record contains but few references to suits between individuals, not that there was a scarcity of controversies or disputes in ancient times—judges having been needed even in primitive society[16]—but because the proceedings were informal and were seemingly conducted without the aid of lawyers.[17]   Mosaic law provided for the hearing and decision of causes by judges,[18] and it is related that "all that had any suits in law came unto" them.[19]   Even women were permitted to bring their suits before the judges, as did the daughters of Zelophehad.[20]   And with respect to "trespasses," the law prescribed that "for all manner of trespass . . . the cause of both parties shall come before the judges."[21] But it was recognized as being inexpedient to "go to law with a judge,"[22] and that one should not so conduct himself that he will "fall into suits."[23]

[§449]   The bringing of a law suit—even the making of a defense in such a suit[24]—is seemingly against the Christian

---

12 Rudd v United States (1909) 173 Fed. 912 (Hook,J)
But a judge should not participate in a case where he has been entertained by one of the parties. See Pearce v Affleck (1812) 4 Binney (Pa.) 344, 349 et seq. (Brackenridge,J)

13 1 RCL 422 (Davids)

14 Deut. 19:18

15 Isa. 42:3

16 See supra §439

17 See supra §433

18 Deut. 1:16
Trial of jealousy, see supra, §113
Trial by gossip, see 16 Tenn.LR (1939) 16 (Sibley)

19 History of Susanna, v 6

20 See supra §139

21 Ex. 22:9

22 Ecclesiasticus 8:14 ("Go not to law with a judge, for they will judge for him according to his honour")

23 Ecclesiasticus 29:19 ("he that undertaketh and followeth other men's business for gain shall fall into suits")

24 Jesus made no defense on his own behalf even when charged with the commission of a crime—when he was "accused of the chief priests and elders, he answered nothing." Matt. 27:12; and see Matt. 27:14; Mark 14:61, 15:3; Luke 23:10; John 19:9

doctrine concerning nonresistence.[25] Jesus commanded that "if any man will sue thee at the law, and take away thy coat, let him have thy cloak also,"[26] and St. Paul, though conceding the "goodness" of law if lawfully used,[27] disapproved of "going to law"—at least of "believers" going to law before "unbelievers."[28]

Under this rule, if a difficulty arises, between two Christians—as where one falls short in the performance of a duty to the other or fails properly to respect his right—a burden rests upon them, no doubt, of meeting together and working out an amicable and reasonable settlement.[29] And where the difficulty is between a Christian and an unbeliever, there must be no controversy.

"If the spirit of the gospel abide with one of the parties, not in word only but in its power, there can be no contest; whatever wrong or injury there may be on the one side—all will be patience and suffering on the other."[30]

[§450] From the beginning, it was a policy of the Christian church to keep litigation within the fold.[31] An injunction of Jesus is considered as having made the church the final arbiter of disputes among its members.

". . . if thy brother shall trespass against thee, go and tell him his fault between thee and him alone: if he shall hear thee, thou hast gained thy brother.

"But if he will not hear thee, then take with thee one or two more, that in the mouth of two or three witnesses every word may be established.

"And if he shall neglect to hear them, tell it unto the church: but if he neglect to hear the church, let him be unto thee as an heathen man and a publican."[32]

Upon this injunction,[33] and upon a later statement by St. Paul, the temporal jurisdiction of the early church was founded.

"Dare any of you, having a matter against another, go to law before the unjust and not before the saints?

"I speak to your shame. Is it so, that there is not a wise man among you? no, not one that shall be able to judge between his brethren?

---

25 See supra §18
26 Matt. 5:40
27 1 Tim. 1:8; and see supra §27
28 See infra §450
29 See infra §451
30 Poor v Poor (1836) 8 NH 307, 29 AD 664, 665 (Richardson,CJ)
31 So that Christians would not resort to heathen courts. See People v Mantei

(1929) 134 (NY) Misc. 529, 236 NYS 122 (Turk,J); and see supra §436
32 Matt. 18:15-17
Reconciliation, see infra §451
33 7 Cal.LR (1918) 103 (Sherman) saying also (p 95) that the very essence of ecclesiastical jurisdiction, with its sanction of excommunication, can be traced to Christ's own words.

"But brother goeth to law with brother, and that before the unbelievers.

"Now therefore there is utterly a fault among you, because ye go to law one with another. Why do ye not rather take wrong? why do ye not rather suffer yourselves to be defrauded?"[34]

In the fourth century,[35] the Roman emperor Constantine gave litigants the privilege of resorting to their bishops, who were authorized to act as arbitrators by consent and whose awards were to be enforced by the civil authorities.[36] And in the ninth century, Charlemagne gave them the right to transfer their causes from secular courts to ecclesiastical tribunals.[37]

In early America—though the country was considered a Christian country and its courts were doubtless regarded as Christian courts—various church authorities exercised consent jurisdiction over controversies among their members.[38] So it has been said of presbyteries and general assemblies that—

". . . although they are not courts of justice, they are bodies enjoying certain rights, established by long custom, and not forbidden by any law. They can inflict no temporal punishment; and their jurisdiction is founded on the consent of the members of the church. No extensive church can preserve decency, good order, and purity of manners, without discipline. It serves to correct a multitude of evils, which cannot and ought not to be subject to temporal cognizance. It corrects them, too, in a manner the most mild, the most private, and the least scandalous and injurious to religion, in a manner that may reform the offender without exposing him to the open scorn and ridicule of the world; circumstances which sometimes render men desperate. A jurisdiction of this kind, exercised only over those who consent to it, certainly must be productive of good effects . . ."[39]

[§451] It is an old doctrine that one should attempt a reconciliation with his adversary before commencing a suit against him at law, or even before making a complaint against him to an ecclesiastical tribunal,[40] where such a course is authorized and he chooses to pursue it.

Mosaic law required that "thou shalt in any wise rebuke thy neighbour"[41] meaning that one should "debate his cause" with

34 1 Cor. 6:1,5-7

35 About 323 A.D.

36 No appeal was allowed to the civil courts.

This legislation was re-affirmed by the emperors Honorius, Valentinian and Justinian.

37 7 Cal.LR (1918) 103, 104 (Sherman)

38 The bylaws or "disciplines" of various sects still provide for the settlement of disputes among their members by church trial. Such trials are thought to be infrequent, however, except as regards doctrinal or moral offenses against the church.

39 M'Millan v Birch (1806) 1 Binney (Pa.) 178, 2 AD 426, 429, 430 (Tilghman,CJ)

40 See supra §450

41 Lev. 19:17

his neighbour himself,[42] and that he should "admonish" his neighbor before threatening him.[43]

Under Christian law, also, one must go to a brother who has trespassed against him "and tell him his fault between thee and him alone."[44]

". . . If thy brother trespass against thee, rebuke him; and if he repent, forgive him.

"And if he trespass against thee seven times in a day, and seven times in a day turn again to thee, saying, I repent; thou shalt forgive him."[45]

It has been said that one should not "regard persons" when rebuking for transgressions.[46] But one should not "rebuke" his "neighbour at the wine" or "give him . . . despiteful words."[47]

If the adversary will not be admonished nor repent, one may properly "give place to the law."[48] A "trespasser" who will "hear neither the man against whom he trespassed, nor his witnesses, nor the church, shall be accounted a 'heathen'."[49] He may be sued if that is deemed expedient.

[§452] In conducting a trial under Biblical law, the judge seated himself upon the judgment seat and the parties came before him.[50] It was incumbent upon a party to "produce his cause"[1]—that is, to make his complaint and offer his evidence,[2] including the testimony of his witnesses[3]—and to "bring forth" his "strong reasons."[4] Before rendering judgment, it was the rule for the judge to state the case of both parties, as Solomon did in the Case of the Two Harlots.[5]

---

42 Prov. 25:9

43 Ecclesiasticus 19:17

44 Matt. 18:15; and see supra §450

45 Luke 17:3,4

46 Two Ways 4:3

Meaning, no doubt, that one should as readily "rebuke'" one who is rich or powerful as one who is poor or weak.

47 Ecclesiasticus 31:31

48 Ecclesiasticus 19:17

49 See supra §450

50 See supra §435

The ancient trial before elders was the forerunner of the trial by jury, which became established in England after 1066. For centuries the jury has consisted of 12 men. In "Guide to English Juries" (1682) it is said "In analogy of late the jury is reduced to the number of 12, like the prophets were 12 to foretell the truth, the Apostles 12 to preach the truth; the discoverers 12, sent into Canaan to seek and report

the truth; and the stones 12 that the heavenly Jerusalem is built on."

1 Isa. 41:22

2 Evidence is offered of "things not seen" (Heb. 11:1) or known to the judge. It is unnecessary to prove matters of common knowledge, which the judge knows or must be supposed to know, as an intelligent member of the community. So a party need not offer evidence of a statement in the Bible in a case where such statement is material. A court or judge will take judicial notice of the contents of the Bible. Herold v Parish School Directors (1915) 136 La. 1034, 68 So. 116, LRA 1915D 941, 943

When it is desired to prove relationship or the date and fact of birth, marriage or death, entries in a family Bible are generally admissible. See annotations in 111 ASR 586, 41 LRA 449, 29 ALR 372

3 See infra §453

4 Isa. 41:22

5 1 Kings 3:23; and see supra §221

[§453]   The parties to a suit were bound to "bring forth their witnesses"[6] to bear witness or declare that which they have heard, which they have seen with their eyes, which they have looked upon, and their hands have handled.[7] Witnesses were expected to be, not false and deceitful, but faithful and true,[8] but two witnesses were nevertheless required, it seems, in order to establish any disputed fact.[9]

Ordinarily a man may be compelled to testify concerning facts within his knowledge,[10] but it is recognized that a minister or priest ought not to be so required as to things told him in confidence, for a man sometimes needs a place for repentance, that he be not like Esau "who found no place for repentance, though he sought it carefully with tears."[11]

[§454]   —— The oath of a witness was originally an appeal to God to bear witness to the truth of his testimony and to visit vengeance upon him if it should be false.[12] Anciently it seems to have been customary for a witness to take such an oath,[13] and this sacramental observance, with some modifications, has continued through the ages.[14]

At common law testimony was not received from any person in a court of justice but under the sanction of an oath,[15] and

---

6 Isa. 43:9 ("let them bring forth their witnesses, that they may be justified")

7 1 John 1:1

8 Prov. 14:5,25

9 See infra §470

10 28 RCL 419

11 Heb. 12:17

12 Atwood v State (1927) 146 Miss. 662, 111 So. 865, 51 ALR 836 (Anderson, J)

13 See Gen. 31:50 ("God is witness betwixt me and thee"); Judges 11:10 ("the Lord be witness between us"); Heb. 10:15 ("the Holy Ghost is a witness") But under ancient Talmudic law, witnesses are said not to have been put under oath. See 38 Case & Comment (1932) No. 2, p 5

14 See 14 Harv.LR (1901) 509 (Thayer)

15 "Every person who does not believe in the obligation of an oath and a future state of rewards and punishments, or any accountability after death for his conduct, is by law excluded from being a witness, for to such person the law presumes no credit to be given. . . . It would therefore be idle to administer an oath to a man who disregarded its obligation. And every person who believes in the obligation of an oath . . . whatever may be his religious creed, whether Christian, Mohammedan, or pagan, or whether he disbelieves them all, is an admissible witness, and may testify in a court of justice, being sworn according to that form of an oath which, according to his creed, he holds to be obligatory. The law which requires that testimony shall be given under oath, has something more in view than to lay the witness under an obligation to speak the truth for fear of incurring its penalties. If it had not, there would be no necessity that there should be any appeal to God, and the form of the oath would be very different from its present form. There can be no doubt but that the law intended that the fear of offending God should have its influence upon a witness to induce him to speak the truth. But no such influence can be expected from the man who disregards an oath. He is, therefore, excluded from being a witness." Curtiss v Strong (1809), 4 Day (Conn.) 51 4 AD 179, 180, where the court found that Ebenezer Robinson, who was offered as a witness, did not believe in the obligation of an oath, or in a future state of rewards and punishments, or any accountability for his conduct after death, at the date of the will, or at any time since. He, therefore, could not be admitted as a witness.

it was held that no infidel could be sworn as a witness.[16] But this rule has been relaxed in England and most of the American states by permitting a witness to make such an oath as accords with his particular belief or merely to affirm that his testimony shall be true.[17]

[§455] Mosaic law provided a kind of appeal to be taken to the chief judge of the land in cases which involved "great matters"[18] or were too "hard" for inferior judges to decide. It is related that the judges chosen by Moses

". . . judged the people at all seasons: the hard causes they brought unto Moses, but every small matter they judged themselves."[19]

And later the rule was established that—

"If there arise a matter too hard for thee in judgment, between blood and blood, between plea and plea, and between stroke and stroke, being matters of controversy within thy gates: then shalt thou arise, and get thee up into the place which the Lord thy God shall choose:

"And thou shalt come unto the priests the Levites, and unto the judge that shall be in those days, and enquire; and they shall shew thee the sentence of judgment:

"And thou shalt do according to the sentence, which they of that place which the Lord shall choose shall shew thee; and thou shalt observe to do according to all that they inform thee:

"According to the sentence of the law which they shall teach thee, and according to the judgment which they shall tell thee, thou shalt do:

16 This rule included Jews for the reason that the Old Scriptures do not teach a future life, and hence there is absent therefrom the doctrine of future rewards and punishments. State v Pitt (1914) 166 NC 268, 80 SE 1060, AnnCas 1916C 422, 424 (Clark,CJ)

17 14 Harv.LR (1901) 523 (Thayer)
In modern Anglo-American law, "Jews may be sworn on the Pentateuch with covered head; Mohametans, upon the Koran; Gentoos, by touching the foot of a Brahmin (or priest); Chinese, by the ceremony of killing a cock or breaking a saucer, the witness declaring that, if he speaks falsely, his soul will be similarly dealt with; a Scotch Covenanter and a member of the Scottish Kirk, by holding up the hand without kissing the Book. Quakers and others, who profess to entertain conscientious scruples against taking an oath in the usual form, are allowed an affirmation —i.e., a solemn religious asseveration that their testimony shall be true." 3 Jones' Evidence in Civil Cases, 4th ed., p 1282

In the District of Columbia in 1866, the form of the oath was: "You do solemnly swear on the holy Evangely of Almighty God, that the evidence you will give in the case now on trial, shall be the truth, the whole truth, and nothing but the truth, so help you God." This was followed by the witness kissing the Bible. Since then the words "the holy Evangely of Almighty God" have been dropped from the oath, and the requirement that the witness actually kiss the book is not now insisted upon. If the witness is of the Jewish faith, instead of being sworn on the Holy Evangely, or as other witnesses are sworn, the Bible is opened, and his hand placed on some part of the five books of Moses, and the oath was, and still is, administered in that way. This is supposed to be the most effective way to make the oath binding on the conscience, swearing by the law, or on the law." 42 Wash.L.Rep. (1914) 771, 772 (Barnard,J)

18 Ex. 18:22 ("every great matter they shall bring unto thee, but every small matter they shall judge")

19 Ex. 18:26

thou shalt not decline from the sentence which they shall shew thee, to the right hand, nor to the left."[20]

In the Case of the Daughters of Zelophehad,[21] it appears that "the chief fathers of the families of the children of Gilead" appealed or reopened the proceeding for the purpose of obtaining a ruling as to the marriage of the daughters.[22]

[§456] The law of damages is that one who injures or wrongs another shall make reparation or restitution.[23] Rules concerning the duty of restitution, and the amount or measure of damages, are stated in the Scriptures.[24] Thus restitution is required of a thief,[25] of one who causes a field or vineyard of another to be "eaten,"[26] or one who kindles a fire which escapes and burns "stacks of corn, or the standing corn, or the field" of another;[27] of a bailee from whom an animal delivered to be kept is stolen;[28] and of one who kills an animal belonging to another.[29] One who commits an assault upon another with a stone or with his fist is required to pay for the loss of his victim's time and to cause him to be thoroughly healed.[30] The owner of an ox that gores another's manservant or maidservant is required to pay thirty shekels of silver to the master.[31] And the seducer of a damsel is required to pay fifty shekels of silver to her father.[32] Similarly, a husband

---

20 Deut. 17:8-11
The "appeal" was seemingly taken by the inferior judge himself to obtain guidance from the higher tribunal, rather than by the unsuccessful party in an effort to overturn the decision against him or to delay its enforcement. The proceeding was similar to that of Texas where the intermediate appellate court certifies questions to the Supreme Court and subsequently decides the case according to the answers of the higher tribunal. See 3 Tex.Jur. 309

21 See supra §139

22 See Num. 36:1-6
This was a proceeding for a "declaratory judgment" to determine the rights of the parties prior to a possible marriage of a daughter to one not of the tribe of her father.

23 See 15 AmJur 388
"A wrong-doer is liable for the damages which he causes by his misconduct." Ehrgott v New York (1884) 96 NY 264 (Earl,J) saying, however, that "this rule must be practicable and reasonable, and hence it has its limitations."
Under the Talmud the correct practice was to compensate a wrong by making a suitable money award and

not by committing a similar wrong in retaliation. The ancient Hebrew legal code was more humane than is generally realized. 38 Case & Comment (1932) No. 2, p 2
The famous Code Napoleon, inspirer of all modern civil law codes, provides that—
(Art. 1382) "Every act whatsoever of a human being which causes a damage to another, obliges the one by whose fault it has happened to make reparation for it," and that
(Art. 1383) "Every one is responsible for the damage which he has caused not only by his own act (par son fait), but also by his negligence or by his imprudence." 36 Case & Comment (1930) No. 2, p 13 (Dox)

24 See 42 Wash.L.Rep. (1914) 772 (Barnard)

25 Ex. 22:3; and see supra §375

26 Ex. 22:5; and see supra §179

27 Ex. 22:6; and see supra §178

28 Ex. 22:10,12; and see supra §155

29 Lev. 24:21; and see supra §288

30 Ex. 21:19; and see supra §177

31 Ex. 21:32; and see supra §287

32 Deut. 22:29; and see supra §182

who slanders a newly married wife is required to pay a hundred shekels of silver to the wife's father.[33]

[§457] —— Restitution plus one fifth is the prescribed measure of damages in a variety of circumstances. Mosaic law provides that—

"If a soul . . . commit a trespass . . . and lie unto his neighbour in that which was delivered him to keep, or in fellowship, or a thing taken away by violence, or hath deceived his neighbour;

"Or have found that which was lost, and lieth concerning it, and sweareth falsely; in any of all these that a man doeth, sinning therein:

"Then it shall be, because he hath sinned, and is guilty, that he shall restore that which he took violently away, or the thing which he hath deceitfully gotten, or that which was delivered to him to keep, or the lost thing which he found.

"Or all that about which he hath sworn falsely; he shall even restore it in the principal, and shall add the fifth part more thereto, and give it unto him to whom it appertaineth, in the day of the trespass offering."[34]

[§458] —— Double damages are imposed upon a wrongdoer in certain cases. Thus it is provided that if a stolen animal be found in the thief's hand alive, "whether it be ox or ass, or sheep, he shall restore double,"[35] and that one who steals out of another's house "money or stuff" that had been delivered to the latter to be kept shall pay double.[36] Another provision in reference to damages for "trespass" prescribes that—

"For all manner of trespass, whether it be for ox, for ass, for sheep, for raiment, or for any manner of lost thing, which another challengeth to be his, the cause of both parties shall come before the judges; and whom the judges shall condemn, he shall pay double unto his neighbour."[37]

[§459] —— In other cases an even greater measure of damages is prescribed. Thus it is provided that "if a man shall steal . . . a sheep, and kill it, or sell it; he shall restore . . . four sheep for a sheep," but if he "shall steal an ox . . . and kill it or sell it; he shall restore five oxen for an ox."[38] And it has been said that if a thief stealing to satisfy hunger is found, he shall restore sevenfold.[39]

---

33 Deut. 22:19; and see supra §184
34 Lev. 6:2-5; and see also Num. 5:6-10
35 Ex. 22:3
36 Ex. 22:7

37 Ex. 22:9
38 Ex. 22:1
39 Prov. 6:31; and see supra §375

CHAPTER 65

CRIMINAL PROSECUTIONS

[§460] Criminal prosecutions are the proceedings by which organized society enforces its laws against crime.[40] The Scriptures repeatedly mention such prosecutions, but they give us few details as to the nature of the proceedings, for it seems that anciently a criminal prosecution—like a civil trial —was informal, as judged by modern standards.[41]

The prosecution was doubtless commenced by an accusation, which may have been made by the victim of the crime, or by his next of kin if he was killed, or by those who saw the criminal act committed,[42] or even by the judge himself,[43] acting upon his own knowledge or upon common report,[44] since the judge was more than an umpire:[45] it was his duty, among other things, to make diligent inquiry as to offenses committed within his jurisdiction and to see that offenders were duly punished.[46]

[§461] The requiring of security to keep the peace was a recognized practice in the time of the early Christians. In the Case of Jason, it is related that—

". . . the Jews which believed not . . .
". . . drew Jason and certain brethren unto the rulers of the city, crying, These that have turned the world upside down are come hither also;
"Whom Jason hath received: and these all do contrary to the decrees of Caesar, saying that there is another king, one Jesus.
"And they troubled the people and the rulers of the city, when they heard these things.
"And when they had taken security of Jason, and of the other, they let them go."[47]

[§462] From earliest times it appears not to have been uncommon for offenders to flee to other lands to escape the consequences of their acts. Thus Moses, after killing an

---

40 See 14 AmJur 753
41 See supra §448
42 See supra §388
43 See supra §369

44 See 1 Cor. 5:1
45 See supra §447
46 See supra §446
47 Acts 17:5-9

Egyptian and hiding him in the sand, "fled from the face of Pharaoh, and dwelt in the land of Midian."[48] Since officers may not pursue a criminal into another country,[49] the fugitive was safe from punishment unless he was seized by officers of the latter country and returned to his own land. Under the Roman rule, provision was made for the return of fugitives. Thus in the time of Simon, it is said that Licius, counsel of the Romans, commanded Ptolemee and other kings subject to Rome to deliver "any pestilent fellows" to Simon the high priest, "that he may punish them according to their own law."[50] It is only in modern times that the nations of the earth have assumed the obligation of delivering these fugitives from justice to the states where their crimes were committed, for trial and punishment.[1]

[§463] Mosaic law provided for a kind of inquest to be held when one was "found slain in the land . . . lying in the field, and it be not known who hath slain him."[2] The first step was to "measure unto the cities which are round about him that is slain," for the purpose of determining that one nearest to the place where the body was found, and the one which should therefore have jurisdiction of the offense and should be held responsible to the victim's next of kin.[3] The inquiry was seemingly conducted by "the priests:" it is said that "by their word shall every controversy and every stroke be tried."[4] When the nearest city or town had been ascertained, it became the duty of its elders to perform an expiation ceremony,[5] and also, no doubt, to search for the killer, and to make reparation if they did not find him.[6]

[§464] One of the ancient rights of an accused person is that of being tried in the neighborhood where the offense was committed, that he may not be required to stand trial among strangers,[7] but among neighbors who are "presumed to know things of the neighborhood."[8] So, under Biblical law, a killer should ordinarily be tried at the gate of the city nearest to the place where the body of his victim was found.[9] But in some

48 Ex. 2:15
49 See People v McLeod (1841) 1 Hill (NY) 377, 25 Wend. 483, 37 AD 328
50 1 Mac. 15:21
1 See 15 RCL 132
2 Deut. 21:1
3 See Deut. 21:2-4
4 Deut. 21:5

5 Deut. 21:6-9
6 See 12 Gr.B. (1900) 198 (Amram)
7 Lyons v Brunswick-Balke-Callender Co. (1942) 20 Cal.2d 579, 127 P2d 924, (Carter,J)
8 Armendiaz v Stillman (1881) 54 Tex. 623 (Moore, CJ)
9 See supra §463

circumstances an offender may be sent to another judge or transferred to another place for trial. Thus it appears that when Pilate learned that Jesus "belonged unto Herod's jurisdiction, he sent him to Herod, who himself also was at Jerusalem at that time."[10] In the case of St. Paul, when the Roman administrator had learned of a conspiracy to waylay and kill the prisoner during his examination, he caused him to be removed from Jerusalem and sent to Felix, governor of Caesarea, and notified the accusers to make their charge before the governor.[11] Later, when St. Paul had appealed to Caesar, he was sent to Rome to be tried.[12]

In sending a prisoner to another judge or place for trial, the crime laid against him should be signified.[13]

[§465]   The trial of an offender was conducted by the judge,[14] or perhaps at times by a court of several judges or elders,[15] sitting at the place of judgment,[16] and, the accused having been found guilty[17]—having been "weighed in the balance and found wanting"[18]—punishment was ordinarily inflicted forthwith.[19] The trial was not a mere game or contest between the accused and the community,[20] but an effort to ascertain the truth[21]—to "weigh" the accused "in an even balance"[22]—according him equal rights[23] and a fair trial,[24] and

10   Luke 23:6,7
11   Acts, chap. 23
12   Acts 25:11,12
13   Acts 25:27
14   See supra §446
15   Proceedings on Sabbath or Sunday, see supra §436
16   See supra §435
17   In voting upon the guilt or innocence of a man, it was an ancient custom to use white or black stones, the white for acquittal, the black for conviction. Rev. 2:17 ("to him that overcometh will I give a white stone")
When judges voted, a plurality of one was sufficient for an acquittal but a plurality of two was needed for a conviction under the ancient Talmudic law. 38 Case & Comment (1932) No. 2, p 5
18   Dan. 5:27
19   See 2 Mac. 6:13 ("For it is a token of his great goodness, when wicked doers are not suffered any long time, but forthwith punished")
20   See supra §447
"The trial of a case involving the death penalty should not be a game." State v Wallace (1942) 131 P2d (Or.) 222, 255 (Kelly,CJ, dissenting)
In America, "the idea that the trial is

a battle, a fair fight, between two parties has taken an exaggerated form." 11 Harv.LR (1897) 297 (Lowell)
21   State v Wallace (1942) 121 P2d (Or.) 222,255 (Kelly,CJ, dissenting)
22   Job 31:6 ("Let me be weighed in an even balance")
"It is certainly the duty of the court to pursue a middle line between the great mass of the community on the one hand, and individuals charged with offenses on the other hand." Spangler v Commonwealth (1811) 3 Binney (Pa.) 533, 537 (Yeates,J)
23   See supra §50
In a criminal prosecution "the principle of equal rights before the law is vital." State v Wallace (1942) 121 P2d (Or.) 222,253 (Kelly,CJ, dissenting)
24   See supra §437
"The doctrine that the end justifies the means has no application to the trial of one accused of crime. As important as it is to society to see that those guilty of criminal activity should be punished, it is far more important to society as a whole that the fundamental principle that every defendant is entitled to a fair trial should be preserved." People v Coleman (1942) 53 Cal.App.2d 18, 39, 127 P2d 309 (Peters, PJ, dissenting)

giving him the benefit of every doubt,[25] but not forgetting the wrong suffered by his victim[26] nor the importance to the community of punishing crimes.[27]

Trials were seemingly conducted with great expedition. The accused was brought to judgment in the morning[29] and the trial was concluded before nightfall.[30] So in the Susanna Case, it appears as though the accusation, trial, conviction, new trial, and release of Susanna, and the accusation, trial, conviction, and execution of her false accusers, all took place on the same day.[31]

[§466] In Primitive law, the various rules which have been evolved to protect persons accused of crime were evidently unknown.[32] But according to Mosaic and Christian law, the accused must be accorded a hearing[33] and permitted to answer the accusation,[34] before he is judged and condemned.[35] And under modern law, it is generally considered that the right to be heard includes a right to be heard by counsel[36] that is, by a lawyer[37]—and not by one only, but by several, it seems, if the accused so chooses.[38]

Moreover, it has long been the established rule that the accused is entitled to confront his accusers at the hearing.[39]

25 See 12 Gr.B. (1900) 506 (Amram)
Where, in a criminal prosecution, the defendant's "life is at stake," the court should "proceed with extreme caution for the protection of all rights of the accused." State v Wallace (1942) 121 P2d (Or.) 222,241 (Brand,J)
Under ancient Talmudic law "the accused was considered to be innocent until he was proven guilty." 38 Case & Comment (1932) No. 2, p 5
26 As did king David, who "was comforted concerning Amnon, seeing he was dead." 2 Sam. 13:39
Justice is due to the accuser as well as to the accused. Snyder v Massachusetts (1934) 291 US 97, 78 L ed 674, 90 ALR 575, 588 (Cardozo,J)
27 11 Harv.LR (1897) 297 (Lowell)
28 See supra §437
Under ancient Talmudic law, a court was not allowed to act on more than one criminal case a day. 38 Case & Comment (1932) No. 2, p 5
29 Jer. 21:12; Zeph. 3:5
30 Under the ancient Talmudic law, "if after hearing both sides, the Court acquitted the prisoner, he was discharged immediately. If the Court could not acquit him, the case was adjourned until the next day. It is interesting to note that on the day the judges condemned a man to capital punishment, they were not permitted to eat nor drink." 38 Case & Comment (1932) No. 2, p 5

31 See supra §§357, 399
32 See 13 Gr.B. (1901) 593 (Amram)
33 Prov. 18:13 ("He that answereth a matter before he heareth it, it is folly and shame unto him"); John 7:50 ("Doth our law judge any man, before it hear him, and know what he doeth?")
34 See Acts 7:1 et seq.
35 "It is a universal and established principle . . . that no man is to be condemned unheard." Bebee v Bank of New York (1806) 1 Johnson (NY) 529, 3 AD 353, 359 (Spencer,J)
36 See 14 AmJur 883
37 See supra §433
38 A defendant has a right to counsel, and it is said that "in the multitude of counselors there is safety." Fidelity & Dep. Co. v Bucki & Son Lumber Co. (1903) 189 US 138, 47 L ed 749 (Brewer,J)

The right to be heard by counsel "would, in the language of St.Paul, 'become as sounding brass, or as a tinkling cymbal' (1 Cor. 13:1) if it did not include the right to a full and confidential consultation with such counsel." State v Davis (1913) 9 Okla.Crim. Rep. 94, 130 Pac. 963, 44 LRANS 1083 (Furman,J)

39 Acts 23:35 ("I will hear thee [Paul], said he [the governor of Caesarea], when thine accusers are also come")

This was the law of Rome in the time of St. Paul, who stated that—

". . . It is not the manner of the Romans to deliver any man to die, before that he which is accused have the accusers face to face, and have licence to answer for himself concerning the crime laid against him."[40]

[§467] Mosaic law provided for the "beating" of a man "worthy to be beaten,"[41] but it did not sanction the chastisement or scourging of an accused or convicted person by way of a "third degree" examination or extra punishment; nor is any instance of the needless and unjust abuse of a prisoner, other than those captured in warfare, recorded in the Old Testament. This practice seems, however, to have become prevalent in later times. Thus it is noticed that Pilate proposed to "chastise" Jesus and release him.[42] And after having yielded to the clamors of the multitude to crucify Jesus, Pilate "scourged" him and "delivered him to be crucified."[43]

"Then the soldiers of the governor took Jesus into the common hall, and gathered unto him the whole band of soldiers.

"And they stripped him, and put on him a scarlet robe.

"And when they had platted a crown of thorns, they put it upon his head, and a reed in his right hand: and they bowed the knee before him, saying Hail, King of the Jews:

"And they spit upon him, and took the reed, and smote him on the head.

"And after that they had mocked him, they took the robe off from him, and led him away to crucify him."[44]

[§468] —— The Roman law, more humane than the custom of the Jews at the beginning of the Christian era, forbade not only the scourging or smiting, but also the "binding" of an uncondemned citizen.[45] Thus it is related that—

"The chief captain commanded him (Paul) to be brought into the castle, and bade that he should be examined by scourging; that he might know wherefore they cried so against him.

"And as they bound him with thongs, Paul said unto the centurion that stood by, Is it lawful for you to scourge a man that is a Roman, and uncondemned?

---

40 Acts 25:16

41 See supra §418
"The Judicial Use of Torture," see 11 Harv.LR (1897) 220, 290 (Lowell)

42 Luke 23:16,22

43 Matt. 27:26; see also Mark 15:15; John 19:1

44 Matt. 27:27-31; see also Mark 15:16-20; Luke 23:11 ("And Herod with his men of war set him at nought, and mocked him, and arrayed him in a gorgeous robe, and sent him again to Pilate"); John 19:2,3

45 Acts 23:2,3 ("And the high priest Ananias commanded them that stood by him to smite him (Paul) on the mouth. Then said Paul unto him, God shall smite thee, thou whited wall: for sittest thou to judge me after the law, and commandest me to be smitten contrary to the law?")

"And when the centurion heard that, he went and told the chief captain, saying, Take heed what thou doest for this man is a Roman.

"Then the chief captain came, and said unto him, Tell me, art thou a Roman? He said, Yea.

"And the chief captain answered, With a great sum obtained I this freedom. And Paul said, But I was free born.

"Then straightway they departed from him which should have examined him: and the chief captain also was afraid, after he knew that he was a Roman, and because he had bound him.

"On the morrow, because he would have known the certainty wherefore he was accused of the Jews, he loosed him from his bands, and commanded the chief priests and all their council to appear, and brought Paul down, and set him before them."[46]

[§469]   In Primitive law, one might be adjudged guilty of a crime though no witness testified against him, for it was thought that the judge—being a representative of God—might know the facts of the case without hearing testimony.[47]   But since the time of Moses, witnesses have ordinarily been necessary to justify a conviction,[48] and "diligent inquisition" has been required for the purpose of determining the guilt or innocence of the accused.[49]   The fact that he does not deny his guilt or makes no answer to questions concerning the crime has been considered as a circumstance from which guilt may be inferred.[50]   But though he may testify,[1] it has long been recognized that he ought not to be required to do so, for if he testifies it may be that his "own mouth" shall condemn him,[2] and in such a case no other witness is required.[3]   Thus it appears that when Daniel had convicted the two old judges who had testified against Susanna "of false witness by their

---

46 Acts 22:24-30

47 See supra §439

48 Num. 35:30 ("Whoso killeth any person, the murderer shall be put to death by the mouth of witnesses")
Number of witnesses required, see infra §470

49 Deut. 19:18
Separate examination of witnesses, see the Case of the Two Old Judges (§357) and the Case of Ananias and Sapphira (§163)
"Children begotten of unlawful beds are witnesses of wickedness against their parents in their trial." Wisdom of Solomon 4:6
Under the ancient Talmudic law, neither slaves nor women were competent to testify. Neither hearsay, nor opinion, nor circumstantial evidence was admissible. A witness could testify only as to what he actually saw and therefore was required to be able to answer the most detailed questions about the case. If any testimony was proven false, the defendant was freed. When the witnesses contradicted each other the accused was acquitted. 38 Case & Comment (1932) No. 2, p 5

50 See 13 Gr.B. (1901) 593 (Amram)

1 Under the ancient Talmudic law, the accused was encouraged to speak on his own behalf, but not to incriminate himself. Conviction could not be had on a confession alone, without corroborating testimony of witnesses. 38 Case & Comment (1932) No. 2, p 5

2 Job 15:6 (" Thine own mouth condemneth thee, and not I. Yea, thine own lips testify against thee"), 19:20 ("If I testify myself, mine own mouth shall condemn me"); Harvey v Territory (1901) 11 Okla. 156, 65 P 837 (Burford,CJ)

3 Matt. 12:37 ("By thy words thou shalt be condemned")
There is nothing in the law counter to this Biblical admonition. Castorina v Herrmann (1937) 340 Mo. 1026, 104 SW2d 297 (Hyde,C)

own mouth," the assembly "arose" against them and sentenced them to death.[4] Jesus also was adjudged guilty of blasphemy because of his own statements before the council.

". . . the high priest . . . said unto him, I adjure thee by the living God, that thou tell us whether thou be the Christ, the Son of God.

"Jesus saith unto him Thou has said: nevertheless I say unto you, Hereafter shall ye see the Son of man sitting on the right hand of power, and coming in the clouds of heaven.

"Then the high priest rent his clothes, saying, He hath spoken blasphemy; what further need have we of witnesses? behold, now ye have heard his blasphemy.

"What think ye? They answered and said, He is guilty of death."[5]

[§470] —— Under Primitive law, it appears that a person accused of crime—even a crime punishable by death— might be convicted upon the testimony of one witness.[6] But if this was the rule in very ancient times, it was changed by Mosaic law, which provides that—

". . . one witness shall not testify against any person to cause him to die."[7]

"At the mouth of two witnesses, or three witnesses, shall he that is worthy of death be put to death; but at the mouth of one witness he shall not be put to death."[8]

"One witness shall not rise up against a man for any iniquity, or for any sin, in any sin that he sinneth: at the mouth of two witnesses, or at the mouth of three witnesses, shall the matter be established."[9]

It was presumed that "the testimony of two men is true,"[10] provided of course that they agreed.[11] Though many witnesses testified against the accused, their testimony was not sufficient to convict him if they "agreed not together."[12] Thus in the case of Susanna, though the defendant had previously bourne a good reputation, the testimony of the "elders" that they had come upon her in the act of adultery was regarded as sufficient until in a further and separate examina-

---

4 History of Susanna, v 61; and see supra §357

5 Matt. 26:63-66; see also Mark 14:61-64; Luke 22:70,71

6 See 12 Gr.B. (1900) 386 (Amram)

7 Num. 35:30; and see McCrary v McCrary (1920) 230 SW (Tex.Civ.App.) 187, 202 (Connor,CJ)

8 Deut. 17:6
"He that despised Moses' law died without mercy under two or three witnesses." Heb. 10:28

9 Deut. 19:15
"In the mouth of two or three witnesses shall every word be established."
2 Cor. 13:1
"Against an elder receive not an accusation, but before two or three witnesses." 1 Tim. 5:19

10 John 8:17

11 Matt. 26:60,61 ("two false witnesses" testified against Jesus)

12 Mark 14:56
Under the ancient Talmudic law, no conviction could be had without the testimony of two witnesses whose testimony had to coincide in every particular. 38 Case & Comment (1932) No. 2, p 5

tion, they disagreed as to the tree under which the alleged offense was committed.[13]

In modern law, one witness is legally sufficient[14] except to prove perjury[15] or treason.[16]   But an analogous rule requires the corroboration of the testimony of an accomplice[17] and that of the complainant in a prosecution for rape.[18]

[§471]   Biblical law makes no provision for a new trial or an appeal in a criminal case.   It was doubtless considered that such proceedings should be concluded before the wrong suffered by the victim was dimmed by lapse of time[19] and the sympathies of wrongdoers' kinsmen and friends had become too greatly aroused.   On the other hand, the law mercifully refrained from subjecting a convicted offender to mental suffering by postponing the execution of his sentence.

But in the case of Susanna, we have seen that a new trial was demanded and granted by common consent, and when the falsity of the testimony of the accusing witnesses was demonstrated the defendant was forthwith released and her accusers were immediately punished.[20]

[§472]   The sentence of death—which, being "the sentence of the Lord over all flesh," is not to be feared[21]—was executed in various ways.[22]   As to several offenses, Mosaic law prescribed that the guilty person should be "stoned with stones."[23]   In executing the sentence to death by stoning, the law provided that—

"The hand of the witnesses shall be first upon him to put him to death, and afterward the hands of all the people. So thou shalt put the evil away from among you."[24]

13 See supra §399
14 Required numbers of witnesses, see
15 Harv.LR (1901) 85 (Wigmore)
15 See 41 AmJur 37
16 U.S. Const. (1787) Art. 3, §3 ("No Person shall be convicted of Treason unless on the Testimony of two Witnesses to the same overt Act, or on Confession in open Court")
17 See 20 AmJur 1087
18 See 22 RCL 1222
19 See 2 Sam. 13:39
20 See supra §§357, 399
   Thus it is seen that the law does not sanction the punishment of one who is shown to have been convicted upon perjured testimony.
21 Ecclesiasticus 41:3

22 Anciently, one found guilty of wilful killing was handed over to the kinsmen of the victim to be put to death. 12 Gr.B. (1900) 197 (Amram)
   Under the ancient Talmudic law, there were four methods of capital punishment: 1, stoning; 2, burning; 3, decapitation—by the sword; and 4, strangling. 38 Case & Comment (1932) No. 2, p 4
23 Lev. 20:2,27
24 Deut. 17:7
   Under the ancient Talmudic law, the witnesses to the crime were the executioners. The culprit was placed on a high platform and hurled to the ground. If this did not kill him, the bystanders threw heavy stones at him until he was dead. 38 Case & Comment (1932) No. 2, p 4

But capital punishment was also imposed in some cases by burning, crucifixion or hanging. Thus, it is provided that the daughter of a priest who profanes herself "by playing the whore" shall be burnt with fire[25] and that "if a man take a wife and her mother . . . they shall be burnt with fire."[26] At the time of Jesus, executions were by crucifixion as well as by stoning, for it appears that Jesus was crucified,[27] but Stephen was stoned.[28]

With respect to executions by hanging, the law provided that—

". . . if a man have committed a sin worthy of death, and he be to be put to death, and thou hang him on a tree:

"His body shall not remain all night upon the tree, but thou shalt in any wise bury him that day; (for he that is hanged is accursed of God;) that thy land be not defiled, which the Lord thy God giveth thee for an inheritance."[29]

25 Lev. 21:9; and see supra §314
26 Lev. 20:14; and see supra §404

27 Matt. 27:35; Mark 15:24; Luke 23:33; John 19:18
The Jews adopted crucifixion only under Roman compulsion. At Rome crucifixion was inflicted upon slaves and brigands, until abolished by Constantine in the fourth century.

28 Acts 6:58
29 Deut. 21:22,23; see also 1 Esd. 6:32, that king Darius of Babylon commanded that whosoever should transgress his commands with reference to the rebuilding of the temple at Jerusalem, "out of his own house should a tree be taken, and he thereon be hanged, and all his goods seized for the king."

CONCLUSION

"LET US HEAR THE CONCLUSION OF THE WHOLE
MATTER: FEAR GOD, AND KEEP HIS COMMAND-
MENTS: FOR THIS IS THE WHOLE DUTY OF
MAN."

ECCLESIASTES 12:13.

INDEX

A

Aaron, §§99, 200, 388
Abdon, §440
Abel, §§281, 327, 369
Abijah, §196
Abimelech, §§112, 148, 208
Abner, §§370, 430
Abortion, §361
Abraham, §§33, 112, 148, 150, 167, 170, 174, 190, 196, 200, 201, 208, 213, 215, 219, 230, 242, 261, 280, 281, 291, 303, 329
Absalom, §§31, 370, 408, 441
Academic freedom, §294, n 5
Accountability for crime, §340, n 19
Accounting by steward, §241
Accounts, written, §149, n 45
Accusation of
offender, §460
servant, §232
Accusers, confrontal, §466
Achan's case, §125
Actions
laws govern, §28
suits, see Suits
Acts
accidental and unintended, §342
speaking by, §127
Adam, §§196, 209, 253, 256, 278, 311, 417
case of Adam and Eve and the Serpent, §§339, 341, 343, 439
Adding words, §42, n 41
Administration of law, §§432-472
Admonition
Mosaic law written for, §40
sons and daughters, admonitions concerning, §224
things written for, not to be ignored, §40
Adonijah, §412
Adoption
children, §219
strangers, §79
Adultery, §§396-400
Afflicted persons, §271
Aged persons, §272
distribution of property, §140
gifts by, §162

Ages
criminal capacity, §340
marriage, for, §190
military service, §117
Agrarianism, §245
Agreements, see Contracts
Agriculture, §§281-283
harvest rules, §274
Ahab, §§96, 112, 168, 340, 381, 420, 422
Ahaseurus, §109, 216, 349, 360
Ahaz, §389
Ahaziah, §86, 93
case of §392
Aid to
animals, §285
criminals, §428
parents, §229
poor, §275
Aliens, see Strangers
Allegiance
king, to, oath, §92
pledge in schools, §296
Alliances, §114
Alms, giving, §270
Altar, §321
Amana Society, §249, n 47
Amasa, §370, 430
Amaziah, §§99, 338
America
Bible as law in, §71
Christian land, §72
colonial grant of law-making authority, §55
religious nation, as, §45
American law
civil obedience, §108
disinheritance of natural heirs, §145
divorce, §205
inheritance, §135
liberty, §25
marriage, ages, §190
polygamy, §197
scriptural influence, §71
source of power, §78
witchcraft, §395
Amnon, §370
Amnon's Case, §408
Amram, §200

Cases—Continued
  Peter, §365
  Queen Vashti, §216
  Rachel, §377
  Rhodocus, §349
  Samuel, §353
  Saul, §96
  Shechem, §182
  Shimei, §110
  Solomon, §392
  Son of Shilomith, §380
  Stephen, §384
  Stick-gatherer, §§388, 436
  Susanna, §399
  Two Harlots, §§221, 439, 452
  Two Old Judges, §357
  Ussah, §342
  Woman taken in adultery, §400
Cat-o-nine tails, beating wife with, §211, n 36a
Cattle
  breeding, rule as to, §284
  caring for, duty, §282
  criminal responsibility, 341
Celebration
  death, §290
  holidays, §318
  wedding, §194
Census, §99
Cephas, §280
Ceremony
  adoption, §219
  purchase and sale of realty, §§169-171
  succession, §142
  wedding, §193
Chalcedon, council at, §189
Change
  judge or place of trial, §464
  law, changes in, §§56-59
  name, of, §280
Charge, priest, to army, §120
Charity, duty, §§18, 275
Charlemagne, §450
Children
  accountability, §340, n 19
  admonitions, §224
  adoption, §219
  aid to parent, duty, §229
  bringing up, natural law, §8
  burial of parent, duty, §230
  criminal responsibility, §340
  emancipation, right, §231
  fatherless, §276
  father's authority over, §223
  heirs, as, §134

Children—Continued
  heritage of Lord, §§209, 361
  illegitimate, §§136, 137
  incorrigible, §351
  marriage, parents' duty as to, §226
  obedience, duty, §228
  orphans, §276
  paternity, §§220, 221
  relationship to parents, §218-231
  rights, §§227, 231
  solicitude concerning, §218
  support, parents' duty, §225
Christianity
  common law, as part of, §73
  communism, §§248, 249
  established faith in early America, §72
Christian law, §17
  divorce, as to, §204
  forgiveness of debts, §266
  Golden rule, §23
  governments ordained, §78
  intent, §29
  interpretation, §24
  judicial proceedings on Sunday, §436
  liberty, §21
  love as fulfillment, §19
  love as rule, §18
  oaths, §151
  observance by nature, §22
  offenses through ignorance, §344
  punishment, as to, §413
  sale or imprisonment of debtor, §267
  swearing, as to, §151
  transgressions, origin, §20
  where found, §17
Christians
  adoption and following of Mosaic law, §17
  America as Christian land, §72
  early, observance of Mosaic law by, §38
  marriage to unbelievers, §199
Church
  communism in early, §248
  interest, taking forbidden, §265, n 32
  places of refuge, §431
  separation of church and state, §86
  trials, §450
  wills, deposit, §143
Circuit judges, §445

Monuments, §292
Moral law, §7
    Golden rule as expression, §23
    Ten commandments as code, §13
Morals
    governmental purpose, §77
    legislature not to disregard, §55
    offenses against, §§358-360
Mordecai, §§219, 228, 349
Mosaic interpretation of law, §16
Mosaic law, §12
    admonition, as written for, §40
    adoption by colonies, §71
    adultery, as to, §§396, 397
    bindingness, §§36-40
    bond-servants, as to, §233 et seq.
    criminal responsiility, §338
        of animals, §341
        of children, §340
    divorce, of, §203
    everlastingness, §57
    governments divinely ordained,
        §78
    inheritance by illegitimates, §136
    intent, §29
    judges under, §440
    judicial proceedings on
        Sabbath, §436
    justice as ideal, §31
    king as amenable to, §47
    law of land, as, §34
    oaths, as to, §151
    observance by Christians, §38
        by Jews, §33
    persons bound to obey, §46
    priests as amenable to, §47
    reaffirmance, §17
    repudiation of certain pro-
        visions, §17
    sanctuary, of, §431
    Talmud, §15
    Ten commandments, §§13, 14
    tribal law, as, §33
    universal law, as, §36
    where found, §12
    writing of, §61
Moses, §§12, 46, 62, 74, 82, 83, 85,
    87, 92, 98, 99, 116 122, 131, 139,
    196, 200, 204 219 254 277, 299,
    327, 370, 376, 380, 384, 388, 400,
    440, 442, 444, 446, 455, 462, 469
    adoption, §219, n 1
    law of, see Mosaic law
Mother, see Parent and Child
    natural custodian of young,
        §223, n 24

Mount Ebal, stones, §63
Mount Sinai
    tables of testimony given upon,
        §62
    touching of, punishment, §393
Mourning for dead, §290
Multiple damages, §459
Murder, §§366-370, and see
    Homicide
Murmuring, §347
    guest, by, §244
Mutilating body, §279

               N

Naaman, §312
Naboth, §§96, 168, 340, 381, 422
    case of, §381
Nakedness, §278
Names
    giving and changing, §280
    lands, naming of, §128, n 28
Naomi, §§191, 274
Nathan, §§91, 96, 378, 398
Nations
    governments, see Government
    leagues of, §114
Naturalization, §79
Natural law, §8
    deducible from Ten Command-
        ments, §13
    freedom, §25
    maintenance of children,
        §225, n 36
    married persons' rights and
        duties, §206
Nature, observance of law by, §22
Nebuchadnezzar, §§280, 422
Nehemiah, §§201, 264, 301
New order, §250
New trial, criminal cases, §471
Noah, §§196, 209, 277, 340
Nonresistance
    duty, §18
    suits, against, §449

               O

Oaths, §150
    allegiance to king, §92
    animals, as between owner and
        bailee, §155
    definition, §150
    Delaware constitution, §72, n 36
    judge, of, §446, n 32
    Mosaic and Christian law, §151

CPSIA information can be obtained at www.ICGtesting.com
Printed in the USA
BVOW02s1759280916

463533BV00001B/10/P